# SUZANNE VON DRACHENFELS

DRAWINGS BY KELLY LUSCOMBE

SIMON & SCHUSTER

*New York London Toronto Sydney*

# The Art of the Table

A Complete Guide to

*Table Setting,*

*Table Manners,*

*and Tableware*

SIMON & SCHUSTER
1230 Avenue of the Americas
New York, NY 10020



This Simon & Schuster hardcover edition August 2009

SIMON AND SCHUSTER and colophon are registered trademarks of Simon & Schuster, Inc.

For information about special discounts for bulk purchases, please contact Simon & Schuster Special Sales at 1-866-506-1949 or business@simonandschuster.com.

The Simon & Schuster Speakers Bureau can bring authors to your live event. For more information or to book an event contact the Simon & Schuster Speakers Bureau at 1-866-248-3049 or visit our website at www.simonspeakers.com.

*Designed by Barbara M. Bachman*

Manufactured in the United States of America

1 3 5 7 9 10 8 6 4 2

Library of Congress Cataloging-in-Publication Data

von Drachenfels, Suzanne, date.
The art of the table : a complete guide to table setting, table manners, and tableware/Suzanne von Drachenfels.
p. cm.
Includes bibliographical references and index.
1. Tableware. 2. Table setting and decoration. 3. Table etiquette.
I. Title.
TX877.V66 2000
642'.7—dc21
ISBN 978-1-4391-6340-5

# Acknowledgments

WHEN THE STUDENT IS ready the master appears. The masters in my life, in order of appearance, are: my son, Dr. James Luscombe, who rescued me many times from mistakes at the computer; Dr. Stuart Miller, literary adviser of Carmel, California, for unerring guidance; Regina Ryan, of Regina Ryan Publishing Enterprises, New York City, agent, teacher, and confidante; Sharon E. Gibbons of Simon & Schuster, editor *par excellence;* Andrea Au, for invaluable assistance above and beyond; Isolde C. Sauer, copy editing supervisor, for the strength of probing questions; Martha Cameron, copy editor, for brilliant attention to detail; my daughter, Kelly Ann Luscombe, for the pure artistry of her talent; and Dr. Jielu Zhao, Head of the Chinese Department, Defense Language Institute, Monterey, California, for invaluable linguistic help with the pinyin and Wade-Giles spelling of the Chinese language. Without their assistance, diligence, accomplishments, understanding, and encouragement, this book would be a dream awaiting reality.

With deepest appreciation, thank you!

*SUZANNE VON DRACHENFELS*

*MONTEREY, CALIFORNIA*

To my children, Jim,
Kelly, Liz, and Tricia for
their encouragement and
understanding
during long silent periods
of writing (and for forcing me
to get a word processor).
To my grandchildren,
Tyler, Jennifer, Kimberly,
Jimmy, Katie, and Christina,
for the pure creativity
they bring to any endeavor.
Finally, to the memory of
my late husband Alec,
the real writer in the family,
for his unflagging interest
and positive suggestions.

# Contents

## PART III: FLATWARE



## PART IV: STEMWARE

## PART V: TABLE LINENS



## PART VI: SERVING TECHNIQUES



## PART VII: DINING FINESSE

## PART VIII: MENU PLAN



## PART IX: TABLE MANNERS

*The joys of the table are superior*
*to all other pleasures,*
*notably those of personal adornment,*
*of drinking and of love, and*
*those procured by perfumes and by music.*

CHAMSEDDINE MOHAMED EL HASSAN EL BAGHDADI
KITABE EL-TIBAH
*1226*

# Preface

Why people write:

*Though for no other cause,*
*Yet for this.*
*That posterity may know*
*We have*
*Not loosely through silence*
*Permitted things to pass away*
*As in a Dream.*

RICHARD HOOKER,
THEOLOGIAN, 1554–1600

THIS BOOK is pure serendipity, something I never intended to do, but once I started I couldn't stop. And like Topsy, it just grew as I considered the millions of people who use tableware daily. When I was a tabletop consultant for a major dinnerware firm, at seminars throughout the country, invariably someone would say, "You should write a book." And so I did.

The more I traveled, the more I realized that everyone enjoys entertaining, but few people are confident about how to handle specific tableware, and many are unsure about table manners. The breakdown of formal structured dining following World War I was coupled with the antitraditional attitudes of the 1960s and 1970s and the employment of women full-time outside the home, and the family unit witnessed erosion. A gap developed in our knowledge of the nuances of dining.

Wherever I spoke, whether at a retail store, a private club, a charitable group, or a corporate meeting, the same questions arose, and always I was asked to suggest a particular book that would explain how to set the table in a variety of social situations. Why, they would ask, do some people eat with the fork in the left hand and others in the right hand? What is wrong with placing the elbows on the table? What is the purpose of holding a wine glass by the stem or the base? Although many fine books are written on the subject of table setting, table manners, and tableware, there was no one volume that started at the beginning and brought the history forward that made sense of today's usage and customs.

Rather than let time-honored methods pass away, I determined to write a book that would give a detailed, comprehensive, and authoritative explanation about tableware and how to use each piece in formal and informal dining. A book that defines the vocabulary of the table setting — terms like *place setting, cover, tableware, stemware,* and *flatware.* A book that reveals the origins of everyday expressions, such as "eating humble pie" and covers the history of table manners so that people can readily understand the commonsense reasons behind today's customs. A book that covers the selection and care of tableware, the choice of table linens, menu planning, the basics of coffee, tea, and wine, and service techniques for all types of entertainment.

It is my hope that brides, who may never have thought about tableware before getting married and establishing a household, will find this book a valuable guide to the selection, care, and use of tableware for formal and informal dining; that the experienced host will find the book a resource of new ideas and a recap of the basics; that young urban professionals who are now part of the corporate scene will find the book filled with confidence-building information; that the food service industry, namely the restaurateurs, service staff, and caterers, will find it a practical guide to the correct way to set a table and present food; that ethnic minorities will find it useful as they learn the dining customs of mainstream America.

For love of the subject a book was written—and I tried to make it as definitive and as complete a guide to the art of dining as possible.

# *The Art of the Table*

# Part I

# Dining Fundamentals

CHAPTER ONE

# WORDS USED IN TABLE SETTING

*Ponder well on this point: the pleasant hours of our life are all connected, by a more or less intangible link, with some memory of the table.*

MONSELET, EIGHTEENTH-CENTURY GASTRONOME

FOOD IS MORE to us than the fuel of life. It is a building block of community, a symbol of hospitality, friendship, and love. Archaeologists believe even early cave dwellers offered food to strangers, hoping to demonstrate the will to peace. After humans learned how to use fire, they moved from survival to social dining, sitting with the clan to eat a kill of cooked meat. Fire brought the invention of clay pots, a discovery that made preparation of assorted foods possible, an array known today as a *meal,* from the Latin word *metiri,* meaning "to measure out" or "distribute among," a word that contains in its etymology elaborately social attitudes.

Today, the table setting has its own vocabulary. Terms such as *place setting* and *service plate* are familiar and easily understood, but others are not as clear. Here are the basics.

- **Cover**—The space allotted the diner on which tableware is placed.
- **Cutlery**—Eating utensils with a cutting edge, such as steak knives.
- **Dinnerware**—A collective term for plates, bowls, cups, and saucers.
- **Flatware**—Utensils manufactured from flattened sheets of metal cut and stamped into form; ware that lays flat on the table, such as a knife, fork, and spoon. Although technically *flatware* applies to utensils without a sharp cutting edge, such as a fork or a spoon, in general usage the term includes all eating utensils, among them the dinner knife.
- **Glassware**—Nonstemmed drinking vessels, such as tumblers and bar glasses; also, glass plates, cups, and bowls.
- **Holloware**—Serveware with height and depth that is hollow in the center; for example, a water pitcher or a coffeepot.
- **Place setting**—The space, or "setting," on the table where the dinnerware, stemware, and flatware are "placed"; *see* **cover.**
- **Serveware**—Utility ware used to serve a meal; for example, platters, trays, and bowls.
- **Silverware**—Flatware made of silver.
- **Stemware**—A glass with a bowl that rests on a stem anchored by a foot; for example, a long-stem wine glass.
- **Suite**—Tableware that matches, such as dinnerware, flatware, and stemware ornamented with the same motif.
- **Table service**—A term that encompasses dinnerware, flatware, glassware, and linens.
- **Tableware**—An inclusive word for dinnerware, flatware, and glassware; the ware from which food and drink are taken.
- **Tumbler**—A nonstemmed glass with a flat or semirounded base, such as a bar glass.

CHAPTER TWO

# THE DIFFERENCE BETWEEN FORMAL AND INFORMAL DINING

The Industrial Revolution that took place in England at the end of the eighteenth century spawned a new prosperity for more people than ever before, and by the nineteenth century a middle class that wished to live and dine like aristocrats had come into being. The majority of these households employed help of some kind and multicourse meals were served formally, course by course, a custom that continued into the early twentieth century. Although both genders were trained "in the service," only men assisted with formal dinner service, a tradition that continues today.

World War I brought increased opportunities for people to work in munition factories and offices, employment that offered better pay, improved work conditions, and greater independence. Live-in help became hard to find. This situation laid the groundwork for informal dining. By the Great Depression, only 5 percent of American households employed domestic help. The labor-saving technology of the mid-twentieth century made daily chores less burdensome; as a result, few households engaged servants and informal dining was the norm.

Following World War II, to conserve on the cost of new homes for returning servicemen, dwellings were constructed without dining rooms, and a space called a *dining area* was reserved at the end of the living room, an expanse less formal than the special room devoted to dining.

Today informal dining is a way of life for all but the rarest occasions. Seldom is help needed to cook and serve a meal (although it is always welcome). Life is more relaxed, menus are simpler, and the table setting is informal. But like formal attire, which is seldom worn but is a necessity for certain special occasions, so too is the knowledge of how to proceed at a formal affair.

## A Formal Meal

*To preside over a political chamber, or to hold a post in an embassy, is to take a course in gastronomy.*

ANTONIN CARÊME, 1783–1833

In the literal sense of the word, a formal dinner is one of strict protocol, like an affair of state, an elegant refined mode of entertainment experienced by approximately 0.5 percent of the population, one reserved almost totally for ceremonial occasions, such as diplomatic affairs, weddings, anniversary parties, corporate banquets, fund-raisers, and catered events.

A formal table setting dazzles the senses with a profusion of sparkling crystal, gleaming silver, glistening porcelain, exquisite floral arrangements, majestic candelabra, and magnificent table decor. Place cards define seating arrangements and menu cards enable the guests to pace themselves through the multicourse meal, where the finest cuisine and wines are served.

To enable the host and hostess to remain seated and relaxed, the meal is prepared by a chef: a *minimum* of four courses, but usually five, six, seven, or more courses are served. To create an atmosphere that is always gracious and nondisruptive, a majordomo oversees the service of food and wine. Maids are engaged to take wraps and provide general assistance. Attendants park cars.

In order to present a multicourse meal at peak flavor and optimum temperature, a formal dinner is served on time and the guests are expected to arrive promptly. Because formal occasions always occur late in the day, cocktails are served at 8:00 or 8:30 P.M. Dinner is announced 30 to 45 minutes later.

A formal dinner involves extensive and expensive preparation, and usually a considerable number of people are seated at different tables. To eliminate confusion about who sits where, a seating plan is provided for a large group, displayed in the foyer on a leather folder or on a small easel-like stand.

To keep the palate ready, hors d'oeuvres and canapés are not served, and the cocktail period is brief, approximately 30 minutes. To expedite service, prepoured drinks are passed on a tray—for example, champagne and a premixed cocktail, such as a martini. The term cocktail first appeared in a New York newspaper, circa 1806, which defined liquor mixed with sugar, water, and bitters as a "cocktail." Eventually the cocktail hour came to mean the 60-minute interval between the arrival of one's guests and the announcement of dinner.

During cocktails the gentlemen stand until the hostess is seated. And the hostess stands until the last guest has arrived (another reason for punctuality). Although the ladies may sit during the cocktail period, generally they stand for ease in conversation with the men. The majordomo checks with the chef to make sure all is ready and announces dinner when the time is right.

For a detailed explanation of the protocol and service, please refer to Chapter 36, "Formal Dinner Service," and Part IX, "Table Manners."

## An Informal Meal

In today's busy world, most people have neither the time nor the inclination to entertain in a formal manner, and an informal meal ranges from an elegant four-course affair served at a fully appointed table, to a simple two-course meal taken before the fire, to potluck with guests contributing dishes, to buffet service of a one-dish meal, to a picnic with tableware made of paper and plastic. When assistance is needed, family or friends may help, although the host cooks the meal. A professional may be hired to serve and clean up.

The hour for an informal gathering is up to the host. Some allot a short time for cocktails and serve dinner early; others favor a longer period for cocktails and present dinner late. To buffer the preprandial drinks and the wine served with the meal, the host may provide hors d'oeuvres and canapés.

Approximately 15 minutes before the meal, the host announces that dinner is almost ready, a courtesy that allows the guests time to finish drinks and conclude a story in progress.

An informal meal is served wherever space allows; at one end of the living room, in the den, or from a kitchen counter with guests eating from plates held on laps. The important point is not the location of the table but the spirit of the occasion!

Because a two-to-four-course meal takes less time to eat than a five-to-seven-course menu, guests sit at the table for approximately 45 minutes. The need to regroup and stretch after dessert is not as imperative as it is in formal dining and after-dinner coffee is served at the table or in another room (hopefully a room free of preprandial paraphernalia).

For additional information, please refer to Chapter 37, "Informal Dinner Service."

# Part II

# Dinnerware

CHAPTER THREE

# FROM POTTERY TO PORCELAIN

MAKE THE MOST OF what you have—that's exactly how primitive potters developed their craft. Using the material at hand, early humans took clay from river beds, beat it for consistency, and left it to air-dry. The history of pottery had begun.

Although the dates of origin vary throughout the world, the evolution of pottery follows a similar pattern from culture to culture. Discovery was by accident, perhaps when food and water were stored in baskets lined with clay. When the baskets were worn out, they were burned; the clay hardened in the fire and pottery was born.

## In the Beginning

The evolution of pottery begins in Neolithic times, circa 10,000 B.C., a period when the climate changed from cold to warm and the first hunter-gatherer cultures began to farm and domesticate animals. With a more settled life and an increase in the food supply, not everyone had to farm. Specialized crafts developed, such as basket weaving, textiles, and pottery, the latter originating in the Middle East. Early pottery was decorated by incision or impression methods; it was cooled in open air to develop red tones or in molten ash to create black tones, a technique Greek potters would adapt for kiln firing. Colors were derived from metallic ores naturally present in the earth, notably copper.

In an agrarian lifestyle, pottery vessels, essential for storage of grains, were shaped by forming pottery from slabs of clay, by winding coils of clay into a form or by casting clay into a stone depression. The coils were laid one on top of the other, then joined and smoothed with liquid clay. Alternatively, ropes of clay coils were wound around a solid core, such as a stone. After the vessel was shaped, the core was removed. In yet another way, clay was molded in stone depressions. Vessels were shaped with pointed ends that stood upright in the ground or in a river bed to provide the cool storage of food.

## Egyptian Pottery

Egyptian civilization began about 4500 B.C. in the rich valley of the Nile River where the stable atmosphere of an agrarian lifestyle promoted the development of glaze and the potter's wheel. Glaze is a waterproof covering that renders clay impervious to liquid absorption. Initially, glaze was made from clay that contained *alkali,* a water-soluble mineral of potassium or sodium carbonate. Historians believe that glaze first occurred naturally when the alkali inherent in the clay emerged and coated the surface of the pottery with a thin frost of crystals that melted into a glassy finish. Glaze composed of quartz and alkali was used to make *faience,* a whitish substance fired at a low temperature, and the precursor of glass. When copper oxide was added to faience, it turned turquoise. But because faience earthenware lacked strength it was use to make small objects, such as beads, amulets, and perfume bottles.

The Egyptians worshipped more than one god, and legend states the earth was shaped on the potter's wheel by Ptah, the Egyptian god of artisans. In the fifth millennium, a fast-spinning potter's wheel was invented; because it was rotated by the feet or knees, it left the hands free to shape the clay. The design remains unchanged to this day, but now an electric motor turns the wheel and gears adjust the speed. The potter's wheel is the most important discovery in the history of ceramics. It improved the symmetry of pottery, promoted thinner vessels, accelerated the speed of formation, and fostered a primitive form of mass production.

The development of the potter's wheel occurred in several places at different times. A wheel dating to 3000 B.C. was found at the mouth of the Euphrates River in the Sumerian city of Ur. The Chinese claim invention circa 2500 B.C., believing the potter's wheel reached Egypt via overland trade routes to Scythia and Bactria. Homer makes the first literary reference to the potter's wheel in the *Iliad,* thought to have been written in the ninth century B.C. The Romans refer to the potter's wheel circa 50 B.C.

Around 3500 B.C. Near Eastern artisans produced bronze, a hard metal made of copper smelted with tin. Bronze was cast in sectional molds made of clay, the segmented bands of which provided the first ornamentation of bronze. And for the next 4,000 years, a period known as the *Bronze Age,* pottery was shaped to resemble bronze vessels and ornamented with punched and stamped designs characteristic of metalwork.

By the end of the fourth millennium B.C. the foundation for modern pottery was laid—kilns, glaze, potter's wheel, and colorants. Thereafter, the progress of pottery shifted from the development of basic methods to the nuances of shape and ornamentation.

## Greek Pottery

In the Old World human social organization spread from the river valleys of Mesopotamia to the northern shores of the Mediterranean, where the Aegean civilizations of Crete, Mycenae, and Greece arose around 3000 B.C. From approximately 2000 to 500 B.C., individual kingdoms rose and fell and tribes migrated from Europe, southwestern Asia, and India into the area that is present-day Greece. Over a period of 500 years, the tribes slowly assimilated the Mediterranean culture, and by 1000 B.C. the base was laid for Greek society and the foundation of Western democracy.

The potters' quarter in Athens was called the *ceramicus,* from the Greek term *keramos,* meaning "potter's clay." Greek potters strove for perfect balance between proportion and function. Their motto was "Nothing in excess, everything in proportion." Form followed function.

The vase was the primary pottery form. The word comes from the Latin *vas,* meaning "useful pot" or "hollow vessel," a versatile shape used in assorted capacities: to hold household substances, as a container in sea commerce, as an article of barter, and as a funerary receptacle in burial rites. There was an enormous demand for these vessels, which fell into four main categories: holders, pitchers, jugs, and dippers, all made with handles. Holders, such as the *amphora,* from the Greek *amphiphoreus,* meaning "jar," were narrow-necked vases made to hold and pour wine, oil, and fish sauces. Pitchers, notably the *hydria,* were used to carry and store water. Jugs, or *kraters,* were large bowls used to mix wine and water. Dippers, called *oenochoe,* were used to transfer wine from a krater to a *kylix,* a shallow two-handled drinking vessel that rested on a footed stem.

Although Greek pottery is admired for its painted ornamentation, utilitarian pottery was left undecorated. Vessels fired in a wood-fed kiln acquired a thin covering burnished to a glossy sheen from the wood ash that fell on them. Pottery made for special purposes was painted with *slip,* fine particles of clay mixed with water to a creamy semiliquid consistency. The ware was fired to a leather-hard state before the slip was applied to a vessel. This kept the slip from spreading the way paint does on paper.

Greek potters ornamented vases with red and black paint and occasional accents of purple or white. Red and black resulted from chemical oxidation in the kiln. In an *unrestricted kiln,* the ends of the furnace are open and complete fuel combustion, or oxidation, takes place. This causes the iron in the slip to turn red. In a *reduced kiln,* the ends of the chamber are sealed; as in a chimney with a poor draw, fuel combustion is incomplete and the kiln is smoky, a condition that turns the iron in the slip to black. When reoxidized, the unpainted body turns a deeper shade of red, but the black decoration remains the same. The development of the controlled kiln was of major importance. It enabled Etruscan and Roman potters to create red, gray, and black glazes; Chinese, Islamic, and European potters would later adapt these glazes to create colors with yellow or gray undertones.

## Etruscan Pottery

From approximately 1000 to 800 B.C. diverse Italic-speaking tribes of Indo-Europeans migrated from the Danube basin into present-day Italy, bringing with them Iron Age skills. The most prominent of these were the Latins, who settled along the west coast of the peninsula south of the Tiber River in the Latium plain. Anthropologists call this early Italic culture *Villanovan,* after the site of important remains. The shapes and decoration of Villanovan pottery, although crude, show the influence of the culture's iron-making skills. Villanovan pottery influenced succeeding cultures, notably the Etruscans and the Romans.

Although the origins of the Etruscan people are uncertain, scholars believe the culture came from Lydia, a country in western Asia Minor bordering the Aegean Sea. Between 900 and 700 B.C., the Etruscans migrated to the Italian peninsula and settled an area known as *Tusci,* modern-day Tuscany. Until late in the fourth century B.C., the Etruscans dominated the Italian peninsula and developed a hybrid pottery influenced by Egyptian, Near Eastern, and Grecian shapes, decorated with the punched and stamped designs characteristic of Villanovan metalwork.

Etrurian potters produced *bucchero* and *bucchero nero,* a name for dark gray to glossy black pottery fired in a reduced kiln. Bucchero was cast in molds and made in simple shapes, such as vessels and portrait heads, and ornamented with relief decoration or incised motifs. In 1769 Josiah Wedgwood, inspired by bucchero, set about to make black basalts, dark ornamental stoneware produced at Etruria, the home of his manufactory in Staffordshire.

## Roman Pottery

The city of Rome was founded in Latium in 753 B.C. The metropolis was named for the Latin prince Romulus. Around 500 B.C. Rome embarked on a period of conquest, finally freeing itself of Etruscan domination in 396 B.C., and imposed the *pax Romana,* or "peace of Rome," throughout the Mediterranean. Because the independent Greek city states had failed to coalesce, rivalries ensued that led to civil war and a political vacuum ripe for conquest. In 146 B.C. the Romans conquered Greece. Eventually Roman rule extended from Britain to the valley of the Egyptian Nile and from the Atlas mountains of North Africa to the Syrian desert.

Because Rome was colonized earlier by the Greeks, the Romans were familiar with their culture and were admirers of all things Greek. However, philosophical differences existed. The Greeks expressed intellectual curiosity for the sake of abstract knowledge, but the Roman viewpoint was practical. Rather than create art for the sake of art alone, Roman art focused on the glorification of the empire. In the medium of pottery, why improve upon perfection? Essentially, Roman potters did little but reinterpret Greek and Etruscan pottery. (The craft was perhaps eclipsed by the Roman domination of glass.)

But the Romans were great organizers and administrators and mass-produced mold-made pottery for the kitchen as well as for storage and transport of goods. For the table, Roman potters molded plates, bowls, cups, and jugs made of red-gloss pottery called *Arretine*. Sometimes Arretine was erroneously called *Samian,* after the red-gloss pottery made from medicinal clay on the Greek island of Samos and stamped with a seal of authenticity. In fact, red-gloss pottery was made in many Roman provinces including Arretium (Arezzo, Italy). Some Arretine is also known as *terra sigillata,* from the Italian *terra,* "earth," and *sigillata,* "seal." Furthermore, Roman potters invented transparent lead glaze, a translucent covering that would influence potters in China, the Middle East, and Europe.

## Chinese Pottery and Porcelain

The Chinese potters were the greatest ceramists the world has ever known. Through centuries of experimentation and rare determination, the Chinese, blessed with the right natural resources in almost every province, advanced ceramics from pottery to porcelain, mastered firing techniques in high- and low-temperature kilns, created lead glaze, invented feldspathic glaze, and developed colorful ornamentation underglaze and overglaze.

The rich tradition of Chinese ceramics begins with imperial China in the reign of Shi Huang Ti (Shih Huang Ti, reign 221–210 B.C.), who formed the first centralized, politically unified, multinational state, with thirty-six provinces. Shi Huang Ti was the fourth monarch, and first emperor, of the Qin (Ch'in) dynasty, which ultimately gave the country its name, China. The Chinese also refer to their land as *Zhong Qua (Zhung Quo),* the "Central Country" or "Middle Kingdom," a land between Heaven and Earth.

The history of Chinese ceramics is divided into three periods, but major advances were made in the Han, Tang, Song, Yuan, Ming, and Qing dynasties.

The first era encompasses the evolution of pottery from prehistory to the sixth century A.D., an epoch that includes the development of stoneware and proto-porcelain in the Han dynasty. The second span is from the seventh through the thirteenth century, a period when ceramic techniques reached a high level of development, notably in the Tang and Song dynasties. The third age, from the fourteenth through the nineteenth century, encompasses the maturation of Chinese ceramics and the development of colorful ornamentation, notably in the Yuan, Ming, and Qing dynasties.

The Chinese names and terms that follow are spelled in pinyin, a system devised by the People's Republic of China for the romanization of Chinese words. The old system of spelling, known as *Wade-Giles*, is given in parentheses.

## *Han Dynasty (206 B.C.–220 A.D.)*

This dynasty is named for the native province of General Liu Bang (Liu Pang), a village official-turned-bandit, who unified China under a centralized government. Today, the main ethnic group in China is called *Han*, recalling the long prosperous period of Han rule. (There are many other ethnic groups native to China—such as the Mongols and the Uighurs—with different cultures and languages.) Confucian and Taoist teachings prevailed and profoundly influenced the arts.

Han potters are noted for the development of tombware, lead glaze, and feldspathic glaze. To help the deceased in the spirit world, live servants were entombed with their masters. Confucius ended this custom between the sixth and fifth centuries B.C. and supplanted it with a tradition of burying miniature clay replicas of humans and animal forms, as well as utilitarian ware and architectural buildings. This practice was known as *ming chi* (pronounced ming-chee). Today, tomb sites are a prolific source of Han ware.

The technology of lead-glazed pottery came from Alexandria via the Silk Road, the trade route that linked China and the eastern Roman Empire via Turkestan. Independently of other cultures, Han potters invented lead glaze, a clear shiny covering that would appear later in the white tin glaze of Islamic potters, in a glaze used by Spanish potters to finish Hispano-Moresque ware, in Italian majolica and Medici porcelain, in the faience and soft-paste porcelain of the French, and in English ironstone. To conceal the impurities in the clay, material that ranged in tone from brown to red to light gray, and also to imitate the patina of bronze, Han potters added the metallic oxides copper and iron to produce glaze colors of green and amber-brown.

Because stoneware is fired at a higher temperature than ordinary pottery, the body resonates, so it is sometimes known as *proto-porcelain.* To adhere to the hard surface, stoneware required a glaze that was harder than a lead glaze—one that would withstand the extreme heat of the high-temperature kiln. Challenged, Han potters invented feldspathic glaze, a rocklike covering made from feldspar, a crystalline mineral found in igneous rock. Feldspathic glaze had far-reaching influence; it was used to cover porcelain in the ninth century by Tang potters, and in the eighteenth century by European potters.

## *Tang (T'ang) Dynasty (618–907 A.D.)*

The Tang dynasty is the first great period of Chinese ceramics, and the Golden Age of medieval China. It was a relatively peaceful and stable period that fostered outstanding creativity in arts and letters, promoted dynamic expansion in political and military arenas, and witnessed territorial expansion. To identify themselves with the attributes of power, ingenuity, and the flowering of ceramics, the "sons of Han" also call themselves "men of Tang."

Trade along the Silk Road had been totally disrupted by repeated Mongolian invasions. Imported materials were unavailable, and the use of lead glaze was discontinued. But in the Tang dynasty the Silk Road was reopened and the safety of trade routes across Central Asia was secured, linking China with countries of the West, notably Iran and India. Foreign trade and cultural exchange followed. Foreigners were welcomed, and all faiths were tolerated. Buddhism, which had been introduced in the first century A.D. from India, was prominent.

With the reopening of foreign trade, lead glaze was reintroduced, but in brighter, clearer colors than before. The stiff shapes associated with *ming chi* in the Han dynasty were interpreted by Tang potters with graceful swelling forms, each part related to the whole. Decoration emphasized relief ornamentation or incised, stamped, or painted patterns. The bases were roughly finished.

The Tang potter is noted for development of stoneware called *Yue (Yüeh),* covered with celadon glaze; a tricolor glaze known as *sancai (san-ts'ai)* or Tang; tomb figures modeled with elegant realism; and the invention of porcelain in opaque and translucent textures. Although stoneware was made in the Han dynasty, Yue ware is finer and more delicate, a semitranslucent resonant proto-porcelain covered with transparent celadon glaze. Sancai, in shades of green, blue, and amber, was applied directly to biscuit, dappled onto the body with a sponge, or painted with a streaked effect the Chinese call "egg-and-spinach glaze." The nobility vied for the most impressive funerals, and magnificent tombware was made in this period—equestrians, concubines, ladies in waiting, and Bactrian camels, elegantly and realistically modeled, many with three-colored sancai glaze.

White, the color of Chinese mourning, was an important color in ancestral worship and burial ceremonies, and some white clays contain both kaolin and feldspar, two essential materials in the production of porcelain. It is generally thought that porcelain was developed by eighth-century potters, who were proficient in firing stoneware at temperatures of 1200°C (2192°F). When they took a natural step and fired the white-clay composition at slightly higher temperatures of 1250–1300°C (2280°F–2370°F), they invented porcelain, the hardest ceramic known.

At first the texture of porcelain was opaque and was occasionally applied over a thick substratum of stoneware. But Tang potters later developed translucent porcelain; translucence is the criterion by which Europeans judged porcelain. In China, porcelain was gauged by resonance; Tang musicians would arrange porcelain cups in groups of eight or twelve to form a scale for tunes played with ebony chopsticks for the court.

## *Song (Sung) Dynasty (960–1279)*

The Song dynasty is known as the first modern period of China, and the Golden Age of Chinese ceramics, a period when the development of stoneware reached its zenith. The first Song emperor, Zhao Guangyin (Zhao Kuang-yin, 960–976), who took the title of Tai Zu (T'ai-tsu), established a centralized bureaucracy staffed by civil servants, and China became a meritocracy. Rather than delegate power to the rulers of feudal kingdoms (an honor bestowed generally on the military), the state conferred wealth, power, and position on those who passed stringent scholastic examinations. Books were more available than ever before, and an elite scholar class emerged. The widely read *Illustration of Antiquities,* written in 1092 by Lu Ta-lin, spurred scholarly interest in the area; one result was that ceramic vessels were often modeled in refined forms to resemble archaic bronzes.

Along the Silk Road, banditry, extortion, and bribery still deterred traffic and trade; as a result, sea-born commerce, controlled by Arab and Indian merchants, developed in the south. In 971, a number of east coast ports opened to foreign ships; among these was Guangzhou (Canton), a port destined in the Ming and Qing (Ch'ing) dynasties to play an important role in export trade.

In the tenth and eleventh centuries, the center of wealth lay in the north, and under imperial patronage potters produced the finest ceramics of the Song dynasty, delicate ware with an almost spiritual aesthetic. Northern kilns were built on level ground with a single chamber known as a *beehive* or a *boot*, made with a single vertical chimney that protruded from the dome. In an oxidized atmosphere, the downdraft fostered glaze colors with warm yellowish undertones, a characteristic of northern Song ceramics.

The Song Chinese were primarily farmers; they lived a settled existence that clashed with the nomadic lifestyle of their Mongolian neighbors to the north. In 1126, the Qin (Ch'in) Tartars invaded China, a conflict that divided China into northern and southern regions and affected the potter's craft. The Song court fled south, where pottery was fired in "dragon kilns," furnaces shaped with long tunnels that descended from the slopes of hills. Dragon kilns were made with individual firing areas that fired pottery, stoneware, and porcelain sequentially, all at the same time. Although technically more advanced than the northern kilns, practicality was more important in southern China than aesthetics, and southern Song ceramics are not as refined as those of the northern Song. Southern kilns were fed with wood that promoted smoke and produced glaze colors with grayish undertones in a closed-kiln reduced atmosphere.

The Song potter emphasized purity of form over decoration and perfected shapes with rounded curves, such as the *meiping (mei-p'ing)* vase, a narrow-necked vase with short shoulders modeled to hold a single flower, forms that were a distinct departure from Tang tombware.

The imperial patronage of potters resulted in a prolific production of fine stoneware decorated with lightly carved or delicately molded motifs (primarily floral), covered with smooth or crackled glazes. Color was applied as an underglaze in a monochrome of jadelike hues, tones known by the name of the kiln: the dark olive green glaze is called *Northern celadon*; gray-green celadon is known as *longquan (lung-ch'üan);* lavender-gray celadon is *jun (chün);* pale lavender to bluish green is *ru (ju),* a glaze that is accidentally crackled; and lavender gray to bluish green is *guan (kuan),* a glaze that is deliberately crackled.

Although stoneware was the primary ceramic of the imperial court, there were two types of porcelains, both ornamented with a monochrome glaze: *ding (ting)* is translucent white porcelain with a faint hint of orange when held to the light, and *yinqing (ying-ch'ing)* is porcelain with a shadowy blue glaze.

For the people, Song potters made coarse stoneware called *cizhou (tz'u chou)* and *temmoku.* Cizhou was made with a light gray or buff-colored body and decorated with the most varied of Song techniques: incised, carved, impressed, slip-painted, or enameled ornamentation in a monochrome or enameled with a limited palette. Temmoku, thick stoneware made for the tea ceremony, is covered with brownish-black glaze.

By the tenth century, local families began to own the kilns, and the ceramic industry evolved from a business that functioned intermittently when the demands of agriculture were low to a year-round operation that provided steady employment for workers who specialized in certain areas, such as mining, purification of clay, modeling, decoration, kiln operation, distribution of product, and transportation.

## *Yuan (Yüen) Dynasty (1271–1368)*

In 1280, the southern Song dynasty fell to the Mongols, and Kublai Khan ascended the throne. Kublai Khan called the dynasty *Yuan,* meaning "first beginning" or "original," and set about to unite China. Within China, the great khan restored and completed the Grand Imperial Canal, an artificial waterway begun in the Sui dynasty (581–618 A.D.) to improve water transportation and promote trade. Kublai Khan also opened up China's borders, opened communication with the West, and stimulated foreign trade. Merchants from far-off Central Asia, India, Southeast Asia, and Indonesia flocked to China.

To take advantage of safe east-west travel, the pope sent Niccolo and Maffeo Polo, two Venetian brothers and merchants, as emissaries to the court of Kublai Khan. In 1271, on a return trip to China, Niccolo brought his son Marco, who later became Kublai Khan's trusted deputy, and for three years ruled as governor of Yuan Chao (Yangchow). After seventeen years of service, the khan granted Marco Polo the right to return to Venice bearing a few gifts of porcelain, including an incense burner now housed in the treasury of St. Mark's Cathedral. On the return voyage, a fight ensued with the Genoese and Marco Polo was taken prisoner. From jail, the great adventurer related his travels to a chronicler with whom he was imprisoned, a story that mentions the *porcelain* bowls of Fujian (Fukien) Province in southern China. Marco Polo coined the term *porcelain* from the Italian-Portugese word *porcellana* for the resemblance it bears to the interior of the translucent pearly-white cowrie shell.

Porcelain was the primary ceramic of the Yuan dynasty. Imperial patronage once so important to the Song potter was irrelevant to the Yuan potter, and ornamentation was more important than form. Yuan potters freely expressed themselves in the bold ornamentation that reflected the stimulus of foreign merchants and artisans—a robust, elaborate, complex style typically arranged in eight zones. The soft jadelike glazes of the Song dynasty were supplanted in the Yuan dynasty by bright, colorful, blue-and-white ornamentation called *Qing Hua (Ch'ing Hua);* monochrome blue and red decoration; and *shu fu,* porcelain modeled with low-relief ornamentation.

Blue ornamentation was made from Persian cobalt, a color applied directly to the body, covered with lead glaze, and fired—a simple and inexpensive one-step method of production. Because the supply of cobalt was plentiful, Yuan blue-and-white ware was made in huge amounts for export, and today the largest collections are found in Iran, Indonesia, and Turkey, notably at the Topkapu Sarayi, Istanbul, and the Ardebil Shrine, Teheran. Monochrome blue and red ornamentation was limited to two colors on a white ground. Shu fu, an ornamental porcelain made for the court, was decorated in low relief and covered with pale bluish-green glaze.

### *Ming Dynasty (1368–1644)*

Eventually, the hardships suffered under Mongolian rule fueled rebellion, and in 1368 the Han Chinese under the leadership of Zhu Yuan-Zhang (Chu Yüan-chang), a peasant priest-turned-soldier, pushed the Mongols out of Beijing and back beyond the northern frontier. Zhu established the Ming dynasty, Chinese for "brilliant." As emperor, Zhu Yuan-zhang took the reign name Hong Wu (Hung Wu), and set about to eliminate Mongol influences and reestablish Han Chinese traditions.

Porcelain was the primary ceramic category in the Ming dynasty, stoneware was secondary, and earthenware was seldom made, except for roof tiles and statues of mythical roof guardians. Vessel shapes were diverse and the contours were varied. Although Ming potters improved upon centuries-old techniques, they are associated primarily with the development of blue-and-white ornamentation, polychrome enamels, and white ware.

Cobalt from Persia was initially the source of blue. However, in 1431, foreign trade was curtailed, and the supply of cobalt grew scarce. Fortuitously, cobalt was discovered in China in the fifteenth century and thereafter local cobalt was used. But when Persian cobalt was available, it was mixed with Chinese cobalt, a combination that produced deep blue with a silvery hue.

Ming potters are noted for polychrome enamels in combinations of colors. *Tang Sancai (San-ts'ai)*, "three-color ware," which was used in the Tang dynasty as an underglaze, was applied as an overglaze enamel in the Ming dynasty, primarily in shades of purple, yellow, and green. *Doucai (Tou-ts'ai)*, Chinese for "contrasting colors," is characterized by a blue outline underglaze, filled in overglaze with enamels of red, lemon yellow, apple green, and aubergine. *Wucai (Wu ts'ai)*, meaning "five-color ware," is a misleading term, for more often the ware was enameled with six or seven colors. The designs were outlined with red or black enamel and filled in with blue, iron red, yellow, turqoise, and green; the palette sometimes included aubergine and black as well.

Firing conditions were far from perfect in the Ming dynasty, and although red was obtained from copper oxide, it often fired to a grayish-red hue, an unsatisfactory color, costly to execute, and discontinued by order of the emperor. As a replacement, Ming potters developed red from iron, an oxide that produced a dull, dark shade. It was not until the nineteenth-century Qing dynasty that red was successfully executed with copper.

Whereas early in the Ming dynasty the porcelain body bore a slight hint of blue owing to impurities in the material, by the seventeenth century the body was improved, and the demand for plain white porcelain superseded that of blue-and-white ware, specifically *blanc de chine* and *An hua*. *Blanc de chine,* a French term meaning "white ware of China," is white porcelain decorated with molded, carved, or engraved ornamentation, used for such items as figures of Guan Yin (Kwan-yin), the goddess of mercy. *An hua*, Chinese for "secret decoration," is a translucent porcelain made with an eggshell thickness, delicate ware decorated with carved ornamentation or painted underglaze with white slip-in motifs visible only when held to the light.

In 1369 Hong Wu rebuilt the kilns at Jingdezhen (Ching-te-chen), and established an imperial porcelain site, the most important ceramic center in China and perhaps the world, where over 3,000 kilns operated. Work was done by serfs under the feudal *corvée* system (i.e., requisitioned or forced labor). Overflow orders were filled by hundreds of private kilns, and to satisfy demand unskilled laborers were employed who tried unsuccessfully to emulate the work of the imperial potteries.

In 1620, with the demise of Emperor Wan Li, power shifted into the hands of eunuchs. Corruption ran rampant and internal strife and economic ruin followed. In 1644, China fell to the Manchus, bringing an end to the brilliant Ming dynasty.

## *Qing (Ch'ing) Dynasty (1644–1911)*

The Qing dynasty marks the final great period of Chinese ceramics. The last imperial dynasty of China was founded by Huang Taiji (Hong Taiji), a Mongol leader who named it *Da Qing (Ta Qing)* for "pure."

Qing potters are noted for the revival of past ceramic traditions, the technical perfection of porcelain, the development of pure white porcelain, mass production, ornamentation with Persian motifs and phrases, and the development of new polychrome and monochrome colors.

In 1674, rebels set fire to Jingdezhen, closing the kilns, but the ceramic center was rebuilt in 1683 by Emperor Kang Xi (K'ang-hsi), a hub where technically perfect porcelain was produced for the court. The *corvée* system was replaced by paid labor. Work was organized into divisions, and porcelain manufacture passed through many stages: shaping, finishing, painting, and firing, tasks supervised by an overseer appointed by the court, some of whom became noted authorities in the field. The specialization of skills fostered improved production methods, evident in a pure white porcelain body. Although ornamentation was executed with exact precision, it bordered on mechanical, and Qing porcelain lacks the spontaneity characteristic of Han, Tang, Song, Yuan, and Ming ceramics.

To satisfy the considerable needs of the court, and to meet the heavy demands of export trade, Qing porcelain was mass-produced. Potters were forced to abandon standards of quality and for the people produced far-from-perfect porcelain. Export ware was characterized by impure bodies flawed with pits and bubbles. To cover the defects, export porcelain was embellished with ornate ornamentation that covered the entire surface.

In 1709, hard-paste porcelain was invented in Germany, and within 50 years porcelain was produced in France, Italy, England, Holland, Vienna, and Copenhagen. Initially, European porcelain was expensive and the manufactories were slow to deliver, but as production increased and the cost went down, so did the demand for Chinese porcelain. To compensate, Qing potters targeted Near Eastern markets, notably India and Persia, and incorporated geometric patterns and Arabic phrases in the ornamentation.

The development of new enamel colors brought a decline in the demand for blue-and-white ornamentation. A polychrome palette took its place. Albert Jacquemart, a French ceramic historian in the eighteenth century, divided the ware into four color families. *Famille verte* (green) featured patterns outlined in blue or brownish-black enamel, filled in with brilliant transparent green, accented with subordinate colors of iron red, violet blue, aubergine purple, and sunny yellow. *Famille jaune* (yellow) was accented with subordinate colors of the *famille verte* palette. *Famille noire* (black) featured a black ground washed over with transparent green enamel, and as accent used subordinate shades of the *famille verte*. *Famille rose* (rose) featured a palette of pink to purplish rose, colors accented with subordinate colors of yellow, green, and blue. *Famille rose* is the only Western influence on Chinese ceramics; it was developed in the seventeenth century by Andreas Cassius of Leyden, Holland, from tin oxide and gold chloride, and introduced circa 1685 to the Chinese court by Jesuit missionaries. The pinkish-purple tones were so popular that eventually the demand for *famille rose* superseded the demand for *famille verte*.

Qing potters also introduced new monochrome colors known as *sang de boeuf* (oxblood red); *flambé,* copper red streaked with purple, lavender gray, and blue; *peachbloom,* a pink to liver-red color mottled with red, green, or brown; and *tea dust,* light brown with a hint of green, a shade that imitated patinated bronze.

In 1912, the Republic of China was established, followed in 1949 by the People's Republic of China, a change that brought an end to imperial China, and to the last great period of Chinese ceramics.

## Islamic Pottery

The progress of Islamic pottery is divided into early, middle, and late periods, one era overlapping another. In the early period potters invented white tin glaze. In the middle period, scratched ornamentation was introduced. In the late period, old techniques were reestablished.

### *The Early Period (Seventh to Eleventh Centuries)*

The early period was preceded by a series of wars that raged in the Middle East from the fourth to the fifth centuries, a conflict that changed the social and political hierarchy of a settled life to that of a nomadic existence dominated by marauding tribes, a law unto themselves, a milieu that inhibited the progress of pottery. But in 622 A.D., the migratory lifestyle changed when the prophet Mohammed united the tribes of the Arabian peninsula into a monotheistic faith under one god, Allah, and established *Islam,* a name that means "submission to God's will." Those who practice the Islamic faith are known as *Muslims,* Arabic for "true believer."

To emulate light gray stoneware and white-bodied porcelain from China, Mesopotamian potters concentrated on the surface of pottery and developed lead glaze, white tin glaze, slip-painted decoration, and luster. The Romans had invented transparent lead glaze, and the Han Chinese had developed colorful lead glaze; now Islamic potters of the Umayyad period (660–750) created clear lead glaze that adhered well to low-fired pottery. The Umayyad were the successors of Mohammed and the first hereditary dynasty of caliphs and Islamic religious leaders. Today, lead-glazed Umayyad tiles are seen at the Dome of the Rock in Jerusalem and at the Great Mosque of Damascus.

To give pottery the white look of porcelain, Islamic artisans opacified lead glaze with tin, a covering known as *white tin glaze.* Islamic potters also painted vessels with slip, ornamentation made from fine clay mixed with water to a thick consistency.

The Koran forbad the use of precious metals to make tableware, so to capture the light that emanates from gold, silver, and platinum, potters created *luster* (from the Latin word *lustrare,* "to light" or "to illumine"). Luster was perhaps the greatest achievement of the Mesopotamian potter. First the potter applied a thin solution of metal oxide over once-fired white tin glaze. Then the ware was fired a second time in a reduced kiln. Lusterware was used in the early period to decorate ceramic ware, such as ewers, bowls, and dishes, and in the middle period to make mosaics and as a ground cover on decorative tiles.

## *The Middle Period (Twelfth to Fourteenth Centuries)*

The dawning of the middle period occurred when the Seljuk Turks, a branch of a nomadic Turkic people who adopted the Islamic faith, overtook the area that is now Iran, Iraq, Syria, and Asia Minor. From 1056 to 1256 they ruled as far west as Anatolia. Under Seljuk leadership, a renaissance of the arts and literature occurred, a golden age of decorative arts that lasted from about 1175 to 1225. New pottery centers were established along the Caspian Sea and the mountainous regions of northern and northwestern Persia (Iran).

Potters of the middle period excelled in incised ornamentation called *sgraffito,* an Italian word for "incised" or "scratched," a form of decoration inspired by cizhou, Song stoneware made for the people. *Sgraffito* created raised edges that acted as dikes and prevented colors from running freely over the glaze. Three distinct styles of *sgraffito* were produced. *Amol* was covered with white slip and incised with simple lines. *Champlevé* featured two-tone decoration in which large portions of green or brown glaze were carved away to reveal the underlying color of the darker body. *Aghkand* featured incised designs in white slip that created raised borders, filled in with colorful shades of green, brown, and yellow, a technique similar to cloissoné.

## *The Late Period (Fifteenth to Nineteenth Centuries)*

From 1220 to 1505 Persia suffered from repeated Mongolian invasion, a period that failed to foster new pottery methods; instead, several old ceramic techniques were reintroduced, each one named for a place, rather than a technique.

*Kubachi* gets its name from the remote metal-working village in Daghestan in the Caucasus, a hamlet noted for its ceramic tiles used to decorate the walls of homes, polychromed in colors of brown, green, yellow, red, black, and white, under a clear crackled glaze. *Gombroon* was made to satisfy the enormous demand for export ware. When the English and Dutch East India companies were unable to get Chinese porcelain, they substituted white ware from Persia made with pierced ornamentation filled in with translucent glaze. The ware was shipped from the port of Gombroon (present-day Bandar Abbas), hence the name. *Isnik* was made in ancient Nicaea near western Anatolia. The colorful polychrome tiles and domestic ware are decorated with an underglaze in brilliant colors, notably cobalt blue, turquoise, green, and purple. Sometimes Isnik is called *Rhodian ware,* an erroneous name attributed to the nineteenth century, from colorful sherds excavated at Lindos on the island of Rhodes. Isnik was also known as *Damascus ware,* a name for white-bodied ware that resembled Isnik, decorated with colorful stylized flowers and leaves outlined in black. *Kirman,* named after a pottery center in eastern Iran, was ornamented to imitate Chinese porcelain, notably in monochromes of celadon or blue on white.

After three hundred years of Mongol invasion, little was left in Persia to foster the ceramics arts. Potters began to migrate to Europe, a flight that ended the rich tradition of Islamic pottery but brought new life to Europe.

## European Pottery and Porcelain

When the western Roman Empire fell to the barbarians in the fifth century, pottery techniques such as the potter's wheel, translucent lead glaze, and slip ornamentation were all but forgotten, and in the early Middle Ages of Europe the development of pottery lay dormant for almost a thousand years. The exception were tiles made by monastic orders for architectural use in churches and monasteries.

Islamic potters who migrated to Spain via North Africa introduced lusterware and white tin glaze. This led to the production of lustered and nonlustered pottery called *Hispano-Moresque ware.* Hispano-Moresque ware was greatly admired in Europe, and from the fifteenth to the seventeenth centuries, huge quantities were produced at Manises, a suburb of Valencia opposite the Balearic island of Majorca. From Majorca the ware was exported to Italy. Because the pottery was transported on Majorcan boats, Italian merchants assumed Hispano-Moresque ware was made on Majorca, and called it *majolica.*

In time the Italians began to manufacture majolica at centers noted for specialized shapes and particular colors, such as Deruta, Faenza, Tuscany, Caffaggiolo, Castel Durante, Gubbio, Urbino, Siena, and Venice. By the thirteenth century, the technique of tin-glazed pottery was spread by Italian potters who migrated northward; potters from Faenza, Italy, introduced tin-glazed ware to France, where it was called *faience.*

Because majolica and faience were essentially the same, today the terms are used synonymously, and the difference between them lies in the years in which each was made. While Italian majolica is associated with colorful tin-glazed earthenware produced in the thirteenth through sixteenth centuries, French faience evokes colorful earthenware made in the seventeenth and eighteenth centuries (and beyond), notably at Lyons, Saint Porchère, Nîmes, and Nevers.

Independent of the Chinese, in the fourteenth century German potters invented stoneware; production was centered in Cologne, Sieberg, and the Westerwald, geographical regions blessed with the right clay and surrounded by forests that provided fuel for the high-temperature kilns. In contrast to majolica, made of soft clay decorated with painted ornamentation applied with a brush, stoneware was made of hard clay decorated with cut, punched, or gouged designs from metal tools. Moreover, while majolica was shaped in simple horizontal shapes primarily as dishes and low bowls, stoneware, a hard ceramic, was produced in vertical shapes, such as jugs and tankards.

But porcelain was always the goal of potters. The Chinese were able to monopolize the technique by spreading the false notion that the clay needed to mature in the ground for decades. The few pieces of porcelain that reached medieval Europe were carried across Central Asia or transported around the Cape of Good Hope by Portugese ships engaged in export trade. By the Renaissance, porcelain was considered one of the world's great wonders, a treasure worthy of a king, a princely prize mounted in gold, silver, or bronze and displayed like a jewel. Demand for porcelain was insatiable and eventually sparked a craze.

The European search for the secret of hard-paste porcelain led to the development of soft porcelain, produced in Urbino from about 1575 to 1587 under the patronage of Francesco de' Medici, grand duke of Tuscany. Medici porcelain was composed of 80 percent kaolin clay and 20 percent ground glass, a translucent body, thickly potted, decorated underglaze with blue ornamentation. Although only sixty pieces of Medici porcelain are extant, about 1673 the secret of soft porcelain was rediscovered in France, knowledge that led to manufactories at Saint Cloud and Chantilly.

Jean Baptiste Colbert, financial minister to Louis XIV in the seventeenth century, advanced the principle of mercantilism, a concept that advocated, as a means to economic stability and power, the sponsorship of local self-sufficient industries. In 1701, Count Ehrenfried Walter von Tschirnhaus, a German physicist and mathematician engaged in porcelain research, suggested to Augustus the Strong, king of

The tankard shown here was manufactured in Germany by Meissen, c. 1715.

Poland and elector of Saxony, that he establish a local manufactory to make hard stones or porcelain. But the king was engaged in war with Charles II of Sweden (1700–1706) and had neither the interest nor the funds to undertake the enterprise.

In the eighteenth century the esoteric science of alchemy supported the idea that it was possible to make certain elements, such as gold or silver, from a combination of the right earthly substances, such as lead or copper, mixed with the elements of water, earth, air, or fire. In 1704, when Tschirnhaus met Johann Friedrich

Böttger, a young German alchemist who boasted he could make gold, history was made, for gold was what the king needed to pay for his foreign wars.

The tale of Tschirnhaus and Böttger is fraught with considerable trauma and includes imprisonment for Böttger, his attempted escape, and the king's wrath for subsidizing experiments that failed to produce gold. But after persistent trials, in July 1708 the two scientists succeeded in discovering the formula for the first hard-paste porcelain produced in Europe. The body was somewhat whiter and smoother than that of Chinese porcelain, but the right glaze remained elusive, and the search was complicated by the death of Tschirnhaus in October 1708. Undaunted, Böttger continued alone and on March 20, 1709, reported he could make "good white porcelain together with the finest glaze and appropriate painting in such perfection as to equal if not surpass the East Indian."

THIS GERMAN PORCELAIN TEAPOT, C. 1765, IS FINELY PAINTED, ENAMELED, AND GILDED.

In 1710, the manufacture of porcelain was patented, and the Royal Saxon Porcelain Manufactory was located at Albrechtsburg in Meissen, a site 12 miles from Dresden, where the king had previously imprisoned Böttger for his failure to make gold. By 1713, porcelain was offered on a commercial basis for sale at the Leipzig fair. Böttger remained in charge of production until he was 37, but on March 13, 1719, he died of alcoholism, an unfulfilled scientist who wanted only to make gold. Above the entrance to his laboratory is this inscription: "God our creator has made of a goldmaker, a potmaker."

To retain a monopoly on the manufacture of porcelain, the formula was withheld from the rest of Europe. Security was extraordinarily tight at the manufactory; the atmosphere was prison-like, and eventually only deaf and mute workers were hired. But despite the strictest of controls, within 50 years, hard-paste porcelain was made in Copenhagen by the Royal Danish Porcelain Factory; in France by the Royal Sèvres Manufactory; in Holland by Weesp, Oude Loosdrecht, and Amstel; in Italy by Capodimonte, Buen Retiro, Doccia, and Vezzi; in Vienna at du Paquier; and in England by Bristol, Minton, Nantgarw and Swansea, New Hall, Plymouth, Rockingham, and Worcester.

## English Pottery and Porcelain

Toward the end of the sixteenth century, two Dutch potters from Antwerp migrated to Lambeth and set about to make majolica, pottery covered with white glaze opacified with tin. The latter was transported from Cornwall by sea, and for ease of transportation, the potteries were located near seaports.

To compete with Chinese export porcelain, in 1671 John Dwight, an English scientist-potter, took out a patent at Fulham, Middlesex, to make stoneware, an earthenware category with the porcellaneous characteristics of translucency and delicacy. His patent read, in part:

> The mistery of Transparent Earthenware, Commonly knowne by the Names of Porcelain or a China and Persian Ware, as Alsoe the Mistries of Stone Ware Vulgarly called Cologne Ware.

Because stoneware withstands heat well, Dwight produced utilitarian shapes that held hot liquids, namely mugs and teapots, as well as decorative busts and statues.

But the English pottery industry did not achieve prominence until the eighteenth century, when in 1720 deposits of ball clay were discovered in England at Devon and Dorset. *Ball clay* is a unique clay used by potters to make thin white stoneware glazed with common table salt. It was also used to make *creamware,* a name for light-bodied earthenware with the white look of porcelain, ware developed by John Astbury and perfected by Josiah Wedgwood. Soon the demand for creamware exceeded the market for delftware, majolica, and faience in England and Europe.

The development of creamware coincided with the Industrial Revolution and the invention of Sheffield, a name for silver fused over copper. For the first time, the common man could afford white-bodied dinnerware—thin, hard, durable, uniformly colored, and well-shaped—and at the same time eat from utensils plated with silver. Creamware was made in utilitarian shapes inspired by silverware, notably tea services, a demand that culminated when Queen Charlotte commissioned a tea set from Wedgwood in 1765, a product known thereafter as *Queen's ware*.

In the nineteenth century, Josiah Spode II developed a hard type of earthenware called *stone china*, a dense body with a grayish or bluish cast. Initially, stone china was known as *opaque porcelain*, *semiporcelain*, *granite ware*, and *ironstone*—ware decorated primarily with transfer prints with oriental motifs. In 1813, Charles James Mason of Lane Delph, Staffordshire, patented the use of scoria (iron slag that remains in the furnace after iron has melted) in the manufacture of earthenware, based on experiments conducted by his father, Miles Mason, and later introduced as "Mason's patent ironstone china." Ironstone was covered with white tin glaze that gave the body the look of opaque white porcelain, a hard durable earthenware suitable as tableware, and widely copied between 1830 and 1880.

Porcelain manufactory was given impetus in 1768 when William Cookworthy, a Plymouth apothecary, discovered a deposit of kaolin at Cornwall, a find that led to manufacture of soft-paste porcelain, bone china, and hard-paste porcelain. Because soft-paste porcelain was composed of kaolin, alabaster, and frit (the latter a glasslike substance), the formula tended to melt or collapse in the kiln. To strengthen the composition, calcined animal bones or powdered soapstone were added. Soon it was evident that bone ash promoted plasticity, fostered elaborate shapes, strengthened the formula, lowered the risk of collapse in the kiln, reduced wastage, and diminished production costs. Around 1794, Josiah Spode II increased the amount of bone ash in the composition and perfected the proportion of bone ash to the porcelain formula. Bone china was produced by Bow, Chelsea, Longton Hall, Lowestoft, Derby, Nantgarw, and Swansea. Porcelain made with soapstone was produced at Bristol, Worcester, Chaffer's Liverpool factory, Lowestoft, Caughley, and Swansea. But manufacture of ware with powdered soapstone eventually ceased and bone china became the standard English body—strong, durable, white-bodied ware that held hot liquids without forming cracks, used to make fine teacups and teapots.

## American Pottery and Porcelain

The American pottery and porcelain industries were overshadowed by competition from abroad and slow to develop any degree of sophistication. Potters and customers alike were scattered in small settlements across the eastern seaboard, deliveries of raw materials were slow, and production was inhibited by England's colonial laws that suppressed the establishment of local manufactories. The range of early tableware was limited. The average household used bowls, mugs, and pots made of crude pottery, while people of means imported pottery from abroad, such as delftware from England and stoneware from Germany.

Late in the eighteenth century, the threat of lead leaching from lead-glazed pottery, coupled with a discovery of a rich new vein of clay that ran from South Amboy, New Jersey, to Staten Island and Long Island, prompted the manufacture of stoneware. In 1738, André Duché discovered a thick vein of kaolin running from Virginia through North Carolina to Georgia. The deposit, called *unaker* by the Indians, launched the American porcelain industry. Duché was the first person to attempt to make porcelain in the New World, but after several attempts at manufacture, begun in Savannah, Georgia, in 1741, he abandoned production.

The first authenticated manufacture of American soft-paste porcelain is credited to Gousse Bonnin, who in 1770 in partnership with George Anthony Morris, established the American China Manufactory in Southwark, a suburb of Philadelphia, and in 1771 advertised the firm could supply dealers with blue-and-white wares. The partnership operated for two years—from 1770 to 1772. Today, only a few pieces of the blue-and-white ware survive.

It wasn't until the nineteenth century that the American ceramic industry achieved any degree of sophistication. The first successful production of American hard-paste porcelain on a commercial basis is attributed to William Ellis Tucker, who in 1827 founded a company in Philadelphia later known as Tucker and Hemphill, a firm noted for the manufacture of dinner services, tea equipage, coffeeware, decorative items, and elegant white pitchers ornamented with gold and floral motifs.

By the mid-nineteenth century, the growing middle class demanded translucent dinnerware, and *parian,* a name for unglazed biscuit porcelain. Ott & Brewer of Trenton, New Jersey, were noted for manufacture of parian figures, such as "The Pitcher," a baseball player modeled by Isaac Broome in 1876, and seen today in the New Jersey State Museum. Generic shapes were popular, such as a presentation pitcher made by Charles Cartlidge & Co. of Greenpoint, New York, a firm that produced hotel pitchers modeled under the spout with molded replicas of the American eagle. In 1870, Karl Muller, a sculptor, joined the Union Porcelain Works (formerly Charles Cartlidge & Co.) and designed the Century Vase, a vessel exhibited at the Philadelphia Centennial of 1876 that honored the newly formed U.S. Potters Association.

Following the Centennial exhibition, the American preference for foreign porcelain led to the manufacture of *Belleek,* a thin type of parian with an iridescent luster and ivory-colored body. In 1889, Jonathan Coxon Sr. and Walter Scott Lenox collaborated in the manufacture of Belleek under the name of the Ceramic Art Company of Trenton, New Jersey. In 1906, Coxon and Lenox changed the name to Lenox, Inc., a company destined to become the leading manufacturer of porcelain dinnerware in the United States. In 1918, President Woodrow Wilson, the twenty-eighth president of the United States, commissioned Lenox to make a 1,700-piece dinnerware service for the White House; this was followed in 1932 by a similar order from President Franklin D. Roosevelt, and in 1951 by an order from President Harry S. Truman. In 1981, President Ronald Reagan commissioned Lenox to make a 4,732-piece bone china dinnerware service hand-painted in the center with a gold seal.

From pottery to porcelain, today dinnerware is made of assorted materials to meet specific needs. Most utilitarian ware is safe in the microwave oven, freezer, and dishwasher. Elegant ware is trimmed with precious metals and reserved for posh occasions.

CHAPTER FOUR

# DECORATIVE METHODS AND STYLES

WHETHER WE ARE STROLLING through a museum, adding to a collection, or browsing through a store, we cannot help but respond to ceramics. The colors, glazes, textures, and shapes touch our senses and give excitement to the table setting with decoration born of old techniques. But so often we fail to fully appreciate a ceramic because we are unfamiliar with a particular technique. The following list of terms can be used for easy reference.

APPLIED DECORATION. A term for ornamentation made separately from the body of ware and attached with liquid clay called *slip*.

BASALT WARE or BLACK BASALTES. From the Latin word *basaltes*, "dark, hard marble," basalt ware is a name for dark stoneware made with oxides of iron and manganese that fire to black. The texture is finely grained, hard enough to polish on a lathe, and ornamented with molded or applied relief decoration. Basalt ware was invented in 1767 by Josiah Wedgwood; it is a ceramic made primarily for display pieces, such as busts, statues, portrait medallions, relief plaques, vases, flower pots, pitchers, and tea ware.

BAROQUE. From the Portugese *barroco*, meaning an irregular "imperfect pearl," the baroque style is bold, curvaceous, irregular in form, and symmetrically balanced—a highly ornate style that flourished in the late Renaissance. In the field of ceramics, the baroque style is epitomized by figures modeled at Meissen, circa 1740, by J. J. Kändler, a master ceramicist of the period.

BELLEEK. Thin-bodied, ivory-colored porcelain made in Belleek, county Fermanagh, Northern Ireland. In 1850, a nearby discovery of kaolin and feldspar spawned an industry for translucent porcelain with the thickness of eggshell. Belleek was made for both utilitarian and decorative purposes, shaped often in the form of seashells or marine life, such as coral branches. The glaze has a nacreous luster, similar to mother-of-pearl. Belleek is still made today.

BISCUIT. A ceramic fired to a leather-hard state but left unglazed. Enamel may be applied directly to biscuit ("on biscuit"), rather than to glaze. *Biscuit porcelain* is unglazed porcelain used primarily to make figures. This type of manufacture was introduced at Sèvres circa 1751. Because biscuit porcelain was unglazed, the composition and execution of the material were perfect and the ware brought a higher price than glazed porcelain embellished with ornamentation.

*BLANC DE CHINE.* A milky white porcelain produced in the Ming dynasty at the Dehua kilns, Fujian Province, and also known as *Dehua*. The unpainted body was covered with a thick lustrous glaze that looked similar to lard, one richer than the normal feldspathic glaze. *Blanc de chine* was decorative ware, used to make Chinese figures, notably Buddha, Guan Yin (Buddhist goddess of mercy), and dogs of Fo, as well as vases, bowls, and incense burners decorated with plum or cherry blossoms, a product still made today.

*BLUMEN.* German for "flowers," *Blumen* is a decorative style dating from about 1720 and inspired by botanical illustrations of anemones, peonies, and roses, depicted in red, blue, green, purple, and violet, and painted singly or in loosely tied bouquets. *Deutsche Blumen* or "German flowers" is a realistic style introduced about 1725 by Höroldt of Meissen. *Indianische Blumen* is a stylized portrayal of flowers, an ornamental mode popular at Meissen around 1740, inspired by Japanese Kakiemon and Chinese famille verte.

CARTOUCHE. From the Italian *cartoccio,* meaning "cartridge" or "roll of paper," a cartouche is a border treatment similar in look to a scrolled sheet of paper, a motif used to frame a central design, such as a crest.

CELADON. A color that ranges in tone from whitish blue to pale green to sea green to deep olive greenish brown. In 1171, Nureddin, sultan of Egypt, sent forty pieces of green-glazed stoneware to Saladin, sultan of Damascus; this is thought to be the origin of the word *celadon*. In the seventeenth century, the cast of a pastoral romance entitled *L'Astrée* by Honoré d'Urfé included Céladon, a shepherd boy who wore clothes decorated with gray-green ribbons.

CHINESE EXPORT WARE. Between the seventeenth and early eighteenth centuries tremendous growth occurred in export trade between China and Europe. To satisfy the enormous demand in Europe for porcelain tea ware and dinner services, the kilns at Jingdezhen engaged in mass production. Ware made by special order for Western tastes was modeled from silver prototypes and drawings supplied by the East India Company.

To meet production deadlines, the kilns were forced to hire less-than-skilled laborers. Impure clay was used that frequently resulted in a porcelain body with a grayish-white or bluish-white cast. Shapes were roughly modeled, and to keep many of the pots from sticking in the kiln, they were fired on sand, a method of manufacture that fostered rough, gritty bases. Oftentimes, the glaze was contaminated with small holes, similar to pin pricks, and workers covered imperfections with gaudy decoration to conceal defects.

Blue underglaze ornamentation was decorated primarily at Jingdezhen. Polychrome enamels were executed at Guangdong (Canton). Popular export styles included armorial, Canton, Carrack, Fitzhugh, Jesuit, Lowestoft, Nanking, and Swatow.

- *Armorial ware* featured a coat of arms or a family crest, copied by Chinese artisans from Western drawings or bookplates. Westerners without such family heraldry used a cipher or a portrait, a style known as *pseudo-armorial*. Symbols of historical interest were also featured: for example, the Society of the Cincinnati, a fraternity of select officers who served in the American Revolution, among them George Washington, a collector of armorial ware.

- *Canton ware* is associated primarily with blue-and-white stock patterns that varied slightly. The ornamentation featured landscapes and figures in a stylized border; common decorations were pine trees, willows, a pagoda, distant mountains, river banks, a teahouse. A figure may be seen in the window of the teahouse, or there may be three fishermen on the rocks or on a bridge. A variation of this type of ornamentation, called the *willow pattern* in England, was adapted to English tastes by Thomas Minton, who made an engraving for Thomas Turner. It was introduced at Caughley circa 1780.

> *Two pigeons flying high,*
> *Chinese vessels sailing by,*
> *Weeping willows hanging o'er,*
> *Bridges with three men, if not four.*
> *Chinese temple, there it stands,*
> *Seems to take up all the land.*
> *Apple tree with apples on,*
> *A pretty fence to end my song.*

- *Carrack porcelain* evokes blue-and-white porcelain with a grayish-blue hue made in the reign of Emperor Wan Li, (1573–1620). The ware is also known as *Kraak porcelain,* a term coined in the sixteenth century by Dutch traders engaged in East India trade. Carrack porcelain was traded from the Portugese base in Macao and exported to Europe on Portugese ships called *carracks*.

  Dutch pirates captured and plundered two Portugese carracks off the coast of Malaya, the *San Yago* in 1602 and the *Santa Caterina* in 1604. Shortly thereafter, over 150,000 pieces of porcelain of all kinds were auctioned at Middleburg and Amsterdam to buyers in northern Europe, among them representatives of King James I of England and Henry IV of France. The cache included underglaze blue-and-white porcelain. The close association with the recently plundered carracks caused the name to stick.
- *Fitzhugh* is the name of a Welsh family who for three generations engaged in export trade with China. Between 1779 and 1781, Thomas Fitzhugh

placed special orders for a pattern that came to be known by the family name. The border treatment featured a delicate lattice-like diamond pattern called a *diaper.* Mythological symbols, pomegranates, flowers, and Buddha's hand citron, were interspersed along the border or around the well of the plate. The center of the plate featured a medallion, notably an emblem or a cipher, surrounded by four groups of flowers with symbolic significance. Fitzhugh was enameled primarily in shades of blue, although red, green, and brown were used occasionally.

- *Jesuit porcelain* is a type of Chinese export ware, notably tea ware, ornamented with Western religious subjects supplied by French Jesuit priests, among them allegorical and mythological themes taken from well-known European paintings, such as the work of Watteau, along with engravings published in the late sixteenth century, notably those of Père Nadal of Antwerp. French Jesuit priests were extremely influential at the Chinese court and were encouraged by Louis XIV to settle in China. Jesuit porcelain was decorated in shades of black and gray with an occasional accent of gold. Black decoration was known as *encre de chine,* the French term for india ink. Gray ornamentation that replicated stone relief, such as the bas relief of antique stoneware, was called *en grisailles.*
- *Lowestoft* is the name of a small manufactory in East Anglia on the south coast of England. Between 1757 and 1780 the manufactory produced soft-paste porcelain ornamented with floral motifs and Chinese patterns. When the factory closed, Robert Allen, a former employee, worked on his own as a decorator of blank ware, white porcelain glazed but not ornamented, some of it exported from China, and also engaged in the sale of Chinese porcelain. In 1863, when William Chaffers, author of *Marks and Monograms on Pottery and Porcelain,* suggested a possible link between hard-paste porcelain produced at Jingdezhen and English soft-paste porcelain made at Lowestoft—a connection that was never proven—"Lowestoft" became a misnomer for export porcelain.
- *Nanking porcelain* was made in the latter half of the eighteenth century and the early nineteenth century at Jingdezhen but shipped from the port of Nanking. The ornamentation, primarily Chinese landscape scenes with buildings, similar to Canton ware, was rendered in blue and white, although border patterns, such as Fitzhugh, were also made at Canton.

- *Swatow* is roughly potted export ware shipped from the port of Swatow in Guandong Province, southern China, and transported to India and Japan. Swatow was made of unrefined clay, modeled in large sizes for export trade, and exuberantly ornamented in underglaze blue and white or enameled in a polychrome of turquoise, red, and black. Swatow was fired on sand and the bases were gritty.

CHINOISERIE. The European idealization of Chinese motifs, chinoiserie evokes fantasy scenes of China, such as landscapes with distant pagodas, beautifully robed figures, and mythical Chinese monsters, a decorative style developed in the eighteenth century by J. G. Höroldt, chief decorator at Meissen.

DELFT. Until porcelain was invented in Europe in the early eighteenth century, tin-glazed earthenware was as close as most Europeans came to owning white-bodied ware. To imitate porcelain, potters from Delft, a small town near Rotterdam, covered earthenware with white tin glaze and an overglaze of cobalt blue or polychrome enamels, resulting in a product also known as *poor man's porcelain*. Because tin oxide was somewhat scarce at the time, the glaze was expensive, and Delft was often glazed only on the front side. However, to give the covering a smooth, glassy finish and to enhance the brilliance of the colors, some of the dishes were given a second coating of translucent lead glaze.

The difference between Delft and tin-glazed majolica lies in the quality of the clay. While majolica was made from ordinary clay modeled with a thick coarse texture, Delft was made from refined clay thinly potted to resemble porcelain. The finest Delft was produced between 1640 and 1740.

DELFTWARE. Delftware was introduced to England in the late sixteenth century by itinerant Dutch potters, a name for white tin-glazed earthenware ornamented with blue and occasionally with polychrome enamels. Although Delft and delftware look similar, delftware is uncapitalized because it is a product of several different cities, such as Lambeth, London, Bristol, and Liverpool, as opposed to enameled tin-glazed ware that is made in the Dutch town of Delft.

ECLECTIC. From the Greek *ekletikos*, "to select" or "to pick out," eclecticism is a style picked out from many periods, starting in the Renaissance with the Italians who rediscovered the classicism of antiquity, followed in the seventeenth century by the baroque that drew from classicism, inspired in the late eighteenth century primarily by rococo grotesques, and in the early nineteenth century by the Victorian interest in historic, naturalistic, and exotic styles.

ENAMELS. Enamels are opaque pigments made of powdered glass colored with metallic oxide, such as copper, suspended in an oily medium. Enamels are usually applied over glaze and fired at a low temperature, but sometimes are applied directly to biscuit. The ornamentation is unprotected and enamels are used primarily to ornament decorative objects.

*EN CAMAÏEU.* A French term for monochrome painting, *en camaïeu* encompasses several shades of one color, such as tonal variations of blue or pink.

GLAZE. A liquid coating of glass that renders ceramics impermeable to liquid absorption, glaze is painted, dusted, or sprayed onto ware. The surface sheen is glossy or matte. There are six types of glaze. Different application methods are used for each type.

- *Alkaline glaze* is a covering made from the fusion of sand and alkali (soda). In the drying process, the alkali in the clay body rose to the surface and created a transparent glassy coating, a process known as *evaporation glaze.* This glaze was used in antiquity by Egyptian, Syrian, and Persian potters.
- *Wood ash glaze* is a crude form of *applied glaze* created by ash falling on pottery fired in a wood-fed kiln. Wood ash glaze is a thin covering that burnishes to a glossy sheen. It was used by ancient Greek, Etruscan, Roman, and Chinese potters.
- *Lead glaze* is a translucent covering with a clear shiny finish made from the fusion of sand and lead oxide. It was used in ancient Rome, China, Mesopotamia, medieval Europe, and England. Today lead glaze is *applied* to ironstone, creamware, semiporcelain china, and bone china.
- *Tin glaze* is a translucent lead glaze opacified with the ashes of tin. This white glaze was invented by Islamic potters; they ground glaze into a fine powder, mixed it with water, dipped pottery into the solution, *applied* color-

ful ornamentation, and fired the ware. Tin glaze was introduced to Moorish Spain where it was used to make Hispano-Moresque ware; it was also used to make Italian majolica, French faience, Dutch Delft, and English delftware.

- *Salt glaze* is made by throwing common table salt into the kiln at its maximum temperature; this gives the ware a thin hard transparent covering with a matte finish the texture of orange peel. Salt glaze was developed in the fourteenth century by German potters; the process is known as *vapor glaze.*
- *Feldspathic glaze* is made of powdered feldspar mixed with lime, sand, potash, and small amounts of other materials; this translucent covering is *applied* to hard-paste porcelain. In a high-temperature kiln, the glaze sinks into the ware, fuses with it, and forms a thin, hard, glassy covering.

GREEK VASE PAINTING. The style of Greek vase painting is divided into five categories, in the following order of development:

- The *geometric style* incorporated triangles, zigzags, swastikas, and meander patterns, such as the key-fret design, a style that prevailed from 900 to 700 B.C. Around 750 B.C. vase painters replaced geometric motifs with geometric stick figures of humans and animals depicted in silhouette form.
- The *Asiatic* or *Oriental style* is based on rounded forms. This style evolved in the late eighth century B.C. when Corinthian vase painters were influenced by commerce with countries of the eastern Mediterranean. In 776 B.C. the Olympic Games were inaugurated, a Panhellenic festival that drew attention to physical beauty, and vase painters created rounded anatomical contours in symmetrical compositions of curved forms depicted in sinuous twisted and bent positions.
- The *black-figure style* developed about 600–550 B.C. This was a precise incised type of vase painting that fostered linear figures with stiff expressions, static vestment folds, and a flat two-dimensional look devoid of spatial representation. In a reduced atmosphere (smoky kiln), the incised lines turned black and provided contrast with the red background.
- The *red-figure style,* initiated about 650 B.C., is a painted style that fostered a three-dimensional look. It is a fluent style with freer emotional expression

and greater anatomical detail than that of the incised black-figure style. The figures were painted in light red on a black background.

- The *painted style* is the final phase of Greek vase painting, an ornamental method developed toward the end of the fifth century B.C., a style reserved primarily for vases used at funerals and religious ceremonies. The painted style featured a white ground; the decoration was outlined in black and filled in with soft colors. The scenes lack spatial depth.

GROUND. A term for the background color of a design.

GUILLOCHE. From the French *guillocher,* meaning "to ornament with lines." A guilloche is a border treatment composed of two or three intertwined bands, such as ribbons, that produce a series of interlocking circles.

HIGH-TEMPERATURE COLORS. Porcelain is glaze-fired at 1100 to 1450°C (2012 to 2642°F), temperatures that dissipate most colors; underglaze ornamentation is characteristically pastel. The exception is the application of colors that need high temperatures to mature: blue made from cobalt, green from copper, yellow from antimony, purple from manganese, and red from iron—colors known as *grand feu,* for "high-fired." However, iron red is a hard color to control underglaze; more often it is applied overglaze and fired in a low-temperature kiln.

HISPANO-MORESQUE WARE. A lustered or nonlustered tin-glazed earthenware made in Valencia, Granada, and Seville by Moorish potters in the twelfth century. Lustered Hispano-Moresque ware featured Christian-Spanish-Moorish decoration, such as Western heraldic emblems applied in the center of vessels surrounded by Near Eastern designs of interlacing leaves, scrolls, and geometric patterns. It was modeled in immense sizes for aristocratic display or given as royal gifts.

IMARI. Japanese Imari is export porcelain produced after 1700 at Arita, Nabeshima, Hirado, Okochi, and Mikawaguchi and shipped from the port of Imari. The ornamentation was inspired by Japanese textiles, decoration noted for overcrowded designs that concealed the underlying quality of the porcelain. The Imari palette centered on blue with a blackish hue applied underglaze, with an enameled overglaze of dark red and gold. Gilded decoration required a third firing, and Imari ornamented with gold was expensive. Imari is divided into color families: underglaze blue and white *(sometsuke)*; three-color polychrome enamels *(sancai)*; five-color polychrome enamels *(gosai)*; brocaded designs *(nishikide)*, and brocaded ornamentation in gold on a red ground *(kinrande)*. Between 1639 and 1854, Japanese ports were closed to foreigners. The exception was the port of Nagasaki, and then only a few merchant ships were allowed access. To capture the market for Japanese Imari, Chinese potters produced underglaze blue-and-white porcelain enameled overglaze with rusty red and gold, a style that came to be known as *Chinese Imari.*

INTAGLIO. From the Italian *intagliare,* "to cut in" or "to engrave." Intaglio ornamentation is carved below the surface of the ware. This sunken style was first developed by Roman potters.

JAPONAISERIE. A decorative term for European designs inspired by Japanese ornamentation, a style popular from about 1860 to 1900.

JASPERWARE. A name for fine-grained stoneware produced circa 1774 by Josiah Wedgwood. Products were made primarily for display, for example, cameos, portrait medallions, buttons, vases, candlesticks, chimney friezes, and furniture plaques and occasionally tea sets, dessert sets, and water pitchers. Barium sulfate was added to the composition, a formula that produced a slightly translucent body that fired to white. Metallic oxides were added as colorants, such as Wedgwood blue, sage green, olive green, pink lilac, golden yellow, and black—colors chosen to match color schemes favored by the Adams brothers. Because the metallic oxides were expensive, after 1780 jasperware was made with a solid white body and dipped into colored slip.

JEWELED PORCELAIN. A decorative technique developed by Cotteau around 1781 at Sèvres. Drops of translucent colored enamel were applied over gold foil and fused, a method that resembled jewel-encrusted ornamentation.

KAKIEMON. Japanese porcelain decorated in polychrome enamels by members of the Sakaida Kakiemon family, a style rendered primarily in underglaze blue overglazed with enamel colors of iron red, bluish green, light blue, and grayish yellow, many of the enamels translucent. Occasionally, the ornamentation was outlined in black, and gold was used as accent. The finest Kakiemon was made between 1680 and 1720, decorated with asymmetrical motifs primarily of flowers, birds, and butterflies, a style that drew attention to the texture of the glaze and revealed the underlying beauty of the porcelain, a distinct departure from the crowded designs of Imari based on brocade. Kakiemon is still made today.

KILN. From the Latin *culina,* "cookstove." A kiln is a specially designed furnace in which pottery and porcelain are placed to remove moisture from the clay and to harden or vitrify the body. Generally, the fuel is contained in a separate chamber. The flow of air is controlled by vents.

*LAUB- UND BÄNDELWERKE.* A German term for "leaf and strapwork," *Laub- und Bändelwerke* is an ornamental style derived from metalwork. In the decorative arts, strapwork is a narrow band folded into assorted shapes, such as crossed and interlaced forms. Initially, *Laub- und Bändelwerke* was a simple leafy design or ribbon-like decoration that evolved in the second quarter of the eighteenth century as a complex cartouche used to frame pictorial reserves, such as a landscape scene or a harbor motif.

LOW-TEMPERATURE COLORS. Colors fired at a temperature lower than the fusion point of the glaze are known as *petit feu* or "low-temperature" colors. They are applied overglaze after the ware is fired, then fired a second time at a temperature low enough to cause the enamels to adhere to the surface, a method that fosters detailed ornamentation. The colors may also be painted on raw glaze and fired with the glaze in one operation, a less costly method of production, in which broad washes of colors are applied to simple designs, one that allows no room for errors. Because the colors are fired at a reduced temperature, they do not dissipate and are brighter than high-temperature colors. (Note, however, that blue, green, red, yellow, and purple are colors that mature at high temperatures.)

MAJOLICA. In 1851, Minton & Co., a Staffordshire pottery firm, produced brightly decorated earthenware reproductions of Italian majolica, for display at the Great Exhibition, the first world fair, held at the Crystal Palace in London. Minton's exhibit spawned the English craze for majolica. The primary difference between Italian and English majolica lies in the type of glaze and the placement of the decoration. *Italian majolica* is covered with white tin glaze decorated with bright, colorful enamels. When it is fired, the glaze and ornamentation sink partially into the pottery, a method that helps to protect the decoration from wear. Occasionally tin-glazed majolica is covered with clear lead glaze for added protection. In contrast, *English majolica* made by Minton is hand-painted under clear lead glaze, a method that displays the colors but protects the decoration from wear. Italian majolica is more often made in simple shapes that rely on color for ornamentation, such as dinnerware, whereas English majolica is noted for relief decoration, such as plates ornamented with molded or pressed figures.

NEOCLASSIC. A revival style that followed the excavations at Pompeii in 1750, it is associated with the classical lines of ancient Greece and Rome.

OXIDATION. From the Greek word *oxys* for "acid" or "sour," oxidation occurs when the oxygen in air combines with a specific element, as in an oxidized kiln where the unrestricted flow of air combines with the colors of the decoration to produce ornamentation with yellowish undertones.

PARIAN. In 1838, William Copeland advanced the development of Parian, a name for porcelain once fired but left unglazed. Parian was used primarily to model figures, its name attributed to white marble quarried on the Greek island of Paros in the Aegean Sea. Although Parian closely resembled biscuit porcelain, it was fired at a lower temperature.

*PÂTE DURE* and *PÂTE TENDRE.* European porcelain is known as *pâte dure,* a French term for "hard-paste porcelain," or *pâte tendre,* French for "soft-paste porcelain."

*PÂTE-SUR-PÂTE.* A French term meaning "paste-upon-paste." Low-relief ornamentation is made from the buildup of white slip on a colored ground.

PEARLWARE. An earthenware category developed in 1779 by Josiah Wedgwood, pearlware was made with a greater amount of flint and white clay than creamware, giving it a whiter, less yellowish cast than creamware—one more like porcelain. The glaze contained a faint hint of blue made from cobalt, a metallic element that promoted an additional whitening effect. Oftentimes the bluish glaze accumulated near the base. Pearlware made between 1840 and 1868 was inscribed on the underside with the letter *P.*

RESERVE. An area within a design left blank to receive decoration, such as flowers or a landscape scene.

ROCOCO. From the French word *rocaille,* "rockwork" or "shellwork," rococo is a curvaceous ornate style based on delicate rock work, shells, and foliage, ornamentation characterized by the letters *C* and *S.* Although rococo was popular toward the end of the baroque period (circa 1715–1774), it featured rounded lines that curved upward along an asymmetrical scroll, while baroque was characterized by straight or curvaceous symmetrical lines.

SLIPWARE. A name for clay mixed in different proportions with sodium silicate and water to form a semiliquid substance with the consistency of cream. Slipware is used as decoration, to join pieces, or to cast ware. It was a popular ornamental method in the seventeenth century, primarily in England and North America, for providing a contrast of color, such as dark slip applied over a light body. Pottery ornamented with slip was decorated by dipping ware into slip or brushing slip onto ware; or thickened slip was piped onto ware in the form of dots and lines, a style called *slip-trailed.*

TRANSFER PRINT. A decorative technique attributed to John Brooks, an Irish engraver employed at the Battersea Enamel Works, London, around 1753, who used the transfer print to decorate metal objects. An engraved copper plate was covered with colorful ink. An imprint of the inked design was stamped on tissue-thin paper. The paper was moistened and transferred while wet to a biscuit body. When fired, the paper burned away, but the imprinted design adhered to the surface and was filled in by hand with enamels. Compared to hand-outlined ornamentation, the transfer print promoted reuse of copper plates, fostering inexpensive decoration and affordable ceramics. In 1756, John Sadler and Guy Green of Liverpool patented the process. However, the method was confined primarily to small plates, usually of pastoral scenes. But around 1770, Josiah Spode successfully adapted the transfer print to larger surfaces covered notably with blue printed designs.

Transfer prints were used before lithographic decoration, the latter a method used today in which paper-backed sheets are pressed onto overglazed ware, a process known in the United States as *decalcomania.*

UNDERGLAZE BLUE-AND-WHITE ORNAMENTATION. The crisp contrast of blue decoration on white influenced ceramic ornamentation in the Near East and caused a craze in Europe that lasted through the eighteenth century. The outstanding periods of blue-and-white underglaze occurred in the Ming dynasty in the reigns of Yung Lo (1403–1424), Hsuan Te (1426–1435), Cheng Hua (1465–1487), Jia Qing (1522–1566), and Wan Li (1572–1620).

- *Yung Lo blue-and-white porcelain* is recognized by bright blue cobalt dotted with small dark flecks of different intensities. The technique, known as *heaped and piled,* was caused by minute impurities in the cobalt that exploded in the kiln and created black dots, a decorative method eventually copied.
- *Hsuan Te blue-and-white porcelain* dates from the classic age of blue-and-white ornamentation and features a deep shade of sapphire blue accented with heaped and piled dots.
- *Cheng Hua blue-and-white porcelain* is blue with a soft silvery hue, a color derived from a mix of Chinese cobalt and Persian cobalt; it is devoid of heaped and piled dots.
- *Jia Qing blue-and-white porcelain,* considered the finest made, is recognized by a warm, intense shade of dark violet blue.
- *Wan Li blue-and-white porcelain* was exported to Europe and England by the thousands, copied by Dutch potters at Delft, and replicated in still life representations of the period.

YIXING (YIH-SING). The clay of Yixing (pronounced "ee-sing") is called *zisha,* Chinese for "purple sands." The ware has hues of red, brown, yellow, and gray and is said to brew the most flavorful tea. The teahouses of Yixing were gathering places for business meetings and social events, and it was not unusual for guests to supply their own teapots and tea leaves; the teahouses had only to provide boiled water. The teapots were just large enough to hold one serving and modeled in dainty, fanciful forms of nature, such as fruits or vegetables, decorated with incised motifs or ornamentation applied in low relief. The curved spout was shaped to fit the mouth, and tea often was sipped from the spout. The vessels were made of unglazed stoneware, and when they were rubbed with the hands, an oily patina developed that was believed to enhance the flavor of tea. When the unglazed interiors were wet from infusion, the pots were said to possess a musky odor with a faint hint of carnation.

CHAPTER FIVE

# THE DIFFERENT CATEGORIES OF DINNERWARE

HAVE YOU EVER WONDERED why one set of dinnerware lasts forever and another breaks easily? Why the chipped areas of certain ceramics absorb food oils and others remain impermeable to liquid absorption? Why the textures of some ceramics are thick and others are translucent? Why some sets develop fine lines and others show minute scratches made from normal use of a dinner knife? The answers to these questions lie in the nature of the clay.

The term *ceramic* applies to fired clay, a property that, in varying degrees, withstands high temperatures. Clay is classified in two major categories known as *primary clay* and *secondary clay*, each with unique properties. Primary clay is used to make porcelain, bone china, and china. Secondary clay is used to make majolica, faience, creamware, ironstone, semiporcelain, and stoneware. Often both types of clays are combined in one ceramic. The general characteristics of primary and secondary clays are given below.

# Primary Clay

Primary clay is known as *kaolin*, from the Chinese *kao* for "peak" and *lin* for "hills," meaning "high ridge" or "stone of the hilltops." It is named for the Gaoling Mountain in Jiangxi Province, China, where it was first found. Derived from volcanic rock, such as granite rock, it is a strong, hard, white-burning clay that the Chinese call the "bone of porcelain." Kaolin deposits are rare, found only in certain areas of the world: in England at Cornwall and Devonshire; in France at Limoges; in Germany at Dresden, and in the United States in North Carolina, and to a smaller degree in Georgia, New Jersey, and Staten Island.

Clay is an earthy substance composed primarily of alumina and silica, minute particles likened to flat, hexagonal plates that slide around on each other when lubricated with water. Kaolin is not transported readily by the elements of nature—wind, rivers, streams, glaciers—and the clay particles are large and irregular in form. Because the particles cannot make point-to-point contact, they settle into a disordered structure through which water cannot pass easily. Kaolin lacks plasticity, although the kaolin from China is easier to model, and softer, than European kaolin.

To promote plasticity, feldspar is added to the porcelain formula; feldspar is a mineral that contains silicates of aluminium and makes up approximately 60 percent of the Earth's crust. Feldspar is also known as *petuntse,* from the Chinese word *pai-tun-tzu,* meaning "little white bricks." In Europe, petuntse is known as *china stone,* and kaolin as *china clay*.

Like kaolin, feldspar is found in granite rock, but it is at an earlier stage of decomposition than kaolin and hence is not as hard. While kaolin turns hard in the kiln and retains its shape, feldspar turns soft, wraps around the needle-like rods of kaolin, promotes plasticity, lowers the point of fusion, and binds the ingredients together. The Chinese say feldspar is the flesh of porcelain.

Because feldspar contains silica, a glassy mineral, it also aids translucency. Translucent porcelain is appropriate for all dining occasions, formal and informal. Opaque porcelain gives the table setting a less dressy look.

Kaolin is a refractory clay; this means that it is heat-resistant and hard to melt. Porcelain is fired at high temperatures—approximately 1300 to 1400°C (2372 to 2552°F). In the kiln, kaolin vitrifies. This glasslike quality is what makes porcelain dinner plates impervious to scratches from normal use of a dinner knife. When porcelain is chipped, the exposed area is hard with a smooth, dense texture that does not absorb food oils or liquids.

The porcelain formula is known as *paste,* with a composition that is hard or soft. The typical hard-paste formula contains fifty percent kaolin, twenty-five percent feldspar, 20 percent quartz, and 5 percent other material. The paste vitrifies at a high, or "hard," temperature, hence the name. Bone china vitrifies at a lower temperature than hard-paste porcelain, a "soft" temperature of approximately 1260°C (2300°F). Although bone china is also known as *soft porcelain,* do not confuse the term with "soft-paste porcelain," a porcelain type that is no longer manufactured; it is made with frit, a glassy powder mixed with clay.

Bone china is made with the addition of calcined bone ash, mainly the ash of oxen or cattle. When bone is divested of all gelatinous matter, it contains lime and phosphates, and the ash is used as *flux,* a substance that promotes fusion of materials at a lower temperature than porcelain, stabilizes production, and eliminates waste. The amount of bone ash in the formula is determined by the manufacturer and varies from approximately 35 percent to 50 percent. The higher the bone ash content, the better the quality of the ware. Typically, high-quality bone china is comprised of 50 percent animal bone ash, 30 percent kaolin, and 20 percent feldspar. Bone china is a stronger ceramic than porcelain; it has greater tensile strength but is not as hard.

Porcelain is very slightly whiter than bone china. Although kaolin fires to white, the clay possesses a few impurities and under direct sunlight the porcelain body reveals a slight bluish-white cast, a color similar to skim milk. The body of bone china is a creamy-white shade, similar to the color of whole milk, a hue made with the addition of bone ash. Although both whites are compatible with all colors of the table setting, for aesthetic reasons porcelain and bone china are covered with clear glaze.

## Secondary Clay

Ceramics made of secondary clay—majolica, faience, creamware, ironstone, semiporcelain, and stoneware—are categorized collectively as *earthenware.* Majolica and faience are also known as *pottery,* a term sometimes used loosely for all ceramics.

Secondary clay is swept from the site of decomposition by wind, streams, rivers, and glaciers. It is called *sedimentary clay* because it is reduced to sediment by the forces of nature. In the weathering process, the clay particles are reduced in size, the shapes are rendered into similar forms that make point-to-point contact, fall into an ordered mass of parallel planes through which water passes easily. With the exception of stoneware, all earthenware is porous. For this reason, secondary clay is highly plastic, takes well to modeling, and is used to make dinnerware and utilitarian items.

In transport, secondary clay picks up mineral impurities, such as iron oxides and vegetable matter, that change color in the kiln, and the body ranges in tone from dark to light. Dark-colored secondary clay contains a high proportion of iron oxides that produce a reddish shade, a color the clay retains after it is fired. Because secondary clay is porous, to avoid collapse in the kiln it is fired at a low temperature, approximately 1000 to 1080°C (1830 to 1980°F). Dark-colored secondary clay is used to make dinnerware such as majolica and faience and to produce utilitarian items, such as drain pipes, roof tiles, flower pots, garden ornaments, and terra cotta bricks (from the Italian, meaning "baked earth").

Fine-grained light-colored secondary clay is called *ball clay*, which is a sedimentary clay found near water that contains a high proportion of decomposed vegetable matter and is used to make creamware, ironstone, and semiporcelain. In a natural state, ball clay ranges in color from gray to brown to blue to almost black. But in the kiln the colors burn out and ball clay fires to an off-white body with a bluish-gray or brownish-yellow cast. Ball clay is extremely plastic and possesses a high rate of shrinkage; kaolin or feldspar are added as strengtheners, and the ware is fired at approximately 1100 to 1200°C (2101°F to 2190°F), almost to the point of vitrification.

## Glazing and Firing

The Chinese say glaze is the skin of ceramics. Glaze contains alumina, silica, and flux. Alumina is a silvery metal found in sand (silica) and various minerals; it acts as a chemical binder to control viscosity. Glaze grips the surface of clay, fills the pores with a glasslike coating, and renders ceramics impermeable to liquid absorption. In the kiln, chemical changes occur in clay. For glaze to adhere to the body, the composition of each must be similar; otherwise they shrink at different rates and fine fissures appear called *crazing*. Glaze may also detach and flake off, or "crawl," leaving bare spots.

Because glaze contains silica, a substance that dissipates at high temperatures, flux is added in order to lower the melting point. Flux also defines the name of the glaze: hence, feldspathic glaze, lead glaze, salt glaze. Feldspathic glaze is used to cover porcelain, lead glaze is used on bone china, and salt glaze is used on stoneware.

Porcelain is fired a minimum of two times, at low and high temperatures. The low-temperature firing produces biscuit, rendering porcelain in a leather-hard state, one that holds shape but is still absorbent; low-temperature firing strengthens the body for easier handling and reduces the risk of breakage in the second firing. Feldspathic glaze is applied for the second, high-temperature firing, also known as the *glaze firing*, a period when the glaze seeps into the body and fuses with it. Feldspathic glaze looks like the pores in skin and is thinner and more brilliant than lead glaze. The high-temperature firing makes the porcelain body rock hard for permanent shape retention.

Like porcelain, lead-glazed ceramics are fired twice, but first at high and then at low temperatures. The first firing hardens the ware; the second firing makes the glaze adhere to the body. Lead glaze partially sinks into the body or rests on top; it gives a covering that is thicker and richer than feldspathic glaze.

Earthenware (except stoneware) is covered with lead glaze, a finish that adheres to ceramics glaze fired in a low-temperature kiln. Lead glaze is transparent or opaque. Transparent lead glaze reveals the body color and is used to cover dinnerware made of light-colored clay: creamware and semiporcelain, as well as bone china. When lead glaze is opacified with tin ash, white tin glaze is produced, a finish used to cover majolica, faience, and ironstone. But regardless of transparency or opacity, lead is a soft metal and lead-glazed dinner plates are subject to minute marks made from normal use of a dinner knife.

Salt glaze is made of common table salt and produces a transparent covering with a semimatte gloss, a finish found only on stoneware. When the sodium in salt combines with the silica in clay, it creates a thin, glasslike covering that fits the surface of stoneware like skin. Because salt glaze does not distribute evenly, the covering is slightly rough and granular with a pitted texture, like orange peel.

Although stoneware is technically considered earthenware, in reality it lies midway in strength and porosity between porcelain and earthenware. It is strengthened with kaolin and feldspar to form a dense, hard, durable product that vitrifies at high temperatures of approximately 1200 to 1300°C (2190 to 2460°F).

## Summary of Ceramic Types

The strength, body color, texture, ornamental color, and glaze associated with ceramic categories are summarized below. When specified by the manufacturer, certain wares are safe in the freezer, conventional oven, microwave oven, and dishwasher.

### *Porcelain*

**Strength** Porcelain is the hardest of all ceramics. The body is vitrified and withstands the rigors of daily dining, yet is appropriate for the most elegant occasions.

**Body Color** In an unglazed state the porcelain body is white, and when chipped the fracture does not draw the eye. Unless the chip is in a dangerous place, such as on the rim of a cup, articles made of porcelain provide years of service.

**Texture** The fracture of chipped porcelain is smooth to the touch, with a shell-like conchoidal shape that does not absorb food oils or discolor. Porcelain textures are both translucent and opaque. Translucent porcelain is delicate, and when tapped gently on the rim resonates with a bell-like tone, a texture appropriate for all table settings, formal and informal. Opaque porcelain is thick and does not resonate; it has a density that is appropriate for informal meals from elegant to casual.

**Ornamental Colors** Porcelain is glaze-fired at a high temperature that dissipates most color and typically is decorated with soft shades. The exception is strong color that needs high temperatures to mature: blue from cobalt, green from copper, purple from manganese, yellow from antimony, and red from iron. However, iron red at high temperatures is hard to control and is more often used to ornament ceramics glazed at low temperatures.

GLAZE Feldspathic glaze fuses with the body, so porcelain dinner plates do not show minute marks made from normal use of a dinner knife. The finish is hard, glassy, smooth, and transparent.

### *Bone China*

STRENGTH Bone china is made with calcined bone ash, a porcelain category that possesses the greatest tensile strength (ability to resist stress lengthwise) of all ceramics. Wedgwood, makers of fine bone china, have demonstrated that four to six bone china after-dinner coffee cups can support a Rolls-Royce without breaking.

BODY COLOR Bone china features a milky-white body color that does not draw the eye when chipped.

TEXTURE The texture of bone china is translucent or opaque. Translucent bone china is appropriate for formal and informal dining, and opaque bone china is compatible with casual table settings when less-than-delicate table appointments are used. When chipped, the density of the fracture neither absorbs food oils nor discolors.

ORNAMENTAL COLORS Bone china is glaze-fired at a lower temperature than porcelain, one that does not dissipate color. Typically it is ornamented with rich jewel tones, such as turquoise blue or ruby red.

GLAZE Bone china is covered with lead glaze, a finish that promotes a smooth, glassy surface appropriate for all dining occasions. Because lead is a soft metal, bone china dinner plates are subject to minute marks made from normal use of a dinner knife. However, the marks are extremely slight and should not deter one in a choice of dinnerware.

## *China*

**Strength** Technically, china is a different ceramic than porcelain, but because the ceramic bodies are both hard and vitrified, they look the same, and the terms are often used synonymously.

**Body Color** The formula for china contains kaolin that fires to white, a color that does not draw the eye when the body is chipped.

**Texture** The density of china is opaque or slightly translucent, textures appropriate for casual or elegant dinnerware. When chipped, the exposed surface does not absorb food oils, nor does the texture discolor.

**Ornamental Colors** China is fired first at high and then at low temperatures. The low-temperature glaze firing fosters colors that do not dissipate and promotes a wider range of color hues than porcelain. Typically, china is ornamented in bright colors, such as Christmas red.

**Glaze** China is a porcelain category covered with lead glaze, a glaze that rests on the surface, does not bond with the body, and is less durable than feldspathic glaze.

## *Majolica and Faience*

**Strength** Majolica and faience are earthenware categories made of softer clay than creamware, ironstone, semiporcelain, and stoneware, and are fired at lower temperatures. In the kiln, majolica and faience harden but do not vitrify; the wares are brittle, prone to chipping, and unsuitable for everyday use.

**Body Color** Majolica and faience are made of darker clay than creamware, ironstone, semiporcelain, and stoneware, and when the body is chipped the exposed surface draws the eye.

**Texture** The textures of majolica and faience are porous; when chipped they reveal a granular texture that absorbs food oils, is not resistant to stains or food acids, and exposes discolorations.

**Ornamental Colors** Majolica and faience are glaze-fired at low temperatures that do not dissipate color. They are typically ornamented with bright colors that add great personality, charm, and fun to the table setting.

**Glaze** Majolica and faience are glazed with white tin glaze, a shiny surface that partially sinks into the body or rests on top. Lead and tin are soft metals, and the glaze is subject to minute scratches made from normal use of a dinner knife.

### *Creamware*

**Strength** Creamware is made of ball clay, a clay with a high rate of shrinkage and too malleable for use alone. To strengthen its composition and reduce shrinkage, nonplastic material, namely kaolin, is added to the formula. The paste is fired at a higher temperature than majolica and faience, and creamware is a harder, more durable ceramic with a composition similar to stoneware. However, creamware is fired at a lower temperature than stoneware and is not as strong.

**Body Color** In the unfired stage, ball clay ranges in color from gray to brown to blue to almost black, a clay potters call *blue clay*. In the kiln, ball clay fires to a light cream with a slight yellowish tinge—hence, the name *creamware.* When chips occur, the exposed surface does not draw the eye.

**Texture** Although the texture of creamware is opaque, the texture is relatively thin compared to majolica, faience, ironstone, and stoneware, a look that is appropriate for informal dining, from elegant to everyday. When chipping occurs, the fracture absorbs some food oils and there is mild discoloration.

**Ornamental Colors** Creamware is covered with transparent lead glaze, a translucent covering that reveals the light body color that accents all colors of the table setting.

GLAZE Lead glaze is a transparent soft covering, and dinner plates made of creamware are subject to minute scratches made from normal use of a dinner knife.

## *Ironstone*

STRENGTH Ironstone is made of ball clay mixed with feldspar, a mineral called *china stone*. Hence the name *ironstone,* a stronger, heavier earthenware category than majolica, faience, and creamware.

BODY COLOR The body of ironstone is light-colored with a bluish or grayish tone. When chipped the exposed surface does not draw the eye.

TEXTURE Ironstone is made with a thick, opaque texture, a density appropriate for informal table settings. When chipping occurs, the exposed area is susceptible to some liquid absorption and to slight discoloration from food oils.

ORNAMENTAL COLORS Ironstone is covered with white tin glaze. a neutral covering that accents and blends with all colors of the table setting. Colored decoration is seldom used. Rather, ironstone is decorated with relief ornamentation.

GLAZE White tin glaze is softer than feldspathic glaze, and over time ironstone dinner plates may show minute scratches made from normal use of a dinner knife.

## *Semiporcelain*

STRENGTH Semiporcelain is made of ball clay strengthened with kaolin, the clay used to make porcelain. It is fired at a high temperature that semivitrifies the body. Hence the name *semiporcelain* or *semivitrified porcelain*. Semiporcelain is harder than creamware, majolica, faience, and ironstone.

BODY COLOR Kaolin adds whiteness to the semiporcelain formula and the body color is light. When chipped, the fracture does not draw the eye.

TEXTURE Semiporcelain is semivitrified; it has a strong body that withstands potting in thinner textures than majolica, faience, creamware, and ironstone. The surface is smooth, similar to porcelain, with an opaque texture that gives the table setting a dressy ambience. Semiporcelain is a bridge between heavy earthenware and delicate porcelain. When chipped, the exposed area is slightly porous and less subject to discoloration from food oils than other light-bodied earthenwares.

ORNAMENTAL COLORS Semiporcelain is glaze-fired in a low-temperature kiln, one that does not dissipate color. The ornamentation is normally rendered in brighter colors than porcelain.

GLAZE Semiporcelain is covered with lead glaze, which is soft, and the dinner plates are subject to minute marks made by normal use of a dinner knife.

## *Stoneware*

STRENGTH Stoneware is a strong ceramic made of secondary clay mixed with kaolin, quartz, aluminum oxide, and feldspar. Hence the name *stoneware,* a ceramic with the weight and feel of stone. The formula is fired at a high temperature and stoneware is vitrified, a quality that promotes durable dinnerware that can withstand the rigors of everyday use.

BODY COLOR Depending on the impurities in the clay, such as iron oxides, the body color of stoneware ranges from dark reddish brown to light bluish gray to buff, and when chipped the exposed surface may draw the eye.

TEXTURE Although early Chinese stoneware ("proto-porcelain") was potted with a slight translucency, today stoneware is made with opaque textures that are thick or thin. Thick-density stoneware is made as large containers, such as garden pots. Thinly potted stoneware is made as dinnerware, a texture appropriate for informal dining, from country to casual to rustic oriental.

When chipped, the vitrified texture of the exposed area is not subject to discoloration from food oils, nor does it absorb liquids.

**Ornamental Colors** Stoneware is fired at a high temperature that dissipates most colors and is typically decorated with soft colors. The exception is color that needs a high temperature to mature, such as blue, green, yellow, purple, and red.

**Glaze** Although stoneware is hard enough to leave unglazed, for aesthetic reasons it is given a salt glaze. This results in a hard covering with a rough orange-peel texture that makes dinner plates impervious to scratches made by normal use of a dinner knife.

CHAPTER SIX

# PLATES: PIECE BY PIECE

*He may live without books, what is knowledge but grieving?*
*He may live without hope, what is hope but deceiving?*
*He may live without love, what is passion but pining?*
*But where is the man that can live without dining?*

EDWARD ROBERT BULWER LYTTON
(PSEUDONYM OWEN MEREDITH), LUCILLE, I, 1860

AND WHAT IS DINING without plates or dishes? And what is the difference between them? A plate (from the French *plat,* "flat") is approximately ½-inch deep. A dish (from the Latin *discus,* "circular shape") is up to 1½ inches deep.

Plates are made in twelve sizes for table use: service plate, dinner plate, luncheon plate, round salad plate, crescent salad plate, fish plate, dessert plate, cheese plate, fruit plate, tea plate, bread-and-butter plate, and fruit saucer.

Until the time of the Industrial Revolution, plates were made in large and medium sizes, but the growing middle class wanted plates for service of specific foods, such as fish, oysters, dessert, and fruit. By the nineteenth century, plate sizes were governed by the time of day they were used: large plates for dinner, smaller plates for luncheon, and undersize copies of both for breakfast and afternoon tea. By the mid-nineteenth century, plate sizes were standardized. Today, plates are manufactured in slightly larger sizes than those made a century ago, when multicourse meals were served and a number of small plates were needed.

To allow for slight variances in plate dimensions, approximate figures are given here. Although two plates may appear to be the same size, one may have a broader rim or a narrower well than another.

## Service Plate

The service plate is the largest and most expensive plate to manufacture because it has a shape with a large well prone to warp in the kiln. (When moisture evaporates, clay shrinks. If shrinkage occurs at an uneven rate, the plate warps. The loss of warped material, plus increased labor and energy, add to production costs and retail.)

Although contemporary service plates range in size from 11 to 14 inches across, and the well is about 8 to 9 inches in diameter, antique service plates measure about 11 inches across and the well is approximately 6 to 6½ inches, a difference that affects the way the plates are used. The well of contemporary service plates is capacious enough to hold a combination of foods, namely, a main course comprised of meat, vegetables, and garnish. The well of antique service plates is too small to use as a dinner plate, and they are used solely as an underplate for an appetizer course.

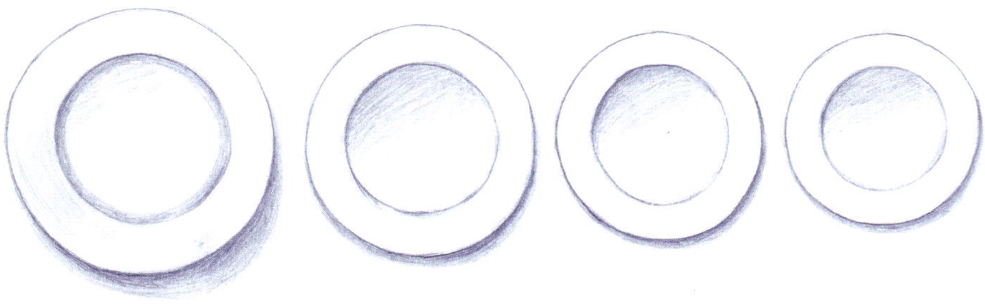

THE PLATES USED IN TABLE SETTING, SHOWN IN ORDER OF DESCENDING SIZE: SERVICE PLATE, DINNER PLATE, LUNCHEON PLATE, ROUND SALAD PLATE, CRESCENT SALAD PLATE, FISH PLATE, DESSERT PLATE, CHEESE PLATE, TEA PLATE, FRUIT PLATE, BREAD-AND-BUTTER PLATE, AND FRUIT SAUCER.

The service plate is laid in the center of the cover *before* the diners come to the table, but the way it is used is different for formal and informal dining. At a formal table laid with a profusion of flatware and stemware, the service plate decorates the cover with color and design, and the rim should frame the appetizer plate with a surround of no less than 1 inch. Otherwise, the decorative effect of the service plate is lost. Without a service plate in the center of the cover, the place setting looks like a frame without a picture.

In formal dining, food is never placed directly on a service plate. Rather, the service plate is a base on which to lay the plate for the appetizer course and is cleared from the table after the first or second course is finished. Picture a formal dinner that begins with a course of hot soup. Since soup splatters, the service plate is soiled easily, and at the end of the course it is cleared from the table with the soup plate. Because one of the dictates of hospitality decrees that there should never be an empty space before a guest at the table, after the service plate and soup plate are cleared, the plate for the next course is laid on the table immediately. But when the meal begins with a cold first course, such as fish, followed by a hot course of soup, the fish plate is removed at the end of the first course, and the service plate is left on the table to hold the soup plate. At the end of the soup course, the service plate and soup plate are cleared together, and exchanged immediately for the plate on which the next course is served.

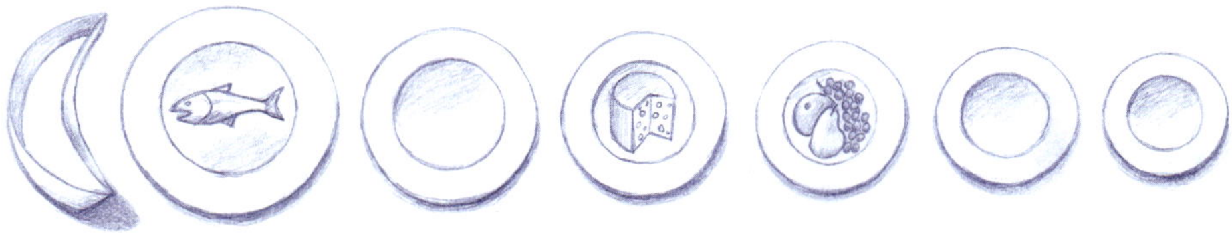

At an informal meal, the service plate is an optional accoutrement of dining. Although traditionally the purpose of the service plate is to hold the plate for the appetizer course, at an informal meal it is used in whatever way makes sense, for example, as a dinner plate, buffet plate, placemat, or platter. But when a service plate is used in a traditional sense, it is laid on the table in advance of seating and should set the mood for the occasion: for example, gold-banded service plates for an elegant meal, and wooden service plates for casual affairs. Oftentimes, dinner plates are used as service plates to hold a first course.

Service plates are known by a host of names—*buffet plate, charger plate, cover plate, lay plate,* and *place plate,* terms that confuse the novice. The first one, a buffet plate, dates back to the sixteenth century, when Pierre Buffet, a French chef who at one time worked in Verona, Italy, introduced the credenza course to the French court; this was a cold course, such as antipasto, served from a sideboard, a piece of furniture made with drawers and shelves that held linens and valuable silver. In ecclesiastic use, the credenza is a small table placed on the side of the communion table to hold bread and wine that is to be consecrated; in a secular capacity the credenza was used in the Middle Ages and the Renaissance to hold food to be tested for poisoning. Eventually, the plate on which a credenza or cold course was served came to be known as a *buffet plate,* after the furniture from which it was served. Today a buffet plate is an oversized plate used to serve a one-dish meal from a sideboard, buffet, or credenza.

The *charger plate,* from the Italian *caricare,* meaning "to load," was a large round platter used in medieval England to carry a load of food to the table, such as a joint of meat. Records from the Pewterer's Company of London note that chargers were made in 1438 as small oval platters 8 to 13 inches across, round plates 13 inches and over, and large plates 18 inches or more. Today, charger plates 11 to 14 inches in diameter are used as service plates, and those 18 inches or larger are considered platters.

The *cover plate,* from the French *couvert,* "covered" or "hidden," began as a plate that kept food hot and circumvented attempts to poison the king. To avoid the threat of fire, palace kitchens were located a good distance from the dining hall (at Versailles a quarter of a mile away), and in the long stretch hot food cooled. To promote a warm meal at best, the king's plate was "covered," and to preclude contamination by miscreants, his flatware was "hidden" in a napkin. In the reign of Louis XIV, the public was invited to watch him take his dinner, a repast known as the *grand couvert.* The midday fare, which the king took privately in his bedroom, was called the *petit couvert.* Today, the cover plate is a large plate laid in the center of the place setting to cover the empty space and provide a base on which to lay the plate for the appetizer course.

*Lay plate* is a term from the Middle Ages when dining tables were made of heavy wooden boards laid temporarily on trestles. After the meal, the boards and trestle were removed and the space was used for other purposes, such as dancing. Setting the table was known as *laying the table,* and large platters loaded with food were called *lay plates.* Today, the lay plate is a large plate laid at each place setting as a base for the appetizer plate.

*Place plate* is a term that emanates from a time when the service plate was removed from the cover immediately after a diner was seated, and replaced promptly by another large plate on which was laid the plate for the appetizer course. Today, many fine restaurants continue the custom of setting a service plate at each place. The moment the diner sits down, the waiter either removes the place plate or leaves it as a base on which to place a preprandial drink or appetizer course. The place plate is cleared just before the main course is served.

## Dinner Plate

In antiquity food was placed directly on the table or served in bowls (although records from the wedding banquet of Caranus of Macedonia reveal food was served on platters made of silver, bronze, and crystal). Bas reliefs from Khorsabad, Iraq, show Assyrian noblemen eating from individual trays and the poor sharing small plates. Moreover, archaeological findings have uncovered Assyrian plates made of stone, alabaster, and bronze. In Rome, royalty and aristocrats dined from gold, silver, glass, and pottery plates, while slaves ate from wooden bowls.

In the fifth century, when Europe was overrun by barbarians, the individual plate almost disappeared from the table, not to reappear until the sixteenth century. But in the Middle Ages, some amenities did return to the table—for example, plates made of whole-wheat flour, rye, or barley, baked in a round loaf called a *boule,* the French word for "ball." The boule was aged for four days, then sliced horizontally into rounds 2 to 3 inches thick with a 6-inch diameter; or cut into rectangles 4 to 6 inches wide by 6 to 10 inches long. The slice was called a *trencher*, from the French word *trancher*, meaning "to slice." The heavy crust kept the sauce, gravy, and juices that emanated from boiled food within the trencher, a design that evolved into the rim-shape plate. When the trencher was too soggy to hold food, a fresh one was supplied, cut from loaves stacked vertically along the wall of the dining hall. Furthermore, trenchers were used as napkins, hot pads, and hollowed-out dishes to hold salt or candles.

Fresh trenchers were provided with the fruit and cheese course at the end of the meal, and leftover trenchers, in good condition, were collected in a *voyder*, a wide, deep, decorative container made of wicker, wood, or metal.

Before the meal began, the chaplain placed a trencher on the alms bowl that was kept on a nearby cupboard. A loaf of bread was laid on top the alms bowl with trencher, and at the end of the meal the bowl was used to collect leftover trenchers, along with the fresh trencher and loaf of bread, and distributed by an almoner to the poor waiting at the manor house gates. Humble households often saved leftover trenchers and added them to beer, ale, or wine as a supplement at breakfast. Trenchers beyond salvage were thrown to the dogs wandering among the tables fighting for morsels of food.

In the Middle Ages, banquets were the primary means of hospitality and entertainment, and as decoration trenchers were tinted with colors derived from herbs, leaves, and flowers, such as green from parsley, mint, spinach, and hazel leaves; yellow from saffron and dandelion; gold from egg yolk and dandelion; lavender from violets; red from roses; and blue from heliotrope.

*When meate is taken quyte awaye*
*And Voyders in presence,*
*Put you your trenchour in the same*
*And all your resydence.*
*Take you with your napkin and knyfe*
*The croms that are fore thee,*
*In the Voyder your napkin leave,*
*For it is a curtseye.*

*John Russell*, Boke of Nurture, *c. 1430*

Early in the fourteenth century, wooden and pewter trenchers were occasionally placed underneath bread trenchers, a solid base on which to cut slabs of meat into bite-size pieces. By the fifteenth century, wooden trenchers featured an indentation in the center, and by the sixteenth century trenchers were fashioned in a circular shape with a narrow rim.

Across the waters in America, settlers ate from both sides of wooden trenchers. The top part was called the *dinner side*, and the bottom surface the *pie side*. And in some areas when courting couples shared the same plate, they were considered engaged. Wooden tableware was called *treen,* ware made from a tree. Linden and poplar trees were particularly favored because they did not impart the taste of wood, and also were less odorous. Those too poor to own treens ate from a long heavy board carved with bowl-shaped indentations about 18 inches apart. But when fortunes improved, treens and boards were replaced with plates made of pottery or pewter.

The first ceramic plates were modeled in Europe in round, oval, and oblong forms, shapes made with wide rims and deep wells that held liquids that escaped from boiled or roasted food (the primary methods of cooking). The round-rimmed plate with a deep well (a shape similar to today's soup plate) originated in Italy in the sixteenth century, and by the seventeenth century it was the accepted form throughout Europe. The flat-rimmed plate with shallow indentation (a shape similar to today's dinner plate) was introduced in France toward the end of the seventeenth century, and by the nineteenth century the form was accepted throughout the Western world.

The custom of a separate plate for each course is traceable to François I of France, who, in 1536, ordered six plates for service of individual courses, a tradition accepted at the French court in the seventeenth century and adopted by royalty throughout Europe, a convention that continues today.

The dinner plate is used more than any other plate, and it is the wise host who collects extras. It is used to serve the main course at all meals, formal and informal. Although antique dinner plates vary from approximately 9½ to 10½ inches in diameter, modern dinner plates measure 10 to 11 inches across.

*Entrée,* French for "enter," is a culinary expression attributed to the seventeenth century when menus were comprised of three courses, each containing dozens of dishes. The middle course, the roast or game course, began with the "entrance" of light dishes called *entrées,* similar to today's hors d'oeuvres.

Today, at a formal dinner in a private residence, the entrée is the third appetizer course (just as it was in the seventeenth century), such as creamed chicken in vol-au-vent cases, and as such is served on a medium-size plate, notably a salad plate. But in a restaurant, the main course often follows two appetizer courses, usually soup and salad. Typically, the entrée consists of cooked meat served with vegetables, starch, and garnish, and as such is served on a dinner plate.

## Luncheon Plate

*So munch on, crunch on, take your nuncheon,*
*Breakfast, supper, dinner, luncheon!*

ROBERT BROWNING, THE PIED PIPER OF HAMELIN, 1842

Although three meals are served today—breakfast, lunch, and dinner—in the eighteenth century the three meals consisted of breakfast, dinner, and supper. In an age without electricity, food was prepared in daylight, and the main meal was served at midday or in the early afternoon, (sometimes at 3 P.M.). It was called *dinner* after the Latin *disjejunare,* meaning "away from the fast." In the long stretch between breakfast and dinner, an informal snack called *nunchin* was taken midday, notably by servants who arose in the dark and needed something to keep them going during the day. In time, nunchin developed into a substantial meal called *nooning,* from the Latin *nona,* meaning "ninth hour," a word based on the Roman system of counting hours from sunrise. Jane Austen referred to nunchin as the midday meal; in a letter written in 1808 she refers to nunchin as "noonshine," and in *Sense and Sensibility,* written in 1811, she calls the noon meal "nuncheon."

Eventually the midday snack was called *lunch* from *lunshin,* a word meaning "lump" or "a lump of food." To quote Samuel Johnson's *Dictionary of the English Language* (published 1755), lunch or lunshin was "as much food as one's hand can hold." Today's "luncheon," from the Norse-British word *lounge,* meaning "a lump of bread and cheese," is the name of the midday meal.

In 1860, Isabella Beeton, author of *Household Management,* an exceedingly successful cookbook, wrote: "Luncheon is an inconsequent meal." However, by the late nineteenth century, luncheon evolved as an important meal served by ladies of leisure who entertained at midday those they might not have to dinner. Today, as the majority of women work outside the home, fewer luncheons are given at home, and the luncheon plate is used less than in previous years. But those lucky enough to own luncheon plates find the size perfect for small portions. Luncheon is a lighter, simpler meal than dinner, a repast served on a plate about 9 to 9½ inches in diameter. Although the luncheon plate is used for formal and informal meals, it is not essential for either occasion.

## Round Salad Plate

In medieval England, vegetable dishes were served raw, baked, or boiled. These dishes were called *sallets* and, like salads of today, were dressed lightly with oil and vinegar, salt and pepper, and perhaps a pinch of sugar.

Today the round salad plate is made in two sizes. The larger salad plate is about 8 to 8½ inches in diameter, a dimension manufactured primarily by English and European dinnerware firms. The smaller salad plate measures approximately 7 to 7½ inches across, an all-purpose plate made by American manufacturers for both salad and dessert.

The way the salad plate is presented is different for formal and informal dining. At a formal meal, the salad plate is laid before the guest after the main course is cleared, and an arranged salad is presented to the diner on a platter. At an informal meal, the salad plate functions to serve salad presented before the main course, as a side dish with the main course, or following the main course to stimulate the palate. But when salad is the main course, it is presented on a dinner plate.

## Crescent Salad Plate

The crescent salad plate is made by English dinnerware firms. It is approximately 4½ to 6 inches at its widest point by 7 to 8 inches long. Its quarter-moon shape fits snugly against the upper rim of the dinner plate, where it is laid to decrease the possibility of spills. In America, the crescent plate is used at informal meals to hold a side dish, such as salad, a vegetable, or a sauce, but it is not used in formal dining because the shape is out of proportion when laid in the center of the cover.

# Fish Plate

In the Middle Ages, Wednesday, Friday, Saturday, Lent, and church holidays were fast days. *Fast,* from the Anglo-Saxon word *faest,* means "to secure." It was intended to fix spiritual insight through mortification or self-denial, such as abstinence from specific foods, notably animal flesh, fish, and dairy products. During fast, one meal a day was served from meatless foods listed by the church as acceptable.

By the ninth century, fish was exempted from abstinence and was included in the diet, notably on Fridays to commemorate the crucifixion. Transportation in the Middle Ages was poor, and those who lived inland sustained live fish in a vivarium, or fish pond. Moreover, to ensure a weekly diet of fish, feudal castles and estates stocked moats and streams with freshwater fish such as carp and trout and charged the tenants a fee to fish.

By the thirteenth century, fish was included in monastic diets. To relieve the monotony of dried and salted fish, many an abby maintained three freshwater fish ponds, such as one for pike, a second for trout, and a third, called a *stew,* from the Middle English word *stuwe* for "fish tub," divided into sections for a variety of fish.

In the nineteenth century, when trawlers replaced sailboats and ice was used as a preservative, ocean fish were available to a wider market and plates were made solely to serve fish as an appetizer course. Today, the fish plate is a specialized plate about 8 to 9 inches in diameter. It is not made as part of a dinnerware set, but it is recognizable by ornamentation in a fish pattern. The fish plate is not essential for formal or informal meals; when served as an appetizer, fish is presented on any medium-size plate, such as a salad plate or a dessert plate. If fish is the main course, it is presented on a dinner plate.

# Dessert Plate

From the Middle Ages through the Renaissance, the aristocracy served dessert on small wooden trenchers made of beech or sycamore, round plates called *roundels,* ornamented with gilded flowers, fruit, or astrological signs and often painted on the underside with a short verse (many of a risqué or bawdy nature). Following dessert, roundels were turned over and the poems were read aloud, or the stanzas were sung by the guests to music. Hence, the term *roundelay* for a short, simple song with a phrase repeating at intervals.

By the sixteenth century, in addition to wooden roundels, dessert plates were wrought of pewter, such as those made between 1553 and 1554 by the Pewterer's Company of London, plates approximately 7 to 8 inches in diameter, the size of dessert plates today.

By the seventeenth century, dessert was a multidish course. Because the banquet table was heavily ladened with dozens of serving dishes, to give the servants time to clear the table the final course was served in another room, a course called *dessert* from the French *desservir,* meaning "to clear the table." Dessert was magnificently displayed in different locations: in a "withdrawing" room, a small intimate room to which people withdrew after dinner, in a garden pavilion or on a roof top, such as at Longleat House, Wiltshire, England.

Dessert services were modeled in a profusion of shapes, such as plates, bowls, compotiers, baskets, large and small tureens, cups, and pyramids. Grapes were served on plates made in the shape of grape leaves. Puddings, such as syllabub, were served in large bowls. Stewed fruit was presented in compotiers. Fresh fruit was placed in porcelain baskets. Wet sweetmeats (preserves or ice cream) were served in large and small tureens, and ices in individual cups. Dry sweetmeats (cakes and candy) were presented in compotes stacked like pyramids. The dessert service was not merely extensive, but elaborately ornamented.

Toward the end of the eighteenth century, the multidish dessert course began to wane in popularity, and by the nineteenth century dessert was a one-dish course served in the dining room on a medium-size plate decorated with simple but elegant ornamentation. By the second half of the nineteenth century, dessert plates were made to match the dinnerware pattern. Today, dessert plates are once again ornately decorated, a plate designed to end the meal with flair, like the grand finale of opera. They are specialized plates about 7¼ to 8½ inches in diameter, used at formal and informal meals, and not made as part of a dinnerware set.

# Cheese Plate

*Dessert without cheese is like a beauty with only one eye.*

ANTHELME BRILLAT-SAVARIN (1755–1826),
FRENCH GASTRONOME

The cheese plate is recognized by ornamentation in a cheese pattern, a specialized shape about 7¼ inches across, used in formal and informal dining, and not made as part of a dinnerware set.

# Tea Plate

*Polly, put the kettle on, we'll all have tea.*

CHARLES DICKENS, BARNABY RUDGE, 1841

Before lunch was an established meal in the nineteenth century, tea was taken in the late afternoon to tide one over during the long stretch between the morning and evening meals. Tea plates are more often found in England and Europe than in North America. They are a specialized shape, about 7 to 7½ inches in diameter. The purpose of the tea plate is to hold the teacup without a saucer. Some tea plates feature a shallow well.

# Fruit Plate

*In an orchard there should be enough [fruit] to eat, enough to lay up,*
*enough to be stolen, and enough to rot upon the ground.*

SAMUEL MADDEN, BOSWELL'S LIFE OF JOHNSON, 1783

In the Middle Ages, Bishop Venantius Fortunatus wrote a letter to the Abbess of Poitiers describing a first course of peaches. In the Italian Renaissance, fruit was used to make preserves, pastes, syrups, and candy, and the pear grove, so often depicted in paintings, was the queen of the orchard. In the seventeenth century, soup made of pureed fruit was served to start a meal. By the eighteenth century, fruit was served at the end of a meal to cleanse and refresh the palate. In the nineteenth century, fresh fruit was served as a final course on special fruit plates. Today, fruit is served anytime during a meal, from a first course of cold soup served in a bowl to a final course on a small plate.

The fruit plate is about 6¼ to 8 inches in diameter, a specialized plate not made as part of a dinnerware set, recognized by ornamentation in a fruit pattern. It is used in formal and informal dining.

## Bread-and-Butter Plate

*I never had a piece of toast*
*Particularly long and wide,*
*But, fell upon the sanded floor,*
*And always on the buttered side.*

*James Payn, editor,* Chambers's Journal, *1859–1874*

In the Middle Ages, trenchers were made of brown bread, and not eaten except by the poor. The bread served to accompany a meal was made of white flour and laid on the table to the left of the place setting, where the bread-and-butter plate is placed today. The freshness of bread equated to rank. Freshly baked bread was served to the lord of the manor, one-day-old bread was provided honored guests, and those of lower rank received bread three days old.

Because bread is dry, for palatability it is covered with an oily spread, such as butter. But up to the eighteenth century, butter was churned by hand, a laborious, time-consuming chore. Refrigeration was unknown and butter turned rancid quickly. To economize, a small mound of butter, called a *pat*, was presented on a plate approximately 2½ to 3½ inches in diameter, a dish called a *butter pat.*

In the nineteenth century, to satisfy the Victorian craze for novelty, the butter pat evolved into two plates: one for bread and the other for butter. However, after World War I, dining became less formal and a single plate 6 to 7 inches in diameter was made to hold both bread and butter.

Today, the bread-and-butter plate is used to separate bread and butter from sauce, gravy, and juices that emanate from foods on the plate. Although the bread-and-butter plate is an optional accoutrement at formal dinners in Europe, in a private residence in North America it is not laid on a formal dinner table because the menu is planned to provide sufficient taste and texture without the need for bread and butter. Thinly sliced melba toast may be passed with the soup course, the fish course may appear in a pastry shell, and toasted crackers are passed with cheese, along with butter at room temperature. When dry toast and crackers are served at a formal dinner, they are placed on the tablecloth. However, at a formal dinner in a restaurant or club, bread often is provided to cleanse the palate between different wines and to tide one over during the long lapse between courses.

Because luncheon is comprised of fewer courses than dinner, bread and butter are always served, whether the meal is formal or informal. Moreover, bread and butter are served at informal dinners. But when a plate is not provided for a slice of bread or a roll, it is laid on the tablecloth or the rim of the dinner plate, where the butter is also placed.

## Fruit Saucer

In the Middle Ages and the Renaissance, meat was far from fresh. Sauce was served to cover the taste, to enhance the flavor of dried food, and to aid digestion. *Sauce,* from the Latin *salire,* meaning "to salt," meant not only a saline seasoning but also a liquid seasoning, such as spices mixed with wine, prepared by the yeoman of the sauces in a small room or house:

> One little timber building, commonly called the Saucery House, conteyning foure little roomes used by the Yeoman of the Sauces.
>
> *Survey of Nonesuch,* 1650

The yeoman, dressed in livery, delivered sauce to the table in "saucers," small, round, deep dishes approximately 6 inches in diameter, served after meat was placed on the trencher.

In the sixteenth and seventeenth centuries, sauce dishes were made in shallow, round, or oval shapes approximately 5 to 8 inches in diameter, often with two handles. In the *Universal Etymological Dictionary* (published in 1728), Nathan Bailey defines the small shallow bowl as "a Little Dish to hold Sauce." In the reigns of George I (1714–1727) and George II (1727–1760), it was used to serve pickles.

Today, the sauce dish is known as a *fruit dish*, *fruit saucer*, *side dish*, or *berry bowl*, a small shallow dish about 4 to 6 inches in diameter by 1 inch deep, a shape that holds approximately 6 ounces of sauce. The purpose of a fruit saucer is to separate juices that flow from raw or cooked food from other foods. Because a formal meal is served course by course, side dishes are not used, and a fruit saucer is provided only at informal meals.

CHAPTER SEVEN

# BOWLS: LARGE TO SMALL

*The bowl is a vessel circular,*
*For food seldom perpendicular.*

SUZANNE VON DRACHENFELS

THE SPHERE IS a fundamental form of the potter's craft. When cut in half the sphere is round, a shape heightened, flattened, widened, or narrowed to form a bowl, from the Anglo-Saxon word *bolla,* meaning "round vessel." Bowls modeled for table use are made with and without handles to hold broth, such as a soup bowl or a soup cup; to rinse the fingertips, such as a finger bowl, and to hold solid foods, such as a ramekin. To insulate the table and balance the place setting, soup

BOWLS USED IN TABLE SETTING, SHOWN IN ORDER OF DESCENDING SIZE: SOUP PLATE, COUPE SOUP BOWL, SOUP-CEREAL BOWL, COVERED SOUP BOWL, LUG SOUP BOWL, CREAM SOUP BOWL AND SAUCER, BOUILLON CUP AND SAUCER, FINGER BOWL, AND RAMEKIN.

bowls, soup cups, finger bowls, and ramekins are placed on underplates, even those made with companion saucers.

## Soup Bowls

*Good soup draws the chair to it.*

GHANIAN PROVERB

In the Middle Ages, *soup*, from the Latin *suppare*, "to soak," was poured over toasted bread for nourishment. This was called a *sop* because it soaked up the broth.

Soup is served in seven different vessels: the soup plate, coupe soup bowl, soup-cereal bowl, covered soup bowl, lug soup bowl, cream soup bowl, and bouillon cup. The shapes are determined by the texture and the temperature of the soup. Soup with a chunky texture, such as vegetable-beef soup, retains heat well and is served in a wide, shallow bowl, a shape that releases heat easily. Soup with a smooth texture, such as pureed soup, is presented in a deep bowl, a form that conserves hot and cold temperatures. To preserve the temperature of thin liquids, clear soup or jellied broth are served in a small, narrow cup.

The way the handles of soup bowls and soup cups are shaped determines the way the vessel is used at the table. Soup bowls and soup cups made with vertical open-loop handles, such as the cream soup bowl and bouillon cup, occasionally are lifted at the table and the broth is drunk from the bowl or cup. Soup bowls made

with solid horizontal handles, such as the lug soup bowl, are tilted at the table to capture a last morsel or two, such as the onion in onion soup.

The average soup bowl holds a volume capacity of approximately 8 to 12 ounces, and the soup cup holds about 4 ounces of liquid.

### *Soup Plate*

The soup plate is a wide, shallow bowl made with a flanged rim, a shape called a *soup plate* rather than a *rim soup bowl* because the form and shallow depth are similar to a rim-shaped dinner plate. The soup plate looks larger than it is. Overall the diameter is approximately 9 to 10 inches, the rim is 1 to 2 inches wide, the depth is up to 1½ inches deep, and the well is 6 to 7 inches across.

Although the soup plate is used at informal meals, it is the only soup bowl used in formal dinner service. To cushion the affect of preprandial libations and to sustain one through various wines served at a formal dinner, soup is fortified with particles of food and a small serving is presented in a soup plate. Moreover, the broad rim is easy for a server to grasp and keeps fingers away from the contents of the bowl.

### *Coupe Soup Bowl*

*Coupe,* from the French *couper,* "to cut," is a saucer-like shape approximately 6 to 9 inches across. The rimless form is best described in the French expression *sous la coupe de quelqu'un* meaning "under one's thumb," a shape that places the server's fingers in close proximity to the contents of the bowl. The bowl is used only for informal dining.

### *Soup-Cereal Bowl*

The soup-cereal bowl is made with or without a rim; the former gives the table setting a dressier look. The purpose of the soup-cereal bowl is to serve food taken with a fork, such as salad or pasta, or eaten with a spoon, such as soup or cereal. This bowl is used only at informal meals and is also known as an *oatmeal bowl.* The soup-cereal bowl measures approximately 5¾ to 8¾ inches in diameter; its shape slightly narrower and deeper than the soup plate and coupe soup bowl.

## *Covered Soup Bowl*

The covered soup bowl is made to keep soup hot from kitchen to table, a specialized shape not made as part of a dinnerware set and used only at informal meals, elegant or otherwise. Guests remove the lid, rest the cover, rim side down, on the side of the underplate, and replace it before the table is cleared. The bowl measures about 4½ to 6½ inches across, and the depth is approximately 2 to 3½ inches. It is narrower and deeper than a soup plate, a coupe soup bowl, or a soup-cereal bowl.

## *Lug Soup Bowl*

The lug soup bowl is a specialized bowl not made as part of a dinnerware set. It is narrower and deeper than a soup plate, a coupe soup bowl, a soup-cereal bowl, or a covered soup bowl, approximately 4½ to 5½ inches in diameter and 2½ inches deep.

*Lug,* from the Swedish word *lugga,* meaning "to pull," is a solid horizontal handle placed on the side of the bowl to lift the vessel from the oven. To withstand oven temperatures, the lug soup bowl is made with a thick opaque texture that retains heat well, a density incompatible with the delicate appointments of an elegant table setting. The lug soup bowl, used only for casual dining, such as to present an individual serving of French onion soup put under the broiler to melt cheese, is also known as an *onion soup bowl.*

## *Cream Soup Bowl and Saucer*

The cream soup bowl is a modern-day adaptation of double-handled vessels made centuries ago, namely the *écuelle,* loving cup, caudle cup, posset pot, and porringer, shapes derived from the Greek *kantharos,* a shallow two-handled vessel.

The *écuelle,* French for "bowl," "basin," or "dish," features two open-loop or flat pierced handles made for sharing by two people, plus a close-fitting cover and a companion stand that often served as a food warmer. Hence, the French expression *manger à la même écuelle,* meaning "to live in one another's pocket." In the Middle Ages, the number of guests invited to a banquet often was determined by the number of *écuelles* available, a figure multiplied by two (one handle per person).

The tall loving cup of today was initially a shallow vessel, a shape used in the fifteenth century as a model for the cream soup bowl. Originally, shallow loving cups were wrought of silver; they were vessels made to serve brandy, and used by bridal couples to toast each other—hence "loving cup" and "bridal cup."

*Caudle,* from the Latin *caldus,* meaning "warm," was a hot beverage served in the Middle Ages to invalids, a drink composed of oatmeal, broth, milk, sugar, spices, wine, or ale and the forerunner of porridge. Tea caudle, a beverage made with the addition of tea and eggs, was administered to women who had just given birth and to convalescents. By the early seventeenth century, caudle was served in elaborately ornamented bowls approximately 6 to 8½ inches deep and 3½ to 6½ inches wide. Later, the caudle cup featured a shallow bowl made with two horizontal handles.

*Posset,* from the Anglo-Saxon word *poshote* (*pos* for "head cold" and *hote* for "hot"), was a drink similar to caudle, a hot beverage made of curdled milk spiced with wine, a liquid served in a deep cup called a *posset pot* (and also known as a *posnet cup*). Because the posset pot and caudle cup are similar in shape, the two forms are often hard to distinguish. However, the posset pot is usually pear-shaped, a vessel made with two handles, and sometimes with a spout from which a convalescent too weak to sit up could drink liquid. Both caudle cups and posset pots featured high domed lids ornamented with a knob and decorative finial. The vessels were accompanied by companion saucers and usually sold in sets or as part of a coffee or tea service.

*Porridge,* from the vulgar Latin *porrata,* meaning "leek broth," was a hot food made with boiled oats, spices, wine, beer, or curdled milk. In the late seventeenth century, porridge was served in small, shallow vessels called *porringers,* an adaptation of the French word *potager* for "soup dish," a vessel approximately 4 inches in height and width, with two horizontal handles pierced or solid, and a cover, a shape also known as an *eared dish.* In colonial America, single-handled porringers, approximately 2 to 9 inches across, were used primarily as shallow bowls to serve cereal to children.

Today, the double-handled cream soup bowl is slightly narrower and deeper than a soup plate, a coupe soup bowl, a soup-cereal bowl, a covered soup bowl, and a lug soup bowl. It is made in small and large sizes and accompanied by a companion saucer.

Because the flavor and texture of cream soup are too rich and heavy to start a meal where multiple courses are served, the cream soup bowl is not used at formal dinners. However, the small size, which measures approximately 4 to 5 inches in diameter, is used to serve a first course of pureed soup at meals where a simple, light menu is offered, namely, a formal or informal luncheon or an informal dinner. The volume capacity of the large cream soup bowl is almost double the smaller size, a bowl used at informal meals to present a hearty main course.

### *Bouillon Cup and Saucer*

The bouillon cup measures approximately 3¾ inches in diameter and features a companion saucer about 5½ inches across. The shape of the bouillon cup is similar to a teacup, only the bowl is narrower and deeper. It is made to sustain the temperature of hot broth or the consistency of jellied soup.

Bouillon is drunk entirely from the cup or sipped from a spoon, one or the other but never both. To test the temperature, a single sip is taken from the spoon. When bouillon is drunk from the cup, the cup is held by one or both of the open-loop handles, whichever is more comfortable.

The bouillon cup is not used at formal dinners because the consistency is too thin to start a multicourse meal where two or three wines are served. However, at formal luncheons and informal meals, generally one wine is served to accompany the lighter menu, and the bouillon cup is ideal for a small serving of thin soup.

## Finger Bowl

*Finger bowls: sign of wealth in the household.*

GUSTAVE FLAUBERT (1821–1880),
DICTIONNAIRE DES IDÉES REÇUES

Until the seventeenth century the majority of people ate with fingers, and *ablution,* from the Latin *ablutio,* meaning "to wash," was an essential part of dining. Warm water, often scented with herbs and flowers, was poured from a tall narrow jug called a *ewer,* a vase-shaped vessel with a globular body mounted on a high pedestal base fashioned with a high-curved handle and an arched spout. A servant, called a *ewerer,* poured water over the guests' hands into a basin known as a *laver.* Hence, *lavabo,* the French word for basin.

*A basen ewer and towell to array your cupbord.*

BOKE OF NURTURE, 1577

The vessel from which water was poured was sometimes made of agate or unicorn horn (narwahl tooth), substances believed to change color if contaminated with poison. At the high table, the water used for ablution was tasted for poison by a ewerer and not used again. As an added precaution, the ewerer kissed the towel on which the lord of the manor wiped his hands.

*Thanne somme of yow for water owe to goo. Somme holde the clothe,*
*somme poure uppon his hande.*

BABEES BOKE, *SIXTEENTH CENTURY*

In medieval France, ablution was announced by a blare of trumpets, a custom known as *sounding the horn for water*. Amid great ceremony, the nobility lined up in order of rank to wash their hands. In the reign of Elizabeth I (1533–1603), guests washed their hands before, during, and after a meal, but the queen ate with her gloves on, exchanging them between courses for fresh pairs.

In the seventeenth century, when the fork was accepted by the nobility of Europe, the practice of ablution began to wane. Old advertisements for English and Irish glass attributed to the last third of the eighteenth century mention "water glasses" in the shape of tumblers. Tobias Smollet in *Roderick Random* (1766) states: "I know of no custom more beastly than that of using water glasses in which polite company spirt and squirt and spue the filthy scourings of their gums."

In 1784, François La Rochefoucauld-Liancourt noted after a visit to England, "Dinner is one of the most wearisome of English experiences, lasting as it does for 4 or 5 hours. . . . After the sweets you are given water in small bowls of very clear glass in order to rinse out your mouth, a custom that strikes me as extremely unfortunate. The more fashionable folks do not rinse out their mouths but that seems to me even worse; for, if you use the water to wash your hands, it becomes dirty and quite disgusting."

By the nineteenth century, it was customary for English and French tables to feature individual finger glasses, vessels known also as *finger cups* and *wash-hands glasses*, shapes accompanied by saucers. From the finger glass, a sip or two of water was taken, swished around in the mouth, and spat into the saucer (similar to a wine tasting). The water that remained in the glass was used to rinse the fingers.

Eventually, the finger glass was replaced by the finger bowl, a dining accoutrement not everyone knew how to use. Confusion evidenced by a certain senator, who after watching President Martin Van Buren (1837–1841) use a finger bowl, rolled up his sleeves and washed from his fingertips to his forearms. Miss Eliza Leslie, a nineteenth-century etiquette author, noted the man who mistook a slice of lemon floating in his finger bowl for lemonade, stating, "Well! If this ain't the poorest lemonade I ever tasted." And in Mark Twain's *The Prince and the Pauper* (1882), we read of the person who drank from the finger bowl.

The finger bowl is a gracious custom seldom used today except at a formal dinner that concludes with a course of fresh fruit, particularly in the United States, where the final course is so often dessert taken with a utensil.

The finger bowl is a shallow vessel made of crystal or silver lined with glass, a container about 4 inches in diameter by 2¼ inches high, a bowl used to rinse the fingertips only, and filled with just enough water to cover them. To prevent water from overflowing the bowl, the fingertips are rinsed one hand at a time and wiped on a napkin held low in the lap. The lips may be patted gently with moistened fingertips, and the mouth blotted with a napkin.

The bygone custom of floating flowers in a finger bowl for fragrance is not

At a formal dinner, the finger bowl is presented on a medium-size plate lined with a doily, usually with the fruit course. The fruit fork and fruit knife are placed on the left and right sides of the plate, respectively.

The utensils are removed from the plate and laid on the table on the left and right sides of the plate. To clear the plate for service of fruit, the doily and bowl are lifted from the plate simultaneously.

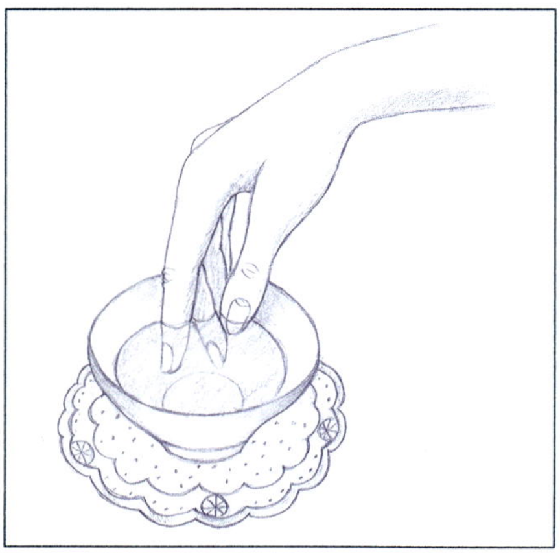

The doily is placed on the upper left side of the cover, and the finger bowl is laid on top. The fingertips are rinsed, one hand at a time.

recommended today because the floral essences compete with the aroma of food. However, to assist the cleansing act, at the host's option, a slice of lemon is floated in the finger bowl.

The finger bowl is used differently in formal and informal dining. At a formal affair, a finger bowl is placed on a medium-size plate laid with utensils for the fruit course. The fruit fork is placed on the left side of the plate, and the fruit knife is laid on the right side. The diner removes the utensils from the plate and lays them on the table on the left and right sides of the plate, respectively.

To prevent the finger bowl from slipping on the underplate, at the host's option, a doily is used as a liner. To make room for a piece of fresh fruit, the diner transfers the finger bowl to the upper left side of the place setting. With one hand he lifts the finger bowl and simultaneously raises the doily with the other hand, placing the finger bowl on it. Although presentation of a finger bowl does not mandate use, nonetheless the diner must clear the space for service of the course and lift the bowl to the proper place. However, when a finger bowl is presented on a plate without flatware, the finger bowl is used in this position and is not moved.

At an informal meal when a finger bowl is presented, it is laid on a plate without utensils, and placed to the left of the cover or wherever space permits. Infor-

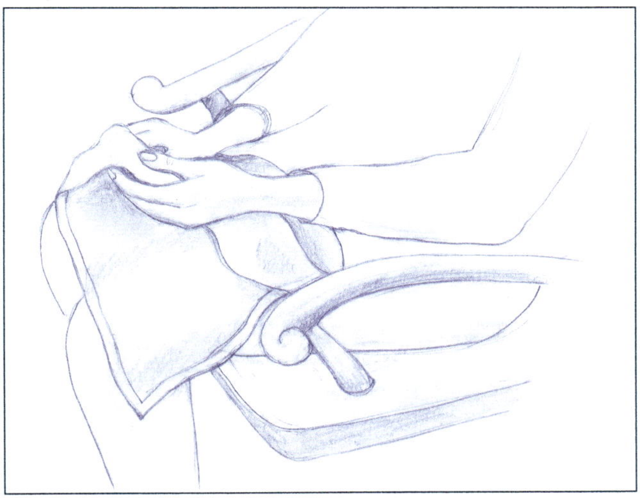

THE FINGERTIPS ARE DRIED ON A NAPKIN HELD LOW IN THE LAP.

mally, any small container is appropriate as a finger bowl, such as a small porcelain box at an elegant affair or a seashell at a fish dinner. Hot finger towels are a practical alternative to finger bowls, moistened, wrung out, heated in a microwave for a few seconds at 50 percent power, and presented rolled on a tray or in a bowl. The host hands the towels to the guests with tongs, and recirculates the container to collect them.

## Ramekin

*The ramekin or ramequin,*
*Pronounce it as you please,*
*'Tis a dish for food*
*Made of cream or cheese.*

SUZANNE VON DRACHENFELS

The ramekin is a small flat-bottomed bowl with vertical sides, a vessel made to serve baked dishes composed largely of cheese, milk, or cream, such as custard, flan, crème brûlée, or cheese soufflé.

*Ramekin* derives from the German word *rahm,* for "cream"; a *ramkin* is a Dutch dish comprised mainly of cheese. In France a *ramequin* is a small dish used to serve cheese tart. In England, a *ramekin* is a small bowl used to serve a savoury, a highly seasoned cheese dish, such as Welsh rarebit, served warm or cold as an appetizer to stimulate the palate before the main course or to aid digestion at the end of a meal.

The ramekin is made in small and large sizes approximately 3 to 4½ inches in diameter by 1½ to 2 inches deep. The small ramekin holds around 4 ounces filled almost to the rim. The large ramekin holds about 8 ounces filled to the top.

The ramekin is made with and without a narrow rim. The rimmed ramekin made with companion saucer is more often found in older sets of dinnerware, a shape that gives the table setting a dressy look. The rimless ramekin made without a saucer is used at informal meals, and for balance is placed on a medium-size underplate, such as a salad plate or a dessert plate.

CHAPTER EIGHT

# CUPS: ONE AND ALL

UNTIL THE AGE of Exploration in the seventeenth century, Europeans took beverages cold. The new international trade brought hot beverages to the table, namely, coffee, tea, and chocolate. Whereas cold beverages were served in tall cylindrical vessels, such as goblets, beakers, and tankards, hot drinks brought a need for short bowl-shaped vessels called *cups*, from the Sanskrit *kupa*, meaning "water well," and the Latin *cupa*, meaning "tub" or "cask."

Coffee, tea, and chocolate were expensive commodities to import and distribute; only the affluent could afford to serve such beverages. To conserve on the cost, the first European cups were small, approximately 2¾ inches high, a size that accommodated 2 to 3 ounces. By the eighteenth century, road conditions had improved, and so had the distribution of food, and the common people found they too could afford to drink coffee, tea, and chocolate. By the nineteenth century beverage cups were made in larger sizes to accommodate the increased demand for hot drinks.

Today the cup is made in seven sizes, each with a different volume capacity: breakfast cup, mug, teacup, coffee cup, chocolate cup, after-dinner coffee cup, and demitasse cup. Although the expression "cupful" denotes a half-pint serving, or 4 ounces, the size of the cup is determined by the strength of the drink, the hour the beverage is served, and whether it is thick or thin. Large cups and mugs are made to serve thin beverages taken hot at breakfast and lunch, such as coffee, tea, and cocoa, or cider on a cold afternoon. Small cups are made to serve strong-tasting beverages, such as espresso; drinks with a thick consistency, such as hot chocolate made from paste; and potent drinks made with alcohol, such as grog. But regardless of size,

THE CUPS, SAUCERS, AND MUGS USED IN TABLE SETTING, FROM LARGE TO SMALL, ARE THE BREAKFAST CUP, MUG, TEACUP, COFFEE CUP, CHOCOLATE CUP, AFTER-DINNER COFFEE CUP, AND DEMITASSE CUP.

cups and mugs are filled approximately three-quarters full, except for the demitasse cup, which is filled half full. Moreover, all cups except mugs are made with companion saucers. The dimensions of the following vessels are approximate.

## Breakfast Cup and Saucer

The tremendous demand for coffee in the early nineteenth century called for cups made with a volume capacity double or triple that of regular-size cups, and the breakfast cup was born, a vessel approximately 3¼ inches in height by 4½ to 5¾ inches in diameter. The companion saucer measures 6¾ to 8¾ inches across.

## Mug

*You and he are cup and cann.*

JONATHAN SWIFT, LIBEL ON DR. DELANEY, 1729

The mug is a cylindrical vessel known originally as a *cann* and also as a *tankard*, a vessel used in the Middle Ages. *Canne* is the Anglo-Saxon word for "cup," and the Indo-European term *gan(dh)* means "container," a tall vessel used initially to serve cold drinks. When coffee, tea, and chocolate were introduced to western Europe in the seventeenth century, they were expensive commodities; to conserve on the cost, hot beverages were served in short canns made with metal lids. In France, Sèvres produced a straight-sided "coffee cann," a container approximately 2½ inches in height and width, about the size and shape of today's demitasse cup. In England, Derby made a "breakfast cann" approximately 3 ¼ inches in height and width, a vessel slightly larger than today's regular-size coffee cup.

The original tankard was a vertical wooden tub or a hollowed-out log bound with iron, a container that held 3 gallons of water, used to transport water from city fountains and pipes to the home. The men who transported the water were called *tankard bearers*. By the seventeenth century, the 3-gallon tankard was reduced in size to a vessel that held 2 pints, made with a slightly tapered or globular body fitted with a handle, and sometimes a hinged lid raised by a thumb piece.

*A large vessel for strong drink.*

SAMUEL JOHNSON'S DICTIONARY, 1755

Customarily, silver tankards featured a notch in the base of the handle, a nick that released hot air and prevented the handle from bursting open. The notch was also used as a whistle to indicate the tankard was empty and ready for a refill. Hence the expression to "whet your whistle."

*Hath his tankard touched your brain?*

BEN JONSON

Eventually the tankard was produced in a smaller, straight-sided shape made without a lid, a vessel called a *mug*, from the Old German word *muck* or *mock,* "heavy drinking cup," a form immortalized by Sigmund Romberg in "The Drinking Song" from *The Student Prince.* By the eighteenth century, mugs featured baluster and drum shapes.

In colonial America, mugs were used by taverns to serve ale and beer, in sizes that held a pint or a quart. When a reveler was perhaps a bit inebriated or a touch too noisy, the innkeeper reminded him "to mind his p's and q's," (for pints and quarts).

From the seventeenth to the nineteenth centuries, silver mugs were fashionable christening gifts.

The mug is a heavier vessel than a cup; the walls are thicker and the base is denser. To retain heat, the mug is taller than a cup, made in regular and extralarge sizes. Regular-size mugs are approximately 3 to 4 inches in height by 3½ inches across, a vessel with a volume capacity of around 8 to 10 fluid ounces when filled almost to the rim. Extralarge mugs are the American counterpart of the European breakfast cup, a shape about 4 inches in diameter or more, a size that holds approximately 15 to 20 fluid ounces. To accommodate the shape of the mouth, the mug often flares outward at the rim.

From elegant to casual, the mug is used only for informal dining. But to keep pace with the luxurious attitude of informal dining today, manufacturers often make mugs that match formal dinnerware patterns.

## Teacup

*Look here, Steward, if this is coffee, I want tea;*
*but if this is tea, then I wish for coffee.*

CARTOON CAPTION, PUNCH, 1902

The first teacups used in Europe were handleless bowls imported from China in crates of loose tea, vessels used to measure samples of tea. It wasn't until the eighteenth century that porcelain was invented in Europe, and prior to this tea was served in silver bowls, a drink taken semicold because the handleless vessel was uncomfortable to hold when hot, a condition delightfully illustrated by Richard Collins in *A British Family at Tea,* a painting that hangs today in the Victoria and Albert Museum, London. Three members of a family are gathered around a tea table. One holds the handleless tea bowl with his index finger on the rim and his thumb on the base. The second places his fingers around the middle of the tea bowl. The third person holds the tea bowl by the base alone.

Handled cups were expensive to produce, and only the wealthy could afford to own them. But the Industrial Revolution fostered mass production, and by the late eighteenth century handled cups were affordable for the masses. Originally, the cup handle was held between the thumb and forefinger, and the last three fingers were curled outward to keep them grease-free, a custom that dates to the Middle Ages when food was eaten with the thumb and index finger. Today, the cup handle is held with the thumb and first finger or first two fingers, and the fourth and fifth fingers curl inward toward the palm. In the cold northern countries of Eastern

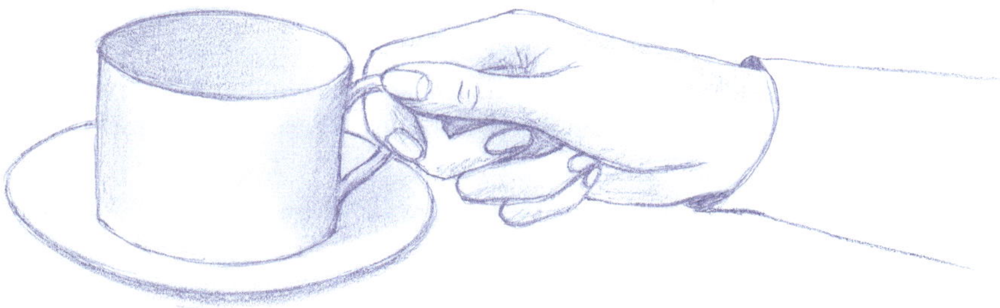

DEPENDING ON THE SIZE OF THE OPENING, THE CUP HANDLE IS HELD WITH THE THUMB AND THE FIRST FINGER, OR THE FIRST TWO FINGERS, AND THE FOURTH AND FIFTH FINGERS POINT INWARD TOWARD THE PALM.

Europe, particularly Russia, hot tea is served in tall glasses placed in metal holders fitted with handles ornately embellished with gold and silver filigree.

The saucer dates back to seventh-century China in the period of Emperor Te Tsung. It seems that a lady was scalded as she handed a tea bowl to her father, so she put the tea bowl on an iron plate. But the cup slid about and the hot water spilled out, so she secured the tea bowl to a small plate with beeswax. This proved messy and time-consuming. So she asked a lacquer merchant to make a small rimmed plate with a depression in the center to hold the tea bowl secure.

By the second quarter of the nineteenth century, bowl-shaped saucers were used as a vessel from which to drink tea, a cooling measure known as *saucering*. Although not sanctioned by fashionable people, saucering persisted among the lower classes well into the twentieth century, a custom that gave rise to the glass "cup plate," a small dish about 2½ inches to 4½ inches in diameter on which the cup was placed while one drank from the saucer.

The moustache cup, a nineteenth-century variation of the traditional teacup, evolved during the Crimean War. At this time, moustaches were in vogue, and to protect a gentleman's whiskers from the liquid in his teacup, Harvey Adams, a Staffordshire potter, designed a cup with a ledge that projected from the rim of one side on which the moustache rested. Between the ledge and the side of the cup was an opening through which tea flowed, a projection that kept whiskers dry. The moustache cup was fashionable up to the end of World War I.

Tea is a beverage cooled slightly before drinking, and to release heat, the teacup is slightly shorter and a little wider than the coffee cup, a shape approximately 3¼ to 3¾ inches in diameter by 2 to 2½ inches in height. The companion saucer measures about 5¼ to 5⅝ inches across. To accommodate the shape of the mouth, the rim of the teacup is often flared outward, a form derived from the beaker (from the Latin *beccus,* for "bird's bill").

Although the teacup is used at informal meals, elegant or otherwise, the flavor is too delicate to follow a heavy multicourse meal, and tea is not served at formal dinners and at formal luncheons only upon request.

## Coffee Cup

*Coffee:*
*Black as the devil,*
*Hot as hell,*
*Pure as an angel,*
*Sweet as love.*

CHARLES-MAURICE DE TALLEYRAND

Coffee is a beverage served from early morning to late evening, and the size of the cup is determined by the time of day it is taken, along with the strength of the brew. Coffee with a brisk taste, a light body, and a high caffeine content is served as a stimulant, notably at breakfast and lunch, in a large cup. Coffee with a strong taste, heavy body, and a low caffeine content is served as a digestive following a multicourse meal, such as after dinner, in a small cup.

> The morning cup of coffee has an exhilaration about it which the cheering influence of the afternoon or evening cup of tea cannot be expected to reproduce.
>
> Oliver Wendell Holmes Jr., *Over the Teacups*

Coffee is at its peak flavor when served extremely hot. To conserve the heat, the cup features a cylinder shape, taller than wide, a size approximately 2½ inches in height by 3¼ inches in diameter. The companion saucer measures around 6 to 6½ inches across.

The coffee cup is made in three sizes, namely, the *regular-size coffee cup,* the *after-dinner coffee cup,* and the *demitasse cup.* The regular-size coffee cup is used at informal meals, the after-dinner coffee cup at elegant informal affairs, and the demitasse cup at formal occasions.

> Coffee has come into general use as a food in the morning, and after dinner as an exhilarating and tonic drink.
>
> Anthelme Brillat-Savarin, *The Psychology of Taste,* 1825

After-dinner coffee is a strong-flavored brew with a low caffeine content served to stimulate digestion at an elegant multicourse meal. The smallish cup measures approximately 2⅜ inches in height by 2½ inches in diameter and holds approximately 3 ounces. The companion saucer is about 4¾ to 5 inches across. Rather than interrupt good conversation and take coffee in another room, after-dinner coffee is often served at the dinner table.

Demitasse is a heavy-bodied brew with a strong taste and low caffeine content. It is served to aid digestion and dispel the lingering effects of alcohol after a formal dinner where several wines are served. *Demitasse* means "half cup" in French, and the cup is approximately 2¼ inches in height and width, slightly shorter and narrower than the after-dinner coffee cup. The companion saucer measures about 4½ to 5 inches across.

Guests at a formal dinner are seated at the table for hours, so in order to provide them with the opportunity to stretch and regroup, and to revive conversation, demitasse is presented in another room. The cup is filled half full (approximately 1.5 ounces). Customarily, at a formal affair, demitasse is followed by brandy or liqueur;

entertainment—dancing or cards—may then commence. A second cup is not offered.

In Edwardian times the dining room and library had a quite masculine architecture that featured paneled walls and molded ceilings, a setting that invited gentlemen to linger after dinner for coffee, port, and cigars. The ladies took demitasse and liqueur in rooms decorated with a feminine air, such as the anteroom of the powder room, the boudoir, or the drawing room. After approximately 20 minutes or so, men and women regrouped for conversation, games, and dancing. Today the preferred way to take demitasse is together in the drawing room.

At an informal meal, demitasse is served away from the table, wherever is convenient.

## Chocolate Cup

*The superiority of chocolate, both for health and nourishment, will soon give it the same preference over tea and coffee in America, which it has in Spain.*

THOMAS JEFFERSON, IN A LETTER TO JOHN ADAMS, 1785

Chocolate is a concentrated food made from the fruit of the *Theobroma cacao,* a member of the Sterculiaceae family, an evergreen tree indigenous to Southeast Asia, Africa, and South America. In 1737, botanist Carl von Linné classified the cacao tree as *theobroma,* meaning "divine food" (and it is). *Theobroma cacao* produces large pods that contain twenty to fifty seeds called *cocoa beans.* The Aztecs crushed cocoa beans between stones, added boiling water, and produced a strong, bitter-tasting drink. Our word *chocolate* comes from the Aztec *xocolatl,* meaning "bitter water."

Chocolate contains theobromine, literally, "food of the gods," a nitrogenous substance similar to caffeine that stimulates the nervous system and dispels fatigue. The Aztec believed chocolate was sent from heaven—and maybe it was. Chocolate was considered an aphrodisiac and Montezuma was reputed to have drunk fifty cups a day.

Columbus carried the cocoa bean from the New World back to Spain in 1492. In 1519, Cortés found cocoa beans widely used in Mexico. Instead of being greeted with gold, he was welcomed with mounds of cocoa beans, for the Aztecs believed the food brought good fortune and strength. From Spain chocolate was introduced to Italy in 1600. When the Spanish Infanta, Anne of Austria, married Louis XIII in the seventeenth century, she introduced chocolate to the French court. The first use of chocolate in England was in 1650 at Oxford, and in 1657 a Frenchman opened a chocolate house on Bishopsgate Street, London.

In the mid-seventeenth century the cost of chocolate dropped, and rather than drink cold beverages at breakfast, such as ale and beer, the gentry drank hot chocolate, tea, or coffee. By the eighteenth century, chocolate was a fashionable drink served throughout Europe, and chocolate houses were popular gathering places for writers, politicians, and gamblers.

In 1780, Dr. James Baker, an American, financed a factory to produce chocolate made soluble by a reduced cocoa-butter content, a product called *baker's chocolate*. Cocoa powder was made in 1828. Because chocolate is naturally acerbic, it is sweetened with sugar, and in 1875, Daniel Peter, a Swiss chocolate manufacturer from Vevey, mixed chocolate with sweetened condensed milk (the latter discovered by Henri Nestlé, a Swiss chemist), a product called *milk chocolate*. In 1888, Milton Snavely of Pennsylvania opened the first chocolate factory in the United States. The rest is delectable history.

Originally hot chocolate was a breakfast drink made from unsweetened chocolate mixed with cream, a mix beaten into a thick paste. Just before serving, sugar and hot frothy milk were added. To accommodate demand, in the second half of the eighteenth century the morning chocolate cup was larger than a coffee cup or teacup. However, the thick paste was slow to pour, and at social affairs in the afternoon, hot chocolate was served in small narrow cups about 3 inches in height by 2½ inches in diameter. The companion saucer measured approximately 4 inches across.

Today, hot chocolate is made from powdered cocoa, a thinner beverage than the original drink; it is served in a large vessel, such as a coffee cup, teacup, or mug. Small chocolate cups purchased in specialty stores are not made as part of a dinnerware set.

CHAPTER NINE

# HOW TO LAY DINNERWARE

*All human history attests*
*That happiness for man,*
*The hungry sinner,*
*Since Eve ate apples*
*Much depends upon dinner.*

LORD BYRON, DON JUAN

THE DINNER TABLE is the heart of the home, a magic place where moments are treasured and memories made. Family events, anniversaries, and holidays are all celebrated at the table, a place where children are taught, business is conducted, and romance is found, a setting that greets with a silent message: "Welcome. A place is prepared for you."

A myriad of traditions surround the service of meals, especially dinner. We dine in a designated area and sit at a table enhanced by the symmetrical alignment of dinnerware. Like a picture slightly askew, an asymmetrical place setting creates subtle irritation, and to promote a harmonious relaxed ambience, dinnerware is laid directly opposite the ware on the other side of the table. When an odd number of people are seated at a rectangular, square, or oval table, the odd-numbered place setting is aligned with the middle of the even-numbered place setting opposite. This is not to suggest that one set the table with a ruler in hand, only that the symmetrical alignment of dinnerware please the eye.

The type of dining occasion determines where to lay dinnerware. At a multi-course meal, notably a formal affair, each course is served one at a time, and dinnerware is laid in the center of the place setting. In formal dining, side dishes are not used, cups and saucers do not appear on the table, and demitasse is served in another room.

At an informal meal, the menu is simpler and the courses are either laid on the table all at once or presented one at a time as in formal service. A meal served all at once requires space, and side dishes, namely, salad plate, bread-and-butter plate, and fruit saucer, are laid to the left of the cover. The left-handed person reverses the placement. Why are side dishes placed opposite the hand with which one eats? Because the placement of ware near the "eating" hand is awkward to manipulate and makes the dishes too close for comfort.

The placement of the cup and saucer is different for company and family dining. Because the majority of people are right-handed, at a company occasion the cup and saucer are placed on the right side, even for a left-handed person; this placement promotes a symmetrical table setting. The cup and saucer are laid to the right of the outside piece of flatware. However, at a family meal, aesthetics are not as important as comfort, and commonsense dictates seating the left-handed person at the end of the table where the cup and saucer are placed on the left (even though the other cups and saucers are on the right).

When hot beverages are served during a meal, such as coffee at breakfast or tea at lunch, the cup and saucer are laid on the table initially. But if hot beverages are served at the end of a meal, such as after dessert, the cup and saucer are brought to the table following the last course.

Here are some guidelines for the alignment of dinnerware.

- *Large plates,* such as the dinner plate and luncheon plate, are laid about 1 inch in from the edge of the table. The exception is the service plate, a capacious plate aligned flush with the edge of the table.
- *Small plates,* such as the salad plate, fish plate, and dessert plate, are laid in the center of the cover, about 2 inches in from the edge of the table.
- *Cups and saucers* are placed approximately 1 inch beyond the outermost

piece of flatware. The top edge of the saucer is aligned with the top rim of the plate or bowl.

- *Cup handles* are faced in a four o'clock position for easy access.
- *Soup bowl and soup cup handles* are aligned parallel with the edge of the table.
- *Bread-and-butter plates* are laid at the top left of the cover, usually above the dinner fork, a placement that avoids overcrowding on the right side, where the goblet and wine glass are placed.
- *Elbow room* requires a minimum of 15 inches between place settings, or approximately 24 inches from the center of one place setting to the middle of the next.

CHAPTER TEN

# THE INTERCHANGE OF DINNERWARE

More people today live in smaller spaces than ever before, a circumstance that leaves little room to store things seldom used. The interchange of dinnerware is a necessity; substitutions are based on proportion, balance, and the size of the serving.

## Plates

### *Large Plates*

The *service plate* is the largest plate, approximately 14 inches in diameter, a size ideal to use as a dinner plate, buffet plate, placemat, and platter. When used as a dinner plate, it can hold generous portions of food, such as a slice of prime rib. As a buffet plate, it balances well on the lap and makes it easier to eat a meal seated on a sofa, chair, stairway, or floor. If it is used as a placemat, the size frames the dinner plate with color and design and remains on the table through the entire meal. Alternatively, the service plate is cleared after the main course and the dessert plate is laid directly on the table. The service plate also works as a small platter to serve canapés, cookies, sandwiches, or food prepared in a ring mold.

The *luncheon plate* and *dinner plate* range in size from approximately 9 to 10½ inches, respectively, dimensions right for serving oysters on the half shell, for use as small placemats on which to lay medium-size plates, such as salad or dessert plates, or as small platters.

### *Medium-Size Plates*

The *salad plate, entrée plate, fish plate, fruit plate, dessert plate,* and *cheese plate* are approximately 8 inches in diameter, a size that lends itself for use as an underplate on which to lay small bowls, such as ramekins and fruit saucers, to hold discarded bones, such as spareribs, or to lay in an entry to receive mail.

The *crescent salad plate* is a suitable size for crudités, sauce, relishes, nuts, candy, and nibbles and is used in the home to hold jewelry, pins, pocket change, and small guest soaps.

### *Small Plates*

The *tea plate, bread-and-butter plate,* and *fruit saucer* are approximately 6 inches in diameter, sizes appropriate to use as side dishes and underplates for small bowls. The fruit saucer substitutes as a finger bowl and also as a vessel to hold butter balls, lemon wedges, sugar cubes, condiments, dessert, ice cream, nuts, or candy.

## *Bowls*

### *Large Bowls*

The *soup plate* and *coupe soup bowl* are large bowls approximately 6 to 10 inches in diameter, shallow bowls used at the table to serve pasta, stew, vegetables, and rolls, and in the home to float candles or short-stemmed flowers, such as camellias.

### *Medium-Size Bowls*

The *soup-cereal bowl, covered soup bowl, lug soup bowl,* and *cream soup bowl* range in size from approximately 6 to 4½ inches in diameter. The soup-cereal bowl and covered soup bowl interchange to serve sauce, chutney, jam, ice cream, nuts, or candy. The lug soup bowl substitutes as a bowl for dips (especially those hot from the oven). The cream soup bowl is an appealing shape to hold condiments or candy and, in the home, to display a small bouquet or hold potpourri.

### *Small Bowls*

The *finger bowl* and *ramekin* are approximately 3 to 4½ inches, respectively. The finger bowl, usually made of glass, substitutes as a side dish to serve cold vegetables or fruit. The ramekin interchanges to serve condiments, dips, ice cream, puddings, nuts, and sauce.

## *Cups*

### *Large Cups*

The *breakfast cup, mug, coffee cup,* and *teacup* hold about 16 to 4 ounces, respectively, shapes that interchange with bowls to serve soup away from the table. Moreover, mugs are used at the table as holders to present edibles, such as carrot and celery sticks, and on a buffet to contain flatware. In the home, mugs are used to hold desk items, such as pens, pencils, rulers, scissors, and letter openers, on a vanity for cosmetic brushes, and throughout the house as small vases for cut flowers.

### *Small Cups*

The *bouillon cup, chocolate cup, after-dinner coffee cup,* and *demitasse cup* hold approximately 4 ounces filled to the rim. At the table small cups hold bread sticks, crudités, cinnamon sticks, and candy canes. They can also be used for hot apple cider. Throughout the home, small cups contain cosmetic brushes, desk items, or tiny bouquets.

CHAPTER ELEVEN

# SERVEWARE: AT THE TABLE AND IN THE HOME

*Serveware* comprises the dishes, platters, and bowls, that hold the food to be served at a meal. The first serveware was made from earthly forms, such as hollowed-out rocks and tree barks, textures that evolved in antiquity into vessels made of gold, silver, and alabaster for royal feasts. Very little is known about serveware in the early Middle Ages of Europe, a period of meager subsistence when food was probably served from a common iron pot.

As a precaution against fire and to avoid unpleasant cooking odors, the medieval kitchen was located a good distance from the dining hall, and serveware was transported by high-ranking servants to a pantry, a small room located between the kitchen and the hall where the dishes were reheated and final touches were made. Most of the food cooled in passage, and the medieval banquet was a moderately warm feast at best.

Precious metals were a measure of wealth, and in the great hall silver serveware was displayed on a trestle table, from the Latin words *transtrum* for "beam" and *tabula* for "board." The trestle table was laid across sawhorses before meals, dismantled afterward, and placed at the side of the room where it was called a *sideboard*, furniture that evolved into a multitiered buffet for display of silver serveware too valuable to use.

The banquet was the primary form of medieval hospitality, a lavish event that symbolized wealth and power. One feast, hosted in 1416 by an English nobleman for

2,162 guests, included 104 oxen, 1,000 sheep, 3,000 chickens, 400 peacocks, and 6,000 sweet dishes. Needless to say, hundreds of pieces of serveware were required.

In 1710 Augustus the Strong, king of Poland and elector of Saxony, gave serveware royal endorsement when he commissioned Johann Jacob Irminger, court silversmith, to make serving dishes in all sizes, "so that foreign courts and persons of noble standing, as well as those of middling estate, may be supplied therewith." But it was not until 1720 that serveware was made as a matched set known as a *dinner service,* with covers removed simultaneously in a grand display. Each cover was held in place with a napkin wrapped around the bottom and tied on top. Soon the ornamentation of the lid was as important as the decoration of the bowl.

The Swan service is the largest porcelain dinner service made *en suite,* a set comprised of 2,200 pieces, modeled from 1737 to 1742 by Johann Joachim Kändler at Meissen, with the assistance of Johann Friedrich Eberlein. The Swan service was a wedding gift from Augustus III, elector of Saxony, to Count Heinrich von Brühl, administrator of Meissen, on the occasion of his marriage to Countess Frances of Kolowrat-Krakowski. An aquatic theme was used, and each piece featured a different motif, such as a swan, dolphin, sea nymph, river god, or seashell, designs inspired by an engraving published in 1700 by Leonard Buggels of Nuremberg.

The typical banquet in the eighteenth century was comprised of three courses of up to 100 dishes each, a menu that required serveware by the hundreds. The courses were served *à la française,* that is, all the serveware for each course was placed on the table at one time. Although the guests did not partake of every dish, they helped themselves and their dinner partners to the serveware placed nearest them.

By the mid-eighteenth century covered serveware was made with warming stands to keep food hot. After each course was cleared, leftover food was taken to a *serre,* a small room where food was kept hot until auctioned or resold by the *maître d'hôtel.*

In the early nineteenth century, dinner service *à la russe* was introduced. In Russian-style service a butler presented platters and bowls to the guests and then returned the serveware to the kitchen. Russian service not only reduced the amount of serveware required for a multicourse meal; it also decreased the number of staff needed to attend the guests, and is a method followed today at formal affairs.

*Serveware* comes from the Latin *servire,* "to serve," and the Anglo-Saxon *waru,* meaning "special merchandise." It is an inclusive term for bowls, beverage pots, compotes, pitchers, platters, salt and pepper dispensers, trays, and tureens. Serveware made with height, depth, and a hollow center is also known as *holloware,* which on average accommodates six to eight people. A basic set of serveware includes the following:

- A large oval platter to serve a roast
- A small oval platter to serve chops or fish
- A deep bowl, approximately 5 to 6 inches deep, to serve soft foods, fruit salad, and deep-dish pie
- A shallow bowl, approximately 1 inch deep, to hold firm vegetables, fruit, rolls, crackers, and cheese
- A small bowl for cold sauce, dips, nuts, and candy
- A sauceboat to serve gravy and hot sauces
- A medium-size pitcher for syrup, gravy, sauce, or honey
- A large pitcher to serve water, iced tea, and other beverages
- A beverage pot for coffee, tea or hot chocolate
- A creamer for cream, also used to serve salad dressing, gravy, sauce, or dessert topping
- A covered sugar bowl that doubles for service of condiments, jam, jelly, nuts, sauce, or dip

Duplicate sets of serveware are recommended for informal dining. At an informal meal, for eight to ten people, duplicate sets of serveware, such as bread baskets or sauceboats, are suggested for each end of the table, a placement that encourages the guests to help themselves and facilitates service. Moreover, when a menu calls for frequent use of a particular sauce, such as drawn butter with lobster, the placement of small bowls at each cover eliminates the need to reach awkwardly or interrupt conversation to request passage. Although duplicate sets of serveware need not match, when two pieces are presented together on a tray, such as a creamer and sugarer, a matched pair makes a unified appearance.

At a formal meal, one butler is responsible for service of four to six people and service begins simultaneously. To accommodate twelve to eighteen guests, serveware is required in triplicate.

Like dress fashions, food goes in and out of style, along with attendant serveware. At one time compotes and nut bowls were an essential part of the table setting. Today they are rarely used. To eliminate the mystery behind each category, serveware pieces are described below; alternative uses for each piece are also provided.

## *Bowls*

*That green cheese was most welcome (with an onion),*
*Coarse maslin bread; and for his daily swig,*
*Milk, buttermilk, and water, whey and whig,*
*Sometimes metheglin, and by fortune happy,*
*He sometimes sipped a cup of ale most nappy.*

OLD PARR OF SHROPSHIRE, SEVENTEENTH CENTURY

Serving bowls are made in shallow or deep shapes. Shallow serving bowls approximately 8 to 9 inches in diameter, with a broad, flat base and sloping sides, are used to serve firm food, such as asparagus, fruit, and rolls. Such bowls are also called *nappies,* from the Middle English *nap,* meaning "bowl." At one time a nappy was placed under a glass of strong ale to catch the overflow of foam. Deep serving bowls accommodate soft foods, such as mashed potatos, rice, pasta, or creamed foods, a shape that holds a serving spoon without scraping the bottom of the bowl.

## *Beverage Pots*

Beverage pots are made in assorted shapes to serve tea, coffee, chocolate, and demitasse. Although the average teapot or coffeepot holds six to eight servings, chocolate pots and demitasse pots hold twelve servings or more. To secure the lid tightly, beverage pots are made with a lip on the inside of the rim, and a spout that is sharply defined to avoid drips. To defray heat away from the handles, silver beverage pots are made with Bakelite handles or with insulator rings in the center of the handles.

*Teapots* were originally modeled after the Chinese wine pot, a small flagon-like vessel with a spout and bail (overhead) handle. In the seventeenth century, tea was an expensive commodity and teapots were wrought in sizes just large enough to hold one serving, a shape approximately 3 to 4 inches in height. When the price of tea fell in the early 1700s, teapots were modeled in larger sizes, and by 1800 they were the size we know today.

Because porcelain was not invented in Europe until the early eighteenth century, when tea was introduced to Europe in the mid-seventeenth century, teapots were made of silver. The ceramic teapots modeled thereafter followed the designs of silver beverage pots, vessels made with a tall cylindrical body, high-domed lid, and a handle placed opposite the spout or at a right angle to the spout; this shape was also used for coffee and chocolate pots. Toward the end of the eighteenth century, when tea drinking was affordable for everyone, teapots made for the lower class were wrought of brass or pewter.

The ornamentation and the shape of the teapot reveal the age in which it was made. In the reign of Queen Anne (1702–1714), simplicity of form rather than surface decoration was stressed, and pear-shaped teapots were made with round or polygonal bodies and high-domed lids. The spout curved, and to prevent the leaves from pouring into the cup, a filter was placed at the junction of the body and spout. By the second quarter of the eighteenth century, teapots were lavishly ornamented in the rococo style. In the reign of George I (1714–1727), teapots were modeled with a spherical form and a straight spout, a shape called a *bullet* in Scotland. The lid was low. Late in the eighteenth century, teapots were made in the neoclassical style that featured gadrooning around the edges and acanthus leaves. Around 1760, the flat-bottomed teapot had a drum-shaped body, a straight spout, and a flat lid; the teapot rested on a matching stand to keep from marking the table. Around 1780, eliptical or boat-shaped teapots were in demand.

By the early nineteenth century, revival styles were the vogue and teapots were ornamented with eclectic decoration and modeled in shapes taken from historical periods, as well as naturalistic and novelty forms, such as melons, cauliflowers, or fish. By the mid-nineteenth century tea was served from an urn-shaped vessel, a style replaced eventually by a tea kettle removable from the base.

Today, the teapot is made with a low bulbous body that flares through the center to allow room for tea leaves to expand during infusion. The spout is situated low on the body, a placement that does not disturb the leaves when tea is poured from the pot.

*Coffee from the top of the cup,*
*Chocolate from the bottom.*

VENETIAN PROVERB

*Coffeepots* were originally modeled after the Turkish ewer, a tall, narrow, cylindrical shape. From approximately 1700 to 1730, the coffeepot was made with a flat, round base and a cylindrical body that tapered upward to a peaked dome. After 1730, the round base rested on narrow feet and the body was pear-shaped. Around 1770, the broad base on which the coffeepot rested supported an urn-shaped body, modeled in a square or rounded form. Today the coffeepot is a tall, narrow shape, similar to a truncated cone, that allows space for the grounds to sink to the bottom and the brew to rise to the top. To prevent coffee grounds from pouring into cups, the spout on a coffeepot is placed high on the body.

*Chocolate pots* were introduced in the late seventeenth century; the vessel had a cylindrical form but was a little smaller in size than a coffeepot. Very often the handle was straight rather than looped, and made of wood for insulation. For ease in manipulation, the handle was placed at a right angle to the spout.

Chocolate originally was made from a thick paste of chocolate mixed with hot milk or boiling water. To accommodate the flow of the beverage, the spout of the chocolate pot was wide and short, a shape replaced in the eighteenth century by a pouring lip. To keep the beverage hot, chocolate pots often rested on three feet that lifted the vessel and provided room underneath for a spirit lamp. Unlike that of coffee, the sediment of chocolate was savored and the placement of the spout varied from low to high on the body.

Just before chocolate was served it was whipped in the pot with a *moulinet,* a thin rod made of wood tipped with silver or ivory. The *moulinet* was inserted into the pot through an aperture in the lid, an opening made with a removable finial, and sometimes attached to a chain that fastened to the handle. Today, hot chocolate is a thin beverage mixed in a mug or cup, and chocolate pots are seldom used.

*Demitasse pots* are essentially small, cylindrical coffeepots, about 7 inches in height, plus lid. Although the shape of the demitasse pot is similar to a coffeepot, it is narrower in circumference and shorter.

# Compotes

The compote is a long-stemmed dish or footed serving bowl related to the *tazza,* a shallow ornamental drinking vessel mounted on a high pedestal foot popular in sixteenth-century Italy. Compotes are used in formal and informal dining to serve candy or glacéed fruit. In the nineteenth century, large compotes were a fashionable part of formal table decoration, a tradition that continues today, and at formal affairs compotes are arranged symmetrically near the four corners of the table, or in a straight line down the center of the table in a placement that alternates with the flowers and the candelabras. As such, compotes remain on a formal table thoughout the meal; after dessert guests help themselves to candy and glacéed fruit, or a butler presents the compote to them.

At informal affairs, compotes are seldom used because they compete for space with serveware. However, small compotes are sometimes used creatively to hold a roll at each place setting, serve condiments and sauce, or present dessert. Or they are stacked to make a pyramid-shaped centerpiece, with the outer edges filled with flowers, fruit, and candy.

# Nut Bowls

At one time nuts bowls were laid on the table to balance the menu with a crunchy texture that provided contrast with the soft consistency of cooked food, a custom replaced today by the crisp texture of crudités. However, when nuts are provided in formal dining, large bowls are placed symmetrically around the centerpiece within easy reach of the guests, or small individual bowls of nuts are placed at the top of each cover, and the guests help themselves during the meal. At informal meals, nuts are served more often as an hors d'oeuvre before dinner. But if nut bowls are provided at an informal occasion, they are placed on the table in the same way as at a formal affair.

# Platters

*Platter,* from the French *plat* for "flat," is a shallow dish made in round, oval, or rectangular shapes, a serveware category made primarily to serve meat and fish dishes prepared without sauce. To direct the juices that flow from food, platters are often made with a well, such as the indented tree design.

Platters are made in sizes that descend from approximately 24 inches or more to 9 inches.

- The 24-inch platter is a generous size to serve a roast garnished with vegetables or a large ham or turkey.
- The 16- to 18-inch platter is an appropriate size to serve hot or cold meat to approximately six to eight people.
- The 14-inch oval platter is right for serving a good-size roast, fish, individually molded salad, sliced fruit, or vegetables to approximately four people.
- The 12-inch platter is used to present canapés, food served in a ring mold, sandwiches, cake, pie, cookies, petit fours, and tarts.
- The 9-inch platter is perfect for condiments and relishes.

The way a platter is used is different for formal and informal dining. At a formal affair, a platter is used to serve the fish course, entrée course, main course, salad course, and dessert course. At an informal occasion, the platter is used more often on a buffet to hold the meat course surrounded with garniture, or assorted cold foods, such as sliced fruit, vegetables, sandwiches, cake, or cookies.

# Salt Cellars and Salt Shakers

*There are six flavors, and of them all, salt is the chief.*

SANSCRIT PROVERB

The six flavors are: sweet, sour, bitter, spicy, bland, and salty. Salt is our first seasoning, a mineral used to preserve food and purify water. By 6500 B.C. salt mining was under way at Hallstein and Hallstatt near Salzburg, the Austrian "city of salt."

The expression "worth one's salt" harkens to a time when salt was currency. Originally, goods and service were paid for with salt; later, Roman soldiers were given an allowance, or a *salarium,* to buy salt—hence the term *salary.* In the *Satyricon,* Petronius coined the expression "not worth his salt," a word for an indolent soldier, or one far from valiant. To spill salt implied recklessness or lack of self-control, a superstition depicted by Leonardo da Vinci in the *The Last Supper,* a scene that portrays Judas spilling salt. The biblical expression "salt of the earth" implies a person of merit or one who is admired. To take something "with a grain of salt" suggests skepticism.

At one time, salt was considered a protection from evil and witches and was used at sacrificial meals where oaths were made. The devil was said to dance on the left side, so to prevent misfortune, a pinch of salt was thrown over the left shoulder, supposedly into the devil's eye. The expression "covenant of salt" derives from sacrificial ceremonies where salt was used to preserve a pact. The Arab saying "there is salt between us" implies trust. In Russia, guests are greeted at the door by a host bearing a tray of bread and salt, a gesture called *khleb-sol,* meaning "bread-salt," a symbol of hospitality representing the staff of life.

In the Middle Ages, during the cold winter months of northern Europe, animals were expensive to feed and fishing was difficult to pursue. To ensure a steady supply of food in the winter, great slaughters and heavy fishing took place in the fall. Much of the meat and fish were cooked and eaten immediately; the remainder was preserved with salt or smoke.

From the Middle Ages to the Renaissance, salt was derived primarily from evaporated salt springs and was known as *brine salt.* "Bay salt" came from sea water, mainly from the Bay of Bourgneuf at the mouth of the Loire River; this was coarse, impure salt usually used to cure food. Salt used at the table was purified.

So vital to life was salt that it denoted rank and defined seating arrangements at table. People of power and importance sat at the high table, "above the salt," while those of lesser rank sat at tables "below the salt." Because salt was scarce, it was prized and served in vessels fashioned beyond all proportion to the amount they held. The containers ranged in height from 8 to 22 inches or more. They were modeled in magnificent shapes and used as centerpieces at the high table: for example, they might be made as a miniature replica of a rigged sailing vessel supported on wheels and rolled along the table. Of particular note is the master salt cellar made by Benvenuto Cellini, a work commissioned by Cardinal Ippolito d'Este, and completed in 1543 for François I of France. Made of gold, enamel, and ivory, the famous salt cellar was a mythological interpretation of the interaction of sea and earth, represented by a nude male and a nude female figure in a reclined position; the vessel can be seen today in the Kunsthistorisches Museum, Vienna.

Salt is a corrosive agent that must be placed in an abrasion-proof container of ceramic, wood, acrylic, or glass. To prevent corrosion the interiors of silver salt shakers are gilded. Salt shakers that are not gilded are wiped clean with a damp cloth to pick up all the salt crystals.

Because salt bears a close resemblance to arsenic, at medieval meals salt was tested by an assayer for poison; after the meal it was locked in the cellar for storage against theft—hence the term *salt cellar*. At one time, salt holders were called *trencher salts*, a name for bread baked with a depression in the center to hold salt. Toward the late seventeenth century, trencher salts were made as larger glass bowls. By the eighteenth century, salt cellars were made of silver, silver gilt, gold, and Sheffield plate, ornamented with elaborate decoration and customarily fitted with glass liners. Today, salt cellars are diminutive bowls approximately 1 to 2 inches high by 2 to 5 inches wide, made of glass, silver, or silver lined with glass.

The salt cellar is used differently in formal and informal dining. At formal affairs, salt is always applied from a salt cellar, a method that provides controlled use of salt. A small spoon is presented in the salt cellar and used to sprinkle salt over food. However, food is never dipped into a salt cellar. At informal meals, salt cellars are seldom used, except at elegant occasions. But when salt is presented in a salt cellar, it is sprinkled over food with a salt spoon. Or, a small mound of salt is placed on the bread-and-butter plate or dinner plate. When a salt spoon is not provided with the salt cellar, a pinch of salt is taken with fingers and sprinkled over food.

The *salt shaker* was originally made as a container to enclose salt for protection from the dampness inherent in cellars. Today, the salt shaker provides a freely flowing source of salt, a dispenser that sprinkles salt evenly over food. However, salt shakers are used only at informal meals, elegant or otherwise.

Since more people use salt than pepper (and most people are right-handed), the salt shaker is placed to the right of the pepper shaker, in a position closer to the right hand. Because salt is finer than pepper, the lid of the salt shaker is punctured with smaller, more numerous holes than a pepper shaker.

When salt is requested at a meal, as a courtesy to the diner the salt and pepper shaker are passed together.

## Pepper Shakers and Pepper Mills

Pepper is a member of the *Piperaceae* family, a tropical vine native to the Indian archipelago; it is a pungent condiment also known as a *peppercorn*. Hipocrates used peppercorns to treat certain ailments.

Pepper is served in a pepper shaker or a pepper mill, and occasionally in a pepper pot. The contemporary pepper shaker is a modification of the old-fashioned caster, a cylindrical container made with a pierced lid and used originally to cast seasoning over food. Although pepper tends to make one sneeze, it loses its pungency when enclosed in a shaker, so this is the preferred method of service. Moreover, pepper has a coarser grain than salt, and the lid of the shaker is made with larger but fewer holes than the salt shaker. The placement of the pepper shaker is to the left of the salt shaker, and for added definition it is angled slightly above the salt shaker. Small salt and pepper shakers, approximately 1½ inches in height, conserve space at a crowded table. They are placed above the cover or between two place settings.

Pepper mills are used to grind pepper into fine or coarse consistencies. While finely ground pepper is less apt to make one sneeze, coarsely ground pepper offers a more pungent taste. Accordingly, pepper mills are appropriate at all meals, formal and informal. Elegant silver or crystal pepper mills befit sumptuous dining, and materials such as wood, acrylic, enamel, pottery, or porcelain are suitable for informal meals. Although salt and pepper shakers are passed together, because the pepper mill is a cumbersome size, it is passed alone.

## Salvers

*A salver . . . is a new fashioned peece of wrought plate, broad and flat, with a foot underneath, and is used in giving Beer or other liquid thing to save the carpit and cloathes from drops.*

THOMAS BLOUNT, 1661

*Salver,* from the Spanish *salvar,* meaning "to save" or "to preserve," is a small footed tray. It was introduced in the mid-seventeenth century to serve food and beverages tested for purity. At one time, protocol decreed that the hands of a nobleman must not touch those of a commoner, and a servant conveyed messages to his lord on a salver. Today, the salver is used in a club or hotel to formally deliver a message; in the home it is used informally to hold miscellanea, such as the mail.

## Sauceboats and Gravy Boats

The sauceboat and gravy boat were initially low oval-shaped vessels made in the late seventeenth century with double spouts and two handles. In the early eighteenth century, the shape changed; vessels were made with one pouring lip and a single handle. In this same period, meat and fowl were carved at the dinner table rather than at the sideboard; this slowed the rate of service and created a problem when sauce and gravy cooled and congealed. In 1780, the duke of Argylle invented a container that preserved the heat by means of a double-layered sealed jacket, a shape similar to a casing filled with hot water. The vessel was called an *argyle* (a slight misspelling of the duke's name); it resembled a small teapot with a lid and spout. Today, sauce and gravy are served as they were in the seventeenth and eighteenth centuries, in open boat-shaped vessels made with one or two spouts. At formal meals, sauceboats and gravy boats are presented to the guest by a butler, but at informal meals the vessels are placed on the table.

## Trays

The tray, from the Anglo-Saxon *treg* or *trig,* meaning "wooden board," is made with a flat surface and two handles for easy handling, a serveware category developed in sixteenth-century Europe and introduced to England via Holland in the seventeenth century. In the late eighteenth and early nineteenth centuries, large wooden trays, called *butler trays*, were designed to rest on a folding support, similar to those used in restaurants today. Although the tray does not contain a well, the edges are raised for safe transport of food and serveware.

At a formal meal, large trays are used to present the main course as well as salads, cheese, and dessert, and to transport a coffee service to another room. At an informal meal, trays are used as above, or on a buffet to serve dry food, such as bread, rolls, cookies, or sandwiches, to hold flatware rolled in napkins, to clear the table, and in a bar to group items.

## Tureens

The origin of the tureen is attributed to Marshall Turenne of France, who supposedly used his helmet to hold soup during a lull in battle. In the reign of Charles II (1660–1685), a time when soup was served at the table from a large bowl, the tureen was introduced to England. In the eighteenth century, dinner services took on a role of importance, and oftentimes the tureen was the principal piece, elegantly rendered for display purposes only with gilded interiors, elaborately sculptured details, and armorial crests. Today, the tureen is a wide, deep, covered bowl made with a ladle and a matching platter. The large tureen is used to serve soup, stew, and punch and to cool champagne. The small tureen is used to hold sauce, gravy, and vegetables.

# Alternative Uses of Serveware in the Home

Serveware is a necessity of dining that becomes a decorative accessory when used throughout the home in a creative capacity, one that adds interest to room decor and enhances the home with seldom-used pieces.

- *Large bowls* hold floral arrangements or plants.
- *Small bowls* are containers for tiny bouquets, small soaps, potpourri, matches, or jewelry on a dresser.
- *Shallow serving bowls* float cut flowers with short stems, such as camellias or gardenias, or hold mail in an entry, flatware and napkins on a buffet, or rolled guests towels in a bathroom.
- *Deep serving bowls* double as wine coolers and vases for long-stemmed flowers or plants.
- *Covered vegetable bowls,* displayed alone on a decorative stand or a trivet, make individual centerpieces.
- *Large compotes* hold clusters of candles, guest towels, mail, or act as a base for a figurine.
- *Small compotes* can be stacked in graduated sizes and filled with nuts, candies, flowers, fruits, vegetables, and greenery, suggestive of topiary.
- *Large pitchers and beverage pots* are vases for loose floral arrangements, such as daisies or roses, and hold long utensils, such as skewers or tongs.
- *Small pitchers and beverage pots* contain tiny bouquets or delicate plants.
- *Platters* frame flatware and napkins on a buffet, hold mail in a hallway, display toiletries in a bathroom, and hold hand towels in a powder room.
- *Salvers* act as underplates for small bowls, hold loose change or perfume bottles on a dresser, receive mail in an entry, and contain incidentals on a desk.
- *Trays* display mixes, napkins, and tools in a bar, and in the home hold perfume bottles, combs, brushes, pincushions, or jewelry boxes.
- *Tureens,* featured alone on an underplate or a stand, make a nonperishable centerpiece or hold flowers, with the lid angled to the side of the base for added decoration.

CHAPTER TWELVE

# HOW TO PURCHASE DINNERWARE

After the centerpiece, dinnerware is the most colorful and pronounced design on the table. It is the first item that meets the eye. To choose dinnerware that will enhance the pleasures of dining for a long time to come, you must consider a number of factors before making your purchase.

## How Will the Dinnerware Be Used?

People purchase dinnerware either for everyday use or for special occasions. Dinnerware used daily is subject to chips, cracks, and fractures. In the order of damage resistance, porcelain is the hardest ceramic, bone china is the strongest, followed by stoneware, semiporcelain, ironstone, creamware, and majolica or faience. Microwave oven and dishwasher safety is a primary consideration in purchasing utilitarian ware.

When one set of dinnerware is selected to meet all dining needs, the most versatile choice is plain white dinnerware, a pick that showcases food. Note the number of restaurants that use white dinnerware, or ware made with a white well banded in color. Not only is white ware easier to coordinate than colorful patterns; it is less costly to produce, it is safe in a microwave oven (as long as it has no metallic ornamentation), and it will not fade in the drying cycle of a dishwasher.

For those who prefer colorful dinnerware, a pattern depicted in one or two colors is easier to coordinate and usually less expensive than ware ornamented with hand-applied precious metal or multiple colors that require separate firings.

But for pure charm and fun, there is no substitute for brightly colored majolica or faience, pottery reserved for occasional use at the informal table setting. However, majolica and faience chip easily, so buyer beware and treat them with care.

Dinnerware selected for special occasions—namely, formal patterns and holiday ware—is often ornamented with precious metals. Although gold, silver, or platinum create an elegant, sumptuous ambience, the metals preclude use in the microwave oven, and hand-washing is recommended.

The most formal dinnerware pattern is one ornamented with a solid-color border trimmed with precious metal, such as cobalt blue edged with gold. For a dramatic pattern, choose a contrast of vibrant colors: dinnerware ornamented with Chinese red and black or a sophisticated combination of colors, such as gray, black, and gold.

Dinnerware selected in a color associated with several holidays offers versatility; for example, green-rimmed plates will do for St. Patrick's Day, Easter, Thanksgiving, and Christmas. When theme-related dinnerware is selected, salad plates are less costly to purchase than dinner plates and offer the same impact.

## Choosing the Right Pattern

To choose a pattern category, such as country, traditional, contemporary, or oriental, peruse magazines devoted to home decor and visit furniture stores and antique shops. Choose a nontrendy pattern, one that allows various options, from elegant to informal, seasonal, or daily use.

Dinnerware falls into three types of design: romantic, classic, and modern. Each type is harmonious with particular flatware and stemware patterns and furnishings. *Romantic* patterns are reminiscent of living things, such as birds, shells,

DINNERWARE DECORATED WITH A ROUNDED PATTERN IS UNIFIED WITH STEMWARE AND FLATWARE DECORATED WITH CURVILINEAR MOTIFS.

flowers, and fruit. The ornamentation is curvilinear and compliments flatware, stemware, and furnishings decorated with rounded motifs.

*Classic* designs are adapted from historical periods, such as the straight lines of neoclassic designs or the curving asymmetry of rococo. When a classic pattern includes both geometric and curving lines, accent the dominant line in the flatware, stemware, and furnishings.

DINNERWARE ORNAMENTED WITH A GEOMETRIC MOTIF IS HARMONIOUS WITH FLATWARE DECORATED WITH AN ANGULAR PATTERN AND STEMWARE MODELED WITH A STRAIGHT-SIDED BOWL.

TO UNIFY ROUNDED AND ANGULAR PATTERNS, ACCENT THE DOMINANT LINE IN THE CENTERPIECE, TABLE ACCESSORIES, AND LINENS.

*Modern* patterns are abstract in concept and often depict geometric motifs that look well with flatware, stemware, and furniture designed with straight lines.

## Choosing the Shape of the Plates

Plates are divided into rim or coupe shapes. To make the right decision regarding the shape, simulate a full table setting in the store.

The rim-shaped plate originated in Europe, where one main course is served comprised of a combination of foods prepared whole, such as a roast presented with starch, vegetables, and garnish. In the West, food portions are cut into bite-size pieces at the table, and the rim-shaped plate is made with a well that collects the juices that flow from the food, a shape harmonious with contemporary, country, and traditional furniture.

The coupe-shaped plate is made without a rim, a sleek line that looks well with contemporary or Asian furniture. The coupe shape accommodates the way food is cooked and served in the East. To conserve fuel and nutrients, in the East food is cut into bite-size pieces in the kitchen and cooked quickly over high heat. In China, three or four main courses are served, and to unify the flavor, aroma, color, and texture into a blend of one harmonious whole, the courses are served all at once.

*Sour, sweet, bitter, pungent—all must be tasted.*

CHINESE PROVERB

To allow space for the courses on one plate, the diameter of the coupe-shaped dinner plate is approximately 1 inch larger than that of the rim-shaped dinner plate.

## Balancing Simple and Ornate Decoration

A table set entirely with plain patterns lacks impact. But a table laid totally with ornate designs distracts the eye, and full appreciation of the table setting is lost. To reach a balance between simple and ornate patterns, keep the ratio two-to-one. Accent two showy patterns with one plain design, or contrast two simple designs with an elaborate motif. This does not suggest that one start over. Instead, use what you

WHEN THE TABLEWARE IS A MIX OF PLAIN AND ORNATE PATTERNS, ACCENT THE SIMPLE DESIGN WITH TWO ELABORATE MOTIFS.

REVERSE THE PRINCIPLE AND ACCENT TWO SIMPLE PATTERNS WITH ONE ORNATE DESIGN.

have, but accent plain tableware with ornate linens and a showy centerpiece, or contrast ornate tableware with simple linens and a plain centerpiece.

## Matched Set or Mix-and-Match Patterns?

First-time buyers aren't sure whether to purchase a matched set of dinnerware or mix several patterns. You should do both. A matched set of dinnerware provides a foundation for the table setting but confines you to a single look. A mix of dinnerware patterns makes entertaining more flexible, but many people are unsure how to create the best mix.

Begin with the dinner plate. The main course is the focal point of the menu, a combination course consisting of meat, starch, vegetable, and garnish, all served on the largest plate. Accordingly, the dinner plate is the plate around which the soup, salad, and dessert plates are mixed and matched.

The exception is the cup and saucer. To avoid too much diversity, when beverages are served at the table, use cups and saucers that match the dinner plate. But when beverages are served away from the table, such as demitasse or afternoon tea, design continuity is unimportant, and an assortment of patterns adds interest to the occasion.

Color is the common denominator. It is easy to mix and match when colors are blended within a given harmony, such as a mix of blue patterns or a match of gold decoration. But when a particular color is unavailable, mix it with a contrasting shade in a solid color. And if all else fails, mix the pattern with clear glass plates.

Mix and match is appropriate for formal and informal dining. At a formal occasion, the table is set with a multiplicity of tableware: candelabra, centerpieces, table accessories, stemware, and flatware. To avoid distracting the eye, at a formal table the dinnerware pattern is the same for each course, and the entire table is laid with like pieces. But at an informal table where fewer courses are served, the table setting is uncluttered, and a mix of patterns adds interest to the meal, as does a different pattern at each cover, the latter unified by the same colors, such as all green patterns or a mix of solid colors in assorted hues.

To avoid repetitious table settings, select formal and informal dinnerware in patterns that mix and match. Moreover, match the background colors: white with white, ivory with ivory. But if the ground colors are slightly off, mix them. They will blend.

## Coordinating the Textures of Dinnerware, Stemware, and Flatware

The table setting is a mass of assorted textures, from ceramic to metal to glass to linens. To unify the finishes, keep like textures with like, namely, smooth surfaces with smooth and coarse surfaces with coarse. Smooth surfaces, such as porcelain, combine well with fine textures, such as silver, crystal, brass, lacquer, and tightly woven linens. Coarse finishes, such as pottery, coordinate well with heavy tableware, such as pewter, thick glass, wood, and loosely woven textiles. Matte and glossy surfaces are unified when one or the other is accented.

## How Safe Is Lead-Glazed Dinnerware?

When the temperature of the kiln is too low or the heat is inconsistent, the lead in lead-glazed dinnerware leaches into food, a phenomenon that causes health problems, such as high or low blood pressure, nausea, diarrhea, cancer, birth defects, and in children mental retardation. Such health hazards are more apt to happen when acid-based foods, such as vinegar, salt, eggs, mayonnaise, orange juice, lemonade, and coffee, are served on lead-glazed ware. To be safe, purchase lead-glazed plates and cups from countries and manufacturers that use advanced industrial technology. In the United States, the manufacture of lead glaze ware is controlled by the Food and Drug Administration.

## Choosing for Quality

Proportion, balance, and craftsmanship are the criteria of quality dinnerware. The plates lie flat on the table and the rims are not warped. The handles are wide enough for a comfortable grip, and the cups rest securely and evenly on the saucers. The glaze does not have spots, is free of pinholes or bubbles, and is not too thin in one area, creating a matte look. The color tones of each piece are consistent. The lids fit tightly.

Second-quality dinnerware is a good buy when the color and pattern please the eye, the condition of most pieces is satisfactory, and the price is reasonable. At the right price, slightly defective ware affords the opportunity to own a trendy pattern, such as a musical theme or a golf motif, or to purchase a particular color just right for several holidays, such as pumpkin-colored dinnerware for Halloween and Thanksgiving or red-rimmed dinnerware for the Fourth of July and Christmas.

# How Many Place Settings to Buy

The term *place setting* denotes the number of pieces required to set a place at the table. Dinnerware is available in three-, four-, and five-piece or more place settings. Lids and saucers are counted as separate pieces. A three-piece place setting consists of dinner plate, cup, and saucer. A four-piece setting contains dinner plate, cup, saucer, and salad plate. A five-piece place setting includes dinner plate, cup, saucer, salad plate, and bread-and-butter plate or soup bowl. English dinnerware firms often make a seven-piece place setting that consists of dinner plate, salad plate, bread-and-butter plate, cup, saucer, and cream soup bowl and stand or soup cup and saucer.

The number of place settings to buy depends on the size of your family (present and future) and your plans for entertainment. Although eight place settings will provide a couple or a single person with several days of use, a large family may use an entire set in one day. Twelve place settings will entertain more people with the same effort expended as it takes to have two couples to dinner.

When resources are limited, buy what is affordable and add to it as circumstances warrant.

## A Starter Set

A set of dinnerware prepackaged with twenty pieces in a box is known as a *starter set,* a unit comprising of four dinner plates, four salad plates, four cups and saucers, and four soup-cereal bowls. Although a starter set may offer bread-and-butter plates instead of soup-cereal bowls, when a choice is offered, choose soup-cereal bowls, which provide more versatility than bread-and-butter plates. Starter sets are made for people with simple dining requirements, such as a student or a newly-wed couple. The unit does not include serveware.

## Serveware

When eight or twelve place settings of dinnerware are ordered at one time, the set often includes matching serveware. A forty-five piece set for eight contains dinner plates, salad plates, cups and saucers, bread-and-butter plates or soup-cereal bowls, plus four matching pieces of serveware: a medium-size platter, open vegetable bowl, covered sugar bowl, and creamer. A ninety-six piece set of dinnerware for twelve contains dinner plates, salad plates, bread-and-butter plates, cups and saucers, soup bowls, and fruit saucers, plus matching serveware, such as a large platter, medium-size platter, open vegetable bowl, covered casserole, gravy boat with stand, sugar bowl with lid, creamer, coffeepot, and salt and pepper shakers.

### *A Completer Set*

Many times five pieces of matching serveware are available for purchase separate from a starter set, ware known as a *completer set*. But completer sets vary in content: for example, a medium-size round platter, open vegetable bowl, covered sugar bowl, and creamer; or an oval platter, two vegetable bowls, gravy boat, and butter dish.

### *Open Stock*

When dinnerware is available for individual purchase rather than by the place setting, the option is known as *open stock*. However, open stock does not mean a pattern is available indefinitely. Once demand for a pattern ceases, the manufacturer cannot afford to actively continue production. When the dinnerware firm states it will not discontinue a pattern, it means they will make it available only when enough orders have accumulated to make production profitable. This may take years.

When a discontinued pattern is no longer available, inquire if a few pieces are available for purchase at the factory. If not, extend an incomplete set with dinnerware made by another manufacturer in a similar design. Or match an incomplete set with a pattern in a solid color.

### *The Cost of Replacements*

Replacements are a subtle expense not included in the initial purchase of dinnerware, notably ware that chips easily, such as majolica and faience. Moreover, imported dinnerware is more expensive to replace than domestic ware. To extend serviceability, purchase extras of pieces frequently used, such as dinner plates and cups and saucers.

Because precious metals scratch easily, plates ornamented with gold, silver, or platinum in the center of the well are prone to marks from normal use of a dinner knife. When replacements are not available, mix the patterns with solid-color ware.

CHAPTER THIRTEEN

# THE CARE OF DINNERWARE

DINNERWARE PROVIDES A lifetime of beauty when proper care is given. But "proper care" depends on a number of factors, including the type of glaze, the use of metals in the design, whether the ware is dishwasher-safe or requires hand care, and the methods of storage.

## Glazes

The ornamentation of dinnerware lies underglaze or overglaze, and sometimes both methods are used. *Underglaze ornamentation* is fired two times, once at a low temperature and then at a high temperature. The purpose of the low-temperature firing is to harden the body and render it into an *absorbent* leather-hard state called *biscuit.* The ornamentation is applied to biscuit and covered with transparent glaze; the decoration lies literally "under the glaze." To make the glaze adhere, the ware is fired a second time at a high temperature. In the high-temperature kiln, the glaze sinks into the body and fuses with it, a process that makes underglaze ornamentation the most durable form of decoration. It has a smooth surface and the glaze is not subject to corrosive food acids or scratches made by normal use of a dinner knife. This decorative technique is safe in a microwave oven and a dishwasher, when stated by the manufacturer.

*Overglaze ornamentation* is fired in a high-temperature kiln first. The purpose of the high-temperature firing is to harden the body and render it *nonabsorbent.* It also promotes brighter color. Glaze is then applied and the ware is fired again, at a low temperature. The glaze does not fuse with the body; rather, the ornamentation rests on top of the ware or partially sinks into the body (a decorative technique known also as *in glaze*). The high-low firing method makes overglaze ornamentation perceptible to the touch, vulnerable to corrosive food acids, and subject to fading in the drying cycle of a dishwasher. Dinnerware with overglaze ornamentation should be rinsed as soon as possible after use. Moreover, the ornamentation is unprotected, and is prone to scratches made from sharp objects, so during cleanup it is never scraped with the blade of a dinner knife. Instead, food debris is wiped with a paper towel, and stubborn spots are soaked and removed with a plastic scouring pad.

## Care of Precious Metals

Today most dinnerware manufacturers specify the proper care of precious metals on the back of plates or on the wrappers in which the ware is packaged. When the term *dishwasher-safe* is not used on the packaging, hand-wash and hand-dry dinnerware decorated with gold, silver, or platinum.

If you're not sure whether to machine-wash or hand-wash metal-ornamented dinnerware, experiment with a small plate, such as a saucer. Place the plate in the back of the dishwasher, well away from the other plates, and leave it in the dishwasher through repeated washings. Cool the plate and compare the decoration to the ornamentation of dinnerware washed by hand. If there are no apparent changes in the color of the metal, and if the sheen is as lustrous as before, the ornamentation is dishwasher-safe.

*Never* place metal-ornamented dinnerware in a microwave oven. A reaction can occur between the metal and the oven that causes sparks. Not only will this damage the microwave, it will leave the ornamentation pitted or mottled. However, it is safe to warm metal-decorated plates in the "plate-warm" cycle of a dishwasher or in a standard oven for 5 to 10 minutes at a low temperature, approximately 150°F (66°C).

Gold sets up better than silver or platinum, and gold is the most popular form of metal decoration. Two types of gold are used: pure gold and bright gold. Pure gold is 22- to 24-carat gold, a metal that wears well and is used to decorate quality dinnerware. When pure gold is fired in the kiln, the heat turns the metal a brownish color and dulls the finish. To impart the yellowish color and mellow sheen associated with pure gold, the metal is burnished by hand. But in the dishwasher drying cycle, the intense heat turns the yellowish color bronze and dulls the finish, so to maintain the quality of pure gold, wash dinnerware ornamented with metal by hand. Once the color and sheen of pure gold are lost, restoration is costly; partial restoration is possible by rubbing gold with silver polish, an all-purpose metal polish, or a special cloth treated to clean gold or silver.

Bright gold is a liquid preparation to which a small amount of gold is added, a method of ornamentation reserved for inexpensive dinnerware. Because of the low-gold content, when bright gold is fired, the preparation does not change color, does not require burnishing, does not turn darker in a dishwasher, and is not susceptible to thumb prints, dents, scratches, or food acids. However, bright gold does not wear well, and in time the low gold content simply wears off.

## Care of Dinnerware in a Dishwasher

The proper care of dinnerware in a dishwasher is as follows:

- Load dinnerware well apart so the vibration of the dishwasher does not make one piece hit and scratch another.
- Make sure the bottom of the dishwasher is free of broken glass or a utensil that may fly up and scratch the glaze.
- To keep metal decoration from becoming too soft, turn off the dishwasher in the drying cycle.
- To avoid thumb prints and scratches, wait for metal-ornamented ware to cool before wiping or unloading.
- Sudden changes of hot and cold temperatures weaken ceramics, and in the process of heating and cooling, the body and glaze expand and contract at different rates and may create a network of fine lines called *crazing.* When earthenware is crazed, hot water and bacteria permeate the lines and collect

around the cracks. For protection, wash crazed earthenware in warm water with a mild detergent (preferably one with a low chlorine content).

- The buildup of film caused by hard water is eliminated by the addition of two teaspoons of water softener to the rinse cycle.

## Washing Dinnerware by Hand

- Prior to washing delicate dinnerware by hand, rinse off any excess food.
- Soak food baked onto ware in detergent and hot water (not boiling water), and remove the spot with a *plastic* scouring pad.
- Cushion dinnerware in a towel-lined sink, or use a plastic basin. Do this particularly with dinnerware that is decorated with gold, silver, or platinum, soft metals that scratch easily.
- A reaction can occur between a rubber mat and precious metals that leaves a brown mark on metal-ornamented dinnerware. Use a rubber mat only to cushion dinnerware not decorated with gold, silver, or platinum.
- Be careful of faucet guards.
- To avoid scratches from abrasive compounds, such as powdered cleanser, use a gentle soap or a mild detergent, one with a low-chlorine content that will not fade or react with the ornamentation.
- To remove stains, such as those made by coffee or tea, or brown spots caused by contact with rusty machine parts or metal pans, choose a non-abrasive cleaner with a *creamy* consistency, and apply it with a soft sponge.
- When a buildup of film occurs, buff delicate dinnerware with a soft lint-free cloth.
- To hide unsightly scratches, use toothpaste as a filler and gently rub the marks. The paste hardens in approximately 1 hour.

## Care of Antique Dinnerware

- The chemicals in detergent and the heat in the dishwasher drying cycle dim or destroy color and can ruin the decoration of antique or hand-painted dinnerware. Hand-washing with a mild soap is recommended.

- Rather than hold an antique cup by the handle, or an old teapot by the spout, support the vessel by placing the fingers around the middle of the vessel.
- Lift antique plates from the bottom, rather than by the rim.
- When a valuable piece of dinnerware is broken, rather than attempt a repair at home, take it to a professional. Glue contains chemicals that may stain and yellow a home-repaired article and render the piece undesirable and worthless.

## Methods of Storage

- The underrims of dinnerware are unglazed. To protect plates stacked for storage, cover them with a paper towel, a paper napkin, a piece of fabric, or a microfoam pad.
- The weight of stacked plates can cause ware to break. To distribute weight evenly, stack pieces of the same size and shape together, such as dinner plates with dinner plates, and soup bowls with soup bowls. To relieve stress, stack plates and bowls in columns of four or six or store plates upright in plate racks.
- The rim is the most vulnerable part of the cup. Rather than stack cups for storage, hang them by the handles, preferably from plastic-covered hooks or store cups in protector cases fitted with foam separators.
- Plastic storage cases buffer and cushion dinnerware and provide quick reference when labeled for content. Moreover, plastic cases are easy to carry to the area of use and save steps when setting the table or putting dinnerware away.
- Ceramic dinnerware is sensitive to changes in temperature. Storage above or near a heating vent or near sunlight causes the body and glaze to expand and contract at different rates and may lead to crazing and cracks.

# Part III

# *Flatware*

CHAPTER FOURTEEN

# FROM SILVER TO STERLING

SILVER IS A precious metal with a grayish-white color. It was first used in religious rituals by cultures who farmed according to phases of the moon, such as the Sumerians. According to Homer's *Iliad,* silver was discovered in Alybe, a mountainous region along the southern shore of the Black Sea. Toward the end of the fourth millennium B.C., silver was exported to southern Mesopotamia and traded for domestic goods; thus, silver was used as an early form of currency.

Silver was assigned a given weight by King Manishtusu of Babylonia (2269–2255 B.C.), who minted coins whose names have come down to us through the Bible as *talent, mina,* and *shekel.* In 6 B.C., King Croesus of Lydia issued coins made of silver alloyed with gold, a light yellow metal called *electrum* by the Romans.

In the early Christian era, the Roman Empire stretched north to England, south to Upper Egypt, west to the Atlantic coast of Spain and east to the Black Sea, a vast terrain that yielded an almost unlimited supply of silver. Wealthy Romans reclined on wooden couches covered with silver and drank from silver vessels. By the first century B.C., silver was so plentiful that free families and Roman slaves alike ate from silver ware. However, by the fifth century, the supply of silver was almost exhausted and mining ceased in Europe, a factor that contributed to the decline of the western Roman Empire. In search of work, goldsmiths migrated from Europe to Constantinople, the center of the eastern Roman Empire.

With the final collapse of the western Roman Empire in 476 A.D., Europe became an area of small independent kingdoms. During the so-called Dark Ages, (roughly the fifth to the tenth centuries), little progress was made in the development of silver, except for *cloisonné* (from the French *cloison,* "partition") the primary craft of the barbarians. Early in the ninth century, deposits of high-grade silver were discovered in the Rhineland, and in an attempt to restore the grandeur of ancient Rome, Charlemagne (742–814 A.D.), king of the Franks and first emperor of the Holy Roman Empire, ordered the resumption of silver mining. But silver was wrought primarily for ecclesiastical purposes by the church, by monks who were also artisans.

By the thirteenth century secular silver was produced for ewers and basins, domestic ware called *plate* from the Spanish word *plata* for "silver." Since not all European countries were rich in silver, owning plate carried rank. The thirteenth and fourteenth centuries were relatively prosperous periods, a time when workers began to leave the confines of feudal communes and move to towns where various skills were taught, among them goldsmithing. Eventually associations were formed called *guilds,* from the Middle English word *gylde,* meaning "payment"—organizations that set standards of workmanship and quality. The Goldsmiths' Guild was established in London in 1238. Prior to the sixteenth century, goldsmiths worked in both gold and silver. However, the demand for silver was so enormous by the sixteenth century, that artisans who designed, made, and repaired only silver articles were recognized in their own right as silversmiths. The term *smith* has the Indo-European base *smei,* meaning "to work with a sharp tool."

Because silver is a harder metal and more abundant than gold, it was made into plate and coin; gold, the softer, rarer, more expensive metal, was wrought into jewelry and decorative objects. The value of coin was based on the purity of the silver in the country of origin, a measure of worth that changed from country to country. In the thirteenth century, English coin was of little value, and in 1215 King John of England commissioned a band of German silversmiths, called *Easterling,* to restore purity to English coin. The coins were initially called *easterlings* after their easterly-dwelling makers, but in time King John ordered the first two letters dropped from the name. This is the origin of *sterling,* the standard of English silver for centuries.

To enforce compliance with the sterling standard, in 1238 Henry III ordered the mayor and aldermen of London to select six goldsmiths as superintendents, or wardens, to monitor the assay of silver and carry out the regulations of the Goldsmiths' Guild. The board of governors, known as the Worshipful Company of Goldsmiths, or the Assay Office, from the Old French word *essai,* meaning "test," tested articles of silver before sale by taking small samples of silver from the underside.

Silver made in compliance with the standards of the Goldsmiths' Hall was impressed with a registered mark. Hence the term *hallmark*, an early form of consumer protection. Hallmarks were used as early as the fifth century in the eastern Roman Empire; in 1275 they were adopted in France, followed shortly thereafter by England and, to a lesser extent, by German kingdoms. By the seventeenth century, hallmarks were used throughout Europe. In 1816, England adopted the gold standard, followed shortly thereafter by most of Europe, and the demand for silver declined, along with use of the silver hallmark. The six most common hallmarks, in order of origin, were the leopard's head, maker's mark, date-letter mark, lion passant, Britannia mark, and duty mark; the study of hallmarks fills volumes, a few of which are recommended in the bibliography at the end of this book.

Henry III also decreed that pure silver was too soft to make into plate unless strengthened with "a good and true alloy," from the French word *alei* meaning "combination." And by law, pure silver was established as 1,000 parts fine, which is 925 parts silver to 75 parts copper. Because copper is harder than silver, the metal added strength without changing silver's whitish-gray hue or ductility.

The thirteenth and fourteenth centuries were the Age of Chivalry, a period when knights rode off into battle clad in silver armor, astride horses caparisoned with silver mounts. Silver was a measure of wealth and power, grandly displayed on open shelves in the great hall. In an opulent setting, wealthy hosts covered their tables with gold and silver tableware. King Charles VI of France gave the entire compliment of gold and silver tableware to his guest, King Wenceslaus IV of Bohemia.

By the sixteenth century, goldsmiths were accorded the same degree of respect as sculptors and painters. Benvenuto Cellini was a Florentine sculptor and the most important goldsmith of the Italian Renaissance. Cellini produced his finest work under the patronage of King François I of Paris, a partially enameled gold table salt sculpted in 1540, today seen in the Kunsthistorisches Museum in Vienna.

The sixteenth century was the Age of Exploration, encouraged by the Treaty of Tordesillas, an agreement signed between Portugal and Spain in Tordesillas, Spain, on June 7, 1494. The purpose of the agreement was to redefine the spheres of maritime activity and divide between Portugal and Spain new territories discovered by Columbus. Pope Alexander VI drew a line on a map that extended from north to south through the Atlantic Ocean. Lands west of the line were given to Spain for exploration, namely the Americas and Mexico (except Brazil). Lands east of the demarcation were given to Portugal, namely Africa and India; Portugal held on to Brazil by right of prior possession.

In the sixteenth century, Spain launched great voyages of exploration to the Americas where large silver mines were discovered in Mexico, Peru, and Bolivia. From South America vast quantities of silver were exported to Germany, and by the second half of the sixteenth century Nuremburg and Augsburg were major silver-working centers. Silver was wrought into preprinted sheets ornamented with decorative motifs to lay as plaques over wooden furniture.

The sixteenth and seventeenth centuries were marked by religious crisis. In England, the king, Henry VIII, declared the Church of England independent of the Catholic Church, and therefore no longer under the Pope's control. Many monks, still loyal to the Pope, protested the king's actions. In response, Henry VIII dissolved the monasteries and confiscated countless articles of silver; today little remains of sixteenth-century English silver except for ecclesiastical plate and articles owned by some of the older colleges at Cambridge and Oxford. Because the silversmith's art was sponsored primarily by the church, the religious turmoil deprived the artisans of patronage. The guilds, now rich and important, encouraged them to come to London, and by the late sixteenth century London was a great silver center.

Across the channel in Europe, a shortage of silver was precipitated by the political and religious turmoil known as the Thirty Years War (1618–1648). The cost of the war, coupled with the excessive display of silver in the reign of Louis XIV, brought a severe dip in the royal coffers of France. To restore financial stability, the king ordered the nobility to relinquish all silver as bullion to make coin, an act that destroyed almost two centuries of French silver. The only silver that survived the period were articles from the provinces, silver given as gifts to foreigners, and items too small to melt. To compensate, French potters fashioned faience from forms drawn from silverware, a source that provided historians with knowledge of the lost articles.

In this period the Protestant group known as Puritans (from the Latin *purus* for "pure") under the leadership of Oliver Cromwell fought the Church of England and the monarchy in bloody civil war. In 1649 England was declared a Commonwealth, ushering in a period of grave austerity for England. The use of silver as a display of wealth and the depiction of Christ ornamented with silver were severely frowned upon. Silver from this period is recognized by plain designs that emphasize form over decoration. As a conservation measure, silver drinking vessels were wrought in a shorter height and made without covers. Great standing salts, once so important to the table, were no longer essential.

Banned by the Republic of the Commonwealth, King Charles II fled to Holland where he stayed with Prince William III of Orange, followed by a prolonged visit with his cousin, King Louis XIV of France. When the monarchy was restored in 1660, Charles commissioned silver wrought in the styles of his homes in exile, ornate decoration known as *Carolean* (Latin for "Charles"). The Dutch influence was seen in silver heavily embossed with repoussé designs punched out from underneath. The French style was opulently interpreted in sculptured baroque scrolls. Such prodigious quantities of silver were produced in the reign of Charles that today the Restoration is also known as the Age of Silver.

In 1662, Charles II married Catherine of Braganza, daughter of King John IV of Portugal, a union that introduced tea to England and stimulated a demand for silver tea equipage, such as silver trays, teapots, coffeepots, chocolate pots, water kettles, hot-water jugs, creamers, tea caddies, sugar basins, tea strainers, and teaspoons, each piece purchased separately as circumstances warranted. Until the eighteenth century tea sets were assembled primarily from unmatched ware.

The aristocracy, whose fortunes were enhanced by large colonial holdings, built great country estates in the seventeenth century and commissioned silver to an extent not since repeated: flatware studded with precious stones; dinner services of 3,000 pieces or more that included plates, dishes, two-handled bowls, cups, trays, tureens, sauceboats, cruets, ewers, basins, and spice boxes; toilette sets of thirty or forty pieces, along with decorative accessories, such as 3-foot-high silver fountains, candelabra, candlesticks, chandeliers, mirror frames, desk items, tobacco boxes, fire dogs, chimney furniture, cane handles, huge 3-foot-wide cisterns, orangery tubs, vases, and silver furniture. In 1676 Nell Gwynne, mistress of Charles II, commissioned a silver bed.

In England, vast quantities of plate had been melted to finance the Civil War (1642–1651), creating a shortage, so silver was clipped illegally from coin. Unable to replace disfigured coins, in 1697 Parliament elevated the standard of silver to 95.8 parts silver, and lowered the alloy content to 4.2 parts copper, a new measure called the *Britannia standard,* hallmarked with "Britannia," the symbol of the empire. Because Britannia silver was softer than sterling it was made into plate, and sterling, the harder metal, was made as coin, shaped with milled edges to eliminate clippage.

The Britannia standard was used mainly in the reign of Queen Anne (1702–1714). To economize on the higher cost of silver, silversmiths conserved on labor and wrought plain silver in shapes that emphasized form and elegant proportions rather than ornate ornamentation. The resulting Queen Anne style required great skill to execute. Although the sterling standard was restored on June 1, 1720, the Britannia standard was not revoked, and silversmiths today continue to work in one metal or the other. Paul de Lamerie, the great Huguenot silversmith, continued to use Britannia metal for twelve years after the sterling standard was restored. Once the Britannia standard was revoked, silver wrought with ornate ornamentation became fashionable.

In the eighteenth century a new silver category was introduced called *Sheffield,* invented in 1743, when Thomas Bolsover, a cutler from Sheffield accidentally fused a silver sixpence to the copper haft of a knife he was in the process of repairing. Sheffield enabled the silversmith to hammer sheets of silver over copper before the articles were wrought, a method that promoted metal with an even gauge and lowered the cost of production. Moreover, articles made of Sheffield required less silver than sterling, and by midcentury the rising bourgeoisie could afford to own silverware, such as knives, hot-water jugs, and inkstands. Although Bolsover used Sheffield to make small items, such as buttons, buckles, and snuffboxes, later Joseph Hancock, an apprentice who worked for a relation of Bolsover's, used the method to make large domestic wares, such as coffeepots, tureens, tankards, sauceboats, and candlesticks.

In France, following the death of the Queen Maria Theresa in the seventeenth century, King Louis XIV married Madame de Maintenon, a governess who held strict religious beliefs. Historians suggest that the stringency of her convictions indirectly influenced the king to revoke the Edict of Nantes in 1685, a decree that had heretofore guaranteed French Protestants the same civil and religious liberties as French Catholics. To avoid compulsory Catholicism and religious persecution, over 250,000 French Protestants, known as Huguenots, fled France for the Low Countries and England. And they took with them great artistic talent and technical skills.

Although the exodus of the Huguenots set back artistic development in France, it advanced the art of other countries. This was reflected in the new silver techniques and designs that appeared in England and Europe, such as heavy-gauge sugar casters decorated with pierced ornamentation, cut-card work, and chinoiserie. The Huguenots' skill and artistry, interpreted in the ornate rococo style, made silver of the late seventeenth and early eighteenth centuries the most sought-after of any in history.

The eighteenth century was the Age of Enlightenment, a period that advanced the principle that human affairs should rule for the good of everyone, a concept that precipitated revolutions in America and France. To finance the Revolution (1789–1794), the French melted down prodigious quantities of silver, and the loss, coupled with plate melted in the reign of Louis XIV, left France with little silver made before 1790. In 1797, French guilds were abolished and the silversmiths were free to work in whatever alloy they chose, some using as little as 80 percent silver.

Whereas the eighteenth century brought the development of Sheffield silver, the nineteenth century witnessed the creation of a new process: *silver plate.* In 1836 and 1840, Elkington's of Birmingham, an English firm run by the cousins George and Henry Elkington, filed for patents to electroplate base metal with another metal, a revolutionary new process that cost approximately one-third less to produce than sterling and led to the mass-marketing of silver articles. It also rang the death knell for Sheffield silver. The electroplate process was franchised to companies in England and Europe. To distinguish plated silver from sterling silver, English and American manufacturers stamped acronyms on the bottom of the ware, such as *EP* for "electroplate," *EPNS* for "electroplated nickel silver," and *EPBM* for "electroplated Britannia metal."

In North America, colonial wealth was measured by the quantity of coin brought from the Old World, and coins provided the primary source of bullion to make domestic plate. The first American silver was made circa 1620 by Thomas Howard of Jamestown, Virginia. In 1652, the British crown empowered the partnership of John Hull of Boston and Robert Sanderson to mint money for the colony of Massachusetts. John Coney (1655–1722) and Jeremiah Dummer (1645–1718) were the first silversmiths born and trained in the New World.

But the most famous American silversmith is the midnight equestrian Paul Revere, the son of an immigrant Huguenot who apprenticed to John Coney of Boston under the French name Apollas de Revoire, a name later anglicized. Although Revere made both secular and ecclesiastical silver, his most famous work is the Sons of Liberty bowl, a vessel also known as the *Rescinders' bowl,* wrought to commemorate a letter sent in 1768 by the Massachusetts House of Representatives to request that the colonies protest unfair British law. A bowl is now on display at the Museum of Fine Arts in Boston.

In the eighteenth century, the colonies were self-governed and regional styles were interpreted by immigrant silversmiths. Silver wrought in Boston, Baltimore, and Philadelphia was fashioned in the Puritan style of England, unadorned and personalized with a single initial. Silver crafted in Nieuw Amsterdam (renamed "New York" in 1664 after the British invasion) featured ornate decoration influenced by opulent repoussé ornamentation. Silver worked by Huguenot silversmiths in the territories of New Orleans, Detroit, Mobile, and later Philadelphia, settled largely by the French, featured the curvaceous rococo style and the classical style of the French Empire.

But in the colonies guilds were unknown and colonial silver (ware made before the American Revolution) was not qualified by a standard of purity. To identify worth, early silver was stamped with the initial or name of the silversmith. When further clarification was needed, an emblem was used or the article was punched with the name of the city or town where it was made. In the nineteenth century, Baltimore established an assay office and between 1814 and 1860 briefly used the hallmark system.

Eventually, the composition of silver was stamped on the back with *C* for coin silver, or *standard* or *premium* for fine-quality silver. But overall, the purity of colonial silver is dubious; between 1792 and 1837 the content dropped from 92.5 percent pure to 89.2 percent pure, and after 1850 it was 90 percent pure. To establish a standard of purity, in 1907 President Theodore Roosevelt signed the National Stamping Act, a law that decreed only American silver 92.5 percent pure could bear the words *sterling* or *sterling silver,* words used today as an American hallmark.

The technological advances made in the Industrial Revolution lowered the cost of silver production. The availability of silver from mines newly discovered in the United States meant that by the nineteenth century silver was inexpensive to own. Manufacturers flourished, and silverware was sold through mail-order catalogs. New flatware patterns proliferated, made for an upwardly mobile middle class who demanded elaborate silver services made in abundant new shapes—ice-cream plates, soup plates, bread-and-butter plates, ice-cream stands, tilting water pitchers, castor sets, revolving fruit knife holders, bone holders, egg coddlers, and napkin rings with tiny vases attached.

Clearly, by the nineteenth century, the silver industry was a mechanized business born of a cottage craft. Silversmiths who designed and made silver by hand were replaced by factory artisans who fashioned silver by machine. Whereas handwrought silver was hammered from a single ingot, in the nineteenth century it was rolled by machine into sheets of uniform thickness, pressed against a chuck of wood that spun at a fast speed producing ware with symmetrical dimensions. By 1830, the production of silver was dominated by a few large manufacturers; the independent silversmith sought employment in silver factories where his designs were advertised and mass-marketed under the company name.

Today, in an age of computerized machines, antique handmade silver is collected for aesthetic appeal, quality craftsmanship, and mellow, lustrous sheen. In centuries past the fashion of silver was more important, whereas today handwrought silver is valued for its craftsmanship, beauty, history, and unique shapes.

CHAPTER FIFTEEN

# DECORATIVE METHODS AND STYLES

LIKE A PENDULUM in motion, the ornamentation of silver swings from symmetrically balanced classical motifs to curvaceous asymmetrical designs drawn from nature, from plain decoration influenced by religious beliefs or a scarcity of silver to elaborate ornamentation in times of plenty. Silver is known as much by the techniques of ornamentation as by the characteristics of the metal. For clarification, the major decorative methods and styles are presented below.

ACID ETCHING. Etched ornamentation begins with a design drawn on the surface of silver. The undecorated area is covered with an acid-resistant substance, such as wax. Acid is applied and eats into the uncoated portion of the metal, etching in the design. The acid leaves a dull surface that contrasts with the shiny luster of the protected area.

*AJOURÉ.* Perforated or pierced ornamentation.

APPLIED DECORATION. Decoration made separately and then applied to the metal, such as cut-card work or silver cast in a mold.

ARTS AND CRAFTS MOVEMENT. An aesthetic founded in 1888 by William Morris, an English artist, poet, and craftsman, the arts and crafts movement was based on the individuality of handwrought products versus the anonymity and perfection of mass-produced machine-made ware. To learn the old techniques, the guild system was revived. Handicraft industries were established and special workshops were set up where the artisans lived, such as the Guild and School of Handicraft, founded by Charles Robert Ashbee at Toynbee Hall, London, and the Kalo Workshop founded by Clara Barck Welles in Park Ridge, Illinois. Although the arts and crafts movement frowned upon industrial methods, such as spinning, pressing, and die-stamping, it sanctioned the hand-finishing of machine-made products. The arts and crafts movement was centered on the decorative arts of England and North America. Silver was characteristically inlaid with semiprecious stones and materials, such as turquoise, agate, quartz, or ivory, chosen more for their color and shape than for their intrinsic value. Celtic motifs were a favorite, for example, a celtic knot tied to give an abstract impression of an owl or a bat; medieval motifs with masculine overtones, such as heraldic lions, were also popular.

ART DECO. The term *art deco* derives from the International Exhibition of Decorative Art *(Art décoratif)* held in Paris in 1925. Art deco was prevalent during the 1920s and 1930s. Initially, it featured symmetrical geometric designs, such as rectangles, squares, circles, and triangles, and the ornamentation of silver was influenced by cubism, expressionism, modernism, and art and designs from the Aztec, pre-Columbian, African, and Egyptian civilizations. Later, the art deco style was interpreted with rounded, symmetrically balanced baroque lines and the curvilinear asymmetry of rococo, designs that manifested in silver ornamented with sleek undulating forms, such as seen in silver toilette sets.

ART NOUVEAU. Art nouveau is a decorative style with romantic overtones, a style that evolved in France between 1880 and 1914. In Germany, art nouveau was known as *Jugendstil* for "youth style." Art nouveau was inspired by four aesthetics that influenced the ornamentation of silver: gothic architecture, such as flamelike designs and leaf tracery; the sculptural symmetry of baroque, such as balanced, raised, curvilinear designs; the asymmetry of rococo, such as intertwined branches and leaves that spiral upward ending in a whiplash curve; and Japanese designs drawn from nature, such as fish, cranes, fans, bamboo, and cherry blossoms.

BAROQUE. From the Portugese *barroco,* meaning an irregular, "imperfect pearl," Baroque decoration is characterized by rounded, sculptured, symmetrical decoration, a European style that flourished in the late Renaissance when classical themes dominated architecture and furnishings. *Baroque silver* implies a curvaceous sweeping style of ornamentation represented by the *C* scroll and *S* curve, decoration heavily interpreted and compactly arranged over a broad expanse of silver, such as a teapot with an all-over design or flatware with handles encrusted with rounded, sculpted decoration.

Baroque art is associated with the court of Louis XIV (1643–1715) and the grandeur of Versaille, a style influenced by Charles le Brun, director of the Royal Academy of Art, who in travels to Italy was inspired by the classical antiquities of Rome. On his return to France, le Brun adapted the balanced geometric lines of Greco-Roman architecture, to symmetrical rounded lines lavishly depicted in a sculptural style. Silversmiths who worked under court patronage used heavy-gauge silver to achieve the sculptural three-dimensional quality. Little remains of baroque silver, as most of it was melted down to finance Louis XIV's wars.

BEADING. A decorative border treatment comprised of small, closely set, round circles of metal.

BRIGHT CUT. A form of engraved ornamentation with narrow zigzags of faceted grooves cut at angles to catch light, a technique that promotes sparkle and shine. Bright-cut silver was popular from 1770 to 1800.

CHASED ORNAMENTATION. *Chased* is from the French word *enchâsser,* meaning "enshrine," an ornamental technique that encloses design but does not remove metal. A blunt-ended punch called a *chaser* is struck on the front of silver with a hammer; the chaser produces shallow lines with soft edges.

CLASSIC REVIVAL or NEOCLASSIC. In an attempt to discover the basis of universal good taste, in the eighteenth century the study of antiquities was encouraged among the nobility, and a classical education was considered the only education. On completion of formal studies, young aristocrats took a "grand tour" of Europe, an excursion that included the archaeological excavations at Herculaneum and Pompeii, discoveries that inspired interest in Greco-Roman art. The study of antiquities trickled down to the middle class who enjoyed new-found prosperity as a result of the Industrial Revolution and were also interested in education and travel, influences that manifested in a revival style called Classic Revival or Neo Classic.

Silver made in the classical style is characterized by flat, restrained decoration that does not overwhelm the article or interfere with the profile of the object, such as pierced, chased, and engraved decoration, and border ornamentation in low relief, such as beaded or reeded edges. The designs are based on geometric shapes, namely the square, rectangle, triangle, octagon, circle, and oval, the latter characterized by cylindrically shaped urns and teapots. Greco-Roman themes were interpreted on a small scale, such as the Greek key, lyre, convex fluting, laurel wreaths, wheat shafts, lions' and rams' heads, shields, and swords.

The revival of classical design swept through France, then England and America and was known by different names in each country and century in which it was popular. In the eighteenth century, French classic design was called *Régence, Louis XVI,* and *Neoclassic*; in England it was known as *classic revival,* and in the United States it was called *federal style*. In the nineteenth century, French classical motifs were called *Empire,* a style that incorporated Egyptian themes from Napoleon's campaigns; in England it was known as *Regency,* a style that incorporated marine themes that commemorated Nelson's victories, and in the United States it was called *American Empire.*

CONTEMPORARY. The ornamentation of modern silver is characterized by simplicity, a style inspired by contemporary architecture with grids, cubes, and modules, as well as decoration from classical antiquity, Egyptian motifs, and American Indian themes.

CUT-CARD WORK. In the mid-seventeenth century, English silver was 95.8 parts pure, a measure known as the *Britannia standard.* Compared to sterling silver, which was 92.5 parts pure, Britannia silver cost more to produce. To economize, English silversmiths cut ornamentation from thin sheets of silver called *cards,* and soldered or bolted them to the body of ware. Today, cut-card work is used to make a network of design, such as leaves and flowers carved in low relief, and to reinforce silver at points of wear.

DUTCH ORNAMENTATION. The joint reign of William and Mary (1689–1702)—Prince William III of Orange, and Mary II, daughter of King James II—was a prosperous time when silver was generously wrought in the baroque style. However, Dutch baroque was a little less formal than French baroque, and silver dubbed "William and Mary" is characterized by ornate scenes of Dutch still life wrought in repoussé, such as toilette sets decorated all over with curving foliage, acanthus leaves, and floral swags.

EMBOSSED ORNAMENTATION (REPOUSSÉ). The decoration of thin sheets of silver with ornamentation punched up from underneath is known as *embossed* or *repoussé*. The method is used to create pictorial patterns in relief.

ENAMEL. Enamel is made of powdered glass colored with metallic oxides, a decorative substance with a smooth, glossy texture fired to the surface of silver at approximately 800°C (1472°F).

Enamels are opaque or translucent. Opaque enamel is applied to silver in three basic ways. *Champlevé* is made with shallow depressions of silver that form edges. The indentations between the edges are filled in with opaque enamels. *Cloisoné* is made with wires secured to metal that form partitions. The space between the wires is filled in with opaque enamels. *En ronde bosse* is a decorative technique that uses opaque enamels to decorate round objects and irregular surfaces. The method encrusts silver with designs in high relief and is also known as *encrusted enamel*.

Two techniques are used to apply translucent enamel to silver. *Basse taille* is a term for silver ornamented with low-cut designs, such as chased, engraved, or stamped motifs. The designs are covered with translucent enamels. *Plique-à-jour* features pierced motifs filled in with translucent enamels. The enamel between the pierced motifs is unsupported and light shows through.

ENGRAVING. The French word *engraver* means "to carve." A sharp tool, called a *graver* or a *burin,* is used to cut thin burrows in silver, a technique that removes only a small amount of metal.

FLUTING. A decorative style composed of vertical or spiral concave grooves.

GADROON. From the French word *godron,* meaning "to crease" or "to pucker," a gadroon is a border treatment made up of convex lobes laid out in repetitive patterns in vertical, diagonal, or twisted motifs, a method developed in the eighteenth century to ornament the borders of silver.

GEORGIAN SILVER. A style developed in the first half of the eighteenth century during the reigns of George I, George II, and George III, it is characterized by large-scaled, well-proportioned silver with heavy masculine overtones. Silver wrought in the reigns of George I and George II was influenced by rococo, while silver made in the reign of George III is decorated in the classic revival style. To make the silver affordable to a growing middle class, Georgian silver was wrought with a thin gauge.

GILDING. The application of gold dust to metal is known as *gilding.* The surface is prepared with sizing, such as glue or varnish, and gold dust is applied with a brush. Before 1840, metal was gilded with mercury, but the poisonous fumes caused side effects, and the process was replaced by the invention of electroplating with gold.

*Parcel gilt* denotes silver partially covered with gold, a coating applied usually as protection against acidic foods that react with silver and create dark spots, such as serving spoons made with gilded bowls and silver handles.

*Silver gilt* refers to silver covered entirely with gold, a method that prevented tarnish, used largely before glass liners accompanied silver that held corrosive substances, such as silver salt cellars.

GOTHIC. In the ornamentation of silver, *gothic style* refers to designs modeled in high relief interpreted with angular lines adapted from ribbed vaulting, flying buttresses, pointed arches, and steep roofs of Gothic twelfth-century cathedrals, a style that underwent revival in the era of nineteenth-century Victorian eclecticism.

JAPONAISERIE. The European adaptation of Japanese motifs, such as bamboo, birds, fans, and cherry blossoms, an ornamental style interpreted in silver made during the arts and crafts movement.

*MARTELÉ.* From the French word *martel* for "hammer," a decorative technique developed by William Codman, an English silversmith employed by the Gorham Company of Providence, Rhode Island, and patented by the firm in 1900. Because each piece of silver was beaten by hand, no two items were alike, and *martelé* gave machine-made ware a soft handcrafted look. The style is associated with the arts and crafts movement and popular up to World War I.

MATTING. A decorative method that creates a matte texture, made by chasing the surface of metal with a series of fine punched dots made with a matting punch.

NIELLO. An alloy composed of lead, silver, copper, borax, and sulfur; a black wax-like substance that accents the ornamentation of inlaid or engraved silver. Niello ware was popular in the Middle Ages and fashionable in nineteenth-century Russia. It was revived in the early twentieth century to accent the ornamentation of art deco silver.

PATINA. Old silver is coveted not only for its craftsmanship, shape, and design but also for surface changes that occur with the passage of time, a process called *patina.* Old silver has a dull grayish-blue hue, with myriad tiny lines that cast a mellow glow, whereas new silver has a bright grayish-white hue. Although the reason for the color differences is unknown, two theories exist. One is that atmospheric conditions, such as sunlight and the impurities in air, cause a microscopic coating of silver oxide to build up over a period of centuries, protecting the underlying metal and casting a bluish hue on the surface of old silver. Silver with good patination resists tarnish better than silver without patina, so patina may form a protective coating. It is also possible that the tiny scratches that develop from frequent use reflect light, projecting a grayish-blue hue on the surface of the metal.

QUEEN ANNE. In the reign of Queen Anne (1702–1714), a higher ratio of silver was used to make sterling, namely 95.8 parts pure silver compared to 92.5 parts silver in sterling. This was called the *Britannia standard.* Silver made by the Britannia standard was softer than sterling and not conducive to ornate ornamentation; it also cost more. To conserve on the higher cost, silversmiths reduced the ornamentation and wrought plain silver with elegant proportions that emphasized form. Queen Anne silver is characterized by superior workmanship, with concave and convex forms represented by the ogee, and cyma curves, two lines that flow in opposite directions.

RAISING. A method used to make holloware, by hammering a sheet of silver against a wooden or metal stake.

REEDING. A decorative style used to ornament silver with narrow, convex, vertical molding laid in parallel lines.

ROCOCO. An ornate style associated with Louis XV, who in 1723 ascended the throne and ushered in a period of sparkling gaiety and informality. Rococo is the final phase of the baroque period, a style represented by lighthearted, dainty, curvaceous motifs, naturalistic in origin and irregular in form, such as shells, vines, leaves, floral swags, rocks, and marine life. The name derives from the French *rocaille,* meaning "shell," and many of the themes center around water. The ornamentation is expressed in low-relief sculptural motifs that incorporate sinuous *S* and *C* scrolls spiraling upward along an asymmetrical path, a style interpreted in silver decorated with repoussé, chased decoration, and applied ornamentation.

STRAPWORK. An ornamental pattern created by interlacing bands of straps.

VICTORIAN SILVER. Named for Queen Victoria of England (1837–1901), Victorian silver is associated with eclectic ornamentation—a nonstyle attributed to the demands of machine-made products. The great advance in industrial technology in the nineteenth century fostered a revival of historical styles, namely European gothic and Renaissance ornamentation combined with Asian, Middle Eastern, and Indian art. Early in the nineteenth century, classical themes dominated, followed by gothic revival, asymmetrical rococo, chinoiserie, japonaiserie, opulent Turkish decoration, Egyptian motifs, and American Indian interpreted in geometric patterns. Moreover, naturalistic shapes were popular, such as centerpieces made in the form of a tree with leaflike dishes and heavily embossed branches; beverage pots with handles, spouts, and feet modeled like tree roots; and low bulbous ware, such as melon-shaped kettles or vessels wrought to resemble floral blossoms.

CHAPTER SIXTEEN

# THE DIFFERENT TYPES OF METAL FLATWARE

METAL FLATWARE IS made of assorted materials, some precious, such as sterling silver and vermeil, others plated, such as silver plate or gold electroplate, or alloyed, such as stainless steel and pewter. But to a larger or smaller degree, all metals possess ductility, malleability, and luster, attributes that imbue the table setting with a distinct ambience.

## Silver

Silver is the queen of metals, a luxury material admired for its grayish-white color and reflective surface, a metal extracted from the veins of ores embedded in rock and also found in the ocean and in dust. A small amount of silver is obtained from argentite, a heavy dark gray mineral. Silver is mined in various parts of the world, notably Australia, Bolivia, Canada, Germany, Honduras, Japan, Mexico, Peru, Russia, Spain, the United States, and Zaire.

The word *silver* is from the Anglo-Saxon *sealfor*. *Silverware* denotes flatware made of metal, such as sterling silver, silver plate, vermeil, gold electroplate, stainless steel, and pewter.

Silver is lighter than gold, and is therefore preferable for articles held in the hand. Silver is also malleable and ductile (plastic); it is possible to beat silver into leaves that are 1/100,000 of an inch thick and to draw it out into a wire finer than a human hair. However, silver in a pure state is too soft to use alone, so it is alloyed with copper, a harder metal that does not change the whitish-gray hue of silver. Here are the various types of silver, listed from softest to hardest.

- *Mexican silver* is 100 percent pure silver, the softest form of silver.
- *Britannia silver* is 95.8 parts pure silver alloyed with 4.2 parts copper.
- *Sterling silver* is 92.5 parts silver alloyed with 7.5 parts copper.
- *Coin silver* is an American term for silver made after 1850; it is 90 percent silver with 10 percent copper.
- *German silver* does not contain silver; it is an alloy containing 50 percent copper and equal parts of nickel and zinc. The alloy was first used in Hildburghausen, Germany, to make inexpensive souvenirs with the look of silver. Later, German silver was used as a base metal to make Sheffield plate, a hard metal that resembles the grayish-white hue of silver. German silver takes a high polish well and is also known as *nickel silver, alloyed silver,* and *argentine silver.*

Silver is subject to scratches that over time develop a fine network of lines to form a *patina,* giving old silver a mellow hue. New silver is recognized by shiny or dull surfaces known as *bright* and *florentine,* respectively. Bright finish has a reflective mirror-like sheen. Florentine is cross-hatched with tiny lines that impart a dull luster.

Because silver is not as rare as gold, it is less expensive to purchase; the price of silverware is commensurate with the weight, the intricacy of the design, and the quality of the craftsmanship. Although the sterling standard is stipulated by law, guidelines are not given for the weight, and the density of silver articles vary from heavy to medium to light.

Silver melts at 961°C (1762°F). Of all metals, silver is the best conductor of heat and electricity; it is not harmed by sudden changes in temperature and adjusts instantly, both in and out of the mouth, to hot and cold foods. It is the perfect metal for the manufacture of flatware.

When heated, silver flows well, molds easily, and retains its shape, qualities ideal for carved ornamentation with deep recesses, decoration enhanced with tarnish, an element caused by the sulfuric fumes of nonmetallic substances, such as rubber, matches, bleach, and disinfectants. Although tarnish is unattractive on plain surfaces, when used as an accent it is a design tool.

Sterling silver knives are wrought with blades made of stainless steel or solid silver. Stainless steel blades are strong and are used for knives that require a sharp cutting edge, such as dinner knives, steak knives, and carving knives. The blade is inserted into two hollow halves of silver, creating a *hollow-handle knife* polished until the seams are invisible. In the burnishing process, the handles become faintly contoured and are slightly larger and wider than knife handles made of solid silver.

Solid silver blades are softer than stainless steel, and are used to make knives, such as butter spreaders, that do not require a good cutting edge (although butter spreaders are also made with stainless steel blades). Silver blades are stamped from one sheet of metal, and a *flat-handle spreader* is slightly narrower and flatter than a hollow-handle knife. Many manufacturers offer a choice between hollow-handle knives and flat-handle spreaders.

## Vermeil

*Why is gold pale? Because it has so many thieves plotting against it.*

DIOGENES, EPIGRAMS, 325 B.C.

Gold is the king of metals and the rarest and most precious metal recognized by its lemon-yellow color and intense luster that takes polishing well and does not tarnish. *Vermeil* (pronounced "vair-may") means "silver plated with gold." Because gold is heavier than silver and weightier in the hand, vermeil combines the lightness and lower cost of silver with the durability, tarnish-free quality, and yellowish color of gold. In the era of stately English homes, silver and vermeil were often stored in separate rooms designated as "white," for the whitish-gray shade of silver, and "gilded," for the gleaming yellow color of vermeil.

Gold is found in volcanic rocks, veins or lodes of ore in the earth's crust; placer deposits (nuggets washed away from lodes by flood waters); copper deposits (but only to a minor degree), and sea water (about one grain per ton of water). However, unlike silver, gold is not susceptible to chemical changes in air, does not tarnish, and is resistant to rust and acids. Finds of gold date to ancient Egypt, Arabia, Nubia,

Ethiopia, other parts of Africa, and areas around the Black Sea and the Mediterranean. In the Renaissance, explorers found gold in the Americas. Today, most of the world's gold supply comes from South Africa, Russia, Canada, the United States, Australia, and the Gold Coast of Africa.

Pure gold possesses density, weight, malleability, and ductility in quantities greater than silver. Gold is 19.25 times more dense than water; it is possible to hammer gold into leaves 1/200,000 of an inch thick and draw a grain into a wire 500 feet long or more. But in a pure state gold is too soft for use alone and is alloyed for strength with other metals, such as silver, copper, nickel, and palladium, a metal susceptible to scratches that over time develop into a fine patina. Although gold-plated silver is easy to manipulate and provides a wonderful showcase for deep, intricately carved designs, its softness makes it impractical for utensils that go into the mouth. Vermeil, a noncorrosive metal, is used to gild the interiors of serving utensils and serveware that may come in prolonged contact with salt or acids, such as nut spoons, sauce ladles, salt cellars, and compotes.

At the table, vermeil imparts a regal glow, a look of solid gold appropriate for table accessories, such as candlesticks and epergnes. It is a metal that lends an opulent air to elegant formal events, such as state occasions.

## Silver Plate

Silver plate is a base metal, or alloy, coated with pure silver in a process that involves electrolytic action. The base metal and a bar of pure silver are suspended together in a chemical solution of potassium cyanide. When an electric current is passed through the solution, ions of silver are evenly deposited onto the base metal through the electromagnetic process. The longer the base metal remains in the plating solution, the thicker the coating of silver. After a certain point (approximately 20 minutes), base metals cease to accept silver, regardless of how many times they are processed, so terms like *double plate, triple plate,* and *quadruple plate* mean little if the base metal is not left in the solution long enough to build up a thick coating.

How does one identify silver plate when it looks the same as sterling silver? *Pure silver* is used to plate base metal, whereas sterling silver is alloyed with copper; silver plate is whiter than sterling. To identify quality silver plate, look for the name of a reputable manufacturer, an indicator of silver plated over a base of thick metal, covered with a dense coating of silver, ornamented by skilled artisans.

Base metals vary in color according to content and imbue silver plate with different hues and attributes. Nickel silver is composed of nickel, copper, and zinc. It is a metal with a silver-white color, hard yet malleable, that acts as a tough bonding agent. Copper is a light-weight and efficient conductor of heat. Zinc is a bluish-white metallic chemical element not affected by dry air; in moist air it forms a self-protective coating of tarnish. Both copper and zinc are resistant to rust. Britannia metal is comprised of 70 to 90 percent tin, plus copper and antimony. Tin is malleable at ordinary temperatures—a soft, silver-white color, that takes a high polish well. Antimony is a silver-white hardener that increases the resistance of Britannia metal to chemical action. Copper bestows a reddish-brown tone on silver plate, and brass, an alloy of copper and zinc, casts a yellowish shade. A base metal of nickle silver, zinc, and Britannia metal imparts a bluish-white cast to silver plate.

Articles that undergo frequent handling, such as flatware and holloware, are plated over nickel silver, a hard base metal that is weighty, rests heavily in the hand, and assists balance (quality silver-plated flatware balances on the fingertips). Articles that receive little or no handling, such as napkin rings, picture frames, and boxes, are plated over brass or Britannia metal, base metals that take well to modeling.

Because of the base metal, silver plate is harder than sterling silver and less malleable. It is difficult to decorate with carved or stamped designs. When intricate motifs are rendered in silver plate they do not possess the same richness of depth as the identical pattern rendered in sterling silver or vermeil.

## Gold Electroplate

Gold electroplate is made by the application of 24-carat gold over a base metal, a process similar to the manufacture of silver plate. A *carat* is a unit of measure used for precious metals and stones. It comes from the Arabic *qirat,* symbolizing fruit of the locust bean tree. Emperor Constantine (280?–337 A.D.) used the *qirat,* or carat, to represent value, the pod of the locust bean carrying a weight of 4 grams.

Gold electroplated flatware provides a rich elegant look suitable for the table setting but at a lower cost than vermeil. Like quality silver plate, the cost of gold electroplate is commensurate with the thickness of the base metal, the density of the plating, and the quality of the craftsmanship. Brand name is important, and reputable manufacturers back gold electroplate with warranties of 50 to 100 years.

Because gold is plated over base metal, gold electroplate is hard and suitable for the manufacture of flatware. But there are fewer flatware patterns available in gold electroplate than in sterling and silver plate. Like pure gold, gold electroplate does not tarnish, is durable, and is highly resistant to stains.

## Stainless Steel

Steel is an alloyed metal, a mix of two or more metals whose combined hardness is greater than its individual parts. Steel is alloyed with iron and a small amount of carbon. Because iron is subject to tarnish and rust, chromium and nickel are added for rust resistance. The term *stainless* means the alloy stains *less* than other metals.

Chromium is the primary alloy of stainless steel; it is a grayish-white crystalline metallic chemical element that forms a protective transparent film against corrosive agents, like rust, when exposed to oxygen. Nickel is a hard, silver-white metallic substance that resists oxidation. To identify the amount of chromium and nickel, quality stainless steel is imprinted on the underside with the numbers 18/8 or 18/10. The first number, 18, indicates the amount of chromium, and the second number indicates the amount of nickel: 18/10 is more lustrous and costlier than 18/8 because it contains a higher proportion of nickel.

Stainless steel flatware is graded as *high* and *low*. Flatware made of high-quality stainless steel undergoes *grade rolling,* a process that imparts degrees of thickness to different parts of the utensils. The spoon is heavily graded at the base of the handle to resist bending, and for comfort in the mouth the bowl is lightly tapered at the edge. To hold a good cutting edge, knife blades are made with a stronger grade of metal than the handles. Flatware alloyed of low-quality stainless steel is made from a single thickness of metal that does not hold its shape well; it is light in the hand and lacks a good cutting edge.

Stainless steel is the hardest and toughest metal used to make tableware; it is hygienic, does not rust, is resistant to stains and acids from fruit, vegetables, and organic matter, and is backed by manufacturers with a lifetime warranty. Furthermore, stainless steel provides care-free maintenance and is resistant to oxidation at high temperatures, such as the heat of the dishwasher drying cycle. However, stainless steel is a hard alloy, less malleable than silver or gold. It does not take well to intricately carved ornamentation, so it is ornamented with contoured or sculptured decoration, and recessed areas are highlighted with black tarnish.

Stainless steel is given a lustrous or a bright finish, each imparting a different ambience to the table setting. A *luster finish* features a satin-smooth matte look, a surface similar to old silver, giving the table setting an informal ambience. A *bright finish* imparts a shiny surface, a look similar to new silver that imbues the table setting with a dressier ambience. To promote a rich look appropriate for elegant yet informal dining, stainless steel may be partially plated with 24-carat gold.

## Pewter

Pewter is an alloyed metal with a grayish color; it is composed primarily of tin and small amounts of antimony, bismuth, and silver or zinc. Tin is a silver-white crystalline metallic element that takes a high polish well and resembles silver. The higher the amount of tin, the better the quality of the pewter, and the more silvery-white the appearance. Fine pewter contains 75 to 90 percent tin. Moreover, tin is a soft metal that takes engraved ornamentation well.

Poor grades of pewter contain a large amount of lead, an alloy with a dark gray color and a dull luster. Lead is an impure metal that centuries ago was discovered to be poisonous. In the eighteenth century the English developed lead-free pewter, a silver-white alloy known as *Britannia metal* (made with 150 parts tin, 10 parts antimony, 3 parts copper, and an optional amount of bismuth and zinc). Britannia metal is a harder metal than leaded pewter, an alloy that has a lighter shade of gray than antique pewter and is known as *poor man's silver*. Today, when lead is added to pewter it is used to impart the dark color of age. This makes it unsuitable for food or beverage service.

Pewter is a darker shade of gray than silver, a tone appropriate for informal table settings, such as a country table setting. It is an alloy manufactured in matte and bright finishes. A *matte finish* with a dull surface imparts a mellow casual look to the table setting. A *bright finish* with a highly polished shiny surface, similar to silver, imbues the table setting with a dressier look.

Although pewter flatware is made with pewter handles prone to dents and scratches, the soft metal is easy to repair. To give strength to the utensils at points of wear, the blades of knives, the tines of forks, and the bowls of spoons are made of stainless steel.

CHAPTER SEVENTEEN

# THE KNIFE

THE KNIFE IS THE earliest known implement, a tool used as an eating utensil before it evolved as a weapon. The word *knife* is from *knif,* a Middle-English word that means "to press together" or "to pinch." *Cutlery* is from *coutellerie,* an Old French word for the business of a cutler, "one who makes knives."

In the Stone Age, knives were made of flint, a hard stone honed to a narrow blade and used as a tool to work antler, bone, and ivory. Neolithic peoples used stone hammers to pound stone knives into sharp-edged tools used to spear and skin animals and divide meat, but knives were rarely used in sacrificial ceremonies or as weapons. By the Bronze Age, single-edged knives were made as tools to prepare and carve food, and double-edged knives featured dagger-like points made for war and for the hunt. In the Iron Age, knives were wrought of fused iron, like the dagger Goliath carried into battle against David.

During the early Middle Ages, the Franks carried an all-purpose knife called a *scramasax;* it was about 20 inches long and hung from the belt. The *scramasax* was used for war and for hunting. So vital was the *scramasax* to life and survival that the blade was often damascened with wavy patterns or engraved in runic script with the name of the owner or with words and notes of a song. Today, *scramasax* can be seen at the British Museum.

By the Middle Ages, European noblemen owned two knives: a large knife used as a kitchen tool and a smaller knife used both as an eating utensil and as a dagger. Poor men owned one all-purpose knife. The medieval host did not supply dinner knives; instead, noblemen carried their own in a dagger-like sheath made of elaborately tooled leather suspended from the belt. Peasants carried knives in their stockings strapped to their legs.

A whetstone was often placed by the entrance to the great hall so that guests could sharpen their knives before a feast. Hence the expression "to whet the appetite" in keen anticipation of food.

Knife handles were cast of solid metal or made from two hollow halves die-stamped from thin sheets of silver into which a blade was inserted. The space between the hollow halves was filled in with resin, an organic substance exuded by plants and trees that melted when exposed to heat. Hence the expression "to fly off the handle" in the heat of anger. Die-stamped handles gave the appearance of solidity without weight.

For the wealthy, knife handles were made of gold and silver embedded with semiprecious stones, such as amber and agate. Henry VIII, in a display of wealth and power, commissioned knife handles encrusted with diamonds, emeralds, rubies, and pearls. In the second half of the eighteenth century, pistol-grip handles were popular, and by the nineteenth century knife handles were made of colored material chosen to commemorate a religious holiday, such as ebony for Lent to represent Christ's suffering on the cross, and ivory for Easter to symbolize his resurrection, as well as mother-of-pearl and bone.

In the Middle Ages, the tip of the knife and the blade were essential accoutrements of the meal, a diet that included for the nobility a great deal of roasted or boiled meat. The tip of the knife blade was used as a fork tine to spear large sections of meat for transfer from platter to trencher plate. The edge of the blade was used to cut portions into bite-size pieces, eaten from the tip of the blade or from the side of the blade. The tip of the blade was also used to take salt from the salt cellar. Although the peasantry were not served a lot of meat, they used the side of the knife blade to eat vegetables, such as garlic.

*If the dish be pleasant, either flesche or fishe,*
*Ten hands at once swarm in the dish;*
*And if it be flesche, ten knives shalt thou see,*
*Mangling the flesche, and in the platter flee.*
*To put there they handes, in peril without fail*
*Without a gauntlet, or else a glove of mail.*

*Anonymous, sixteenth century*

But to use one's knife to cut meat for another without first asking his permission was considered impolite. Another writer explains the niceties.

> But I would not have him be any mans Carver, without asking him first, except it be to one so much his inferiour, as he knoweth will be glad of the curtesie he sheweth him, though he like not the meate. For as to carve to a mans better is presumption, so to ones equal, except by asking first the question.

The dinner knife originated in Italy in the sixteenth century, but only wealthy hosts could supply their guests with utensils. When Cardinal Richelieu, the French statesman and leading minister to Louis XIII, witnessed a dinner guest use the tip of a double-edged knife as a toothpick, he ordered knives wrought with rounded tips and a single cutting edge.

*Pick not thy teeth with thy knyfe,*
*nor with thy fyngers end,*
*But take a stick or some cleane thyng*
*then doe you not ofende.*

BOKE OF NURTURE, *1577*

In an effort to discourage violence, Louis XIV made it a legal offense to use and carry knives with pointed tips, an act that prevented innkeepers from supplying them. Louis XIV was also the first king to provide each guest with a knife, fork, and spoon, and by the eighteenth century suites of matched flatware were fashionable throughout Europe and England.

When the knife was no longer used to spear, lift, and eat food, the tip of the blade changed from round to blunt to square, to a slightly rounded but pointed form. Moreover, the width of the blade changed from narrow and slightly curved, to wide and straight, a form similar to a spatula. Knives were then used to balance food difficult to spear with fork tines, such as peas, rice, and gravy.

*I eat my peas with honey,*
*I've done it all my life.*

*It makes the peas taste funny,*
*But it keeps them on the knife.*

In 1740, Thomas Bolsover, a cutler from Sheffield, England, accidentally fused silver to copper and thus invented what is known today as *Sheffield silver,* which produced harder knives than sterling, used less silver, and lowered the cost of flatware. By the mid-eighteenth century, those of average means could provide their guests with dinner knives. By 1760, dinner knives were made to match dinner forks and soup spoons. In the late eighteenth century the cost of bullion fell, and for the first time, silver dinner knives were available in the middle- and low-price range. Utensils were displayed on the sideboard in a special box made of fine materials, such as mahogany, satinwood, shagreen, or metal.

The English aristocracy of the eighteenth century frowned on the knife as an eating implement and accepted the fork as a refinement of dining. However, the change was slow to reach approval in North America, and in the nineteenth century the dinner knife continued as an eating utensil. Notes this expert on etiquette and wife of a Harvard professor:

> If you wish to imitate the French or English, you will put every mouthful into your mouth with fork; but if you think, as I do that Americans have as good a right to their own fashions as the inhabitants of any other countries, you may choose the convenience of feeding yourself with your right hand, armed with a steel blade; and provided you do it neatly, and do not put in large mouthfuls, or close your lips tightly over the blade, you ought not to be considered as eating ungenteelly.
>
> Elizabeth Ware Farrar, *The Young Ladies Friend,* 1838

Today, knives are made in a host of shapes, some with serrated blades, others with dull edges and pointed or rounded tips. Knives with serrated blades, such as steak knives, section thick cuts of meat. Knives with dull blades, such as dinner knives, luncheon knives, and dessert knives, cut soft or cooked food. Knives with pointed tips, such as a steak knives, fruit knives, and fish knives, carve meat, pare fruit, and separate fish bones. Knives with blunt ends, such as butter spreaders, are made to spread food.

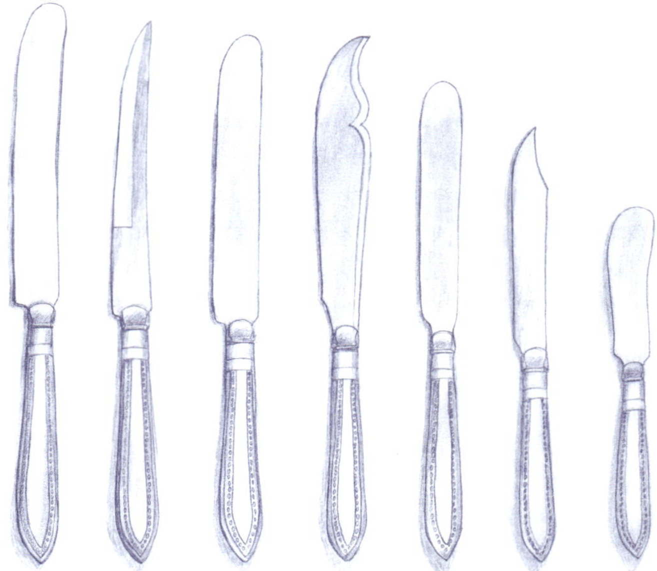

THE KNIVES USED IN TABLE SETTING, SHOWN IN THE DESCENDING ORDER OF SIZE, ARE THE DINNER KNIFE, STEAK KNIFE, LUNCHEON KNIFE, FISH KNIFE, DESSERT KNIFE, FRUIT KNIFE, AND BUTTER SPREADER.

Table knives are made in seven sizes, including, from large to small: dinner knife, steak knife, luncheon knife, fish knife, dessert knife, fruit knife, and butter spreader. Some knives are made as part of a flatware set, while other knives are specialized shapes or only found in older sets of silver. Although the dimensions of knives vary according to the manufacturer, the size of each category is approximately the same. The lengths given below are based on my own collection.

## *Dinner Knife*

The dinner knife is the longest knife in a set of flatware. It is used to cut and push food and is laid on the table at all meals, formal and informal. The exception is when soup is served as the main course, and a dinner knife is not required. The dinner knife is made in two sizes: place size and continental size. The place size measures around 9¼ inches in length and the continental size is about 9¾ inches long.

Before stainless steel was invented in the early twentieth century, knife blades were made of carbon steel, a metal that not only imparted a metallic taste to salad but discolored the delicate lettuce leaves and corroded the blades that came in contact with the acidic salad dressing. To resolve the problem, French chefs tore lettuce leaves into bite-size pieces before adding the dressing, thus eliminating the need for salad knives at the table. Today, when a knife is needed to cut an extralarge salad leaf, such as a piece of romaine or a thick wedge of lettuce, a dinner knife is used. The exception is at a formal dinner when an extra dinner knife is provided for salad.

## Steak Knife

The steak knife is a specialized knife not made as part of a set of flatware. It is approximately 8¼ to 9 inches long and has a sharp tip and a serrated edge to cut thick portions of meat. At a formal meal, a steak knife is not provided because meat is served roasted for the main course, a method of preparation easily cut with a regular dinner knife. However, at an informal meal when thick or tough portions of meat are served, steak knives are an asset.

## Luncheon Knife

The luncheon knife is 8 to 8¾ inches long, a size that balances the proportions of the luncheon plate, which is 8½ inches in diameter. Although the luncheon knife is used at formal and informal luncheons, it is not mandatory for either occasion. Because so many women today work outside the home, there is little demand for luncheon-size flatware, and regular dinner knives are normally used at the midday meal. Luncheon knives are often found in older sets of flatware.

## Fish Knife

*I don't mind eels,*
*Except at meals.*

OGDEN NASH

Before the fish knife was invented in the nineteenth century, the aristocracy used two dinner forks for fish, one to cut a bite and the other to eat. Commoners ate fish from a single fork and used bread as a pusher. When the middle class began to use fish knives, the aristocracy, whose silver was handed down through generations, scoffed at the utensil as too select.

The fish knife is a specialized shape not included as part of a flatware set. Originally, the fish knife was made as a smaller version of the asymmetrical fish server. Today, the fish knife features a wide blade with a dull edge and a tip made with a notched point used to separate the skeleton from the body and lift the bones onto a plate. Fish knives vary in size but usually measure about 8¾ inches long. They are used in both formal and informal dining.

## Dessert Knife

The dessert knife is a specialized utensil not made as part of a flatware set. It is used in formal and informal dining with a dessert fork. The dessert knife measures approximately 8 inches long and features a narrow blade and a rounded or pointed tip. The rounded tip is used to section soft desserts, and the pointed tip to cut firm desserts.

## Fruit Knife

The fruit knife is approximately 6½ inches to 7¼ inches long. It is a specialized utensil not made as part of a flatware set. The fruit knife features a pointed tip and a narrow blade that is straight or slightly curved. Sometimes the edge of the blade is serrated. The fruit knife is used to cut and peel fresh fruit at the table in formal and informal dining.

## Butter Spreader

The butter spreader is approximately 5 to 6 inches long. It is the smallest knife in a set of flatware. The tip of the blade is rounded and some are slightly wider at the tip. The butter spreader is used differently in formal and informal dining. At a formal dinner given in a private home where strict protocol is followed, the multiplicity of courses provides sufficient taste and texture without the need for bread and butter, and a butter spreader is not used. However, at formal luncheons and informal meals, fewer courses are served, bread and butter are provided, and a butter spreader is used. (See also Chapter 6, "Plates: Piece by Piece," for a discussion of bread-and-butter plates.)

CHAPTER EIGHTEEN

# THE SPOON

THE SPOON, FROM the Anglo-Saxon term *spon,* meaning "to chip," was the first eating utensil, a shape made with a small oval-shaped bowl at one end of a handle. Perhaps the first spoon was a depressed piece of stone or a gourd. By the Neolithic era, pottery was a known craft and scoop-shaped utensils were made of clay. The Egyptians crafted spoons in antiquity from assorted materials, such as cowrie shells mounted on stems of stone or wood, spoons carved from ivory, cast in metal, or made from wooden splinters. Occasionally Egyptian spoons were made with a tine at the end of the bowl, a utensil used possibly to extract meat from the shells of snails and seafood.

In ancient Greece and Rome, spoons were made of bone, ivory, bronze, silver, and gold; the latter, a precious metal, was reserved for ceremonial occasions. The shapes of stems were long, narrow, and rounded, and the bowls were modeled in the form of a fig, with pointed tips to spike the shells of eggs (evil spirits were believed to dwell inside the egg, and a cracked shell released the soul). Although the profile of Roman spoons lay generally in one plane, occasionally they were shaped with a bowl lower than the handle, a form known as *keel and disk,* a term evolved from a flat-bottomed boat called a *keel.* Fourth-century Roman spoons made of silver were discovered in 1919 at Dumpelder, East Lothian, Scotland. In 1929, two silver spoons traced to 600 A.D. were found in an Anglo-Saxon ship sunk off Sutton Hoo, Suffolk, England; the spoons were inscribed with the names "Saul" and "Paul." Today, the Dumpelder and Sutton Hoo spoons are in the collection of the British Museum.

Spoons are mentioned in the Bible. In Exodus, the Lord commands Moses to make spoons of gold for the tabernacle. The prophet Nathan used a gold spoon to anoint Solomon king of Israel.

In the Middle Ages, an infant was given a spoon at its baptism. Baptismal spoons were made of silver, for the child of an aristocrat, or horn or wood, for a peasant child. Hence the expression "born with a silver spoon in his mouth." One's spoon was kept for life. The medieval lord did not provide spoons for his guests, and those who ate with him carried their own. Royalty ate from spoons made of gold; aristocrats, from silver, gilt, rock crystal, and coral. The poor took food from spoons made of horn, bone, pewter, brass, latten (a form of brass), or wood, such as cherry, poplar, and boxwood. By the seventeenth century metal spoons made of pewter and latten were common, although silver was the principal metal until electroplating was invented in the nineteenth century.

The primary methods of food preparation in the Middle Ages were boiled and roasted dishes, and to accommodate the texture of soft foods, notably soups, stews, and puddings, spoons were a size similar to today's tablespoon. The spoon was wrought from one piece of metal, drawn out, and hammered into a form with a deep fig-shaped bowl that tapered to a slim hexagonal stem. The handle was round or square and short.

From the fourteenth to the sixteenth centuries, spoon handles terminated in finials soldered to the stem. These knops, or ornamental knobs, came in a number of common forms: a ball; a plain pineapple shape; the *akerne,* an acorn form; the diamond point, a spear; the *wrythen,* a twisted, fluted, globular shape, from the Anglo-Saxon *writan,* "to wind about"; the "maidenhead," a female head, originally an effigy of the Blessed Virgin; the lion sejant, a seated lion; and apostle spoons made in sets of thirteen, each topped with a finial of one of the twelve apostles, plus a master spoon ornamented with a knop of Christ. In the fifteenth and sixteenth centuries, apostle spoons were fashionable baptismal gifts. The godparents would present the infant with a single spoon mounted with the finial of the apostle for whom the child was named. Wealthy godparents gave a set of thirteen spoons, and those of lesser means gave a set of six.

Toward the end of the sixteenth century stiff lace ruffs were worn at the neck, and rather than drink soup from a bowl and risk soiling a fashionable pleated collar, the aristocracy began to use spoons with a larger bowl. Moreover the spoon bowl was changed from fig shape to pear shape. The widest part of the bowl was nearest the junction of the stem.

By the seventeenth century short handles with knops were replaced by longer handles made in broad flat shapes that accommodated cut ornamentation on the end, spatulate forms known as *seal-top* and *slip-top.* The seal-top featured a flat end incised with initials, a shape similar to a sealing-wax stamp. The slip-top spoon, from the horticultural term meaning to "cut" or "prune" and also known as a *slipped-in-the-stalk spoon,* was made with a blunt end carved at an angle. The *puritan,* a plain shape associated with the first half of the seventeenth century and the grave austerity of Cromwell's reign, was made with a square end adorned with a notch.

Two types of handles with rounded ends were popular from the second half of the seventeenth century into the eighteenth century. When Charles II was restored to the throne of England in 1660, the *trifidus* handle was in vogue; it had a rounded end made with two V-shaped cuts that formed three lobes similar to a cleft hoof. The handle was also known as a *trefid* or *trifid,* and as a *pied-de-biche,* meaning "doe's hoof" in French. The *wavy end* handle featured an undulating line.

In the second half of the eighteenth century, handle styles included the *Hanoverian,* a ribbed stem named for the English royal house of Hanover; the *fiddle-head,* a curved handle similar in shape to the scroll of a violin head; the *King's* pattern, ornamented with a shell motif; the *Onslow,* a fluted handle that ended in an Ionic volute (spiral scrolls on Ionic capitals), a pattern named for a member of Parliament in the reign of George II; and *Old English,* a stem that turned down.

To reinforce the junction of stem and bowl, from approximately 1660 to 1730, the underside of the bowl was strengthened with a tapered V shape, a form known as *rattail*. By the eighteenth century the V shape was rounded, a form called a *drop*. Sometimes the back of the bowl was reinforced with an ornamental shell, a configuration called a *shellback*.

From the mid-seventeenth century into the eighteenth century spoons were wrought in more than one size and in specialized shapes known as a *teaspoon, porringer spoon, dessert spoon, tablespoon,* and *mote spoon.* The teaspoon held half the quantity of a tablespoon or a dessert spoon; it was a dimension made to fit a teacup. The porringer spoon was slightly smaller than today's dessert spoon; it was made to eat hot cereal from the double-handled bowl called a *porringer*. To allow a good bite, the dessert spoon was larger than a teaspoon but smaller than a tablespoon, an all-purpose spoon used to eat soft foods. The tablespoon was larger than the other three and was used to eat soup made with particles of food. The mote spoon was similar in size to a teaspoon, only made with a pierced bowl to strain leaves, twigs, and other foreign matter (like small dead insects) from tea poured into a teacup. The needle-like handle was used to relieve motes from the spout of a teapot.

In the second half of the seventeenth century, the shape of the spoon bowl changed from pear to ovoid, forming a longer, narrower bowl similar to the elliptical form used today. To promote balance, the back of the handle was hammered wide, a method that allowed room for engraved ornamentation, such as a monogram or a crest.

By the eighteenth century the profile of the handle changed from flat to curved, a shape that modified the way the spoon was held. Whereas flat-stemmed spoons were held in the palm like a scoop, the curved handle was grasped like a pencil, a shape still in use today.

In the second half of the eighteenth century, elegant entertaining called for specialized spoons, such as a marrow spoon and a caddy spoon. The *marrow spoon,* approximately 9 inches long, featured a slender stem and a shallow bowl at each end; it was a spoon-shaped utensil used to scoop marrow from beef bones or veal shanks. The *caddy spoon* was made with a large shallow bowl and a short handle; it was used to measure tea and its shape derived originally from seashells enclosed in chests of tea and used to gauge the quantity of samples.

To meet the dining needs of a rising middle class, in the nineteenth century machine-made spoons were made in a host of sizes and shapes for various purposes and courses. There were spoons for aspic, bouillon, citrus fruit, ice cream, molded jelly, coffee, cream soup, a moustache spoon with a shaped ledge that separated the moustache from the contents of the spoon, and souvenir spoons that commemorated special events, such as county fairs, holiday resorts, a hero, or an election.

Spoons are used to sip, stir, and sup. Fourteen types are discussed below in order of descending size. Because the dimensions vary, particularly among antique flatware, approximate dimensions are given, drawn from my personal collection.

THE SPOONS USED IN TABLE SETTING, SHOWN IN ORDER OF DESCENDING SIZE, ARE THE ICED-BEVERAGE SPOON, OVAL SOUP SPOON, DESSERT SPOON, PLACE SPOON, CREAM SOUP SPOON, TEASPOON, FIVE O'CLOCK SPOON, ICE-CREAM SPOON, CITRUS SPOON, BOUILLON SPOON, AFTER-DINNER COFFEE SPOON, CHOCOLATE SPOON, DEMITASSE SPOON, AND SALT SPOON.

## Iced-Beverage Spoon

The iced-beverage spoon, also known as an *iced-tea spoon,* is the longest spoon in a set of flatware, a utensil made with a small bowl and a long handle, approximately 7 to 10 inches in length.

The iced-beverage spoon is used to stir sugar in cold beverages served in a tall glass, such as iced tea or iced coffee. It is used only for informal dining. At formal affairs, water, wine, and demitasse are served, and iced-beverage spoons are not needed. In the American south, a region known for hot humid weather, a full set of flatware is often sold with iced-beverage spoons rather than cream soup spoons.

# Oval Soup Spoon

*Beautiful soup! Who cares for fish,*
*Game or any other dish?*
*Who would not give all else, for two*
*Pennyworth of beautiful soup?*

LEWIS CARROLL, ALICE'S ADVENTURES IN WONDERLAND, 1865

The oval soup spoon is similar in size and shape to a tablespoon, only the bowl is a little smaller and tapers slightly to a tip and the handle is shorter. It is made to eat soup, namely, soup made with particles of solid food, such as meat, vegetables, grains, and pasta. The overall length of the oval soup spoon varies from approximately 5¾ to 8¼ inches.

The oval soup spoon is used differently in formal and informal dining. At a formal dinner, soup is served in a soup plate and the oval soup spoon is the only spoon laid on the table. At an informal meal, the oval soup spoon is used to eat any food presented in a large, shallow soup bowl, such as chili, stew, ravioli, and dessert.

# Dessert Spoon

The dessert spoon lies midway in length between the tablespoon and teaspoon, approximately 7 to 7¼ inches long. The shape of the bowl is oval and holds approximately two teaspoons of food, a size that affords a generous bite. The dessert spoon is used in formal and informal dining.

## Place Spoon

The place spoon is an all-purpose spoon slightly larger than a teaspoon but smaller than a tablespoon, a utensil used originally to sip cream soup and eat dessert. The shape of the bowl is oval, and the length is approximately 6½ to 7½ inches.

## Cream Soup Spoon

The cream soup spoon is approximately 6 inches long. It is made with a round bowl to fit the shape of the cream soup bowl. To reach into the depth of the cream soup bowl, the cream soup spoon is made with a longer handle than a teaspoon. Because the bowl of the cream soup spoon is too wide to fit the mouth, pureed soup is sipped from the side of the spoon.

At a formal dinner the cream soup spoon is not used, because cream soup is considered too rich and heavy to start a multicourse meal. However, at a meal with a simpler menu, namely, a formal luncheon and all informal meals, often a first course of cream soup is served, sipped from the side of the cream soup spoon.

## Teaspoon

Tea was introduced to the European continent in the seventeenth century. At first it was very expensive and served in a small cup about the size of today's demitasse cup. To provide the right balance and weight for the small cups, the first teaspoons were about 4¼ inches long, a size similar to today's demitasse spoon. By the eighteenth century, tea was less expensive, and teacups were made in larger sizes, as were teaspoons. Today, the average teaspoon measures approximately 5½ to 6¼ inches in length. The teaspoon is used only in informal dining to stir hot beverages, sip soup, and eat solid food, and it is the wise host who collects extras.

## Five O'Clock Spoon

The five o'clock spoon is a specialized spoon found in older sets of silver. Made for an era when afternoon tea was taken at five o'clock, the spoon is approximately 5¼ to 5½ inches long. Although the five o'clock teaspoon is slightly shorter than a teaspoon, it is a little larger than an after-dinner coffee spoon. Today, those lucky enough to own five o'clock spoons find the size ideal as an extra teaspoon and as a utensil to feed young children.

## Ice-Cream Spoon

The ice-cream spoon, also known as an *ice-cream scoop,* looks like a miniature shovel. It is approximately 5 inches in length and made with a wide shallow bowl to afford a generous bite. The ice-cream spoon is used at informal meals only to eat frozen dessert served on a plate, such as ice-cream roll. In formal dining, two dessert utensils are presented and the ice-cream spoon is not used.

## Citrus Spoon

The citrus spoon, also known as a *grapefruit spoon, orange spoon,* and *fruit spoon,* features an elongated bowl and a pointed tip, a shape used to eat segmented fruit, such as a grapefruit or an orange. The overall length is approximately 5½ to 6½ inches. The citrus spoon is made with a plain or serrated edge. The plain edge is used to eat fruit with presectioned segments, such as a grapefruit half. The serrated edge is used to eat citrus fruit with segments still attached.

# Bouillon Spoon

*She was always fond of putting her spoon into other people's broth.*

F. G. TREFFORD, THE WORLD IN THE CHURCH, 1863

The bouillon spoon looks like a cream soup spoon, only the bowl is smaller and the handle is shorter; it is approximately 5 to 5½ inches long. The bouillon spoon is used at light meals, such as formal and informal luncheons, when clear or jellied soup is served as a first course. However, at a multicourse dinner, notably a formal dinner, bouillon is considered too light to start a meal where numerous wines are served, and a bouillon spoon is not used. Furthermore, at an informal dinner composed of a few hearty courses, bouillon is not normally served because the broth is not substantial enough to begin the simple menu.

# After-Dinner Coffee Spoon

The after-dinner coffee spoon is approximately 4½ to 5 inches long, a length that balances the after-dinner coffee cup. It is used only for informal dining. At a multicourse meal, notably, an informal dinner or luncheon, a small cup of strong coffee is served after the meal to aid digestion, and after-dinner coffee spoons are used.

# Chocolate Spoon

In the seventeenth century, chocolate was introduced to England and Europe; it was a luxury beverage prepared from a paste of chocolate, cream, sugar, and hot milk. The rich paste was thick and to keep it from settling to the bottom of the cup, chocolate was stirred constantly with a small spoon made with a round bowl. In the morning, hot chocolate was served in a tall cup and stirred with a long-handled spoon, approximately 4¾ to 5¾ inches long. In the afternoon, chocolate was served in a small cup and a short-handled chocolate spoon about 4¼ inches long was used.

Because the flavor of hot chocolate is too rich to follow a multicourse meal, the drink is not served at formal affairs. At informal meals, such as breakfast, cocoa is served, a thinner beverage presented in a large cup or mug, and a teaspoon is used to stir it. Generally speaking, the only time a chocolate spoon is used today is when hot chocolate is served in a small chocolate cup, and any small spoon will do, such as an after-dinner coffee spoon or a demitasse spoon.

## Demitasse Spoon

The demitasse spoon, also known as a *mocha spoon* (to stir coffee made with an equal amount of hot chocolate), is approximately 3¾ to 4½ inches long, in proportion with the demitasse cup and saucer used in formal dining. At a formal dinner or formal luncheon, coffee is served in a demitasse cup, and a demitasse spoon is used if sugar is added.

## Salt Spoon

In the eighteenth century, rather than eat in a great baronial hall with family, guests, and servants, the master of the house chose to dine with family and friends in a smaller intimate room called a *dining room*. The great standing salt, once so important on the medieval high table, was no longer in demand, and salt was served from a tiny bowl-shaped salt cellar. In a smaller room, eating habits were more refined, and food was no longer dipped into a salt cellar with fingers; rather, salt was sprinkled over food from a diminutive salt spoon, approximately 2½ inches in length. Initially the shape of the salt spoon resembled a miniature tablespoon, but later it was fashioned in various forms, such as a tiny shell, a small heart, or a miniature shovel. To inhibit the corrosive effect of salt, the interior bowls of silver salt spoons were gilded. Today salt cellars are reserved almost totally for formal dinners or elegant informal affairs, but when provided, a salt spoon is placed in a salt cellar before and after use.

CHAPTER NINETEEN

# THE FORK

*It is coarse and ungraceful to throw food into the mouth as you would toss hay into a barn with a pitchfork.*

ANONYMOUS

THE WORD *FORK* comes from the Latin *furca* for "pitch fork." The two-prong twig was perhaps the first fork. In Egyptian antiquity, large forks made of bronze were used at religious ceremonies to lift sacrificial offerings. One of the earliest dinner forks is attributed to Constantinople in 400 A.D.; it can be seen in the Dumbarton Oaks collection in Washington, D.C. By the seventh century, small forks were used at Middle Eastern courts; one such fork, a small, gold, two-pronged tool, came to Italy in the eleventh century in the dowry of a Byzantine princess who married Domenico Selvo, a Venetian doge. After witnessing the princess use the fork, the church severely censured her, stating that the utensil was an affront to God's intentions for fingers. Thereafter the fork disappeared from the table for nearly 300 years.

They say fingers were made before forks, and hands before knives.
Jonathan Swift, *Polite and Ingenious Conversations,* 1738

In England the fork was slow to gain acceptance because it was considered a feminine utensil. The exception was the *sucket fork,* a utensil used to eat food that might otherwise stain the fingers, such as "a silvir forke for grene gynger" noted in an inventory taken in 1523 of Lady Hungerford's effects. The sucket fork was wrought with two prongs at one end of the stem and a bowl at the other. The fork end was used to spear food preserved in thick, sticky syrup, such as plums and grapes, and the spoon end to convey the syrup to the mouth.

When Catherine de' Medici married Henry I in 1533, her dowry included several dozen dinner forks wrought by Benvenuto Cellini, the great Italian silversmith. The fork began to gain acceptance in Italy by the late sixteenth century, a period when upper-class Italians expressed renewed interest in cleanliness. However, the French court considered the fork an awkward, even dangerous, utensil, and the nobility did not accept it until the seventeenth century when protocol deemed it uncivilized to eat meat with both hands. The way to use the fork remained a mystery, and many sophisticates, notably King Louis XIV, continued to eat with fingers or a knife.

> Then must you learn the use of handling of your silver fork at meals.
>
> Ben Jonson, *Volpone,* 1605

In 1608, Thomas Coryate, son of the Rector of Odcombe, took the "grand tour" of Europe, and on his return published a narrative that included the Italian custom of eating with a fork. Thereafter, Coryate's friends jokingly called the young traveler *Furciferus,* "Pitchfork."

> I observed a custome in all those Italian Cities and Townes through which I passed that is not used in any other country that I saw in my travels, neither doe I think that any other nation of Christendome doth use it, but only Italy. The Italian, and also most strangers that are cormorant in Italy, does alwaies at their meales, use a little fork when they cut the meate . . . their forkes being for the most part made of iron or steel, and some of silver, but these are used only by gentlemen. The reason of this their curiosity is because the Italian cannot endure by any means to have his dish touched by fingers, seeing that all men's fingers are not alike cleane. Hereupon I myself thought to imitate the Italian fashion by this forke cutting of meate, not only while I

was in Italy, but also in Germany, and often-times in England since I came home.

Thomas Coryate, *Coryat's Crudities,* 1611

The modern table setting is attributed to Charles I of England who in 1633 declared, "It is decent to use a fork," a statement that heralded the beginning of civilized table manners. But it wasn't until almost a century later that the fork gained acceptance among the lower class. In England, the acceptance of the fork encouraged preparation of continental recipes, such as *olios* from Spain, a dish made with stewed meat taken with a fork as opposed to mashed food eaten from the blade of a knife. Because the average family owned a limited number of forks, historians suggest that the service of sherbet midway through a meal gave the servants time to wash the forks used earlier on.

The first dinner forks were made with two flat prongs. The earliest two-prong fork to bear an English hallmark and engraved with a coat of arms dates to 1632 and is attributed to the Earl of Rutland. It can be seen today in the Victoria and Albert Museum, London. In the seventeenth century, fork tines were made of case-hardened steel and were fast to wear down. To promote utensils with longevity, early fork tines were extralong in length and made with sharp pointed tips.

But when it came to spearing certain foods, such as peas and grains, the widely spaced two-prong fork was impractical, and between the seventeenth and eighteenth centuries the tines increased in number from two to three and then to four. Moreover, from the late seventeenth century to the mid-eighteenth century, the profile of the fork changed from flat to slightly curved, a shape that accommodated a scoop of soft food, such as peas. But three- and four-prong forks were slow to reach North America, where people continued to eat from a knife blade food that was difficult to spear with a two-prong fork, such as mashed potatoes and gravy.

The way to use the dinner fork remained a mystery well into the eighteenth century. Joseph Brasbridge, a retail silversmith in Fleet Street, wrote of his confusion in a customer's home, "where the cloth was laid with a profusion of plate. . . . I know how to sell these articles, but not how to use them."

The *New York Ladies' Indispensable Assistant,* published in 1852, gave general advice on eating with a fork, knife, and spoon.

If silver or wide pronged forks are used, (for fish), eat with the fish fork in the right hand—the knife is unnecessary. . . . If possible, the knife should never be put into the mouth at all, let the ledge be turned down. . . . The teeth should be picked as little as possible, and never with fork or fingers. . . . Eat peas with a dessert spoon; and curry also."

In the nineteenth century, mass production and the invention of the electroplating process made silver forks affordable to a rising middle class who wished to emulate the nobility and eat with forks made for specific foods, such as berries, birds, cake, cold meat, cucumbers, fish, ice cream, lettuce, lobster, oysters, pickles, salad, sardines, shellfish, strawberrys, souffle, terrapin, tomatoes, and to pass sliced bread at the tea table. Although fork handles were normally made of silver or silver plate, in the nineteenth century organic materials were also used, such as bone, mother-of-pearl, and ivory (the latter often tinted green). Fork tines were shortened and closer together, and remain so today. No longer did fingers touch food, except to pick up small fruit, such as grapes. Nor did servants wash forks during a meal for use with another course.

Today, depending on need, a set of flatware may contain five forks: dinner fork, fish fork, luncheon fork, salad or dessert fork, and seafood fork. But the collector may amass specialized forks—for eating lobster, fruit, dessert, ice cream, pastry, strawberries, snails, and oysters—from antique shops and specialty stores.

The shapes of the fork tines accommodate particular foods. Forks wrought with long tapered tines, such as a dinner fork, are made to spear thick morsels of food, such as steak. Forks with a wide left tine and an optional notch, such as a salad fork, fish fork, dessert fork, and pastry fork, provide extra leverage when cutting food that normally does not require a knife. Forks with curved tines, such as the oyster fork, are made to follow the shape of the shell.

Although flatware is made in continental and American lengths, the American size, also called *place size,* is the most popular dimension. In order of descending size, the measurements of the following forks are given in place size. The dimensions of antique flatware are somewhat different from contemporary utensils. The lengths given here are derived from my own collection.

THE FORKS USED IN TABLE SETTING, SHOWN IN ORDER OF DESCENDING SIZE, ARE THE DINNER FORK, FISH FORK, LUNCHEON FORK, LOBSTER FORK, FRUIT FORK, SALAD FORK, DESSERT FORK, ICE-CREAM FORK, PASTRY FORK, SEAFOOD FORK, STRAWBERRY FORK, SNAIL FORK, AND OYSTER FORK.

## Dinner Fork

The dinner fork measures about 7 inches in length. It is used to eat the main course at all formal and informal meals. The larger continental-size dinner fork balances the profusion of tableware laid on a fully appointed formal table, and although the length is not necessary in formal dining, those who own the continental size use it for posh events. The American-size dinner fork, or place size, is approximately ½ inch shorter than continental size, a length that balances a table set to serve a few courses, namely, the informal table setting, from elegant to casual.

## Fish Fork

The fish fork was introduced around 1870 along with the fish knife. It is approximately 7¼ to 7¾ inches in length and is used in formal and informal dining. To provide leverage in separating fish from the body, the fish fork features an extrawide left tine, and an optional notch, grooved to fit over the bones.

## Luncheon Fork

The luncheon fork is approximately 6¾ inches long, a size in proportion with a luncheon plate, and found more often in older sets of flatware.

## Lobster Fork

The lobster fork is approximately 6¾ to 8 inches long. It is made with one long narrow tine that ends with two hooks or with a long, narrow center tine and two hooked tines on either side; both shapes are used to spear lobster served in a shell. Because the lobster shell is steadied in the hand and the lobster fork is held in the other hand, the utensil is used only in informal dining. At a formal dinner or luncheon, only dry rolls, cheese, crackers, and sometimes fresh fruit are touched with the fingers.

## Fruit Fork

*Fruit is gold in the morning,*
*Silver in the afternoon,*
*And lead at night.*

BISHOP SHUTE BARRINGTON, RULES OF HEALTH, C. 1800

The fruit fork is made with narrow tines and a long slender handle; it is approximately 6¼ inches in overall length. Although the fruit fork is used in formal and informal dining, Americans tend to eat cut fruit with fingers, and the fruit fork is used more often in Europe than in the United States.

# Salad Fork

In the late nineteenth century, refrigerated train cars made salad vegetables more abundant. The salad fork originally featured curved claw-shaped tines and was known as a *lettuce fork*. Today the tines of salad forks are flatter and slightly broader than those of a dinner fork, and the utensil is approximately 6 inches long. To provide leverage when cutting thick veins of lettuce or broad vegetables served in salad, the salad fork is made with an extrawide left tine that is sometimes grooved. For additional strength, the second and third tines of the salad fork are occasionally connected by a rod. The salad fork is used in formal and informal dining. It is also used for appetizer courses other than seafood, such as pâté.

# Dessert Fork

In the eighteenth century, after the main course was cleared from the table, the dinner fork was placed on a fork rest, where it remained ready for the dessert course. Toward the end of the eighteenth century, a smaller fork was introduced for dessert, and the fork rest became obsolete. Today, the dessert fork is a specialized fork approximately 6 to 7 inches in length, that looks similar to a salad fork, only a little narrower. It is not made as part of a flatware set. The left tine is extrawide to provide leverage in cutting firm dessert, such as baklava. The dessert fork is used in formal and informal dining.

# Ice-Cream Fork

Ice cream was introduced to the United States by Thomas Jefferson, who as ambassador to France tasted the delectable dessert, a food kept cold in snow. The ice-cream fork features a wide shallow bowl with three tines at the tip. The spoon part is used to scoop and eat soft ice cream, and the tines to cut, spear, and lift firm bites to the mouth. As two dessert utensils are provided in formal dining, namely a dessert fork and dessert spoon, the ice-cream fork is used only in informal dining. The overall length is approximately 5½ inches.

## Pastry Fork

The pastry fork evolved about 1880. It looks similar to a salad fork, but it is narrower and slightly shorter, approximately 5 to 5½ inches long. To provide leverage in cutting, the left tine is often notched. The pastry fork is used in informal dining, although it is not essential; it is not used in formal dining where two dessert utensils are presented.

## Seafood Fork

The seafood fork, also known as a *cocktail fork,* is a small, narrow, three-pronged fork made with short tines and a long handle; it is approximately 4½ to 5½ inches in overall length. The purpose of a seafood fork is to spear seafood served in a compote or a shell, such as shrimp cocktail or coquille St. Jacques.

The seafood fork is used in formal and informal dining. At a multicourse formal dinner or luncheon, the seafood fork is the fourth fork laid on a fully appointed table. It is placed to the right of the oval soup spoon. Sometimes the tines of the seafood fork rest in the bowl of the soup spoon and the handle is angled to the right, a placement easy for the diner to grasp. At an informal meal, the seafood fork is used as needed.

## Strawberry Fork

The strawberry fork is made with three long narrow tines and is approximately 4¾ to 5¾ inches long. In the late nineteenth century cultivated strawberries provided a new and flavorful version of the fruit, previously only available as wild strawberries.

The strawberry fork is used to pierce fresh strawberries and dip them into condiments, such as powdered sugar, brown sugar, whipped cream, and sour cream.

Because the fruit course is served with two utensils in formal dining, a fruit fork and a fruit knife, the strawberry fork is used only in informal dining.

## Snail Fork

*How ingenious an animal is the snail. When it encounters a bad neighbor, it takes up its house and moves away.*

PHILEMON, FRAGMENT, C. 300 B.C.

The snail fork is approximately 4½ inches in overall length, a small fork made with two long, pointed tines. In formal dining, snails are prepared without shells and served on a snail dish made with indentations to hold the buttery sauce and the meat is eaten with a snail fork. In informal dining, snails are usually served in shells. The diner steadies the shell with metal tongs or a napkin-covered hand, and extracts the meat with a snail fork held in the other hand.

## Oyster Fork

*Oysters are not good in a month that hath an "R" in it.*

JOHN RAY, ENGLISH PROVERBS, 1678

Lord Byron's nineteenth-century work *Don Juan,* which described oysters as an amatory food that heightens sexual stamina, created a mania for oyster forks. By the late nineteenth century, oysters were thought to elevate mental acuity. The oyster fork is a small utensil made with three short wide curved tines, approximately 4 inches in overall length. The left tine is extrawide to assist in cutting the membrane that connects the oyster to the shell. The oyster fork is used only in informal dining. The shell is steadied with the fingers of one hand and the utensil is held in the other hand to extract the meat. Oyster forks are not used in formal dining.

CHAPTER TWENTY

# SERVING UTENSILS

Serving utensils are made to cut, spear, scoop, grasp, spread, strain, and transfer food from plates, trays, platters, and bowls. In the Middle Ages, serving utensils were the possession of the servants, who, after use, wiped the implements clean at the table or washed them at a sideboard. Even so, diners dipped their personal spoons into communal serving bowls.

Serving utensils are placed on the table in the same way as eating utensils, on the right side of serveware (because the majority of people are right-handed). The handles face the diner. When a serving spoon and serving fork are presented together, the placement is the way they are used: the spoon is laid on the right ready to cut and lift and the fork on the left to steady and hold. The utensils are returned to the platter or serving bowl in the same position. When a serving spoon is presented on an underplate, after use the utensil is replaced in the bowl (ready for the next person to use). To protect the hand, the blade of a carving knife faces inward.

So many times serving utensils are passed down through a family and one is not sure how they are used, or an unusual shape catches the eye in an antique store but the purpose is unclear. For clarification, the serving utensils are presented in alphabetical order, and approximate sizes are given.

Asparagus server, berry spoon, bonbon spoon, butter knife, cake knives.

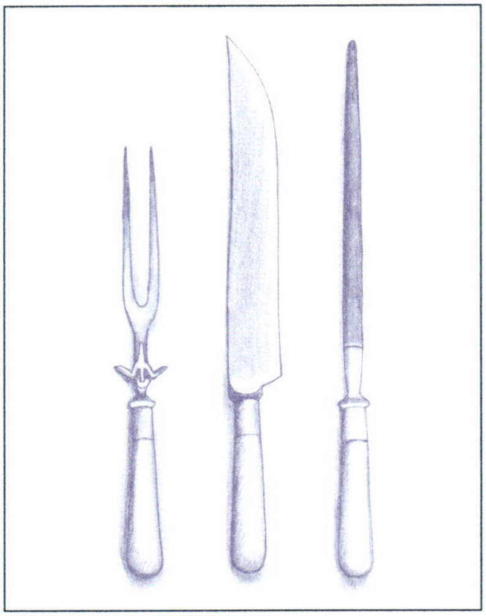

Carving fork and knife with steel.

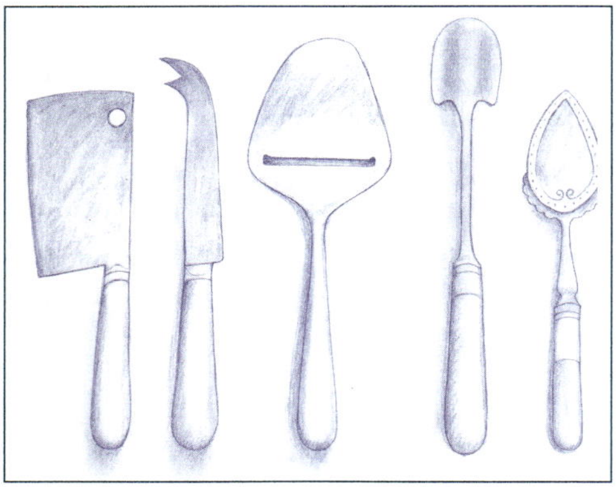

Cheese servers: cleaver, knife, plane, scoop, and triangular cheese knife.

Cold-meat fork, fish servers, flat server, jelly server.

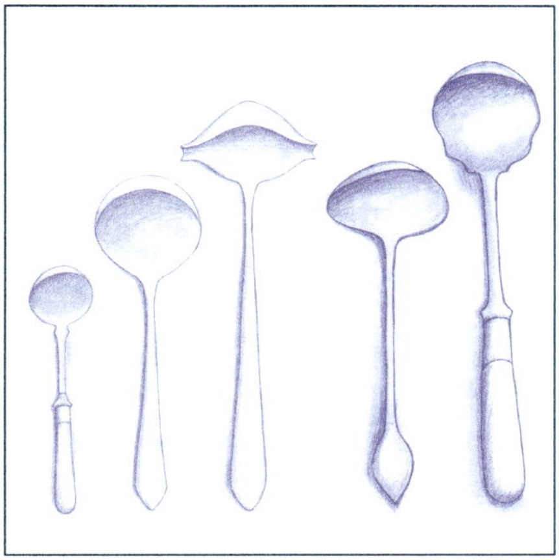

Ladles: small, medium, and large ladles, soup ladle, punch ladle.

Lemon fork, pasta fork, pastry server, pickle fork, serving fork and spoon, stuffing spoon.

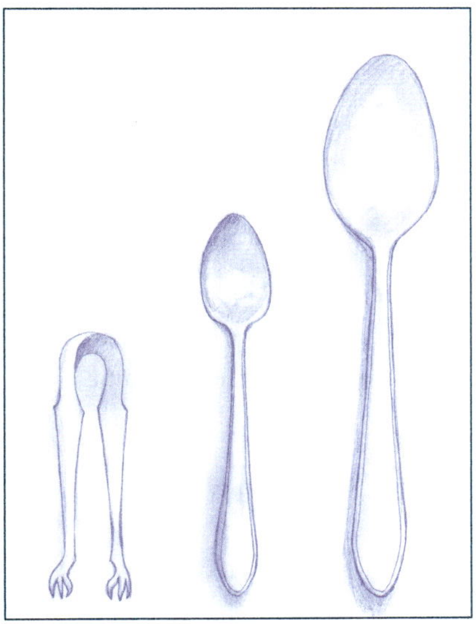

Sugar tong, sugar spoon, tablespoon.

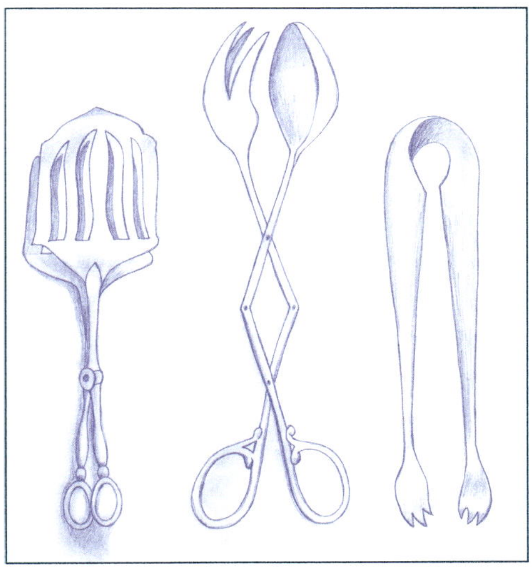

Tongs: flat-bladed tong, scissor tong, and inverted U-shaped tong.

## Asparagus Servers

Asparagus servers come in several forms: as a large fork with four or five wide tines (often stabilized with a connecting bar); as a tong to grip asparagus; and as a flat-bladed utensil with a rolled hood that prevents stalks of asparagus from slipping off the blade. The dimensions range from approximately 9 to 10 inches in length.

## Berry Spoon

The berry spoon is made with a wide shallow bowl in round or shell shapes. It is approximately 7½ to 9½ inches in overall length. The purpose of the berry spoon is to dish up fruit from a serving bowl, so it is also known as a *fruit spoon,* and easily recognized by an embossed fruit pattern on the bowl of the spoon (optional). To inhibit the corrosive effect of fruit acid on metal, the bowls of silver berry spoons are often gilded.

## Bonbon Spoon

The bonbon spoon, from the French word *bon,* "good," is a nineteenth-century term for a small spoon made to serve candy and nuts at a tea table. This utensil, which is also known as a *nut spoon* and a *confection spoon,* has a round shallow bowl that is solid or pierced and attached to a short handle. It is approximately 4½ to 6½ inches long.

## Butter Knife

Originally, butter was served in a chilled earthenware crock and extracted with a drill-shaped pick that was turned like a tool to pierce and withdraw butter from the pot. In the mid-eighteenth century the butter knife was introduced. It has a wide dull blade, a curved edge, and a pointed tip and is strong enough to cut through a hard mass of chilled butter. Today, butter is sold more often in rectangle form, and the butter knife is made with a dull blade to slice butter and a pointed tip to transfer cubes of butter to the plate. It is approximately 7 inches long.

## Cake Knife

The cake knife, which measures approximately 9½ to 14 inches in length, is made with a long blade that reduces the number of strokes required to cut food with a delicate texture, such as angel food cake. Some cake knives feature a serrated edge; in the nineteenth century they were known as *wedding cake knives*. Antique cake knives are wedge-shaped utensils that look like pastry servers; they are approximately 8¼ to 10½ inches long.

## Carving Set

The large two-pronged fork used in the medieval kitchen to lift meat from an open fire was the prototype for the two-prong dinner fork used at the table. By the seventeenth century, the carving fork featured three prongs, as did the dinner fork. And in the eighteenth century, the kitchen fork was made with four prongs, as were dinner forks.

In the Middle Ages, the transport of serveware to the table and the use of serving utensils was an honor accorded the children of the nobility as a way to learn courtly customs. Furthermore, domestic service provided the opportunity to advance politically and professionally, particularly in countries ruled by the law of primogeniture (from the Latin *primus*, "first," and *genitura*, "birth"), a law that prevented division of property by decreeing second-born sons could not inherit their father's estate. (Daughters did not inherit land at all.)

The carver (from the Greek *kerben* "to notch") was chosen as much for pleasant appearance and adept social skills as for his ability to wield a knife with precision. And because of his rank, the carver was the only person permitted to attend the table with an unsheathed knife. Amid great ceremony, the carver entered the hall at the head of a procession that included a taster, a cup bearer, a butler, and a panter (all of aristocratic lineage). With a napkin-covered hand, the carver cut slices of bread for his lord and used the tip of the knife to hand them to the taster for assay. Four trenchers were sliced horizontally, laid before the lord in a square (a form considered more elegant than a round shape). The edges were abutted, and to conceal the borders three smaller squares were placed on top. Hence the expressions "square meal" and "three squares a day."

The panter (from the French *pain,* "bread") carried four knives, the chaffer, parer, tranchor, and mensal. The *chaffer knife* was used to cut bread eaten with the meal, as opposed to bread used as trenchers. The *parer knife* was used to trim a round slice of bread into a square. The *tranchor knife* was used to cut cinders from crusts of bread and to spear uneaten portions of food and put them in a voyder for the poor. The *mensal knife* was used to slice the upper crust of bread, an honor accorded the lord of the manor, who sat at the high table. Hence the expression "upper crust" for a person of high rank.

Carving sets consist of a carving knife and a carving fork. Generally, a *carving fork* is made with a guard, a metal protrusion that extends from the shank, lifting the fork from the table and protecting the surface from soil. Carving forks made without guards are laid on rests, small items about 4 inches long fashioned in assorted shapes, for example, a miniature bar bell or a dog with a long back, such as a borzoi or a greyhound.

Carving sets are made in large and small sizes. The large *carving knife* features a blade approximately 11 to 15 inches long, a length that reduces the number of strokes required to carved thick cuts of meat, vegetables, and fruit, such as prime rib, pumpkin, and watermelon. To hold food securely, the large carving fork features two or three long, widely spaced tines. Often the large carving set is accompanied by a *steel,* a metal implement with an abrasive blade about 14 inches long; the steel is used to sharpen the carving knife. Generally, the carving knife is sharpened in the kitchen, but when a steel is brought to the table it is laid horizontally above the platter with the handle facing left (in a position ready for use).

The small carving set, also known as a *steak set,* is used to cut food of average thickness, such as chateaubriand. The knife is approximately 10¾ inches long, the fork about 9 inches long, and the steel is about 13 inches long.

# Cheese Servers

Cheese is made in assorted textures: soft, creamy, hard, brittle, smooth, firm, crumbly, coarse, and with holes. To accommodate the consistencies, cheese servers are made in numerous shapes as well.

The *cheese cleaver* is a miniature replica of a large meat cleaver. It is approximately 7 inches long and is used to slice hard cheese with a granular, brittle consistency, such as romano or parmesan cheese.

The *cheese knife* is made with a short curved blade that is often serrated and has two or three short tines extending from the tip. It measures 6 to 8 inches and is designed to cut firm cheese with a mealy texture, such as gouda or colby, and to lift sliced cheese to the plate. The cheese knife is a nineteenth-century accoutrement known originally as a *comb top* for its resemblance to a rooster's comb or head feathers.

The *cheese plane,* approximately 8 to 10 inches long, is made with a handle attached to a plane, a shape similar to a small carpenter's tool. The cheese plane is used to slice cheese with large or small holes, such as swiss cheese or gruyere, semisoft cheese, such as monterey jack, and cheese with a hard texture, such as cheddar cheese.

The *cheese scoop,* which is about 6 to 8 inches long, is made with a short curved blade attached to a long handle, a shape similar to a garden trowel. It is used to hold together a serving of crumbly semisoft cheese, such as stilton, or to extract firm cheese from a wax-covered ball, such as edam or gouda. Antique cheese scoops feature retractable pushers worked by the thumb, a shape that resembles an old-fashioned ice-cream scoop.

The *triangular cheese knife,* about 6 to 7 inches long, is made with a wedge-shaped blade, similar to a small putty knife. It is used to cut soft cheese with a creamy interior and an edible crust, such as brie and camembert.

# Cold-Meat Fork

The cold-meat fork measures approximately 8¾ to 9 inches in length. It is made to spear and lift food presented on a platter, such as lamb chops, waffles, or french toast.

# Fish Servers

Fish servers include both a fish knife and a fish fork. The *fish knife,* approximately 10½ to 12 inches long, has a long asymmetrical blade that curves to a pointed tip. The *fish fork* has three or four wide tines and is approximately 8 to 10 inches long.

Originally, the fish knife was called a *fish trowel,* a flat, triangular-bladed knife, sometimes pierced, used to serve fish and soft desserts. Later the fish trowel was called a *fish slice,* and then a *fish server.* In the late eighteenth century, the fish server featured a symmetrical blade decorated with chased and engraved ornamentation or a blade and handle sculpted in a fish design. By the early nineteenth century, the blade became scimitar-shaped and was often sold as a set with a matching four-tine fish fork.

# Flat Server

The flat server is a round or wedge-shaped utensil, some made with a shallow bowl. Its overall length is approximately 6 to 8 inches. The purpose of the flat server is to balance sliced food for transfer from platter to plate. Some flat servers are pierced to drain watery foods, a utensil also known as a *tomato server.* Years ago flat servers were made with tines on the left side to spear waffles or chops.

# Jelly Server

The jelly server, approximately 6 to 7 inches long, is a spoon-shaped utensil with a shallow bowl and pointed tip and a flat edge on one side. It is used to serve molded jelly, such as tomato aspic.

# Ladles

Ladles are serving spoons made with deep bowls in round, oval, or fluted shell shapes and various sizes.

The *small ladle* is used to serve a modest amount of sauce, such as a dollop of mustard or mayonnaise. It is approximately 4¾ to 5¾ inches long and more often found in older sets of silver. Many small antique sauce ladles feature a side spout to pour sauce.

The *medium ladle,* also known as a *cream sauce ladle,* is approximately 6½ to 7 inches long and has a wider bowl than a small ladle to accommodate a larger serving of sauce, such as hollandaise or bearnaise.

The *large ladle,* also known as a *gravy ladle,* about 7 to 7½ inches long, features a wider bowl than the medium ladle, a size that holds an ample serving of sauce or gravy.

The *extralarge ladle,* also known as a *soup ladle* and a *punch ladle,* is approximately 9 to 15⅛ inches long, a length that accommodates the depth of the average soup tureen or punch bowl. The bowl of the soup ladle is a little larger and deeper than the punch ladle bowl and holds approximately 4 ounces of soup. The punch ladle holds about 3 ounces, but the handle is longer than that of the soup ladle to accommodate the depth of the punch bowl.

# Lemon Fork

The lemon fork, approximately 4¼ inches long, is made with three narrow tines to serve sliced lemon. For easy release of the juice, the outer tines often splay outward.

## Pasta Fork

The pasta fork, also known as a *pasta server, pasta scoop,* and *fried oyster server,* is made with a deep oval bowl (often slotted), surrounded by large wide tines. It is approximately 11 inches long. In older sets of silver, pasta forks often feature a curved edge on one side and large wide tines on the other side.

## Pastry Server

The pastry server, also known as a *pie server* or a *cake server,* features a wide spadelike blade made to balance a serving of pastry, such as a piece of pie or cake. It is about 9 to 12½ inches long.

## Pickle Fork

Before the era of refrigeration in the nineteenth century, vegetables and fruits were preserved in jars. The pickle fork had two or three slender tines and a long narrow handle to reach deep into a pickle jar. The pickle fork is approximately 5½ to 8 inches in length.

## Serving Fork and Serving Spoon

In the Middle Ages bathing was a low priority, and historians suggest that the long-handled serving utensils distanced the servers from those whom they served. By the early eighteenth century, the culinary trend toward "made dishes" brought a need for specialized serving spoons to serve soup, stew, and ragout in a size larger than the tablespoon.

The serving fork and serving spoon measure approximately 9 to 10 inches and the utensils are used together or separately. As a set, the serving fork and serving spoon are used as tongs to serve food that requires two implements, such as a tossed salad or pasta. Individually, the serving fork is used to spear food from a platter, and the serving spoon to lift food from a bowl.

## Stuffing Spoon

In the eighteenth century, the stuffing spoon was called a *basting spoon* in England, and a *hash spoon* in Ireland and Scotland, but today it is known universally as a *buffet spoon, casserole spoon,* and *dressing spoon.* The original stuffing spoon resembled a tablespoon only larger, approximately 8 to 9 inches long. However, the modern stuffing spoon measures around 13 inches in length. The stuffing spoon is made with an extra-large bowl and a long handle to reach deep into the cavity of turkey or other fowl.

## Sugar Servers

In the seventeenth century it was said that sugar "nourishes the body, generates good blood, cherishes the spirit, makes people prolific, and strengthens children in the womb."

The original *sugar tong* was made circa 1780 to serve compressed sugar and today is used to grasp cubed sugar, a unit of measurement equal to a teaspoon of granulated sugar. Because cubes are a neater form of service than granulated sugar, tongs are used at formal and informal events. The sugar tong is made with an inverted U shape or with grippers. The inverted-U tong is made with a spring arch that after use is hung over the handle of the sugar bowl or laid by the side of the bowl. It varies in length from approximately 3¼ to 6½ inches. The sugar tong with grippers features various shapes, such as petite shells, fork tines, or tiny oval spoons, and it is shorter than sugar tongs with grooved grippers found in older sets of silver. Originally, the long sugar tong was known as a *sugar nip* or a *sugar cutter.* In the nineteenth century, compressed sugar was sold in the shape of a loaf or a cone. The shapes were nipped with a sugar cutter, and the pieces were placed in a sugar bowl. Because the cone resembled a witch's hat, it was called a *hat.* Hence the expression "I'll eat my hat."

The *sugar spoon* is used to serve granulated sugar, a consistency easy to adjust and faster to dissolve than cubed sugar. The spoon is used at informal meals where people spend less time at the table (although cubed sugar is also served). The sugar spoon, also known as a *sugar scoop* or a *sugar shell,* is approximately 5½ to 6½ inches long.

## Tablespoon

From the Middle Ages to the Renaissance, the tablespoon, a large spoon with a long handle and an oval tip, was the only spoon that appeared on the table and the only spoon used to *eat* food, such as soup, porridge, and pudding, hence the name *table-spoon.* Today the tablespoon, also known as a *vegetable spoon* and a *buffet spoon,* is used only to *serve* food. It is approximately 8½ to 9½ inches long. Tablespoons often are made with a pierced bowl in order to drain food.

## Tongs

*Tong* is from the Indo-European *denk,* meaning "to bite" or "those who bite together." It is a twin-armed implement made in various shapes and designed to grasp and lift portions of food.

The *flat-bladed tong,* about 5 to 10 inches long, is made with two wide blades to grip and serve food, such as small whole potatoes, rolls, pastries, and waffles. Many flat-bladed tongs feature grippers with slots to drain watery vegetables, such as asparagus.

The *scissor tong,* approximately 10 inches long, is a hinged utensil joined together at the handle, a shape similar to scissors. To grasp mixed salads or vegetables, the utensil is often made with a large spoon on one side and a fork on the other side.

The *inverted-U tong* features a sturdy spring arch. It is about 8 to 10 inches long and made with grippers in different forms, such as shells to serve pasta or claws to grasp ice cubes.

CHAPTER TWENTY-ONE

# HOW FLATWARE IS LAID ON THE TABLE

*Flatware:*
*Call it knife, fork, and spoon,*
*Separates earthly man,*
*From the one on the moon.*

*Suzanne von Drachenfels*

THE WAY flatware is placed on the table is based on common sense, comfort, convenience, and symmetrical alignment, a placement that invites diners to relax as opposed to the subtle tension created by a haphazard arrangement. The symmetrical alignment of flatware is easily done when the table is laid with an even number of place settings, but when an uneven number of people are seated, the odd-numbered place settings are laid opposite the middle of the even-numbered place settings.

The lower edges of the utensils are aligned with the bottom rim of the plate, about 1 inch up from the edge of the table. To avoid hiding a utensil under the rim of a plate or bowl, lay it approximately 1 inch away from the side. To eliminate fingerprints on the handle, hold flatware by the "waist," the area between the handle and the eating end of the utensil.

Flatware is laid on the table in the order of use, a placement that starts on the outside of the place setting and moves inward toward the plate. Flatware is never laid on the table according to size. Because the majority of people are right-handed, the knife and spoon are laid on the right side of the place setting and the fork on the left. The left-handed diner reverses the placement.

The *dinner knife* is laid to the right of the plate, with the blade facing the plate, a custom that dates to the Middle Ages when an inward-facing blade indicated good will, as opposed to an outward-facing blade ready for swift retaliation against the enemy.

FLATWARE IS LAID ON THE TABLE ACCORDING TO USE, STARTING ON THE OUTSIDE OF THE PLACE SETTING AND WORKING INWARD TOWARD THE PLATE. THE DINNER KNIFE IS LAID ON THE RIGHT SIDE OF THE PLATE, AND THE BLADE FACES THE PLATE. THE SOUPSPOON IS LAID ON THE RIGHT SIDE OF THE DINNER KNIFE. THE DINNER FORK IS LAID ON THE LEFT SIDE OF THE DINNER PLATE. WHEN SALAD IS SERVED BEFORE THE MAIN COURSE, THE SALAD FORK IS LAID TO THE LEFT OF THE DINNER FORK.

At an informal meal, when salad is served as a side dish with the main course, the dinner knife is used to cut both salad and the main course. But at a posh event, if salad is served after the main course to clear the palate for dessert, and the salad is composed of thick-veined greens, a salad fork is laid next to the dinner plate, and an extra dinner knife is laid to the left of the regular dinner knife. At a formal affair, when a knife is needed for the salad course, it is presented to the diner on a tray.

The *fish knife* and *fish fork* are placed on the table in the order of use. When fish is served as an appetizer course, the fish knife is laid to the right of the dinner knife and the fish fork to the left of the dinner fork. But if fish is served as the main course, the fish knife is placed to the right of the dinner plate and the fish fork is laid to the left of the plate.

The *dessert fork* and *dessert spoon* (or *dessert knife*), are placed differently at formal and informal affairs. At a formal event, the dessert fork is laid on the left side of

If salad is served after the main course, the salad fork is laid next to the dinner plate.

The fish fork and fish knife are laid on the table in the order in which the course is served. When fish is served as an appetizer course, the fish fork is laid to the left of the dinner fork and the fish knife is placed to the right of the dinner knife.

If fish is served as the main course, the fish fork and fish knife are laid to the left and right of the dinner plate, respectively.

the plate, and the dessert spoon (or knife) is placed on the right side of the plate. The diner lays the utensils on the table in respective order.

IN FORMAL DINING, TWO DESSERT UTENSILS ARE PRESENTED ON THE DESSERT PLATE. THE DESSERT FORK IS PLACED ON THE LEFT SIDE OF THE PLATE, AND THE DESSERT SPOON (OR DESSERT KNIFE) IS PLACED ON THE RIGHT SIDE OF THE PLATE.

TO CLEAR THE PLATE FOR DESSERT SERVICE, THE UTENSILS ARE REMOVED AND LAID ON THE TABLE ON THE LEFT AND RIGHT SIDES OF THE PLATE, RESPECTIVELY.

At an informal meal, when two utensils are provided for dessert, the utensils are laid on the table or presented on the dessert plate. The dessert spoon (or dessert knife) is laid on the table above the dinner plate in a horizontal position, handle facing right. The dessert fork is laid beneath the dessert spoon (or dessert knife), handle facing left. The dessert utensils may also be presented on the dessert plate in the same way as formal service.

The *fruit knife* and *fruit fork* are presented on the fruit plate in the same way as dessert utensils.

At an *informal* meal, the dessert fork and dessert spoon are laid on the table initially, or they are presented on the dessert plate. When the dessert utensils are laid on the table, they are placed above the cover in a horizontal position. The dessert spoon is laid above the dessert fork, handle facing right. The dessert fork is laid below the dessert spoon, handle facing left.

The *butter spreader* is laid on the bread-and-butter plate at formal luncheons and all informal meals but is not used at a formal dinner held in a private residence. For additional information, please refer to the bread-and-butter plate, in Chapter 6, "Plates: Piece by Piece."

At a formal luncheon or informal meal, the butter spreader is laid on the bread-and-butter plate in one of three positions: horizontal, vertical, or diagonal. In the horizontal placement, the butter spreader is laid across the top edge of the bread-and-butter plate, parallel with the edge of the table, an alignment that repeats the parallel arrangement of stemware. The vertical placement of the butter spreader echos the perpendicular alignment of flatware. The diagonal placement reiterates stemware aligned at an angle. Although the way the butter spreader is placed on the bread-and-butter plate is a matter of choice, the important point is keep the alignment the same for the entire table setting.

The *soup spoon* is placed on the right of the outside knife.

The *teaspoon, after-dinner coffee spoon,* and *demitasse spoon* are placed on the saucer behind the cup handle. The spoon handle faces the diner in a four o'clock position, ready for use. But when a teaspoon is used as an eating utensil, such as cereal at breakfast, it is laid on the right side of the place setting.

The *iced-beverage spoon* is laid on the table on the right side of the glass. But once used it is not returned to the table. Instead, the iced-beverage spoon is held in the glass while drinking.

The *seafood fork* is laid on the right side of the soup spoon. It is the only fork

THE BUTTER SPREADER IS LAID ON THE BREAD-AND-BUTTER PLATE IN A HORIZONTAL, VERTICAL, OR DIAGONAL POSITION. THE HORIZONTAL PLACEMENT IS HARMONIOUS WITH STEMWARE ARRANGED IN A LINE PARALLEL WITH EDGE OF THE TABLE.

THE VERTICAL ALIGNMENT ECHOES THE PERPENDICULAR PLACEMENT OF FLATWARE.

THE DIAGONAL PLACEMENT ACCENTS STEMWARE ARRANGED IN AN ANGLE.

When hot beverages are served with a meal, such as at breakfast, the teaspoon is laid on the saucer behind the cup handle in a four o'clock position, a placement easy to grasp.

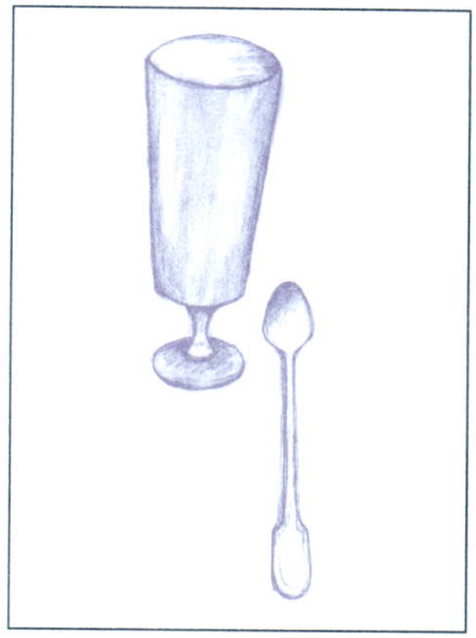

The ice-beverage spoon is laid on the table next to the ice-tea glass.

placed on the right side of the place setting. The fork tines are placed in the bowl of the soup spoon with the handle at a 45-degree angle. It may also be laid next to the soup spoon in a parallel position.

The *salad fork* is laid on the table in the order of progression. When salad is a first course, the salad fork is laid to the left of the dinner fork. If salad is served after the main course, the salad fork is placed to the right of the dinner fork.

The number of utensils laid on the table initially is determined by the number of courses. A place setting for a multicourse meal, notably a formal dinner, is crowded with flatware and stemware; to alleviate clutter, no more than three knives, three forks, and a soup spoon are laid on the table initially. For example, at a six-course meal with three appetizer courses, such as soup, fish, and pâté, plus a main course, salad, and dessert, three forks and knives are laid on the table initially, one for fish, another for pâté, and a third for the main course, plus a soup spoon. The seafood fork is laid on the right side of the cover, if appropriate. When salad is served, the salad fork is presented to the diner on a small tray. The dessert utensils are presented on the dessert plate.

The practice of limiting the number of utensils laid on the table is attributed to the eighteenth-century custom known as *the rule of three,* when the menu consisted of three courses each composed of twenty dishes or more. (On special occasions there

THE SEAFOOD FORK IS LAID ON THE TABLE TO THE RIGHT OF THE SOUP SPOON, AT AN ANGLE OR IN A PARALLEL POSITION. WHEN THE UTENSIL IS LAID AT AN ANGLE, THE FORK TINES REST IN THE BOWL OF THE SOUP SPOON.

IF THE SEAFOOD FORK IS LAID IN A PARALLEL POSITION, IT IS PLACED NEXT TO THE SOUP SPOON.

AT A FORMAL DINNER, A MULTI-COURSE MEAL IS SERVED, BUT TO RELIEVE CLUTTER, THE PLACE SETTING IS LAID WITH NO MORE THAN THREE KNIVES, THREE FORKS, AND A SOUP SPOON.

might be as many as one hundred dishes, although the guests ate only those dishes nearest to them.) To eliminate clutter, the utensils used after the main course were brought on the plates on which the courses were served, a custom that continues today at a multicourse meal.

At a simpler meal, such as a menu composed of soup, salad, main course, and dessert, the table setting is not cluttered and all the flatware is laid on the table at one time. At the host's option the dessert utensils may be brought to the table on the dessert plate. But regardless of the number of courses served and when the utensils are placed on the table, the cover is always laid with a knife and fork. The exception is when hearty soup is the main course and only a soup spoon is needed.

Fork tines may be placed downward, *continental style,* or upward, *American style.* In the continental placement of flatware, the fork is laid on the table in the way it is held, tines downward. In the *American style,* although the fork is used tines downward to cut food, it is held tines upward to eat, and the fork is laid on the table tines upward.

For *temporary placement* of the fork and knife in conversation, in continental style, the fork is laid on the side of the plate with the tines downward and the handle in the eight o'clock position. The knife handle is laid in the four o'clock position. If space permits, the tines are rested over the blade of the knife. In the American style, the knife is rested on the right rim of the plate with the handle in the four o'clock position, and the fork is laid near it, tines upward.

To prevent flatware from falling off when the plate is passed for a second help-

FORKS PLACED TINES DOWNWARD, CONTINENTAL STYLE.

Forks placed tines upward, American style.

Temporary placement of the fork and knife in conversation, continental style.

ing, the fork and knife are centered vertically in the six o'clock position toward the middle of the plate. The important point is to leave enough room to grasp the plate in passage and to provide ample space for the extra serving.

To signal the end of a meal, flatware is placed on one side of the plate diagonally. The utensils are laid parallel with the handles in the four o'clock position on the right rim of the plate. The tips rest in the well of the plate in the ten o'clock position, a placement that secures the utensils when the plate is cleared and leaves enough space for the clearer to get a good grasp. To avoid cuts to the hand, the blade faces inward. Although one sees finished utensils laid in a horizontal placement on

TEMPORARY PLACEMENT OF THE FORK AND KNIFE IN CONVERSATION, AMERICAN STYLE.

When the plate is passed for a second helping, to secure the balance of the utensils, the knife and fork are centered toward the middle of the plate in a vertical position, a placement that allows room for a good grasp, and provides space for the additional serving.

To indicate one is finished eating, flatware is laid on the plate in a diagonal position. The handles of the utensils rest on the right rim of the plate and the tips lay in the well of the plate, a position that allows room for a good grasp when the plate is cleared and secures the steadiness of the utensils.

The soup spoon should be laid in the soup bowl prior to clearing if the underplate is too small to hold it securely.

the top rim of the plate or vertically on the right rim, the positions are less secure than diagonally and leave little room for a good grasp.

When a soup bowl is presented on an underplate, such as a dinner plate, the soup spoon is laid on the underplate when the course is finished. But if the underplate is too small to balance the spoon, the spoon is laid in the bowl.

CHAPTER TWENTY-TWO

# THE WAY TO USE FLATWARE

THE WAY A UTENSIL is shaped determines how it is used. Form follows function. Knife blades are made to cut and push food. Fork tines spear and lift morsels. Spoons are used to stir, sip, and sup. But regardless of shape, once a utensil is used, it is not laid again on the table. Rather, a soiled utensil is laid on the plate or bowl it is provided to accompany. Furthermore, an implement is never rested angled half on a plate and half on the table.

The description of how to use flatware that follows is for the right-handed diner; it is reversed by the left-handed person.

## The Dinner Knife and Dinner Fork

The dinner knife and fork are held continental style at all meals, formal and informal. In the continental style, the fork is held in the left hand, tines downward, a custom that evolved in the seventeenth century when European aristocrats accepted the fork as a utensil to eat meat. Prior to the seventeenth century, the fork was considered foppish, and nobility and commoners alike ate with the fingers. The kitchen fork was the only fork used, a large utensil held in the left hand tines downward to hold a slab of meat that was being carved.

When the dinner fork was accepted by the aristocracy, the kitchen method prevailed at the table. The fork was held in the left hand, tines downward to eat. The

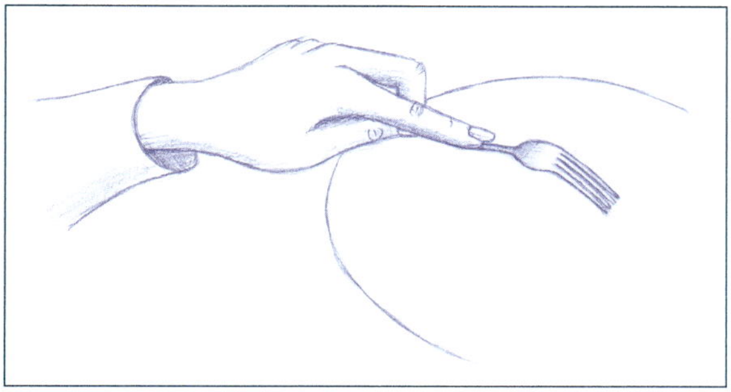

In the continental style, the fork is held in the left hand, tines downward.

knife was held in the right hand to cut meat and push morsels against the back of the fork. But in the eighteenth century the custom changed. After food was cut with the knife, the utensil was laid on the right rim of the plate. The fork was transferred to the right hand and the tines were turned upward to eat. By the mid-nineteenth century, the upper class ceased to transfer the fork from one hand to the other, particu-

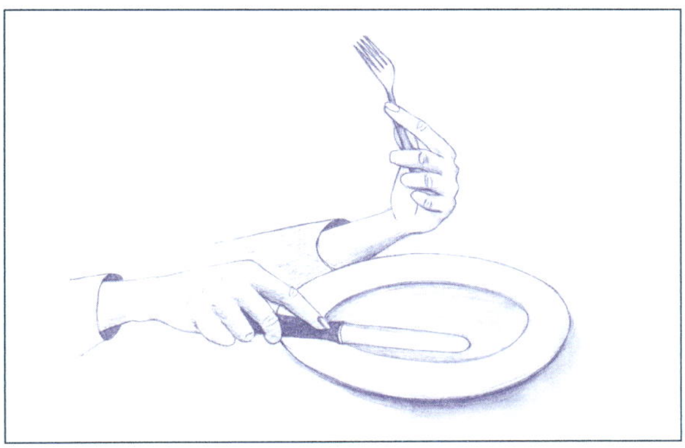

The continental style eliminates the zigzag transfer of a utensil from one hand to the other and creates a smooth ambience at all meals, particularly at a multicourse formal affair. The fork is held in the left hand, tines downward, and the knife is held in the right hand, low to the plate. Left-handed diners reverse the procedure.

At informal meals, the dinner fork may be held tines upward, American style.

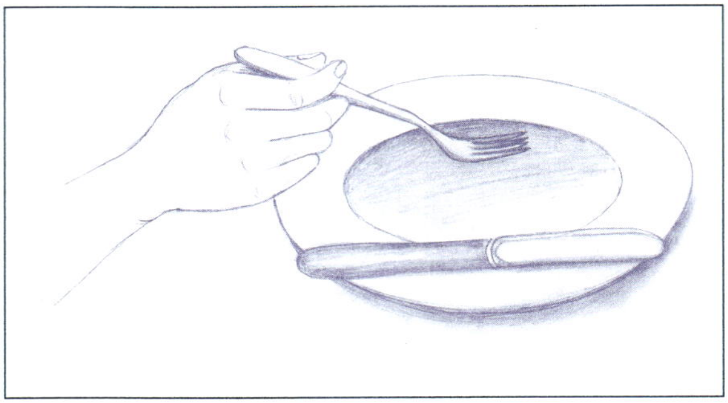

larly after Charles Day declared the method "vulgar" in *Etiquette and the Usages of Society.* Today, the continental style prevails at all meals, formal and informal, because it is a natural, nondisruptive way to eat.

The index finger extends along the top of the blade. To assist the fork, the knife is held low to the plate, an inch or two above. The fork tines are pointed downward to spear and convey food to the mouth. When the knife is not needed, for example, to eat omelette, it remains on the table and the fork is held in the right hand, tines upward.

At informal meals the dinner fork may be held tines upward, American style. This style of eating evolved in the eighteenth century from the continental method. Although many of the colonists ate from the blade of a knife, those who emulated the aristocracy rested the knife on the right rim of the plate, transferred the fork to the right hand, and twisted it tines upward to eat.

But in the nineteenth century, the European deportment of utensils changed, and among the nobility it was fashionable to use the dinner knife as little as possible. The fork was held in the right hand tines upward to eat, a style adopted in France by the bourgeoisie and transported across the waters by those who came to North America.

However, when European nobility adopted the custom of holding the fork in the left hand tines downward to eat, Americans continued to hold the fork in the right hand tines upward, a style that affords deft manipulation of the fork in the hand over which the majority of people have control. The American style also takes longer to manipulate and slows the rate of consumption.

In the early twentieth century, Emily Post, the doyenne of etiquette, labeled the transfer of fork from one hand to the other "zigzag eating," a style disruptive to a formal, multicourse meal. Today, American style is used when a few courses are served and the continual transfer of the fork does not disrupt the meal. But when all is said and done, it is simply easier and more natural to eat continental style.

In the American style, the fork is held like a pencil, and never as if to stab food. The shank extends between the thumb and the second and third fingers. The fourth and fifth fingers rest in the hand. For leverage, the index finger is extended along the back of the fork, as far from the tines as possible. The knife is held with the handle cupped in the palm of the hand, along with the third, fourth, and fifth fingers.

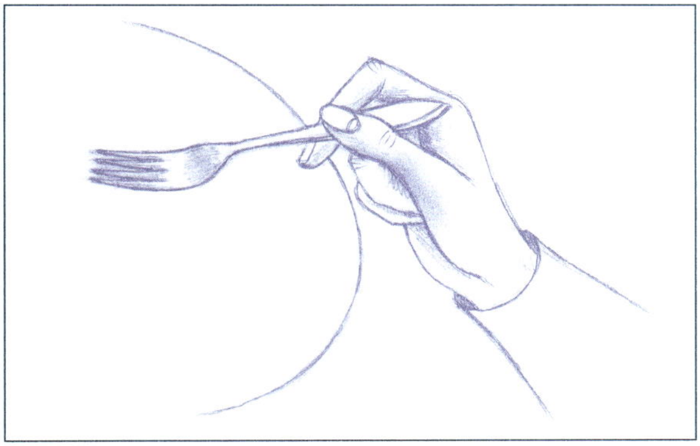

In the American style, the fork is held like a pencil, and never as if to stab food.

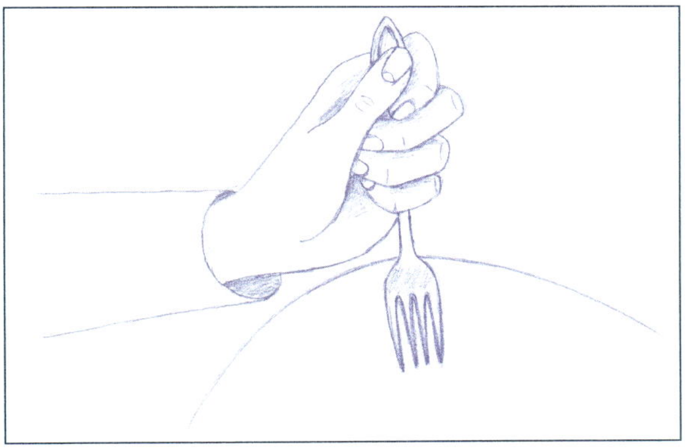

The second finger is placed on the back of the blade. The thumb is held against the side of the handle.

THE KNIFE IS HELD WITH THE HANDLE CUPPED IN THE PALM OF THE HAND, ALONG WITH THE THIRD, FOURTH, AND FIFTH FINGERS. THE SECOND FINGER IS PLACED ON THE BACK OF THE BLADE. THE THUMB IS HELD AGAINST THE SIDE OF THE HANDLE.

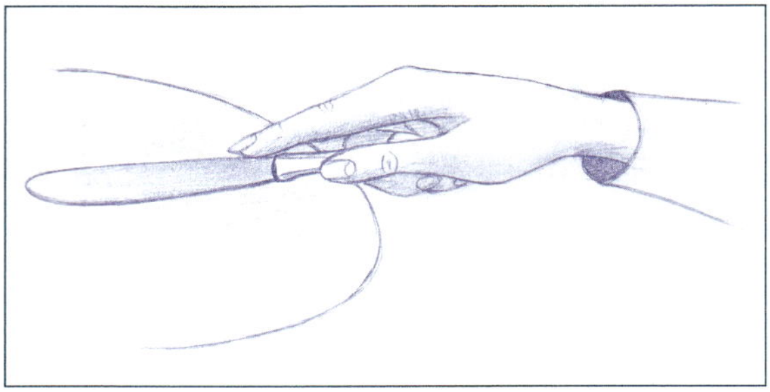

## Soup Spoons

The soup spoon is made with oval or round bowls to accommodate the consistency of soup. The oval soup spoon features an oval bowl, a shape used to eat soup made with particles of food from the semipointed tip. The round soup spoon, such as the cream soup spoon or bouillon spoon, features a bowl with a curved edge, a form used to sip pureed or clear soup from the side of the spoon.

To avoid spills, the soup spoon is filled no more than two-thirds full. But to capture a last spoonful or two, the soup spoon is dipped toward the back of the bowl. To quote an old nursery rhyme:

*Like tiny ships cast out to sea,*
*I dip the spoon away from me.*

# The Use of Two Utensils

Because food is easier to manipulate with two utensils than with one, in formal dining two utensils are presented for the appetizer course, main course, salad course, dessert course, and fruit course.

At an informal meal, one or two utensils are used, whichever is more comfortable. However, the reader will find that two utensils provide greater dining ease than one and may prefer the method.

## *Fish Knife and Fish Fork*

The fish knife is used to separate the soft flesh of the fish from the body rather than to cut a bite. Since leverage is not required to separate fish, the handle of the fish knife is held in the right hand toward the end of the shank, between the thumb and the first two fingers, a position different than the way a dinner knife is held. The tip of the blade is used to fillet fish, lift the skeleton from the body, and ferret out small bones. The fish fork is held in the left hand and used in the traditional way.

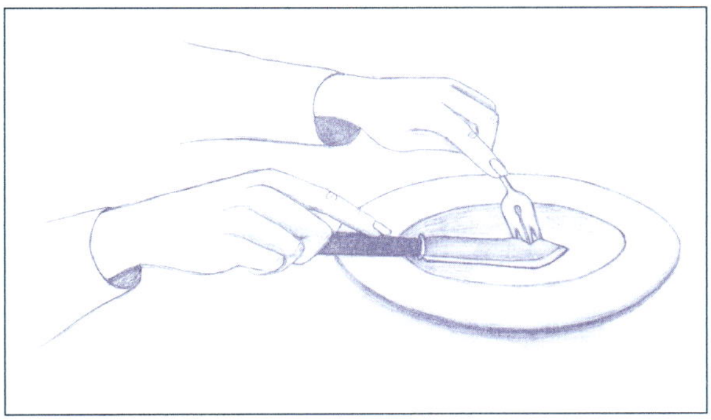

BECAUSE THE FLESH OF FISH IS SOFT, THE TISSUE IS *SEPARATED* INTO BITE-SIZE PIECES, RATHER THAN CUT. LEVERAGE IS UNNECESSARY AND THE FISH KNIFE IS HELD ABOVE THE CUFF OF THE HANDLE.

## *Dessert Fork and Dessert Spoon*

To steady the portion, the dessert fork is held in the left hand, tines downward. The dessert spoon is held in the right hand to cut and convey a bite to the mouth.

### *Fruit Fork and Fruit Knife*

At a formal affair, the fruit fork and fruit knife are presented on a fruit plate with a finger bowl. A piece of fresh fruit is held in the left hand, and the fruit knife is held in the right hand to peel and section. The fruit is steadied on the plate with the fork in the left hand. The fruit knife is held in the right hand to cut a bite, taken from the plate with the fork. Fingertips are rinsed in the finger bowl.

At an informal meal, fresh fruit is cut and sectioned usually with a salad or dessert fork and a dinner knife. A finger bowl is not presented.

## The Iced-Beverage Spoon

Because a soiled utensil is not laid on the table after it is used, while drinking an iced beverage, the user holds the spoon in the glass against the rim with the index finger (where it remains until the glass is cleared from the table).

CHAPTER TWENTY-THREE

# THE INTERCHANGE OF FLATWARE AND SERVING UTENSILS

*Proportion and balance:*
*The equilibrium of life,*
*Displace the angst*
*Of fork, spoon or knife.*

SUZANNE VON DRACHENFELS

THE INTERCHANGE of flatware and serving utensils is based on proportion and balance. In the United States a teaspoon is presented with a coffee cup because the proportion is the right length to balance in a cup and on a saucer. In France, coffee is served in a smaller cup, and a shorter spoon in presented, a length similar to an after-dinner coffee spoon. But when the perfect utensil for a particular course is unavailable, substitutions are made, based on proportion and balance.

The following substitutions are given for place-size utensils, a length that balances the informal place setting, from elegant to everyday.

# Knives

The interchange of knives is based on the shape of the utensils and the sharpness of the blades. Knives with dull blades are manufactured to cut food made with soft textures, such as aspic, butter, jelly, and cheese. Knives with rounded tips are made to spread foods such as soft cheese, preserves, and dips. Knives with pointed tips are used to spear food, such as butter cubes and slices of cheese, to cut meat and poultry, and to separate fish.

## *Long Knives*

The luncheon knife, dinner knife, and steak knife are approximately 8½ to 9 inches in length, sizes that are in proportion with large plates, namely the luncheon plate, dinner plate, and service plate. The dinner knife can also be used as a knife for salad and fish. The steak knife substitutes as a small carving knife.

## *Medium-Size Knives*

The dessert knife and fish knife are about 7 to 8 inches long, dimensions right for medium-size plates such as the salad plate, dessert plate, fish plate, and entrée plate. The dessert knife can be used as a salad knife, and the fish knife can be used to slice a molded hors d'oeuvre such as pâté.

## *Small Knives*

The fruit knife and butter spreader are approximately 6 to 7½ inches in length, proportions that balance small plates such as the fruit plate and bread-and-butter plate. The fruit knife interchanges as a salad knife to cut firm dessert and slice hard cheese. The butter spreader is used to apply preserves, cheese, dips, caviar, smoked fish, and condiments.

# Forks

### *Long Forks*

The dinner fork and luncheon fork are approximately 7 to 8 inches long, lengths in balance with large plates, such as the luncheon plate, dinner plate, and service plate (when the latter is used as a dinner plate). Long forks substitute as fish forks, to eat salad as a main course, and as dessert forks. When two utensils are presented with dessert, as a substitute for dessert utensils, the dinner fork is paired with a tablespoon.

### *Medium-Size Forks*

The lobster fork and salad fork are approximately 6 to 6½ inches long, proportions in balance with medium-size plates such as a fish plate, a salad plate, and a dessert plate. The lobster fork is used to spear condiments packaged in deep jars, such as olives, pickles, and cocktail onions. The salad fork substitutes as a fish fork, a dessert fork, a fruit fork, and to spear cold meat, sliced vegetables, and fruit.

### *Small Forks*

The seafood fork, ice-cream fork, pastry fork, strawberry fork, snail fork, and oyster fork are approximately 4 to 5½ inches long, lengths in balance with small plates, such as a bread-and-butter plate and a canape plate. Small forks can be used to eat shellfish and to spear pickles, olives, cheese cubes, lemon slices, fruit sticks, and sliced butter.

# Spoons

The spoon ranges in size from approximately 4 to 10 inches and is made in long, medium, and small lengths.

### *Long Spoons*

The iced-beverage spoon, teaspoon, dessert spoon, and oval soup spoon are approximately 8 to 10 inches long. The iced-beverage spoon is ideal to eat parfait or a milkshake, to use as a mixer for drinks, and to reach into tall, narrow jars. The teaspoon can be used to sip soup, eat dessert, cut fruit, and as a utensil to serve relishes. The dessert spoon and oval soup spoon are used to eat cereal and ladle sauce and as serving spoons.

### *Medium-Size Spoons*

The cream soup spoon, citrus spoon, five o'clock spoon, and after-dinner coffee spoon are approximately 5 to 6 inches long, dimensions that balance bowls and cups made with shallow or medium depths. The round cream soup spoon is used to serve sauce and fruit cocktail. The citrus spoon with serrated edge substitutes as a cheese scoop, and those with a plain edge are used to eat fruit tart. The five o'clock spoon interchanges as a teaspoon to eat ice cream and puddings. The after-dinner coffee spoon substitutes as a sugar spoon, to serve condiments from small bowls, and as a "junior" spoon to feed babies.

### *Small Spoons*

The chocolate spoon and demitasse spoon measure around 3¾ to 4½ inches long, sizes that can be used as utensils to serve condiments from tiny bowls, such as mustard, horseradish, shaved chocolate, and cinnamon.

## Serving Utensils

Serving utensils are made in shallow, deep, pierced, or flat shapes. Serving spoons with shallow bowls can be used interchangeably to serve food with little or no liquid, such as string beans presented on a platter or in a flat-bottomed bowl. Serving spoons with deep bowls are used as substitute utensils to serve tiny vegetables and grains, such as peas and rice; soft food, such as mashed potatoes; liquid foods, such as soup; and beverages, such as punch. Pierced serving utensils can be used to serve foods that contain excessive fluid, such as tomatoes and asparagus. Flat serving utensils are used to serve foods with little or no liquid, such as sandwiches, sliced meat, cheese, vegetables, and fruit.

### *Long Serving Utensils*

- The large berry spoon, serving spoon, and tablespoon are approximately 9 to 15 inches and can all be used to serve vegetables, rice, pasta, fruit, pudding, dressing, and casseroles.
- The large serving spoon pairs with the large fork to serve salad.
- The soup ladle and punch ladle are interchangeable utensils, although the bowl of each serves a slightly different quantity. The average soup ladle holds approximately 4 fluid ounces. The punch ladle accommodates about 3 ounces of liquid.
- The cake knife and steak knife feature long narrow blades and can be used to cut food with a thick density, such as crusty bread, sizable winter vegetables, and molded desserts.
- The fish knife and pastry server are wide-bladed utensils used to serve crepes, casserole dishes, frozen desserts, aspic, quiche, open-face sandwiches, pizza, fish, pancakes, and waffles.
- The large fish fork, when paired with the large tablespoon, is used as a salad server.
- Long-handled tongs are used to grip crudités, asparagus, small whole potatoes, sliced fresh fruit, sliced cheese, cheese cubes, chicken wings, sausage, and small desserts, such as petits fours or bite-size tarts.
- The carving fork substitutes as a utensil to spear foods from a platter, such as cold meats, chops, waffles, sliced vegetables, fruit, and cheese.
- The pasta fork is used to serve soufflé and quiche.

### *Medium-Size Serving Utensils*

The length of medium-size serving utensils is from approximately 8½ to 7 inches.

- The berry spoon and jelly spoon are used to serve vegetables, ice cream, soufflé, and dips.

- The cream sauce ladle and gravy ladle are both used to serve sour cream, whipped cream, salad dressing, and dessert toppings.
- The cold-meat fork is used to spear sliced tomatoes, fruit, and casserole dishes.
- The butter knife substitutes as a utensil to cut soft cheese, pâté, and molded jelly.
- The flat tomato server and triangular cheese knives serve molded dishes, such as hors d'oeuvres, salad, aspic, pastries, quiche, eggs, and food arranged on a platter.

### *Small Serving Utensils*

The length of small serving utensils varies from approximately 6 to 2½ inches.

- The bonbon spoon, sugar spoon, and small ladle can all be used to serve croutons, oyster crackers, sauce, condiments, preserves, chutney, relishes, and grated cheese.
- The lemon fork and pickle fork substitute as utensils to serve sliced cucumbers, olives, butter cubes, pickled vegetables, smoked fish, and cheese cubes and to spear sliced fruit, melon balls, or butter pats.
- The cheese knife, jelly knife, and small flat server are used to serve molded hors d'oeuvres, pâté, aspic, and pastries.
- Sugar tongs are used to grip small pieces of candy, string beans, sliced cucumbers, and celery sticks.
- The salt spoon is used to sprinkle shaved chocolate or ground cinnamon over hot beverages, such as after-dinner coffee and espresso.

CHAPTER TWENTY-FOUR

# HOW TO PURCHASE FLATWARE

DINING IS ALL things to all people, from a picnic on the beach using plastic flatware, to a patio party with stainless steel or pewter utensils, to an elegant table laid with sterling silver, silver plate, gold electroplate, or vermeil. To make the right choice, one that long enhances the pleasures of dining, consider the following.

## Choose Your Flatware First

Metal flatware is the hardest and most durable item on the table. Rarely does it undergo severe damage, seldom is it replaced, and for the first-time buyer of tableware, flatware is the place to start. The worst thing that can happen to a set of flatware is the accidental loss of a piece or two.

## Type of Metal

Those who plan to entertain with somewhat formal overtones will want an elegant, luxurious metal, such as sterling silver, silver plate, or gold electroplate. But working couples and busy mothers have little time to entertain and need an easy-care metal that is dishwasher-safe, namely, stainless steel. Although pewter is appropriate for informal table settings, the metal is soft, dents easily, and is suggested only for occasional use, such as to impart a rustic overtone to a French country-table setting.

## Number of Sets of Flatware

When one set of flatware must meet all dining needs, the best choice is stainless steel in a simple pattern that blends with any table decor, from casual to sophisticated and traditional to contemporary. Stainless steel is appropriate for all but the most elegant formal dining.

For those who plan to entertain both elegantly and casually, two sets of flatware are ideal: a precious metal like sterling silver, silver plate, or gold electroplate for posh affairs and low-maintenance stainless steel for daily dining.

## Design Elements

To coordinate the table setting into a harmonious whole, it is important that the ornamentation of the flatware, the color of the metal, and the texture of the material is compatible with the design elements of the dinnerware and stemware. The ornamentation of tableware is curvaceous, straight, or a combination. Flatware decorated with curved lines is harmonious with dinnerware and stemware ornamented with rounded motifs. Flatware decorated with straight lines is compatible with dinnerware and stemware ornamented with angular motifs. But when both curved and straight lines are incorporated in a pattern, choose a dinnerware and stemware pattern that accents the dominant line in the flatware. For balance, keep the ratio between curved and angular designs two-to-one. Accent ornate flatware with plain dinnerware and stemware patterns. Emphasize a simple flatware pattern with ornate dinnerware and stemware.

The color of metals gives the table setting different looks. Precious metals, from the grayish-white hue of sterling silver, to the whitish-gray tone of silver plate, to the yellowish shade of vermeil and gold electroplate, impart a formal luxuriant look to the table setting. Alloyed metals like stainless steel and pewter are a deeper shade of gray and imbue the table setting with an informal ambience.

The texture of metals ranges from smooth to coarse to shiny or dull. To avoid a profusion of textures at a cluttered table setting where a multiplicity of courses are served, match the texture of the flatware with the grain of the dinnerware and stemware. The texture of precious metals, such as sterling silver or vermeil, is smooth and shiny or lustrous, a finish harmonious with translucent porcelain, tightly woven linens, and shimmering crystal. Although plated metals, such as silver plate and gold electroplate, are smooth and shiny, because they are plated over a base metal they do not impart quite the luxurious ambience of sterling silver or vermeil and are appropriate for all but the most formal occasions. And compared to precious or plated metals, alloyed metals, namely stainless steel and pewter, have a coarse texture, a surface compatible with opaque dinnerware, heavy glassware, and loosely woven linens.

When metals with shiny and matte finishes are mixed, match the predominant texture to the surface of the table. Flatware with a shiny finish is harmonious with reflective table tops, such as glass, lacquer, plastic, or polished mahogany. Flatware with a matte surface, such as hammered metal or cross-hatched florentine, is compatible with the patterned grain of dull woods, such as pine or bleached oak.

## Mixing and Matching Flatware

Matching flatware is the foundation of the table setting, but a mix of patterns adds beauty and interest to the presentation of each course. At a formal table set with a profusion of tableware, a matched set of flatware does not detract from the overall beauty of the setting and is recommended. At an informal table, set for no more than four courses, a mix of flatware patterns adds design to the simple table setting and is fun, but keep the mix of metals the same.

## Size

Flatware is made in sizes known as *continental, place,* and *luncheon*.

Continental flatware is the longest length, also known as *European size.* The dinner knife and dinner fork are approximately a half-inch longer than place size and about an inch longer than luncheon size. Although continental flatware balances the proportions of a formal table laid with three or more centerpieces, candelabra, service plates, multiple flatware, stemware, place cards, and menu cards, it is used also at informal table settings. And because of the length, continental size is slightly thicker and heavier than place size and luncheon size. The utensils rest heavier in the hand and promote a luxuriant feel.

Place-size flatware, also known as *American size,* originated after World War II, when most households no longer needed, wanted, or could afford two sets of flatware: a shorter set for breakfast and luncheon and a longer length for dinner. Because of the shorter length, place size flatware is lighter to hold, easier to manipulate, and balances well with a table setting laid to serve the average meal. Of the three lengths, place size is the most popular. When purchased as a set, it is packaged often with a place spoon, a medium-size utensil with a bowl slightly larger than a teaspoon but smaller than a tablespoon, an all-purpose utensil used to eat soup, cereal, and dessert.

Luncheon-size flatware is the shortest length, a size that balances the dimensions of the luncheon plate. It dates from nineteenth and early twentieth centuries when luncheons were a common form of home entertainment. Luncheon-size flatware is often found in older sets. Today most women work outside the home and when luncheons are given they are usually held in restaurants or clubs. But when a luncheon is hosted in the home, in the absence of luncheon-size flatware, place or continental size are used.

## Criteria for Quality Flatware

Well-made flatware is recognized by substantial weight and good balance. Lightweight flatware lacks balance; the knife and fork feel clumsy to hold and uncomfortable, almost as if they might bend.

Quality craftsmanship is recognized by precisely rendered ornamentation with depth and clarity. Both sides of the utensils are attractive. Fork tines are symmetrical, the edges are rounded, perfectly tapered, and polished on all sides. The handles are not so narrow that they will slip through the utensil basket of a dishwasher, and when held, the handle does not press uncomfortably into the palm, especially the knife. The knife blade is broad and possesses a good cutting edge, and where it joins the handle it does not reveal an apparent gap of color. The spoon is deep enough to accommodate a good bite.

## The Number of Pieces in a Place Setting

The term *place setting* is the number of utensils needed to eat a simple meal. The minimum number is three: dinner knife, dinner fork, and teaspoon. A four-piece place setting includes a salad fork, a utensil popular for informal dining because it doubles as a dessert utensil. A five-piece place setting adds a soup spoon, a utensil used to eat cereal and at a multicourse meal that begins with hot soup. A six-piece place setting features a butter spreader, a utensil used by those who prefer to provide a bread-and-butter plate rather than pass prebuttered rolls; this implement also doubles as a spreader for cheese or condiments. A seven-piece place setting includes an iced-beverage spoon, a utensil popular in regions noted for hot, humid climates, or a seafood cocktail fork, an implement sought after by those who live near the water where seafood is a favorite appetizer.

## The Number of Place Settings to Purchase

The way one plans to entertain and the size of one's family (present and future) determines the number of place settings to purchase. Four to eight place settings offer a bride or a working couple several days' use, but the average family may need eight place settings per day. Those who entertain often may want twelve to sixteen place settings.

Flatware sold in the flatware department of retail and specialty stores is sold by the place setting. Flatware sold in the houseware sections is sold in packaged sets.

Rather than buy utensils by the individual piece (as open stock) or one place setting at a time, purchase flatware by the set and save approximately 30 percent. Catalogs sell five-piece place settings in sets of four, eight, twelve, and sixteen, at prices lower than retail stores.

## Matching Serving Utensils

A set of matching serving utensils is purchased as part of a set of flatware, acquired individually at extra cost, or bought as a "hostess set."

Matching serving utensils found in a flatware set include:

- In a 43-piece service for eight, three serving utensils: tablespoon, sugar spoon, and gravy ladle
- In a 44-piece service for eight, four serving utensils: tablespoon, sugar spoon, gravy ladle, and cold-meat fork
- In a 45-piece service for eight, five serving utensils: two serving spoons, (solid and pierced), serving fork, meat fork, and butter spreader
- In a 64-piece service for twelve, four serving utensils: tablespoon, sugar spoon, gravy ladle, and a cold-meat fork
- In a 66-piece service for twelve, six serving utensils: two serving spoons (solid and pierced), cold-meat fork, pie server, sugar shell, and a butter knife
- In a 90-piece service for sixteen, two hostess sets: two serving spoons, two cold-meat forks, two pie servers, two sugar shells, and two butter knives
- In a 101-piece service for twelve that includes twelve extra teaspoons, twelve iced-beverage spoons, and twelve cocktail forks, five serving utensils: serving spoon, butter knife, sugar spoon, serving fork, and pie server

When matching serving utensils are purchased as a hostess set, a four-piece set typically contains a tablespoon, sugar spoon, gravy ladle, and cold-meat fork; a six-piece set usually contains a pie server, pierced tablespoon, solid tablespoon, cold-meat fork, butter spreader, and sugar spoon.

## How to Supplement a Discontinued Pattern

Rather than purchase a trendy pattern with a short production run, avoid discontinuance and choose a timeless pattern produced almost indefinitely.

Sterling patterns are seldom discontinued, but when demand for a particular pattern ceases, the manufacturer keeps the dies and fills special orders when requests justify the expense of production or periodically makes old silver patterns available. Flatware made of silver plate is often almost an exact copy of sterling silver, so when a replacement is unavailable, purchase the missing piece in sterling. Stainless steel is sold primarily by the set, and when a flatware pattern is discontinued, generally replacements are not available.

## The Shape of Knife Blades

When matching a new set of flatware to an old pattern, make sure the shapes of the blades are similar. Knife blades are made in shapes known as *French style* and *place style.* French-style blades feature a curvaceous edge and a rounded, blunt tip, a style of blade made in the late nineteenth century. Place blades are made with a straight or modestly curved edge and a somewhat pointed tip, a style produced in the early twentieth century.

## Sterling Silver or Silver Plate?

A good buy is judged by several criteria: weight, balance, comfort in the hand, manufacture (handmade or hand-finished versus machine-made), and quality craftsmanship. Although sterling silver is a precious metal alloyed with copper for strength, and silver plate is pure silver plated over an alloyed base, if the prices are similar and if the weight of silver plate is heavy, the balance is good, the utensil is comfortable to hold, and the workmanship is excellent, silver plate is a better buy than mass-produced, lightweight sterling silver that is wobbly in the hand and poorly finished.

## Why Costs Vary

The amount of silver used to make a pattern and the labor and time required to execute a particular design figure in the cost of the finished product. The ornamentation of silver essentially involves three techniques: the indentation of silver, the removal of silver, or the application of silver, methods known respectively as *chased, engraved,* or *applied ornamentation*. Chased ornamentation is indented or pushed out, and does not involve a loss of silver, an ornamental technique that is *less expensive* to execute than engraved or applied decoration. Engraved ornamentation cuts into metal and involves a loss of silver, so it is *more expensive* than chased decoration. Applied ornamentation is the application of decoration to metal, such as mold-made ornamentation, cut-card work, or enamel, methods that require additional metal or material and are the *most expensive* patterns to execute.

## Monogrammed Flatware

The placement of the monogram on the handle depends on the way the fork is held. In continental style, the monogram is placed on the back of the handle because the fork is held tines downward to eat and the utensil is laid on the table in the same way. In American style, the monogram is placed on the front of the handle because the fork is held tines upward to eat and the utensil is laid face upward on the table. The exception is a highly ornate pattern that leaves little room on the front for a monogram; the letters are therefore placed on the back of the utensils.

To unify the monogram with the pattern, make sure the lines of each are similar. Angular monograms are harmonious with decoration rendered with straight lines. Flowing script coordinates with utensils ornamented with rounded decoration. The most common monogram is a single letter. When three initials are used, make sure they do not spell a word that detracts from the dignity of the pattern, such as B-A-D. If so, execute the monogram in a single letter.

CHAPTER TWENTY-FIVE

# THE CARE OF FLATWARE

ANYTHING WORTH HAVING is worth taking care of. But when it comes to flatware, some metals require more care than others. Sterling silver and silver plate tarnish, whereas vermeil, gold electroplate, stainless steel, and pewter are comparatively easy to care for.

Tarnish is created by warm air, dust, and sunlight. Heated air contains a small amount of carbon and sulfide (a mixture similar to smog), which react chemically with the surface of silver and cause tarnish to develop. Although tarnish creates a film that diminishes the luster and whitish color of silver, in an ornamental capacity it highlights the recesses of deeply carved ornamentation with a darker hue.

## How to Retard Tarnish

- *Display or store silver away from heat or sunlight.* The ideal temperature to display or store silver is 18°C (65°F). Because heat promotes tarnish, in winter months silver is prone to tarnish more when windows are closed, heating registers are open, and fireplaces emit smoke.
- *The best tarnish retardment is the daily use of silver.* Repeated washings keep silver tarnish-free up to 6 months. After that it may require polish to improve the sparkle.
- *Tarnish-preventive bags inhibit tarnish.* Tarnish-preventive cloth is made of cot-

ton flannel embedded with tiny particles of pure silver that attract tarnish-making gases away from silver and inhibit tarnish. Because washing dislodges the particles of silver embedded in the fabric and renders it ineffective, tarnish-preventive cloth is never washed. To make a storage area tarnish-free, buy the fabric by the yard and tack it to the top, bottom, and sides of a drawer or cupboard. Leave enough material to make a flap as an opening. When tarnish-preventive cloth is glued to a surface, make sure the glue is *nonsulfurous*. Otherwise the glue may leach through the cloth and render the material ineffective.

- *Use silver protection strips, camphor cakes, and camphor gum.* To neutralize tarnish for up to 6 months in a cabinet or cupboard, purchase silver protection strips from household catalogs and camphor cakes and camphor gum from pharmacies.
- *Never lacquer flatware or serveware.* Lacquer seals the surface of silver and prevents tarnish, but it is recommended only for articles seldom held in the hand, such as a picture frame, a box, or a napkin ring. Because lacquer is susceptible to scratches, once the seal is broken, tarnish forms around the cracks and spreads underneath. Should this happen, take the piece to a silversmith, who will strip and resilver the article.

## How to Clean Silver

- *Wash sterling silver in hot sudsy water, followed by a hot rinse and hand-drying.* Sterling silver is a soft metal, softened further when subjected to the heat of the dishwasher drying cycle, and hand-washing is recommended. Moreover, the motion of the dishwasher subjects the soft metal to scratches and dents, and when left to steam-dry, the water spots leave marks that etch the surface. Because the alkaline content in some detergents is harmful to sterling, a mild detergent without bleach is recommended. Detergents with bleach remove oxidation.
- *Do not wash silver on a rubber mat.* Rubber contains sulfur that darkens the surface of silver and leaves black marks only a silversmith can remove.
- *Never wash silver and stainless steel together.* An electrolytic reaction occurs

when silver and stainless steel are washed together. Ions of silver disassociate, transfer to stainless steel, and leave silver articles pitted. Should this happen, take the ware to a professional silversmith, who will buff ware made of sterling silver and resilver items made of silver plate.

- *Use a nonabrasive tarnish remover.* There are several ways to remove tarnish, with a tarnish-preventive liquid, a nonabrasive metal polish with a base of jeweler's rouge, or silver mits made of tarnish-preventive cloth.
- *To enhance patina rub silver lengthwise.* Silver is a soft metal that scratches easily. To enhance the patina (the small scratches that promote a mellow glow), rather than polish silver in a circular or crosswise motion, rub lengthwise.
- *Promote the same patina for all utensils.* The easiest way to promote the same patina for all utensils is to lay flatware on its side in a divided drawer or storage chest, a method that keeps the same utensils from constant use. When flatware is stored in a stacked position, the weight of the top pieces scratches the bottom utensils.
- *To clean the crevices of silver.* To reach into the recesses of deeply carved ornamentation, dip a soft brush, such as an old toothbrush, into silver polish. Wash the article in hot soapy water, rinse, and wipe with a soft cloth that will not scratch the surface.
- *Don't use silver dip, except between fork tines.* The chemical composition of silver dip reacts with the metallic structure of silver and leaves a dull white finish on the surface (however the film is removable with silver polish). Moreover, silver dip removes the black tarnish used as a decorative tool to accent the deep recesses of silver ornamentation.
- *Never soak knife blades above cuff level in hot water.* The knife blade is made with a *tang,* a metal point that projects from the blade where it is inserted into the handle. The handle and blade are joined with cement and covered with silver, producing a small ledge called a *cuff.* When the knife handle is soaked in hot water above cuff level, the heat may disintegrate the cement or cause swelling that forces the tang and handle apart.
- *Remove wax from silver.* Wax sometimes gets into candlesticks, but it breaks off quickly when silver is placed in the refrigerator. Any remaining wax washes off in hot soapy water.

## How to Inhibit Corrosion

Sulfur and acids are corrosive agents found in eggs, fruit (notably citrus fruit), mayonnaise, mustard, salad dressing, salt, salt air, vinegar, newspaper print, plastic, rubber products, and flowers arranged in a silver container.

- *Rinse silver tableware soon after use in hot soapy water.* Use a mild detergent (one made without bleach) and avoid soaking silver for a prolonged period of time, such as overnight, as the chloride (salt) in the water may cause the silver to pit.
- *Line a silver bowl or vase.* The acid in fruit and flowers etches silver, and when a silver bowl or vase is used as a container for fruit or flowers, line it with a bowl or jar made of glass.
- *Protect against salt and salt air.* Sodium chloride can pit silver with gray dots. In the early stages, gray spots are removable with silver polish, but when silver is deeply pitted take the piece to a silversmith for a professional polishing. Otherwise, the spots will enlarge and salt will destroy the metal.
- *Empty silver salt shakers soon after use.* To inhibit the corrosive effect of salt, after use, wipe the interior of silver shakers clean with a damp sponge.

## The Proper Storage of Silver

- *Store silver in acid-free tissue paper or tarnish-preventive bags.* For those who live near the sea, to protect silver from the corrosive effect of salt air, store silver in bags made of tarnish-preventive material.
- *Never store silver in plastic.* Moisture is trapped in plastic bags, sticks to the surface of silver, and marks the metal. Should this happen, take the article to a silversmith for a professional polishing.
- *Never store silver in newspaper.* Today newspaper ink supposedly does not rub off, but why take a chance? Printers ink can mark silver, and leave discoloration almost impossible to remove.

- *Before storing sterling silver flatware, count the pieces.* To make sure a utensil isn't thrown out during cleanup (I did this twice as a bride), count the number of utensils before putting silver flatware away.

## The Care of Vermeil, Gold Electroplate, Stainless Steel, and Pewter

- *Vermeil* is gold-plated silver. Both of these are soft metals susceptible to scratches and dents, and hand-washing is recommended. However, gold does not tarnish and vermeil is resistant to acid and stains.
- *Gold electroplate* is a base metal covered with gold, but the surface is susceptible to scratches and dents made in a dishwasher and hand-washing is recommended.
- *Stainless steel* is a hard metal that does not rust, stains less than other metals, retains a high luster, and offers carefree maintenance in a dishwasher.
- *Pewter* is a soft alloy, prone to dents and scratches made by the jostling motion of a dishwasher, and hand-washing is recommended. Although the blades, fork tines, and bowls of the spoons are made of stainless steel for strength, the handles are pewter and are therefore soft.

# Part IV

# *Stemware*

CHAPTER TWENTY-SIX

# FROM GLASS TO CRYSTAL

*The first artificer in glass . . . was facilitating and prolonging the enjoyment of flight, enlarging the avenues of science, and conferring the highest and most lasting pleasures; he was enabling the student to contemplate nature, and the beauty to behold herself.*

SAMUEL JOHNSON, RAMBLER NO. IX

NATURE IS THE first artificer of glass, which is a naturally occurring substance made when lightning fuses sand into long slender tubes called *fulgurites* (from the Latin *fulgur,* "lightning"). Rapidly cooled volcanic rock produces *obsidian,* a hard black glassy substance named for Obsius, an Ethiopian. The material was initially used to make knives, arrowheads, and jewelry and as a form of money.

## Phoenician and Egyptian Glass

According to Pliny the Elder, a first-century Roman naturalist and writer, Phoenician mariners accidentally produced glass in 3500 B.C. The sailors were beached by the Belus River in Cendebia (Syria), a marshy district below Mount Carmalus. To support an iron cauldron for cooking, the sailors took blocks of natron (native soda) from the ship's cargo and used dried seaweed to build a fire. As the fire burned down, the soda, seaweed, and sand melted into a liquid that hardened into glass.

During the fourth dynasty in Egypt (c. 2613–2494 B.C.), solid glass faience was developed. Egyptian faience was made of crushed quartz (of which ordinary sand is the main ingredient) and alkali (the ashes of plants and trees). To hide the impurities inherent in the materials, copper oxide was added as a colorant; this metallic substance fired to turquoise blue. Initially faience was made as turquoise-colored beads, probably by Syrian potters who used glass to glaze pottery.

The significant history of glass begins in the Eighteenth Dynasty (c. 1580–1350 B.C.), when artisans, inspired by pottery and metalwork, threaded molten glass around a core made of sand, clay, and camel dung and reheated, rolled, and smoothed the form on a flat surface. When it was hard, the core was scraped from the inside, a technique used to make small vessels, such as containers for perfume, oil, and cosmetics. Today, a core-formed glass bottle incised with the cartouche of King Thutmose III (1501–1447 B.C.) is on view at the British Museum. Around 1500 B.C., hollow glass vessels were formed in a mold in a process known as *cast glass*. The surface was smoothed and polished with an abrasive wheel.

Next to rock crystal (transparent quartz), glass was the only clear solid material known at the time. It was a luxury item enhanced with silver and gold and made as beads, bracelets, amulets, cups, goblets, bowls, bottles, flasks, and furniture inlay. The throne of Tutankhamen (reign 1361–1352 B.C.) is inlaid with gold, calcite, faience, and glass.

## Roman Glass

Glass came to Rome via Phoenician mariners who used glass containers to hold supplies as they traded goods in countries around the Mediterranean.

In 50 B.C., the glass blowpipe was invented; this enabled glass to be blown into a given shape rather than being formed around a central core. The process is thought to have developed in Sidon, then a Syrian colony of Rome. According to legend, a glassmaker attempting to clear a gather of molten glass from the end of a hollow pipe blew into the pipe and inflated the bubble, an act so simple and efficient it is still used today. The blow pipe is the single most important invention in the history of glass. It took glass out of the realm of luxury and made possible the mass production of inexpensive utilitarian shapes for the common people: bottles, plates, spoons, tumblers, flasks, ointment jars, lamps, and vases.

By the first century A.D., Roman glassmakers (called *vitrearii,* from the Latin *vitrum,* "glassware") had perfected the Egyptian techniques of glass decoration and developed most of the methods in use today: glass inlay and overlay, filigree ornamentation, enamel and gilded decoration, the enclosure of gold leaf between two layers of glass, mosaics, window glass, and glass carved, cut, and engraved to imitate precious stones. (Etched ornamentation was developed in the seventeenth century, and art glass in the nineteenth century.)

Rather than transport breakable glass to the outer reaches of the empire, Roman glassmakers spread the techniques of glassmaking to provinces located near water transportation and blessed with the right mineral resources, notably the Low Countries, Germany, France, and England. So great was the influence of Rome from the first century B.C. to the fifth century A.D. that provincial glass was known as *Roman glass* and regional styles failed to develop. Glass made in one region was hard to distinguish from glass produced in another region.

Today, a vast amount of both iridescent and noniridescent Roman glass survives. Iridescent glass is a by-product of burial; carbonic acid in the soil corrodes the surface, splits rays of light that fall on glass, and creates a prismatic rainbow effect. Noniridescent glass is a work of art that survived above ground, such as the Lycurgus cup, made in the fourth century A.D., a magnificent vessel that can be seen today in the British Museum.

The Lycurgus cup was made from two layers of glass, one superimposed on the other in a method called *overlay.* The top layer of the vessel was connected to the bottom layer by thin bridges of glass, decorated with a scene that depicted the death of Lycurgus, king of Thrace, at the hands of the maenads, nymphs who attended orgiastic Dionysian rites. When lit from the front, the Lycurgus cup is olive green to pea green, but when lighted from the back the color is wine red to deep purple, a tone made by the presence of minute particles of colloidal gold (small insoluble particles that remain suspended in liquid and do not sink to the bottom). Depending on the light transmitted through the particles, two or more colors become visible.

In its natural state, glass is greenish or brownish amber. Its color derives from the impurities inherent in the material, such as iron and aluminum. To conceal these contaminants, glass was originally colored. However, in 2 A.D., Roman artisans invented *crystallinum,* a name for lightweight transparent glass that was decolored with the addition of antimony or manganese, a grayish-white metallic chemical element known as *glass soap,* because it neutralized the impurities and made glass clear.

By 50 A.D. clear glass dominated the market for glassware, and luxury items were decorated with enameled, engraved, and facet-cut ornamentation. Glass cutters were called *diatretarii,* artisans noted for the production of *vasa diatreta,* meaning "open-work vessel" in Latin. Unlike the Lycurgus cup made from two layers of colored glass, these vessels, or "cage cups," were made from one sheet of colorless glass undercut in a lattice type ornamentation that stood free of the body, a network that produced a halo of interlaced circles connected to the body by tiny, almost hidden, glass pegs. Today, nineteen cage cups are extant.

In the fourth century A.D., the vast Roman Empire was divided into western and eastern factions, a division that brought an end to the Roman domination of glass. During the early Middle Ages, glass was once again an expensive commodity, made in simple, coarse shapes. The new center of glass development shifted to the Middle East, where Islamic glassmakers produced new shapes and mastered the art of enamel ornamentation.

## Islamic Glass

On July 16, 622, Mohammed and his followers withdrew to Medina, the Muslim holy city 280 miles northeast of Mecca, a migration that marks the beginning of Islamic rule in the Middle East. The Muslims were very tolerant of the traditions and art of other countries and artistic freedom flourished. From approximately the seventh century to fourteenth century artisans excelled in making fine glass. The most important glass centers were located in Syria at the eastern end of the Mediterranean, in Mesopotamia at the lower end of the Tigris and Euphrates Rivers (part of modern Iraq), and in Persia (modern-day Iran).

Between the eighth and twelfth centuries, Islamic glassmakers developed an intricate, all-over style of repetitive patterns, one in which decoration was subordinate to form. They gained worldwide recognition for glass superbly carved with motifs of birds, animals, and the tree of life pattern among others, work exemplified by Hedwig beakers, thick-walled vessels made of transparent glass cut in high relief with scenes of lions, eagles, griffins, and palm leaves. The beakers are named after Hedwig, patron saint of Silesia and Poland (d. 1243), who was thought to have owned one. Today fewer than twenty examples are extant; one is on view in the Schlesisches Museum, Breslau, Germany.

Luster is the greatest contribution of Islamic artisans to glassmaking. Metallic salt is painted on the surface of once-fired glass, which is then refired in a reduced (smoky) kiln. In the kiln, the glass absorbs the metallic substance and leaves a thin covering of metal that produces a silvery or golden hue, often iridescent in tone.

In 750 A.D., the capital of Islam was transferred from Damascus to Baghdad, near Persia, where the decorative arts flourished. Islamic glassmakers began to produce polychrome enameled and gilded motifs in intricate designs, the finest the world has ever seen. This ornamental technique was prominent in the thirteenth and fourteenth centuries. Mosque lamps of exceptional beauty were made in the shape of urns and hung from the ceiling by chains attached to handles on the rim; when lighted, the lamps illuminated the mosques' interiors with colorful geometric patterns. The lamps were enameled with the donor's name, a dedication to a sultan, a palace dignitary, a verse from the Koran:

> God is the light of heaven and earth. His light is like a niche in which is a lamp, the lamp encased in glass, the glass like a glittering star.

In 1258, the Mongols invaded Persia, wreaking devastation that brought an almost total halt to the production of Islamic glass. When Tamerlane conquered southern and western Asia in 1402, he took Syrian glassmakers as hostages to Samarkand in Uzbekistan, an act that ended the Eastern domination of glass. By the fifteenth century, leadership in glass had shifted to the European continent.

## European Glass

After the fall of the western Roman Empire, regional styles began to develop in northern Europe and England. Glassworks were located in forests, and the presence of iron in the silica produced glass in shades of green or brown, a coarse, heavy style known as *Teutonic,* represented by cone-shaped beakers with pointed ends. As a cooling measure, the pointed ends were placed in the ground or in the beds of rivers or streams. Although little progress was made in the development of glass between the fifth and the tenth centuries, the forested areas provided the fuel that sustained the art in Europe.

Early in the Middle Ages glass was made primarily for the church. Itinerant glassmakers made colorful glass mosaics and stained-glass windows decorated with biblical illustrations that served to educate people who could neither read nor write. Medieval glass was also made for utilitarian purposes, such as crude bottles and simple green or brown goblets. German vessels were made with *prunts,* glass pads applied to the exterior of goblets for easy handling by greasy fingers.

When the northern European tribes invaded the Italian peninsuala in the fifth century A.D., thousands of refugees took refuge in the low-lying lagoon of Venice where the sand and alkaline sea plants provided an excellent source of glassmaking materials. When the crusaders took Constantinople in 1204, fugitive glassmakers migrated to Venice and brought with them glassmaking skills, among them the art of enameled ornamentation. This decorative technique spread to Bohemia and Germany in the fifteenth century, to central Europe in the sixteenth to eighteenth centuries, and finally to England in the latter half of the eighteenth century.

By the mid-thirteenth century, the art of glassmaking was highly advanced in Venice. By 1255 there was a complex guild system that specialized in different types of glass, such as jewelry, bottles, mirrors, lenses, and windowpanes. However, the prolific number of furnaces that burned day and night in the wooden glasshouses posed a threat to the lives of the citizens. On November 8, 1291, the doge and the Great Council forbade the furnaces to operate within the city, and the glasshouses were moved to Murano, a neighboring island about three miles outside the city. This move not only centered the glass industry in one area; it also prevented the establishment of glasshouses elsewhere and assured the secrecy of new glass techniques.

In 1317 Venetian ships with holds laden with glass trade goods landed in Flanders, thus introducing the delicate Venetian glass to the continent and England. To keep outsiders from learning the formula for Venetian glass, the export of materials and cullet (waste glass) was forbidden. As a further precaution, glassmakers were ordered to work behind iron bars in a mile-long stretch carefully controlled by guards who reported to the feared Council of Ten. To encourage loyalty among the workers, and to compensate them for their loss of freedom, in 1376 the Venetian Senate elevated glassmakers to the status of burghers, or citizens of Venice. The daughters of *vetrajos,* master craftsmen, were granted the right to marry noblemen; this was a major privilege in such a restricted society, affording glassmaking families the ability to enter the aristocracy.

Around the fourteenth century, Venetian artisans invented *cristallo,* a relatively clear glass made with *barilla,* soda ash imported from the saltwater marshes near Alicante, Spain. The Romans had made soda glass but the technique was lost for centuries and rediscovered by Venetian glassmakers, who used manganese as a decolorizer. *Cristallo* was clouded with impurities caused by the yellowish-brown ash produced by *barilla;* it was not clear by today's standards but was considered "water-clear," nevertheless. Color was not added to conceal the impurities, and the clarity of *cristallo* brought a decline in the demand for colored glass as a base for enameled ornamentation.

Soda glass was thin and ductile. In its molten state it had to be worked quickly before it turned rigid. It relied on form as decoration, rather than the application of surface ornamentation. Today, Venetian soda glass is characterized by goblets shaped with fantastic winged stems and dragon motifs inspired by the legend of St. George, the dragon slayer—martyr and patron saint of Venice.

With the invention of *cristallo,* Venice became the major source of luxury glass, and to maintain its monopoly, in 1454 Venice decreed under Article 26 of the Statutes of the Inquisition of State, that glassmakers who emigrated to other countries incurred the penalty of death. However, glassmakers succumbed to the lure of bribes. Those who escaped emigrated to the Netherlands, England, France, Germany, Bohemia, Austria, and Spain, where they taught Venetian glassmaking skills that resulted in an elegant, fluid form of glass called *façon de Venice,* a French term for "in the Venetian style."

In 1453 the Turks captured Constantinople, and Islamic glassmakers once again fled to Venice, bringing with them a sense of color and shape that resulted in a blend of Persian and Venetian artistry, notably in the art of enameled decoration. Islamic artistry was absorbed into all aspects of the applied arts. It can be seen in the arabesque, a complex design of intertwined foliate and geometric forms adapted by Renaissance artisans from Moorish architecture, a design style that spread northward from Venice to other countries of Europe. From the fifteenth to the seventeenth centuries, Venice, queen of the Adriatic, dominated the art and commerce of glass.

But the winds of change lay on the horizon, when in the late sixteenth century,

Vasco da Gama discovered a new sea route to the Far East via the Cape of Good Hope. Rather than pay taxes for goods shipped through Venice, which was poised geographically between Western Europe and Asia, the Europeans were now able to trade directly with the Far East, and the dominance of Venetian glassmaking began to wane. By the seventeenth century, the richly forested areas of central and northern Europe emerged as major glassmaking centers, aided by the skills of immigrant glassmakers from Venice and Altare, a glassmaking center located near Genoa.

Altare, situated where the Alps meet the Apennines, was settled in the eleventh century by migrant glassmakers from Normandy. Outside of Venice, the town was the most important glassmaking center in Italy. Unlike the Venetians, who zealously guarded the formula for *cristallo* and the techniques of glassmaking, the Altarians encouraged glassmakers to emigrate to northern Europe and teach the skill. Many a Venetian glassmaker who fled his country in the fourteenth century settled in Altare, which soon became a major center of Venetian-style glass. By the fifteenth century, Altare rivaled Venice in artistry.

In 1621, Antonio Neri, an Italian priest and chemist who once worked in the glasshouses of Florence, Flanders, and Pisa, wrote *L'Arte Vetraria* ("The Art of Glass"), the first book of instruction written for glassmakers, a work that, among other things, contained the formula for Venetian *cristallo*. *L'Arte Vetraria* was translated throughout Europe. Historians believe that the book was directly responsible for new discoveries in Germany, Bohemia, and England.

The seventeenth century brought tremendous changes to the composition of glass, namely the development of *potash-lime glass* in Bohemia, and the invention of *lead crystal* in England. Venetian *cristallo* used soda ash, an alkali exported from marine areas located around the Mediterranean. It was costly to import to northern Europe, and not always easy to get. As a substitute, northern glassmakers looked inland to forested areas for a source of alkali and began to use the ash of wood and plants, such as beech, oak, straw, rushes, and bracken, alkali called *potash* because it contained potassium carbonate.

Potash glass turned rigid fast, was difficult to manipulate, and was made in a coarse, heavy style. The Germans called it *waldglas*, green "wood glass," and the French called it *verre de fougère*, amber-green "fern glass." But in the early seventeenth century, Bohemian glassmakers added lime (chalk) to the potash composition and produced glass that was clearer and more brilliant than *cristallo*, *waldglas*, or *verre de fougère*. Its surface was hard enough and dense enough to take carved, engraved, and cut ornamentation well. Soon cut ornamentation became the hallmark of Bohemian glassmakers, supplanting the demand for glass ornamented with enameled motifs.

Bohemia, a country bordered by forested mountains rich in mineral resources, such as sand, manganese, and lime, was a natural environment for the glass industry to succeed. Manufacture was sponsored by royalty and the nobility, who granted glasshouses the "privilege" to found establishments on their vast estates (a privilege that also cleared their land for agricultural purposes). Furthermore, the nearby mountain streams supplied hydraulic power that drove the cutters' lathes (formerly hand-turned by assistants). Glassmakers would work in a forested locale until the supply of wood ran out, and then they would move on.

To satisfy the considerable needs of the aristocracy for cut glass, artisans sought a man-made substitute for rock crystal toward the end of the sixteenth century. Rock crystal is a hard, semiprecious stone that is mined rather than made, and the supply is limited. One of the glassmakers' goals was to ornament glass using the same methods lapidarists used to cut and polish precious and semiprecious stones.

In the early seventeenth century, Emperor Rudolf II of Prague, a great patron of the arts who amassed one of the world's most magnificent collections, invited a group of artists and craftsmen to his castle at Hradschin to develop lapidary techniques on potash-lime glass. Among those invited was Caspar Lehmann, a master engraver, glassmaker, and well-known lapidarist from Uelzen who was the first to successfully adapt wheel-engraved ornamentation to glass. In appreciation for his superb technical skills and great artistic talent, Emperor Rudolf knighted Lehmann in 1609 and granted the artisan a lifetime patent for the process. Today, the only remaining work signed by Lehmann is a footed glass beaker carved with allegorical figures, a vessel made in 1605 for State Counselor Wolf Sigimund of Lowenstein and his wife, Lady Susanne of Rogendorf. It can be seen in the Prague Museum.

On his demise, Lehmann's patent, or "privilege," transferred to George Schwanhardt, his apprentice and senior assistant, whose work remains unexcelled, and then to Schwanhardt's son Henry. Schwanhardt used diamond-point engraving to execute detail, a technique he combined with polished engraving to create a contrast of matte and shiny finishes.

In 1622, following the turbulent years of the Counterreformation and the Thirty Years War, Schwanhardt left Prague for his native Nuremberg, and by the mid-seventeenth century, Nuremberg was a glass-cutting center, built on the unrivaled techniques of Lehmann and Schwanhardt.

# English Crystal

The English glass industry owes a debt of gratitude to Queen Elizabeth I, who in 1575 granted Giacomo Verzelini, a Venetian glassmaker, a 21-year right to make glass, a right based on the promise that he would instruct English glassmakers on the techniques of making Venetian glass, a style that dominated English glassware for 100 years.

The depletion of forests in the seventeenth century posed a major problem for the English Royal Navy, which needed wood to build its ships. In 1615 the government passed a law that forbade glassmakers and metalworkers from using wood to fuel their furnaces. Coal became the main source of fuel in England, and by the eighteenth century coal-bearing areas, such as Stourbridge and Newcastle, evolved as major glassmaking centers.

In 1673, while attempting to find a substitute for Venetian *cristallo,* George Ravenscroft developed *flint glass.* He substituted calcined flint and potash for sand and soda ash, the main substances in *cristallo.* But the imbalance of materials in the composition caused a glass sickness called *crizzling,* a name for fine cracks made by a high proportion of alkali that leads to the gradual disintegration of glass. Although flint glass was not made after the eighteenth century, the term continued well into the nineteenth century, particularly in North America, where it was used to mean quality lead crystal.

On May 16, 1674, Ravenscroft, a glass trader, importer of Venetian mirror, and former resident of Venice, took out a 7-year patent to make a "perticuler sort of Christaline Glasse," in Savoy, London, a manufactory later transferred to Henley-on-Thames. To remove the crizzling from flint glass, Ravenscroft substituted sand for flint and used lead oxide as flux. The result, in 1676, was lead crystal, a clearer, heavier, thicker glass than *cristallo* and potash-lime glass and most important, a glass that incorporated raw materials indigenous to England.

But because lead crystal was not as malleable as *cristallo* or potash-lime glass, a new style of goblet called a *baluster,* was developed. This stemware had a sturdy, well-proportioned form. Moreover, the refractive property of lead crystal fostered scientific advances in the production of optical glass. This, coupled with the brilliance of facet-cut crystal at the table, caused England to dominate the glass industry for over a century and a half. By the end of the seventeenth century, the demand for facet-cut English crystal superseded the market for Bohemian glass decorated with engraved ornamentation.

On May 29, 1677, Ravenscroft reached an agreement with the Worshipful Company of Glass Sellers of London (incorporated in 1664) granting the inventor the right to impress a seal on glasses of his making. Ravenscroft chose the raven as his mark, symbol of his name and the heraldic emblem in his coat of arms. Although "raven's head-glasses" are rare, some can be seen at the Corning Museum of Glass, Corning, New York.

## Irish Crystal

In 1745, England levied a glass excise tax based on the weight of glass. Although the tax excluded the manufacture of Irish glass, it prohibited the export of Irish glass to England. But when free trade between Ireland and England was established in 1780, within five years glasshouses were founded in Cork, Belfast, Dublin, Newry, and Waterford, manufactories that produced lead crystal with a faint bluish-gray color or a smoky tone attributed to atmospheric conditions. Moreover, early crystal was cut primarily in the sheds of the workers' homes, a cottage industry that contributed great individuality and considerable charm to old Irish crystal. Although the glassworks at Cork, Belfast, Dublin, and Newry have long since ceased to operate, glassmaking continues today at Waterford. (The company closed in 1851 and reopened in 1951 under the name of Waterford Glass, Ltd.)

About 1825, when glassworkers in England complained about the high cost of duty, the Irish crystal industry began to wane, and soon a glass excise tax was levied, an assessment that brought an end to the Anglo-Irish collaboration. Although the Tax was repealed in 1845, by that time trade in Irish crystal had declined to a point where manufacture was no longer profitable.

## American Glass

The American glass industry was primarily one of struggle and collapse and did not take root until the late eighteenth century, the era of industrialization. Even then, most glasshouses were stories of growth and decline, and little progress was made in the production of glass until the end of the nineteenth century, when mechanization stabilized the industry. By the twentieth century, the United States was a world leader of glass manufacture.

Glass was the first American industry encouraged in the seventeenth century by the English Board of Trade when England was engaged in a period of expansion and colonization, an era that brought a shortage of wood to build ships. To preserve the forests as a reserve for the Royal Navy, the English turned to coal-burning furnaces and used for supply the virgin forests of the New World, where they also encouraged the production of glass.

The first American glasshouse was built in 1608 at Jamestown, Virginia, staffed with eight immigrants from Germany and Poland hired by the London company to make glass beads, bottles, and crude drinking vessels. However, the workers did not get along, and for economic reasons many moved to pursue other occupations, notably farming. From the start, glassmaking was an impractical venture, particularly given the distance and hazards involved in shipping breakable products to England. In 1609 the glasshouse at Jamestown closed.

A second glasshouse was established in 1621. It was staffed with glassmakers from Italy and lasted 14 months, until the Indian massacre of 1622. Although other glasshouses opened in the interim, all met with failure, and the colonists were dependent on England for their supply of utilitarian glass—bottles and window glass.

English policy changed in the eighteenth century: the manufacture of glass in the colonies was forbidden, but the use of American raw materials to make glass in England was sanctioned. Moreover, North America was considered a market for English glass. After the American Revolution, Congress refused to pass protective tariffs, and American glasshouses were undersold by the British. But in the face of these tremendous odds, three German glassmakers met with considerable success in the New World: Caspar Wistar of New Jersey, Henry William Stiegel of Pennsylvania, and John Frederick Amelung of Maryland.

The Wistarberg Glassworks was the first glasshouse to operate over a long period of time (37 years). Founded in 1739 in Alloyway Creek, Salem County, New Jersey, the company operated until 1776, when it closed, possibly because of the disruptive conditions of the American Revolution. Wistar, born in Germany in 1695, was a prosperous brass button manufacturer from Philadelphia, who imported four glassmakers from Germany and Holland to teach him how to make flint glass in utilitarian shapes, primarily bottles, bowls, drinking glasses, pitchers, and window glass.

To meet competition from abroad, early American glass was made to emulate European ware, and Wistarberg workers produced styles popular in Germany and Holland. An American style did not yet exist. The exception is *South Jersey glass*, free-blown by Wistarberg workers in their spare time from leftover material, glass made as gifts for family and friends. To earn extra income workers sold their Jersey glass at the company store. The style was utilitarian and the products were everyday: pitchers, bowls, vases, and candle holders in natural shades of bluish-green, aquamarine, amber, and brown. No two pieces were alike; glass sets, such as a creamer and a sugar bowl, were unmatched, ornamented primarily with threaded decoration such as the *lily pad*, an innovative American technique made by attaching a small gob of glass to the underside of the base and pulling it up and over. Today, Jersey glass is a folk art, a product made of unrefined material and natural colors. Benjamin Franklin used Wistar glass to conduct electrical experiments.

Henry William Stiegel of Cologne, Germany, a self-proclaimed baron, operated three glasshouses in Pennsylvania, one at Elizabeth Furnace and two at Manheim. The factories operated from 1763 to 1774. Stiegel was the first American glassmaker to standardize production methods, maintain rigid quality controls, advertise extensively, and employ field agents in major cities. However, he overextended himself financially, and in 1774 died in debtor's prison.

Stiegel glass was clear or artificially colored. Stiegel employed skilled craftsmen, mainly from England, Ireland, and Germany, to make glass in shapes similar to English and European ware. For the Pennsylvania Dutch customers, Stiegel decorated glass with enameled peasant styles popular on the Continent. To accommodate English patrons who resided in New York and Philadelphia, Stiegel produced flint glass in large sturdy shapes favored in England.

The New Bremen Glass Manufactory was founded in 1784 by John Frederick Amelung in New Bremen, Frederick County, Maryland. The company was named after the town of Bremen, Germany, home of Amelung's financial backers. The New Bremen Glass Manufactory began operations a year after the American Revolution ended and continued to operate until 1795, when it was sold. Amelung, a glassmaker, arrived in the New World with his brother, seven relatives, and sixty-one glassworkers from Bohemia and Germany. He was an entrepreneur dedicated to the production of clear glass in utilitarian shapes, such as bottles, bowls, and stemware. His work was noted for its colored glass in shades of amethyst, grayish blue, cobalt blue, and green, luxury free-blown glass, and the finest wheel-engraved presentation pieces made in the United States before 1800, the first signed and dated glass.

Many glassmakers settled in Pittsburgh, a glass center blessed with deposits of coal and nearby water transportation. By the late eighteenth century glass made between the Allegheny Mountains and the Mississippi River was known as *Midwestern glass,* and from Pittsburgh to Louisville, glasshouses sprang up along the Ohio River, each specializing in glass blown in *hinged molds.* Liquor was increasingly packaged in glass bottles and flasks in the Midwest.

The American glass industry suffered in the eighteenth century from lack of government financial support and fell into a severe decline. But in the nineteenth century a series of federal laws and events stimulated the production of glass: the Embargo Act of 1807 imposed by President Jefferson against Britain and France; the Nonimportation Act passed in 1811 by Congress; and the War of 1812, which blockaded the English navy and eliminated British competition. In 1824, Congress passed a tariff on glass imports, and by 1840, mechanization of the glass industry assured that business would be profitable. Eighty-one factories were in operation.

In 1827 the machine press was developed by Enoch Robinson. It was considered the most important glass-making discovery since the blowpipe and the greatest American contribution to glassmaking. The machine press lowered costs, tripled glass production, and enabled the glass industry to evolve from a handicraft art to an industrialized business. Iron molds carved with elaborate designs were reused over and over promoting cost economies, and two dishes a minute were made that required little or no hand-finishing. Manufacturers supplied a newly affluent middle class with inexpensive copies of luxury glassware, and for the first time, glass tableware was mass-produced in different shapes. By 1850, the average homemaker owned a suite of glassware that contained glasses made for service of white wine, red wine, and dessert wine.

In 1903, Michael Joseph Owens of Toledo, Ohio, perfected the first *automatic bottle machine,* an invention that promoted mass production of uniform containers, and by the 1920s bottles and jars were a disposable item. Without touching human hands, a conveyer transported glass from the melting tank, to the bottle machine, to the annealing oven. In 1940, Owens perfected the first fully automated *glass-blowing machine,* an invention that stimulated mass production of new glassware shapes.

Today, glass is handmade or machine-made. It is used to make tableware, jewelry, laboratory equipment, optical glass, photosensitive glass, conduits, television tubes, computer screens, insulation, building blocks, textile fibers, pipe and pipe fittings. These are only a few of the modern-day uses of glass.

CHAPTER TWENTY-SEVEN

# DECORATIVE METHODS AND STYLES

THE DIFFERENCE in glass so often lies not in the material, but in the method of ornamentation. But when one is unfamiliar with the mechanics of decoration, the terms mean little or nothing.

The application of decoration to glass is made while the material is hot; this is done with art glass, cased glass, colored glass, crackle glass, *crystallo céramie,* enameled glass, *filigrana* and *latticinio,* flash glass, frosted glass, gilded decoration, gold-between-glass, luster glass, milk glass, *lattimo,* mosaics, *millefiori,* and stained glass. The exception is the application of paint to cold glass. The removal of glass to make decoration is done when the material is cold; ornamentation is carved, cut, embossed, engraved, etched, or sandblasted. Glass ornamented by shape alone is formed while the material is hot; this category includes *cire perdue* and *pâte de verre.* Often, several techniques are combined in one glass or a particular style of decoration is characteristic of a country: hence, Bohemian glass, English crystal, French crystal, German glass, Irish crystal, Swedish crystal, and Venetian glass. To help the reader appreciate the decorative methods, the techniques and lore are described below in alphabetical order.

ART GLASS. From antiquity through the eighteenth century, the design and ornamentation of glass depended on the technical skill and artistry of the glassmaker. In the nineteenth century, designers and artists such as Eugène Rousseau and Emile

Gallé turned to molten liquid as a medium of expression. The designer-artist interest, coupled with technical advances in the chemistry of color made in the nineteenth century resulted in glass made for decorative purposes only. This style, known as *art glass,* featured unusual finishes, such as iridescent glass with a rainbow finish, notably Tiffany glass and Aurene glass; glass with a lustrous surface, such as Satin glass; and shaded bicolored glass, such Amberina, Burmese, and Peachblow.

- *Iridescent glass* evolved from an interest in the discoveries of Heinrich Schliemann at Pompeii and Herculaneum in the nineteenth century. In Roman glass, the carbonic acid inherent in the soil splits the rays of light falling on the glass to create the iridescent surface. In nineteenth-century iridescent glass, the molten glass is sprayed through a flame with metallic salts, such as silver or bismuth. The molten glass absorbs the salt, and when it is fired in a reduced atmosphere (closed kiln), it acquires an iridescent surface. Louis Comfort Tiffany is the best-known maker of iridescent art glass, ornamented primarily in a sinuous art nouveau style in shades of blue and green.
- *Favrile,* the most famous iridescent Tiffany glass, gets its name from *faber,* a German word for "color," and the Old English word *fabrile,* meaning "hand-wrought." Trained in the fine arts, Tiffany gave shading and depth to favrile by varying the tones and placement of color so that the color was in the glass and not on the surface. *Aurene* (from the Latin *aureus,* "golden") is an iridescent glass in shimmering shades of yellow, violet, and pink.
- *Amberina* is goldish-red bicolored glass made by reheating portions of glass, a technique that changed the color of the reheated part. Usually the top part of the article was reheated and the body shaded from a darker base to a lighter color near the rim. Amberina was made quite by accident when a gold ring fell from a worker's finger into a batch of glass. Gold is alloyed with copper for hardness, and in a reduced atmosphere copper fires to red. The result was that the gold-ruby compound created a base of yellow amber that shaded to ruby red at the top.
- *Burmese* is bipartite glass made with the addition of uranium oxide, a style that shaded from greenish yellow at the base to a top of delicate pinkish rose. Burmese was developed in matte and glossy finishes, a process patented by the Mount Washington Glass Company, New Bedford, Massa-

chusetts, and licensed to Thomas Webb & Sons of Stourbridge, England. After the English firm presented the glass to Queen Victoria, it was marketed as "Queen's Burmese," bipartite glass that shaded from a base of semiopaque salmon pink to a top of lemon yellow.

- *Peachblow* is a name inspired by an auction held in New York on March 18, 1886, for the effects of the Mary J. Morgan estate. One of the items was a small porcelain vase, dating from the reign of Emperor Kang Hsi (1661–1722), 8 inches high by 3 inches in diameter and glazed with "peachbloom," a pink glaze mottled with deeper red. The vase sold for $18,000, a sum that received considerable press. Soon "peachblow" was adopted as the name for bipartite glass with a base of cream or bluish white and a top of peachy pink or violet red.

BOHEMIAN GLASS. Bohemian glass evokes images of thick, hard glass with cut and engraved ornamentation, a decorative style that evolved in the early seventeenth century when Bohemian glassmakers developed potash-lime glass. The brilliant colorless glass was ornamented in an elaborate style unsurpassed in the depth of the designs and the play of light and shade. But in the second half of the seventeenth century, the demand for Bohemian glass began to wane. The market was superseded by lead crystal, which was easier to decorate with facet-cut ornamentation. Advances made in the chemistry of color in the early nineteenth century revived the Bohemian glass industry. Louis Lobmeyr, a glass designer and manufacturer from Vienna, hired talented glassmakers to produce colored glass. The nineteenth-century colored glass from Bohemia was less ornately executed than the seventeenth-century glass. Blue milk glass was decorated with colorful enamels in the Biedermeier style, and flash glass was decorated with cut motifs, notably ruby red glass.

CAMEO GLASS. A carved technique made with two or more layers of glass ornamented with several colors, cameo glass was known to the Egyptians, but in the period 25 B.C.–50 A.D. the Romans truly mastered the art, cutting glass to resemble carved gemstones, banded stones, and shell cameos. Between the ninth and eleventh centuries, Islamic glassmakers also mastered the art of cameo glass, and the technique was revived in the eighteenth century by Chinese glassmakers who carved Peking glass with colorful relief ornamentation. Snuff bottles about 3 inches high were particularly popular. In the nineteenth century, mechanization of the glass industry brought mass production of cameo glass, primarily as vases, biscuit barrels, and scent bottles decorated in the art nouveau style.

Cameo glass is exemplified by the Portland vase, perhaps the world's most famous vase, a small two-handled amphora approximately 10 inches high that dates to Roman antiquity. Its base is cobalt blue overlayed with white. In the nineteenth century, John Northwood, a skilled craftsman and admirer of Greek art, produced an exact replica of the Portland vase. The original is in the British Museum's collection.

Cameo glass is a difficult technique to execute. The layers of glass, superimposed one on the other, must have the same coefficient of expansion; otherwise they crack. The pattern is outlined on the top layer and the surround is carved by a wheel, leaving a design in relief. Alternatively, the pattern is acid-etched. Usually white glass is applied over colored glass. (See also *crystallo céramie, flash glass,* and *cased glass.*)

CASED GLASS. Like cameo glass, cased glass is made with two or more layers of glass, each a different color. The inner layer is blown inside a cup-shaped blank of outer glass, and the two are inflated together. Normally the outer layer is made of clear glass and the ornamentation is cut through the top layer to reveal the underlying colors. According to the design, additional decoration is added by enameling, gilding, or engraving.

*CIRE PERDUE. Cire perdue* is French for "lost wax," a technique that was perfected by Roman artisans. A model of the finished article is made in wax. The wax model is covered with plaster to make a mold. The mold is heated, and as the wax model melts it drains through an opening in the mold. The mold is then filled with molten glass, poured or blown in. When it is hard, the mold is opened, and the finished glass model is removed. The mold is destroyed, promoting one-of-a-kind articles characterized by great detail.

COLD PAINTING. Rather than firing painted ornamentation to the surface of glass for permanency, cold painting affixes enamels to the surface of glass with an adhesive, such as oil or varnish, an impermanent method that wears off easily. Perhaps the most famous example of cold painting is the Daphne ewer, a Roman vessel made between the second and third centuries A.D.

COLORED GLASS. Copper, manganese, cobalt, and iron are the principle metallic oxides used to color glass. In a reduced kiln (closed kiln), copper yields red, and in an oxidized atmosphere (open kiln), copper becomes bluish green or turquoise. Manganese produces purple and brown. In concentrated form it turns black, and in small quantities, it is a decolorizer. Cobalt produces blue with a reddish tinge. Iron produces shades of green, a color that takes on bluish tones when heated in a reduced atmosphere.

The increase in glass technology in the nineteenth century brought chemical control of colors that fostered mass production of colored glass early in the century. Whereas art glass featured unusual finishes and shaded colors, colored glass is represented by tonalities of color interpreted primarily in shades of red, green, blue, and yellow, such as *Rubinglas* and *uranium glass*. Moreover, nineteenth-century colored glass was made to simulate other materials, notably semiprecious stones, precious metals, porcelain, and stoneware; these decorative styles were called *lithyalin, mercury glass, opaline,* and *hyalith,* respectively.

- *Rubinglas* is a German name for ruby red glass that evolved from sixteenth-century alchemical experiments. In 1679, Andreas Cassius of Leyden, Holland, invented a rose-pink color French Jesuits introduced to the court of China, where it was used to ornament porcelain in a color palette called *famille rose.* But the decorative technique was complicated, and in 1679 Johann Kunckel, director of the prestigious Potsdam Glass Works and a distinguished chemist and glass technician who had successfully produced ruby glass, investigated the method and revealed the information in a publication entitled *Ars Vitraria Experimentalis.* In 1685, Cassius published *De Auro,* a book that described the addition of colloidal gold to a ruby red compound. Because gold is alloyed with copper for hardness and copper turns red in a reduced atmosphere, the special composition was called *Goldrubinglas.* In 1832, Friedrich Egermann of Haida, Bohemia, a glass technician who once worked as a porcelain painter at Meissen, substituted copper for gold and produced a ruby red color he used to stain the surface of glass, an ornamental method called *Rubinglas.*
- *Uranium glass* is a yellowish-green shade developed by Joseph Riedel of the Riedel Glassworks in northern Bohemia and manufactured from 1830 to 1848. Uranium glass was made by the addition of uranium to the batch, a

composition that produced colors called *annagelb* and *annagrün,* an amalgam of Anna, the name of Riedel's wife, and the German words *gelb* for "yellow" and *grün* for "green."

- *Lithyalin* is opaque colored glass developed to simulate the striped marbled surface of agate, a semiprecious stone. Lithyalin was streaked with tones of green, yellow, deep blue, and purple. Occasionally gold was used as an accent. Lithyalin was developed by Friedrich Egermann at his factory in Blottendorf, Bohemia. The process was patented in 1828.
- *Mercury glass* is made to emulate silver, a precious metal. Silver nitrate is applied to double-walled glass through a hole and sealed to prevent tarnish. Mercury glass provided a low-cost alternative to silver and silver plate and was used by Thomas Leighton, superintendent of the New England Glass Company, to make silvered door knobs. However, the demand began to wane after 1877, when silver was first electrodeposited on glass, an invention less expensive to execute.
- *Opaline* is glass opacified with bone ash, a decorative technique that produces glass with a milky-white appearance similar to translucent porcelain. Like the play of color in fire opals, when held to the light opaline reveals a slight touch of red because of the bone ash in the composition. Opaline glass should not be confused with opalescent glass. Opaline is opaque glass, either white or colored, and opalescent glass is clear or colored glass decorated with milky-white ornamentation with opalescent qualities.
- *Hyalith* is varicolored opaque glass made to simulate stoneware, a decorative style introduced in the early nineteenth century by Count von Buquoy. Buquoy perfected hyalith at the Georgenthal and Silberberg glassworks located on his vast estate in southern Bohemia. In 1803, Buquoy's director, Bartholomas Rosler, introduced red hyalith, a name for colored glass that emulated *rosso antico,* red stoneware produced by Josiah Wedgwood. In 1817, Rosler introduced black hyalith, a name for dense black glass accented occasionally with gilded ornamentation, inspired by black basalt, a dark stoneware also produced by Wedgwood.

CRACKLE GLASS. In the sixteenth century, Venetian glassmakers invented *vetro a ghiacciaio,* or "ice glass," a decorative style known in France as *verre craquelé,* one that refracted light and created a sparkling effect. Crackle glass was made by immersing a bubble of hot glass in cold water and quickly reheating it to create a network of fine cracks and fissures. *Encrusted glass* was created by rolling the hot glass on fine pieces of clear or colored broken glass, which fused to the outer surface. (See also *frosted glass*.)

*CRISTALLO.* The Italian word *cristallo* means "crystal" or "clear glass," a name for translucent lightweight soda glass. The Egyptians were the first to make soda glass, but the Romans added manganese oxide as a decoloring agent, an element that neutralized iron and other impurities in the composition and produced clearer glass. In the fifteenth century, Venetian glassmakers rediscovered the Roman technique and produced *cristallo,* so named because the glass resembled rock crystal. In a molten state, *cristallo* was soft and easy to work into thin fluent forms that bore a slight tinge of gray or brown owing to impurities in the material.

*CRYSTALLO CÉRAMIE.* In 1818, Barthelemy Desprez, a French sculptor, enclosed ceramic ornamentation within glass, a process patented under the name of *crystallo céramie,* a French term for "crystal ceramic." Essentially, *crystallo céramie* is cased glass inlaid with ceramic cameos and medallions, usually carved of unglazed white stoneware that takes on a grayish silver-white hue from air trapped under the crystal. In North America, *crystallo céramie* was known as *sulphide* or *cameo incrustation,* a method used primarily to ornament paperweights, jewelry, tableware, and door handles, to depict profile portraits, and to make decorative objects.

In 1819, Apsley Pellatt, son of the founder of the Falcon Glasshouse in Southwark, England, and a manufacturer of decorative glassware, developed *crystallo céramie* independent of Desprez, a technique he used to ornament paperweights, plaques, tumblers, vases, and lamps inlaid with classical motifs. Today, *crystallo céramie* is seen at the Corning Museum of Glass, Corning, New York.

CUT GLASS. In the latter half of the first millennium B.C. colored glass fell from favor. To promote the refractive quality of clear glass, Roman glassmakers introduced facet-cut ornamentation. By the Middle Ages, cut glass was seldom made except in the twelfth century when Hedwig beakers were produced. However, in the early seventeenth century, Bohemian glassmakers expanded the glass cutter's art with the invention of potash-lime glass, a hard glass receptive to cut ornamentation. In the second half of the seventeenth century, George Ravenscroft invented lead crystal, a refractive glass with a soft thick surface that took cut ornamentation well. As a result cut decoration dominated glassware up until the first half of the nineteenth century. Today, cut glass is a popular ornamental style well suited to stemware, tumblers, decanters, serveware, and decorative accessories.

Rather than allow light to pass through glass, cut ornamentation refracts light. Decorative styles include hollow cut, miter cut, and panel cut.

- *Hollow-cut ornamentation* is made with an abrasive cutting wheel shaped with a slightly rounded edge, one that produces oval and circular cuts sometimes called *printies, balls,* or *olives.*
- *Miter cut ornamentation* employs a pointed wheel that produces various V-shaped cuts: the *prismatic cut* features deep horizontal grooves; the *star cut* radiates from a central point; the *diamond cut* is recognized by diagonal grooves that criss-cross at right angles; and the *strawberry-diamond cut* is made with flat areas crosshatched with diamond cuts.
- *Panel cuts* are formed by a flat-edged wheel that grinds slight indentations, an ornamental method used to make shallow depressions on crystal shaped with curved surfaces, such as the bowls of stemware.

*ÉGLOMISÉ.* A technique named for Glomy, a French mirror and picture framer, *églomisé* incorporates the application of silver or gold foil to the reverse side of cut or engraved ornamentation. The decoration is then backed with red, blue, or black lacquer.

EMBOSSED ORNAMENTATION. Embossing is a form of raised, sculptural decoration. The design is protected with a resist of wax, and the surrounding area is dissolved with hydrofluoric acid. When the wax is removed, the pattern stands out in relief.

ENAMEL. Enamel is made from a paste of powdered glass colored with metallic oxides, mixed in an oily medium, and applied after glass is fired. The glass is then refired for a short time at a temperature low enough to soften the enamels but high enough to fuse the colors without distortion to the surface of glass. In antiquity, Roman glassmakers mastered the art of opaque enamel, and by the Middle Ages transparent enamel was developed, a medium used to create fine lines and shadows on stained-glass windows. In the Renaissance, Venetian artisans found enamel the ideal medium for decorating delicate brittle *cristallo.* In the sixteenth century, German glassmakers used the broad surface of large drinking vessels as a canvas for enameled ornamentation, depicting lively scenes with strong colors.

In 1660, Johann Schaper, a glass and porcelain enameler from Nuremberg, introduced *Schwarzlot,* "black lead," a dark transparent enamel inspired by line engravings. This method fostered shaded ornamentation with greater detail and sensitivity than previously known. Schaper used *Schwarzlot* to interpret miniature painting on glass vessels and also incorporated the blackish-brown and grayish-brown tones with a palette of colorful ornamentation.

In the seventeenth and eighteenth centuries, talented enamelers from Bohemia, Germany, and Austria obtained blanks from glasshouses and porcelain manufactories and enameled undecorated ware at home. These artisans were called *hausmaler,* meaning "home painters." Hausmaler produced enameled ornamentation of such skill, detail, and sensitivity that their work was often signed. Well-respected *hausmaler* include Daniel Preissler and his son Ignaz, both of Bohemia and Silesia, and Abraham Helmhack of Nuremberg.

In the nineteenth century, the supply of wood in the forested regions of northern Bohemia began to dwindle, and many glassworkers turned to glass painting. Best-known of these are Samuel Mohn, who used translucent enamels to paint realistic scenes in minute detail, along with his son, Gottlob Samuel Mohn, and Gottlob's student, Anton Kothgasser of Vienna.

ENGLISH STEMWARE. In the late seventeenth century George Ravenscroft invented lead crystal, and by the eighteenth century, crystal drinking glasses were the primary product of English glasshouses. Because lead crystal is heavy and not conducive to the ductile, fluent forms associated with Venetian crystal, English stemware is characterized by thick, sturdy, well-proportioned shapes that feature plain bowls, a style that emphasizes the clarity of the material and the form of the vessel. The decoration is primarily in the stems and is of four main types.

- *Baluster,* from the Italian *balaustro,* "pillar," is a pillar-type stem often ornamented with a knop, a round architectural form that decorates the upper balusters of stairways. The baluster stem with knop was adapted in a variety of ways: inverted, adorned with an acorn-shaped knop, or decorated with several knops.

- *Air twist* is a decorative stem originally made by accident when the base of a vessel was inadvertently pricked by a wire. The threadlike orifice is drawn out in a twisting motion into the stem.
- *Enclosed tears* is an ornamental term for a stem decorated with comma-shaped spheres. While soft, the glass is indented with a tool and the depression is covered with molten glass. When the stem is drawn out, the air in the indentation forms a tear-shaped bubble.
- *Facet-cut stemware* grew out of a need to conserve glass. Because of the popularity of lead crystal, both domestically and abroad, demand was great, and up to the middle of the eighteenth century English stemware was made with an unlimited supply of glass. In 1745 England levied an excise tax based on the weight of glass. Thereafter, heavy lead crystal was very costly to produce. To conserve weight, glassmakers decreased the lead in the composition, a step that also reduced the clarity. To compensate for this loss of brilliance, artisans enhanced the refractive quality with facet-cut ornamentation. Although the glass excise tax was repealed in 1845, facet-cut ornamentation continued as a major decorative technique.

ENGRAVED GLASS. A decorative method that cuts shallow ornamentation in glass using an abrasive wheel or a diamond-point stylus.

*Wheel-engraved ornamentation* is first drawn on glass, and the design is cut by a rapidly rotating wheel made of stone or copper, a technique that produces fluent lines and renders decoration with intricate detail, such as monograms, floral motifs, or landscape scenes. Wheel-engraved ornamentation renders design with an opaque grayish matte finish and creates a dull surface that is usually left unpolished to accent the refractive quality of the colorless background.

Stone wheels are used to make deep cuts, and copper wheels to execute engraving. The wheel is lubricated by water or a mixture of linseed oil and emery powder and held on a spindle rotated by a treadle. The wheel is applied to the far side of glass; the cutter looks through the glass while he or she works, a method that requires extreme dexterity, strength, and artistic talent. The roughness or fineness of a cut is commensurate with the coarseness of the abrasive; the deeper the cut, the higher the relief.

Wheel-engraved work was known in Egyptian and Roman antiquity. The technique was used in the seventh and eight centuries by Islamic glassmakers and revived in the fifteenth century by Bohemian artisans. By the seventeenth and eighteenth centuries, the invention of thick potash-lime glass in Bohemia increased the popularity of engraved ornamentation and demand began to supersede that of enameled decoration. The free robust style of Frans Greenwood of Rotterdam and the work of Jacob Slang, also of Holland, were particularly valued.

In the nineteenth century, glass was engraved with a sculptural look in high relief, a decorative style called *Hochschnitt,* meaning "high cutting," and in low-relief ornamentation known as *Tiefschnitt,* meaning "low cutting." Today, both *Hochschnitt* and *Tiefschnitt* glass can be seen in the Corning Museum of Glass, Corning, New York.

The *diamond-point stylus* is a method of engraved ornamentation rediscovered in the sixteenth century by Venetian artisans, an interest perhaps stimulated when diamonds were introduced to Europe from India (through Venice, the east-west port of trade). The scratched technique was more suitable for delicate Venetian *cristallo* than wheel-engraved work. Essentially, the stylus is a sharp diamond splinter used to tap tiny dots onto the surface of glass in an ornamental process called *stipple engraving.* The sharp needle-like stone is mounted in a holder, and the design is hand-inscribed on glass, similar to the way a pencil is held, only with more pressure. Shading is achieved by spacing the dots. The closer the dots, the whiter the ornamentation. Venetian artisans scratched *cristallo* with dots of such gossamer delicacy that they looked as if they were breathed onto glass. The pattern is fully visible only when the glass is held to the light.

The technique of stipple engraving was carried to northern Europe by itinerant Italian glassmakers, and in 1646, Anna Roemer Visscher, a well-known German glass engraver, introduced stipple engraving to Holland. By the eighteenth century stipple engraving was the favored way to depict portraits and coats of arms, a technique perfected in the eighteenth century by Frans Greenwood of Rotterdam, and in the second half of the eighteenth century by David Wolff.

ETCHED ORNAMENTATION. In the seventeenth century, Henry Schwanhardt invented a way to remove glass in a bath of hydrofluoric acid, a process called *etched ornamentation,* from the German *essen,* meaning "to eat." Etched ornamentation proved a faster, more economical method of ornamentation than engraved decoration, a technique used primarily to interpret pictorial motifs on large surfaces of glass.

Although etched ornamentation appears similar to engraved decoration, it is shallower, and compared to the deeper lines and rounded edges of wheel engraving, the edges are sharp and vertical. The motif is drawn on the surface of glass with a graver, a sharp, pointed steel rod inserted in a brass tube. The unadorned surface is protected with a resist unique to the artisan, such as wax mixed with motor oil, liquid bitumen, or lead foil. Hydrofluoric acid is applied to the design. The acid eats into the motif. The depth of the ornamentation is controlled by the strength of the acid and the amount of time the glass remains in the bath.

In the nineteenth century, etched glass was made by abrasion. Roughly grained sand was forced at high pressure through a sand gun onto the surface of crystal. The decorative surround was protected with a resist substance, and when removed, the matte finish of the design contrasted with the gleaming surface of the glass.

*FILIGRANA* AND *LATTICINIO.* In Grecian and Roman antiquity, artisans decorated glass with lacy patterns; hence *latticinio,* meaning "lace glass." In 1527 the brothers Filippo and Bernardo Serena applied for a patent to ornament clear molten glass with threads of milk glass or multicolored glass. Interestingly, Venetian artisans used *latticinio* to make all-over lacy patterns, and English glassmakers adapted the technique to the stems of crystal in a style called *air twist*.

Today *latticinio* is a decorative technique associated with clear glass ornamented with lacy patterns known as *filigrana,* meaning "filigree" or "thread-grained," a netlike ornamentation made from canes of opaque white or colored glass, the latter primarily of blue.

FLASH GLASS. A name for two layers of colored glass. The top layer is "flashed" with a film of glass in a different color than the bottom layer. Flash glass is a decorative technique that produces glass thinner than cased glass or glass overlay. It is made by dipping the outside surface briefly in a batch of molten liquid. The motif is drawn on the top layer, and to reveal the clear layer underneath, the design is carved away or removed by acid.

FRENCH CRYSTAL. Until the end of the eighteenth century, manufacture of fine lead crystal evaded France, and glass vessels were made of *verre de fougère,* or fern glass, a name for simple glass fluxed with alkali of ferns. To compete with the beauty of imported crystal, in the eighteenth century the Académie des Sciences offered a prize to those glasshouses whose work rivaled that made in England, Germany, and Bohemia.

In 1765, the Archbishop of Metz, who owned the town of Baccarat, established the Saint-Anne factory, an establishment that in 1822 was officially renamed the Compagnie des Cristalleries de Baccarat. In 1767, the Verrerie Royale de Saint Louis was also established in Baccarat. To encourage large-scale production, Louis XVI sponsored the two companies, but with the beginning of the French Revolution his efforts were halted. However, as emperor, Napoleon encouraged the arts, and by the early nineteenth century French crystal rivaled the finest imports. The crystal was decorated with neoclassical designs and ornamented with portrait cameos rendered with silver-white sulfides, along with colored glass, notably opaline. Today, French crystal denotes luxury glass that emphasizes ornamentation over form, decorated with cut, colored, and gilded designs.

By the mid-nineteenth century, writing paper was less expensive than previously, and letter writing was a favorite pastime, a hobby that led to the popularity of crystal paperweights. Baccarat, Saint Louis, and Clichy paperweights with encased ornamentation, such as *millefiori,* commemorative portraits, birds, reptiles, fruits, and flowers, were sought after.

FROSTED GLASS. In the sixteenth century, Venetian glassmakers perfected *vetro a ghiacciaio,* or "ice glass." Today, frosted glass is made by several methods: sandblasting, acid fumes, or the application of powdered glass to the surface. Sandblasting promotes a rough texture. Acid fumes create a smooth, semiopaque surface. Powdered glass gives a matte finish. (See also *crackle glass.*)

GILDED ORNAMENTATION. The application of gold decoration to glass is made by mixing gold leaf or powdered gold with a fixative, such as honey, egg white, or mercury, and applying it with a brush to the surface of cold glass. After application, the article is fired a second time at a low temperature. When removed from the kiln, gold is dull and gilded ornamentation is burnished to a lustrous sheen.

GOLD-BETWEEN-GLASS. In Egyptian antiquity, glassmakers applied gold leaf between two layers of glass. This technique, called *fondi d'oro,* or "gold glass," was perfected in ancient Rome. In the eighteenth century, gold glass was revived by Johann Joseph Mildner, a glassmaker at the Gutenbrunn Glasshouse in the lower Austrian district of Ottenschlag; the technique was called *Zwischengoldglas,* "gold between glass" or "gold sandwich glass." Mildner decorated the outside of glass with gold or silver leaf engraved with motifs accented with red lacquer. A clear glass sleeve was placed over the glass, and the rim was sealed with lacquer. Often the bottom space between the two walls was also decorated.

IRISH CRYSTAL. In 1780, when Ireland was granted free trade with England, many glassmakers moved from England to Ireland to escape from the English excise tax. In Ireland they were able to produce glass that was heavier, more ornately decorated, and cut with deeper grooves than English crystal. From 1780 to 1825 the Irish glass industry prospered. It was noted for quality ware, such as centerpieces, pickle jars, salt cellars, jelly glasses, custard dishes, decanters blown in vertically ribbed molds, and hand-cut canoe-shaped fruit bowls mounted on pedestal bases. Today, Irish crystal is associated with fine lead crystal decorated with cut ornamentation or interpreted with plain designs.

LUSTER. Luster is an iridescent sheen developed by Islamic glassmakers, who brushed the surface with a thin application of metallic salts made from copper, gold, silver, or platinum. After application, the glass was refired at a lower temperature in a closed kiln. Copper yielded a yellowish-red to deep coppery-red luster. Gold produced luster with ruby-red tones. Silver created straw-colored luster, and platinum exuded a silver iridescence.

MILK GLASS AND *LATTIMO.* In antiquity, Egyptian glassmakers produced white "milk glass," a decorative category used later by Chinese artisans to imitate white-bodied porcelain. In the sixteenth century, Muranese glassmakers, fascinated by Chinese porcelain, opacified glass with bone ash, antimony, or zinc, a composition that produced milk-white glass called *lattimo* (from the Italian *latte,* "milk"). In the late seventeenth century, Bohemian glassmakers opacified glass with arsenic and tin oxide, a composition called *Milchglas,* that revealed a touch of fiery red when held to the light. At the Potsdam Glass Works near Berlin, enameled *Milchglas* was known as *Porzellanglas,* a product the English advertised as "mock china." Today, milk glass is opacified with tin oxide.

*MURRHINE,* MOSAICS, AND *MILLEFIORI.* In Egyptian antiquity, the aristocracy collected bowls carved from plain or striated semiprecious stones, luxury vessels that inspired Alexandrian glassmakers to develop *murrhine,* a term for delicate multicolored glass with jade tones and transparent hues characteristic of fluorite. Small fragments of colored glass were arranged side by side on a marble slab, heated slowly in a furnace, and fused. The softened glass was removed and draped, or "slumped," over a simple form, such as a cup, plate, or bowl. When cooled, the core was removed and the vessel was polished until smooth.

In an attempt to reproduce *murrhine,* in the first century B.C. Roman glassmakers blew multicolored glass into thin forms bundled together and fused, a technique that created a single thick rod called a *cane.* The cane was drawn out into a narrow width and cut crosswise; the sections were arranged vertically in or around a mold; then the canes were heated slowly until fused, producing polychrome glass called *mosaic.*

Egyptian *murrhine* was limited by the size, thickness, and shape of the vessel over which the glass was draped, but the dimensions, density, and configurations of Roman mosaics were unlimited. Canes were arranged in floral patterns known as *millefiori,* meaning "thousand flowers." Although *murrhine* is no longer made, mosaics and *millefiori* continue as popular decorative techniques to ornament glassware and jewelry.

*PÂTE DE VERRE.* Literally a "paste of glass," *pâte de verre* is a French term for powdered colored glass mixed with a binder and cast in a mold, a technique used in ancient Egypt to make vessels, furniture inlay, and ornamental objects, such as miniature masks and bas-relief plaques. In the nineteenth century, Henri Cros and his son Jean were interested in reproducing colored Greek and Roman statues, so they revived the art of *pâte de verre,* a method used to produce statuettes, sculptures in bas-relief, small medallions, and decorative accessories.

STAINED GLASS. Stained glass is made by spraying the outer surface of once-fired clear glass with stain made from metallic oxides. The glass is fired a second time at a low temperature. The earliest stained glass is attributed to French artisans in the mid-twelfth century who made windows of white and tinted glass for the Cathedral of Saint Denis in Paris. That glass was enameled with illustrations of biblical stories and replaced wall paintings as a way to instruct illiterate people. When compared to the small, round romanesque windows of the eleventh century, the spear-shaped gothic construction indigenous to western Europe in the twelfth century fostered windows with long, large surfaces on which to portray a single figure or a narrative scene. By the nineteenth century, stained glass provided Bohemian glassmakers with a colorful background for enameled, engraved, or cut ornamentation. Stained glass was also left unadorned, and the glass admired for the beauty of the colors.

STUDIO GLASS. In the 1960s, Harvey Littleton, a glass artist who once apprenticed at the Corning Glass Works and whose father was a glass scientist at Corning, attended a workshop hosted by the Toledo Museum of Art. At the workshop Littleton met Dominick Labino, a scientist and vice president of research for the Johns Manville Fiber Glass Corporation. Littleton used a small furnace invented by Labino to melt 50 to 150 pounds of glass, demonstrating that it was possible to fire a small quantity of glass in a limited space. This meant that a glassblower could work alone in a small studio workshop.

The meeting inaugurated the American studio glass movement, an aesthetic that recognized the glassblower as an artist equal to a painter or a sculptor. Today, at hundreds of colleges and technical schools, classes are now offered in glass design, hand-blown glass, and glass decoration.

SWEDISH CRYSTAL. Between 1915 and 1917, Orrefors Glassworks hired two artists, Simon Gate and Edward Hald, to design and work directly with glassblowers. This concept was later adopted by other Scandinavian glasshouses, such as Kosta and Boda. The engraved style associated with Swedish crystal evolved around 1920, when a group of glass engravers came to Sweden from Czechoslovakia and developed ornamentation based on delicate, spare, simple designs made primarily for display. During the late 1930s and 1940s Swedish glassworkers developed a distinctive style based on classic forms and contemporary shapes that emphasized the clarity of the material rather than ornamentation. Today, Swedish crystal is executed with strong lines that emphasize form; the style is devoid of decoration but accents the sparkling, refractive quality of the material, or is engraved with a simple design that does not overpower the beauty of the form and detract from the purity of the material.

VENETIAN GLASS. The beauty of Venetian glass lies in the translucency of the material and the graceful fanciful forms into which it is blown—for example, goblets fashioned with convoluted stems shaped like dragons and mythical creatures. Venetian glass was made of sand fluxed with soda, a category called *cristallo,* made to resemble rock crystal, a semiprecious stone. However, because *cristallo* was thin and brittle, decoration was rendered by shape alone or ornamentation was interpreted with shallow stipple engraving or colorful enamels and gilding. Unlike lead crystal, Venetian soda glass does not resonate and the surface is lustrous rather than brilliant.

In the sixteenth century, Venetian glass was fashioned to resemble onyx, agate, and chalcedony. In the seventeenth century, Venetian glass was made with minute copper scales, a decorative technique that imitated aventurine, a translucent quartz flecked with bits of mica.

CHAPTER TWENTY-EIGHT

# THE DIFFERENT CATEGORIES OF GLASS

*Glass is more gentle, graceful, and noble than any metal and its use is more delightful, polite, and sightly than any other material at this day known to the world.*

*Antonio Neri*, A Short History of Glass, *1612*

PICTURE LIFE WITHOUT GLASS, a world devoid of windowpanes, lightbulbs, eyeglasses, microscopes, telescopes, airplanes, cars, radio, television, motion pictures, and computer monitors, to name only a few of the modern-day uses of glass. Then ponder the pleasures of dining with glass. View the color of wine in a clear glass vessel. Follow the slow rise of champagne bubbles in a tall glass. Admire the sparkle of crystal and the infinite reflections of mirrors.

Glass is formed by a fusion of silica and alkali, together with small amounts of other materials. Silica is a hard, glassy mineral obtained from disintegrated rock, such as quartz, flint, and, most commonly, sand. It is used for its strength-giving properties. Alkalis are soluble minerals: carbonates of sodium (soda ash), potassium (potash), calcium (lime), and lead oxide, a substance that reduces the melting point of hard materials and promotes fusion at a lower temperature.

Glassmaking materials are put together in a *batch,* from the Middle English word *bache* meaning "to bake." Because a batch contains metallic substances, such as iron, in its molten state the composition is known as *metal,* a term coined by English glassmakers to distinguish the material in the furnace from the finished object. The metal is highly plastic and can be blown, drawn, molded, pressed into form, or spun into fine threads.

But glass hardens without crystallizing, and once hardened it is amorphous or formless. Essentially, glass is a supercooled liquid, a product that goes from liquid to solid without changing structure. Because glass does not possess a crystalline structure, it shatters when broken (unlike ceramics, which break because the clay particles fall into an ordered structure). The amorphous quality, however, means that broken glass can be recycled: it can easily be remelted and reused.

Waste glass is known as *cullet,* from the French *cueillette,* "act of gathering." Cullet is cleaned, melted, and added to new batches of glass made with the same composition. Typically cullet makes up one-quarter to one-half of the batch. Cullet melts quickly, promotes fusion of material at a low temperature, saves fuel, and improves the clarity and quality of clear glass. However, due to imperfections it may possess, cullet is not added to colored glass.

Once glass is shaped it is annealed in a *lehr* or *leer oven.* The lehr oven carries glass slowly on a conveyor belt through a series of gradually decreasing temperatures; this method cools glass evenly, relieves internal stress, and strengthens it so the material resists cracks and breakage when it is cold.

## The Major Glass Categories

Glass is known by the type of alkali it contains. *Soda glass* was originally made from sodium obtained from the ash of marine plants, but today, chemical soda is used for commercial purposes. Soda glass is the most common glass category, typically composed of 72 percent silica (for strength), 15 percent soda (the major flux), 9 percent lime (a stabilizer), and 4 percent other materials. It is easy to melt, clear, hard, and resistant to scratches, but it has only limited sparkle, and when struck on the rim it does not give a musical ring. Soda glass is ductile and maintains its plasticity through a wide range of temperatures. It is inexpensive to make and is used for utilitarian ware, such as glass tableware, serveware, kitchenware, bottles, jars, windowpanes, lightbulbs, and Christmas ornaments.

*Potash glass* is made from potassium carbonate, an alkali obtained from wood and plant ash found in inland regions. Potash is a heavier alkali than soda ash and is used to produce glass that is thicker and more brilliant than soda glass, one with a hard surface conducive to cut and engraved ornamentation. However, potash glass turns rigid faster than soda glass, lacks ductility, and is difficult to manipulate into fluent forms.

*Lead crystal* is associated with luxury tableware, notably stemware, dinnerware, serveware, decanters, candlesticks, napkin rings, salt and pepper shakers, and bowls. The typical formula contains 55 percent silica, 33 percent lead oxide, 11 percent potassium (potash), and 1 percent other materials. Although crystal may contain as little as 10 to 15 percent lead oxide, *lead crystal* must contain 24 percent lead or more. *Full-lead crystal* is 30 to 33 percent lead—more than that makes the crystal too soft. Lead not only promotes clarity, brilliance, thickness, and weight, but the oxide fosters a softer surface than soda glass or potash glass, one receptive to deep facet-cut ornamentation. When struck gently on the rim, delicate crystal resonates with bell-like tones. However, thick shapes, such as heavy bowls, do not have a musical ring.

*Borosilicate glass* is a twentieth-century invention. It was perfected in 1910 by Eugene C. Sullivan and William C. Taylor of the Corning Glass Works, and is generally known by its trademark name Pyrex. Borosilicate glass contains approximately 80 percent silica, 4 percent sodium oxide, 2 percent alumina, 12 percent boron oxide, and 2 percent other materials. The boron oxide is a nonmetallic chemical that occurs in combination with other elements. The batch melts at a higher temperature than soda glass and lead crystal, the rate of expansion and contraction is lowered, and borosilicate glass is three times more resistant to thermal shock. It resists hot and cold temperatures, making it ideal for bakeware, coffee makers, teapots, cookware, and storage containers for the freezer.

# How Glass Is Shaped

## *Blown Glass*

Luxury glass is free-blown and shaped without tools or it is mouth-blown with the aid of a team. Free-blown glass begins with a gather of glass suspended on the end of a hollow pipe. The glassblower blows air through the pipe and the pressure causes the glass gathered at the end to take form. This technique is used to shape one-of-a-kind articles without assorted tools, a skill dependent on the glassmaker's artistic eye and expertise, and costly to execute and purchase.

Less expensive luxury glass involves a team of three to six workers known as a *shop,* a crew who use a *chair,* a special wooden bench fitted with long flat arms. Often, the size of a manufactory is known by the number of chairs. The shop uses tools that have changed little over the centuries, such as the blowpipe and pontil rod. The *blowpipe* is a hollow metal rod about 4 to 6 feet long, and approximately ¾-inch in diameter. The blowing end is fitted with a wooden mouthpiece. The gathering end features a metal ring.

The metal ring is dipped into molten glass by the master glassblower, who is called a *gaffer,* a term adapted from "godfather." The molten liquid gathered on the metal ring is called variously a *gob, glob,* or a *blob*.

When air is blown through the wooden mouthpiece, the gob inflates and forms a small bubble, called a *parison.* Depending on the size of the finished article, the gaffer sits or stands on the chair and, holding the rod in his hands, rolls his arms up and down the long arms of the chair. This rotates the bubble on the *marver,* the flat plates of polished metal or smooth marble that extend from the arms of the chair. The parison takes on a cylindrical shape, and the gaffer swings and spins the pipe to create a form, similar to the way a child forms a soap bubble.

The *pontil rod* is a solid iron rod, also known as a *punty* or a *ponty.* It is a little shorter than a blowpipe and slightly smaller in diameter. The pontil rod is used to carry and manipulate small amounts of glass and is attached to the end of a partly formed article. Because molten glass is heavy and sticky, cools quickly, and stiffens rapidly, to maintain or renew plasticity, the pontil rod is used to reheat it in a *glory hole,* a small opening in the side the furnace. Slightly cooled articles are reheated in the glory hole to remove tool marks and add brilliance to dull surfaces; this is known as *fire polishing*. Hence the name *glory hole* for the glory of the beauty the small furnace brings to the piece.

The pontil rod is used to give final shape to an article, to create ornamentation by twisting, pulling, and bending the molten glass; it is used to apply handles, to work the upper part of an item and finish a rim, and to apply stems. In two-part stemware, the stem is drawn out from the bowl in one piece and the foot is added. To make three-part stemware, the stem is made separately, a technique that accommodates more elaborate ornamentation.

After the article is cooled it is removed from the pontil rod with a gentle knock of the tool, a step known as *knocking off* or *cracking off*, a process that leaves a pontil mark on the base, a rough circular scar characteristic of old glass. In the second half of the eighteenth century, pontil marks were ground off, a process that left a smooth circular area, and by the mid-nineteenth century the pontil mark had almost disappeared. Today the pontil mark is used to give new glass the look of age.

Next, the glass is slowly cooled in the annealing oven and then it receives additional decoration and polishing.

## *Molded Glass*

Machine-made glass is faster, more efficient, and less costly to execute than blown glass. Compressed air injects glass into a mold, giving the glass uniform shape and ornamentation in one operation. The decoration is impressed on the inside and outside of the article simultaneously in a fully automated process, or the article is impressed on one side only. This method is used to make inexpensive bowls, dishes, ashtrays, bottles, jars, serveware, lightbulbs, and Christmas ornaments.

Today, soda glass is used to make utilitarian machine-made items. Borosilicate glass is reserved for glass that can tolerate temperature extremes. And luxury crystal is hand-blown by a single artisan or by a shop of workers.

CHAPTER TWENTY-NINE

# STEMWARE: SHAPE AND PURPOSE

GLASS STEMWARE IS A drinking vessel made with a bowl that rests on a stem, a shape anchored by a foot. The purpose of stemware is to serve cool beverages, such as water, iced tea, and wine. Just as a cup handle protects fingers from heat, the stem provides a way to hold cool drinks without warming the contents of the bowl. The exception is the brandy snifter, a vessel cradled in the palm of the hand to enhance the flavor of brandy, whose taste is improved by heat.

Glass drinking vessels were originally made with rounded or pointed bases. Round-based glasses were called *tumblers*. They were cylindrical vessels with heavy rounded bases. When they were full, the weight of the liquid prevented the vessel from tipping over, but when they were empty, the short, shallow vessel tumbled. Today, a tumbler is any drinking vessel made with a heavy base and straight sides or walls that taper slightly. To keep beverages cool, vessels with pointed bases were planted upright in the ground or in the bed of a river but were never laid on the table. Instead, the vessel was quickly drained for a fast refill.

It wasn't until the late Middle Ages that glass vessels with horizontal or domed bases were made. To create a thick rim that protected the base from chipping, the edge of the foot was folded over or under. In Venice, the folded base helped to balance delicate stemware. In England, the foot was folded in widths of ¼ inch to ½ inch, a thick rim that added weight to the vessel. But in 1745, England levied an excise tax on the weight of glass, and the plain horizontal base was adopted.

The bowls of contemporary vessels come in three main shapes. The *bucket-shaped bowl* is similar to a modern-day bucket, with a horizontal base and almost vertical sides. The *tulip-shaped bowl* resembles a tulip, a form derived from the ogee, or S-shaped, double curve made with a rounded base and sides that curve inward. The *flared bowl* is shaped like a trumpet or a funnel, a long, narrow form made with a pointed or slightly rounded bowl that either flares outward at the top or remains straight.

In the Middle Ages, glass was a luxury product and vessels were made with large bowls for sharing. By the eighteenth century, stemware featured bowls in large, medium, and small sizes. Large bowls were for beverages taken throughout the day such as beer, ale, and mead. Medium-size bowls were for beverages with a low alcohol content, notably wine. Vessels with small bowls were used for drinks high in alcohol, such as cordials and liqueurs.

Today, stemware with a large bowl is reserved for nonalcoholic beverages, such as water and iced tea. Stemware with a medium-size bowl is made for drinks low in alcohol such as table wine and sparkling wine. Stemware with a small bowl is used for drinks with a moderate to high alcohol content, such an aperitifs and dessert wine. Stemware with a tiny bowl is made for drinks high in alcohol, specifically cordials and liqueurs. The exception is the brandy snifter, which may have either small or large bowls.

The purpose and size of stemware is presented below in the order in which the vessel is used at the table, from preprandial drinks to those served after dinner. The dimensions vary slightly between antique stemware and contemporary shapes, and approximate capacities are given.

## Aperitif Glass

The *aperitif* (pronounced ah-pare-i-teef) is a drink fortified with approximately 15 to 20 percent alcohol. Its purpose is to "open" the gastric juices and stimulate the appetite before a meal. Common aperitifs include sherry, Dubonnet, and Campari. Because aperitifs are high in alcohol, only 2 to 3 ounces are poured and the aperitif glass is small. But when champagne is served as a preprandial drink, because the alcohol content is lower than that of an aperitif, the champagne glass is used, a larger vessel filled almost to the rim. The only time an aperitif glass is placed on the table is when sherry is served to accompany a course in which sherry is an ingredient, such as oxtail, lentil, or black bean soup.

*Top row, left to right:* THE APERITIF GLASS, WHITE WINE GLASS, HOCK WINE GLASS, RED WINE GLASS, CLARET GLASS.
*Bottom row, left to right:* ALL-PURPOSE WINE GLASS, MAGNUM WINE GLASS, WATER GOBLET.

*Top row, left to right:* CHAMPAGNE GLASSES IN SHAPES KNOWN AS COUPE, TULIP, HOLLOW-STEM, TRUMPET, AND FLUTE.

*Bottom row, left to right:* LIQUEUR AND CORDIALS GLASSES IN A 1-OUNCE AND 2-OUNCE SIZE, THE DESSERT WINE GLASS, AND BRANDY SNIFTERS IN SMALL AND LARGE SIZES.

# *Water Goblet*

*Here's that which is too weak to be a sinner,*
*Honest water, which ne'er left man in the mire.*

SHAKESPEARE, TIMON OF ATHENS

*Goblet* is from the Old French *gobelet* for "cup" and *gobbet* for "mouthful." Because water is drunk throughout a meal, the goblet is the largest vessel in a set of stemware and holds approximately 6 ounces when filled three-quarters full.

In the Middle Ages, water was badly polluted in cities and a major source of intestinal disease, such as cholera. For health reasons, fermented drinks, such as ale, beer, cider, mead, and metheglin, were served at meals in goblets.

> He pours down goblet after goblet. The second to see where the first has gone; the third to see no harm happens to the second; a fourth to say there's another coming; and a fifth to say he is not sure he is the last.
>
> Charles Lamb

*Ale,* a Middle English word for "bitter," often preceded the names of special holidays or festivities; hence Easter-ale and wedding-ale, the latter giving rise to the modern term *bridal,* from the Old English custom of selling ale at weddings and donating the proceeds to the bride. Ale was also called *nog* or *noggin,* a small serving equal to a quartern (a quarter of a British pint). From an old English drinking song:

*Before we think of joggin,*
*Let's take a cheerful noggin.*

The word *beer* may come from the west Germanic word *beuza* for "foaming," a drink made from ale and hops. *Cider* means "sweet fermented juice." It was made from apple and pear juice, and called *perry* when the beverage contained more pears than apples. *Mead,* from the Indo-European word *medhu* for "honey," was made of honey, boiled water, and yeast; this fermented beverage had an alcohol content of approximately 8 percent. It was given to newlyweds to encourage romance during the first month of an arranged marriage, hence, our word *honeymoon*. *Metheglin,* from the Welsh *meddyg* for "healing," was essentially mead flavored with herbs.

In the Middle Ages the rich drank from goblets made of gold, silver, and Venetian glass, while the poor drank from vessels made of pewter, earthenware, horn, wood, coconut shells, pigskin, or leather. Pigskin tankards were called *piggins*. And leather vessels waterproofed with coal tar or black pitch in a treatment called *jack* were known as *blackjacks*.

Medieval goblets were kept on a sideboard, and when a sip of water was requested, a goblet was brought to the table by a butler, or "bottler," the person in charge of drinks. Goblets were shared, and to ensure ample liquid for everyone, medieval manners decreed that one not imbibe more than three times during a meal. The capacious goblet permitted a hearty guzzle or two before the vessel was relinquished. When a lady requested a drink, a butler held a napkin under her chin.

People ate with the fingers in the Middle Ages, and the communal drinking glass was greasy to hold. To afford a good grasp, German glassmakers applied glass protuberances to the outside of beakers, pads called *prunts*. According to a sermon delivered in 1564 by Mathesius, a German minister, "prunts also make glasses easier for drunken and clumsy people to hold."

Why is wine presented in a "glass," and water in a "goblet"? The answer lies in the nature of the material. Because metal imparts a metallic taste to wine, acidic beverages are served in glass vessels. Conversely, water does not extract a metallic taste from metal and is served in numerous materials, among them glass and metal—a custom that continues today.

The goblet is always used in formal dining, but at an informal meal it is an optional table appointment. A multicourse menu incorporates a variety of seasonings and to refresh the palate and cleanse the taste buds between wines, water is served. At a meal composed of a few courses, water is not served and goblets are not needed, unless the menu includes salty or spicy dishes, for example, Mexican, Chinese, or Thai food.

## Iced-Tea Glass

*Tea: The infusion of a China plant*
*Sweetened with the pith of an Indian cane.*

JOSEPH ADDISON, THE SPECTATOR

Iced tea is a twentieth-century American drink, concocted in the summer of 1904 by Richard Blechynden, a British colonial living in Calcutta who was employed by an Indian tea firm to promote the company's product at the Louisiana Purchase Exposition in St. Louis. Because the weather in St. Louis is hot and humid in summer, the public showed little interest in tasting samples of hot tea. In desperation, Mr. Blechynden poured hot tea over ice and served the drink in a tall glass. An American tradition was born.

The iced-tea glass is a long, narrow vessel with a short stem, a shape made to accommodate ice cubes. Because water and wine are the only beverages served at a formal table, the iced-tea glass is reserved for informal dining, from elegant to casual. The shape is ideal for cold beverages of any kind, such as tomato juice or iced coffee.

## Wine Glasses

*It is difficult to enjoy a good wine in a bad glass.*

EVELYN WAUGH, WINE IN PEACE AND WAR

Homer's *Odyssey* and *Iliad* provide us with the first recorded reference to a wine glass, a two-handled cup that evolved into a silver vessel, such as the one given by Caranus of Macedonia to guests at a wedding banquet. Anacharsis of Athens served wine in small cups made of silver gilt. By the Middle Ages, wine was drunk from goblets made of glass. In the seventeenth century, stemware was fashioned specifically to serve wine, a luxury only wealthy hosts could afford. By the eighteenth century, the prosperity engendered by the Industrial Revolution enabled the expanding middle class to supply each guest with an individual wine glass. Vessels were no longer shared.

Although the average wine glass holds 8 to 12 ounces when filled to the rim, the flavor of wine deteriorates when exposed to oxygen, and only 3 to 4 ounces are poured. To enhance flavor, wine is served cool, and to preserve the temperature the wine glass is usually held at the bottom of the stem between the thumb and the first two fingers. The wine glass may also be held with the thumb on the foot and the index finger or the first two fingers underneath the base, but it is rather awkward and likely to spill.

To test the quality of French wine, the Paris Institut National des Appellations d'Origine (INAO) designed a wine glass with an egg-shaped bowl, relatively short stem, and wide base. The bowl allows room to swirl the wine and release the bouquet upward to the nose, a shape considered ideal by oenophiles. The INAO glass is made of undecorated clear glass to reveal the clarity and color of wine.

The shape of the rim affects the taste of the wine. The flavor of wine is encountered primarily on the tongue, and only secondarily by the nose. Sweet flavors are tasted on the tip of the tongue; acidic tastes (tartness) are encountered on the sides and upper sides of the tongue; salty tastes are sensed on the front and sides of the tongue, and bitter tastes are experienced on the top sides of the tongue and the back center of the top of the tongue.

The wine glass is made in assorted shapes to balance the flavor and bouquet and promote the best characteristics of specific wines. Some bowls are wide and round, others are deep and narrow, and the rims curve inward or outward to varying degrees. Simply stated, a glass with an inward-curved rim, such as a tulip- or balloon-shaped wine glass, directs the flow of wine to the center of the tongue for the best balance of fruit and acid. The outward-flared rim, such as the trumpet wine glass, directs wine to the tip of the tongue where the taste of sweet wine is savored; this shape releases the bouquet of aromatic wines, such as aperitifs, dessert wine, liqueurs, and cordials. The *copita,* a vessel with an almost straight rim, is used to sip sherry.

### *White Wine*

The *white wine glass* is made with a bowl slightly smaller in diameter and with sides a little straighter than a red wine glass, a shape that concentrates the flavor and releases the delicate bouquet. Toward this end, approximately 3 ounces of white wine

White wine is served chilled. To preserve the temperature, hold the glass by the stem between the thumb and the first two fingers.

Alternatively, place the thumb on top of the base and the index finger underneath.

Or place the thumb on top of the base and the first two fingers underneath.

are poured into the glass. However, the difference in size between the white wine glass and red wine glass is so negligible that either wine can be served in the same size glass, but to concentrate the delicate bouquet, approximately an ounce less of white wine is poured than red wine.

The *hock wine glass* features a bowl with a somewhat squat shape that rests on a long stem. Originally, hock, a somewhat sweet white wine, was made at Hochheim on the Main, a vineyard town in the bend of the Main River, Germany. Hockheimer was anglicized as Hockamore, and then shortened to hock. Today it refers to white wine from the Rhine Valley. Initially, the hock wine glass featured a green bowl to conceal the cloudiness of the wine. But today, the clarity and color of hock are improved, and it is served in a vessel with a clear glass bowl. For decoration the stem is often colored green, although colored stems also distort the color of the wine.

## *Champagne*

*Here's to champagne, the drink divine*
*That makes us forget our troubles:*
*It's made of a dollar's worth of wine*
*And three dollars worth of bubbles.*

The *champagne glass* is made in seven shapes. The *tulip glass* is widest in the middle of the bowl with a rim that curves inward, a form that directs the taste of champagne to the center of the tongue for best balance of fruit and acid, and concentrates the bouquet, a glass preferred by wine connoisseurs.

The *flute* and *trumpet glasses* feature long, narrow bowls, a form based on the *rhyton,* an ancient vessel attributed to the primeval custom of drinking from the horns of animals. The flute shape accommodates the slow rise of bubbles to the rim, a form that promotes effervescence, and prolongs the cool temperature at which champagne tastes best. The trumpet shape features sides that flare outward for faster release of the delicate bouquet. When drinking from either glass, the head is tilted backward, a position that allows champagne to flow over the tongue.

The *saucer, sherbet,* and *coupe glasses* have wide, shallow bowls, a form supposedly modeled after the right breast of Marie Antionette. Benjamin Disraeli, writing to his sister in 1832 about a dinner party given at Bulwer's, observed: "We drank champagne out of a saucer of ground glass mounted on a pedestal of cut glass." Because champagne glasses with wide shallow bowls concentrate the bouquet less effectively than other glasses and disperse the bubbles rapidly, the shape is not recommended by wine connoisseurs. To imbibe, the head is bent over the glasses, a position that promotes poor flow of champagne over the tongue.

The *hollow-stem glass* features a bowl that extends to the base. The long bowl is held between fingers, which generate warmth. Because wine loses flavor when it loses its chill, champagne served in hollow-stem glasses is not favored by wine buffs. Moreover, the narrow reach is hard to clean. But for sheer drama no other champagne glass can compare. To provide continuous effervescence of bubbles, manufacturers often make hollow-stem champagne glasses with a small protuberance that projects upward from the inside of the base.

### *Red Wine*

Compared to the delicate bouquet of white wine, the bouquet of red wine is quite pronounced. To release the abundant aroma, red wine is served in a glass with a slightly larger bowl and a little taller overall than the white wine glass. Because the red wine glass is known by various names, making the right choice can be daunting.

The *claret glass,* from the Latin word *clarus* for "clear," is used for the purplish-red wine produced in the Bordeaux region of France. Claret is a dry wine with a more delicate bouquet than burgundy. For concentration of aroma, the diameter of the bowl is approximately half an inch to one inch smaller than a burgundy glass, and to release the delicate bouquet the sides of the claret glass are a little straighter. However, the difference in size between a claret glass and a burgundy glass is negligible. In the United States manufacturers primarily produce a burgundy glass, and in England and Europe manufacturers often make a claret size and a burgundy glass.

The *burgundy glass* is slightly larger than the claret glass and is named for red and white wine produced in the Burgundy region of France. The wine has a heartier bouquet than claret, one that needs less concentration in the bowl.

The *Paris glass* is an all-purpose wine glass used by the sidewalk cafés and wine bars of Paris to serve red and white wine. The bowl is neither large nor small, made with an inward-curved rim that concentrates the bouquet.

The *magnum wine glass,* from the Latin word *magnus,* "great," is an oversized wine glass with an inward-curved rim. Reserved for an aromatic burgundy with an abundant bouquet, this glass holds 8 to 10 ounces or more when filled half full.

## *Dessert Wine Glasses*

*He is believed to have liked port,*
*But to have said of claret that*
*"It would be port if it could."*

RICHARD BENTLEY

Dessert wine is a sweet-tasting wine with a high alcohol content. A few ounces are served in a glass made with a slightly smaller bowl than a white wine glass. However, the shape is specialized, and more often dessert wine is served in the white wine glass.

In the mid-nineteenth century, after the table was cleared for dessert, fruit, crackers, and walnuts were passed, and to compliment the flavors, a decanter of port was placed before the host who poured for the person seated to his right. The host then filled his own glass and passed the decanter to the left around the table, a clockwise custom attributed to a time when ships were steered by oars carried on the right side and moored in port on the left side. Another tale credits the custom to the sun's orbit. Traditionally, a decanter of port never rests on the table until it is returned to the host.

## *Cordial Glasses*

*The cordial drop, the morning dram, I sing,*
*The midday toddy, and the evening sling.*

ANONYMOUS, BALTIMORE WEEKLY MAGAZINE, *1830*

*Cordial,* from the Latin *cordis* for "heart," is a sweet libation with a high alcohol content. The name derives from a time when records were learned by heart and passed on orally. In the Middle Ages, cordial waters were made of honey, sugar, and wine flavored with aromatic herbs and spices, drinks that served to stimulate and warm the heart made from recipes conveyed orally. In the seventeenth century, English housewives made cordials from fruit grown in home gardens. These were fermented drinks that Gervase Markham, author of *Country Contentments,* called "the pretty secrets of curious Housewifes." Today, cordials are served to warm the heart with a sense of conviviality and occasion and to act as a digestive following a heavy meal.

Cordial glasses, also known as *liqueur glasses,* are the smallest glasses in a set of stemware. Although some cordials are larger than others, the larger size holds approximately 2 ounces of liqueur, and the smaller size, called a *pony,* serves about 1 ounce. In the seventeenth century, the cordial glass was known by a host of names.

A *dram* is an apothecary term equal to 60 grains or approximately one-eighth of an ounce, a scant serving presented in a long-stemmed vessel made with a small bowl. The glass is approximately 6 to 8 inches high with thick walls, a shape called a *sham dram* in the early nineteenth century, that magnify the capacity of the bowl and promote sobriety through repeated toasts.

A *nip* is a measure of wine equal to one-sixth of a quartern, a fourth part of a British pint, approximately 4 ounces, a drink served in a small glass.

A *joey* was an English fourpenny piece, and the cost of a cordial served in a tumbler-shaped vessel.

*Firing glasses* and *toasting glasses* were made with rounded bucket-shaped or conical bowls with short stems and heavy bases. Firing glasses were about 4½ inches high, and toasting glasses were approximately 6 inches high. Rather than applaud a toast, firing glasses featured thick bases that withstood excessive pounding on the table, a cacophony of sound similar to the volley of musketry firing; these shapes were also known as *bumping glasses* or *bumpers.* Toasting glasses were made with thick walls to restrict the capacity of the bowl and aid the sobriety of the toastmaster at social occasions. The glasses were favored by political and social clubs and often decorated with emblems.

*Jacobite* and *propaganda glasses* were inscribed with a portrait, a motif, a line, or a word to commemorate a political persuasion, event, or personal sentiment. Originally the glasses were used by groups dedicated to the return to the throne of James II, who fled to France in 1688. To commemorate the ascension of James II's son, James Stuart (known as the Old Pretender), Jacobite glasses were engraved with his portrait or with a likeness of his grandson, Charles Stuart (the Young Pretender). When a sympathizer drank from a glass inscribed with a single rose, the emblem of England, in essence he drank a secret toast to "his King across the water." Two rose buds symbolized the Young Pretender. The thistle represented Scotland. A stricken oak symbolized the fallen house of Stuart. (The Stuarts ruled England and Scotland from 1603 to 1714, except during the period of the Commonwealth.)

*Amen glasses* were engraved with lines from the Jacobite anthem that commemorated the Jacobite rebellion of 1715 in Scotland under the Earl of Mar. When an inscription ended with "Amen," the glass was called an *amen glass*. Today, both Jacobite and amen glasses can be seen in the Victoria and Albert Museum, London.

## Brandy Snifter

*Claret is the liquor for boys;*
*Port for men;*
*But he who aspires to be a hero*
*Must drink brandy.*

JAMES BOSWELL, LIFE OF SAMUEL JOHNSON, 1791

The brandy snifter, also known as a *brandy inhaler*, is a short-stemmed glass with a tulip or balloon-shaped bowl. Because brandy is about 40 percent alcohol, only 1 or 2 ounces are poured, and the size of the snifter is unimportant. The salient point is to serve brandy in a glass with an inward-curved rim to concentrate the heady bouquet. The small brandy snifter, approximately 4½ inches in height, is the size recommended by experts. The large brandy snifter, about 12 inches high, features a wide mouth that rapidly dissipates the bouquet. Connoisseurs suggest the larger size as best reserved for goldfish.

Brandy is aged in oak barrels, which add to the complex flavor. The taste is enhanced when it is served warm or at room temperature. To generate warmth, the short stem is held between the fingers and the bowl is cradled in the palm of one or both hands. Brandy may also be heated over a small alcohol burner.

CHAPTER THIRTY

# HOW TO PLACE STEMWARE

STEMWARE IS PLACED on the table in a way that is comfortable, convenient, and symmetrical, an arrangement determined by the dining occasion. At a formal affair, because the majority of people are right-handed, stemware is aligned symmetrically at the top right of the cover. However, in Europe stemware is often placed above the dinner plate, a position that may catch the sleeve in the contents of the plate. In informal dining, particularly a family meal, comfort is more important than the aesthetics of symmetry, and stemware is placed to accommodate the handedness of the diner.

The arrangement of stemware is based on space. At a formal multicourse meal, there is a profusion of tableware, including a water goblet and two or three wine glasses. To conserve space, stemware is arranged in the shape of a triangle or a diamond. In the *triangle arrangement,* the dessert glass forms the highest point. The water goblet is angled to the lower left of the dessert glass, and the glasses for red and white wine are placed on the lower right side. When sherry is served, the sherry glass is placed on the lower right of the white wine glass. The *diamond shape* is the same as the triangle arrangement, except the white wine glass is angled to the lower left of the red wine glass, and the sherry glass to the lower left of the white wine glass.

At a simple meal, two or three courses are served and less stemware is required. Usually one wine glass is used and perhaps a water goblet. The table setting is uncrowded and there is room to arrange stemware in any way one chooses, such

In the triangle placement, the dessert glass is the highest point. The water goblet is angled to the lower left, and the glasses for red wine, white wine, and sherry are placed to the lower right.

The diamond arrangement begins with the dessert glass at the highest point. The water goblet is angled to the lower left; the red wine glass to the lower right of the dessert glass; the white wine glass to the lower left of the red wine glass; and the sherry glass to the lower left of the white wine glass.

as in a straight line parallel with the edge of the table or a diagonal line angled toward the table's edge.

Stemware is placed on the table in the order of use. Because water is taken throughout a meal, particularly a four- to five-course meal that incorporates a variety of seasonings, the goblet is placed in a position closest to the hand, approximately 1 inch above the tip of the dinner knife to eliminate hitting the goblet when the dinner knife is lifted for use. However, at a simple two- to three-course meal, fewer seasonings are incorporated in the menu, and generally water is not served unless the menu is spicy. But when water is served, the goblet is placed above the tip of the dinner knife.

Wine glasses are placed on the table in the order that accommodates the service of wine. Normally at a simple meal, one wine is served, and the way the wine glass is placed on the table is not important. But a typical multicourse menu begins with light courses, proceeds to the main course, and is followed by a light course or two. To accommodate the course in service, the appropriate wine glass is placed nearest the hand, a position that works from the left toward the water goblet.

WHEN A MEAL HAS ONLY A FEW COURSES, THE SIMPLE TABLE SETTING ALLOWS SPACE TO ARRANGE STEMWARE IN ANY WAY THAT PLEASES THE EYE, SUCH AS IN A DIAGONAL LINE THAT POINTS TO THE EDGE OF THE TABLE.

- The *sherry glass* is placed on the table when sherry is served to accompany a course in which sherry is an ingredient, usually an appetizer of soup. On an uncrowded table, the sherry glass is placed on the right side of the white wine glass, in a position closest to the hand. However, when space on the table is crowded, the sherry glass is placed to the left front of the white wine glass.
- The *white wine glass* is arranged in the form of a triangle or a diamond. In the triangle arrangement, when a sherry glass is placed on the table, the white wine glass is positioned to the upper left of the sherry glass. If a sherry glass is not placed on the table, the white wine glass is placed to the lower right of the red wine glass. In the diamond arrangement, the white wine glass is placed to the lower left of the red wine glass.
- The *red wine glass* is placed also in a triangle or a diamond. In the triangle arrangement, the red wine glass is placed to the upper left of the white wine glass, generally above the spoon. In the diamond arrangement, the red wine glass is placed to the upper right of the white wine glass.
- The *dessert wine glass* is angled to the right rear of the water goblet when space is at a premium. Otherwise, it is placed directly to the right of the water goblet.
- The *champagne glass* is placed on the table to the right of the water goblet when champagne is the only wine served with a meal. If champagne is served to accompany a particular course, such as an appetizer or dessert, the champagne glass is placed on the table in the order of use.
- The *juice glass* is placed in the center of the cover on a small underplate when juice is served as a first course: for example, tomato juice at dinner or orange juice at breakfast. If juice is served to accompany a meal, the glass is placed directly on the table at the top right of the cover.

CHAPTER THIRTY-ONE

# THE INTERCHANGE OF STEMWARE

IN THE LATE nineteenth century, stemware was made in assorted shapes and sizes not only to serve beverages but also to present solid foods. Today, the custom continues and stemware is used to serve certain types of food, such as seafood cocktail, sorbet, condiments, sauce, and soft desserts. Moreover, stemware is used in the home to hold flowers, potpourri, guest soaps, cotton balls, cotton swabs, jewelry, cosmetics, paperclips, and matchbooks.

But when is stemware used in a traditional way, and when is it used creatively? The answer lies in the dining occasion. At an elegant multicourse affair, stemware is used in the capacity for which it was made; water is served in a water goblet, wine in a wine glass, and champagne in a champagne glass. But at an informal meal, from patio to posh, the creative use of stemware not only adds interest to the table setting, it injects the moment with fun. Water goblets may be used to serve muesli at breakfast or dessert at dinner; balloon-shaped wine glasses may hold cold soup at luncheon, and saucer champagne glasses are fine for sauce and candy.

For easy reference, stemware is divided into shapes with large, medium, and small bowls.

## Large Bowls

Stemware that holds a large volume of liquid is made with a sizable bowl. These include the water goblet; iced-tea glass; the flute, tulip, and hollow-stem champagne glasses; and the large brandy snifter.

- The water goblet, iced-tea glass, and flute champagne glass can hold spears of raw vegetables or bread sticks. Large stemware with a thick density doubles as a vessel to hold flatware on a buffet. In the home, large vessels make excellent bud vases.
- The tulip champagne glass holds candy, nuts, potpourri, and guest soaps and can serve as a candleholder.
- The hollow-stem champagne glass can be used to hold rock candy, bubble bath, olives, and cocktail onions.
- The large brandy snifter can be used for long loaves of bread, bread sticks, and rolls or to float flowers, hold a floral arrangement, or house a collection of matchbooks.

## Medium Bowls

Stemware made with medium-size bowls includes the white wine glass, hock wine glass, red wine glass, magnum wine glass, dessert wine glass, coupe champagne glass, and small brandy snifter.

- The white wine glass and hock wine glass can hold soft desserts, fruit compote, sauce, candy, and nuts. They can also be used to hold flowers, potpourri, and bubble bath.
- The red wine glass and magnum wine glass can be used to serve seafood cocktail, cold soup, and soft desserts.
- The dessert wine glass is the right size to serve sherry or to hold a votive candle.

- The coupe champagne glass is ideal for condiments, seafood cocktail, sorbet, frozen daquiris, and ice-cream sundaes.
- The small brandy snifter is a good size and shape for sauce, candy, condiments, potpourri, and flowers.

## Small Bowls

Stemware with small bowls, namely aperitif, cordial, or liqueur glasses, can hold condiments, sauce, minibouquets, or cotton swabs.

CHAPTER THIRTY-TWO

# HOW TO PURCHASE STEMWARE

Stemware is a dining accoutrement that punctuates the table setting with height and sparkle. The choice of pattern depends on personal taste and affordability. Before purchasing a set, consider the following.

## How Often Will It Be Used?

The first consideration is personal lifestyle. The host who entertains often may want inexpensive glassware that goes into the dishwasher and is easy to replace. Those who entertain occasionally, but lavishly and elegantly, may want handmade crystal ornamented with precious metals; it will require hand-washing, but the infrequent use is worth the extra care.

## Long Stems or Short Stems?

The length of the stem creates different looks at the table. Long stems lift the look of the table setting and are particularly suited for sumptuous dining with formal overtones. However, short-stemmed antique glassware and tumblers are often seen on fashionable tables. They add an heirloom touch to sophisticated dining. Short stems are less stately and more appropriate for informal dining, from casual to elegant.

## The Weight of Stemware

The weight of stemware affects the ornamentation. Thin crystal is conducive to shallow-cut and enameled ornamentation and feels light in the hand. Thick crystal accommodates cut decoration with deep grooves and feels heavy in the hand.

## Clear Stemware or Colored Stemware?

Clear stemware does not compete with the color of wine or distort its clarity; it is recommended for formal or informal multicourse meals where several wines are served. Clear glass blends with any dinnerware pattern, harmonizes with all table decor, and does not divert the eye from the beauty of a fully appointed table setting.

Colored stemware punctuates the table setting with color and design. However, white wine looks pale in dark-colored glass and red wine takes on a muddy appearance. But for those who prefer colored stemware under any circumstances, to preserve the color and clarity of wine, serve water in colored goblets and wine in clear glass. Save colored wine glasses as a decorative tool for a simple table setting.

## Shape and Density

The shape of the perfect wine glass is similar to an egg, longer than it is wide, a form that directs the bouquet of wine upward to the nose. The rim is 2 to 3 inches in diameter. The density of the ideal wine glass is paper-thin. White wine is served chilled, and red wine tastes best at a temperature slightly cooler than the average room (approximately 18°C or 65°F). A thick texture absorbs the coolness, whereas a thin texture keeps the coolness in the wine.

# A Matched Set or Mix and Match?

Stemware is visible throughout the meal, and a matched set does not divert the eye from the appointments of the table setting, particularly a multicourse meal where a profusion of tableware is used. But at a meal where a few courses are served, the table setting is simple and a mix of stemware adds interest. Moreover, stemware such as aperitif and cordial glasses is used away from the table. It is not seen collectively, and a mix of patterns is festive.

When a pattern is discontinued, or stock is depleted and shipments are slow, extend an incomplete set by matching it to a similar pattern in another set. Often the differences are slight. However, make sure the shapes of the bowls, the stems, and the bases are the same.

# How to Mix and Match Stemware

In a set of stemware, the water goblet, the largest vessel, is the focal point of a mix-and-match collection. For best results keep the mix of stemware patterns two-to-one. Balance ornate dinnerware and flatware with plain stemware. Accent plain dinnerware and flatware with stemware decorated in an elaborate pattern.

In a mix of stemware patterns, keep the *design* of a particular piece the same for the entire table setting: for example, matching water goblets and wine glasses ornamented with the same decoration.

Keep the surface *sheen* of tableware alike. Mix brilliant crystal with glistening dinnerware and gleaming silver. Match dull surfaces, such as machine-made glass with unglazed stoneware and matte-finished flatware.

Keep tableware *textures* alike. Mix thin crystal with delicate dinnerware and flatware in a normal size. Match bulky glassware with thick textures, such as heavy pottery and coarse flatware.

Keep the *scale* of stems similar. At a table laid with a profusion of tableware, rather than divert the eye with a mix of assorted heights, keep the length of the stems the same. However, for those who own an assortment of long and short stems, to avoid a profusion of design, match the dinnerware and flatware patterns and mix the height of the stemware.

## Stemware Should Complement Dinnerware and Flatware Patterns

To establish design compatibility, take a small plate and a few utensils to the store and simulate a place setting with the chosen stemware.

The bucket and flared forms of stemware feature *flat-bottomed bowls* with straight sides, a line that is harmonious with dinnerware and flatware decorated with angular lines. The tulip bowl is *rounded,* a form harmonious with dinnerware and flatware ornamented with curvaceous patterns drawn from nature, such as flowers and seashells. When a stemware pattern features a combination of straight and rounded lines, keep the shape of the bowl similar to the predominant line of the dinnerware and flatware.

## The Number of Pieces per Place Setting

A suite of stemware has a minimum of three pieces: goblet, champagne glass, and wine glass. A four-piece place setting contains a goblet, champagne glass, wine glass, and a cordial glass. A five-piece place setting incorporates a goblet, champagne glass, wine glass, cordial glass, and iced-beverage glass. A six-piece place setting features a goblet, champagne glass, wine glass, cordial glass, iced-beverage glass, and a second wine glass.

# Open Stock

Stemware purchased by the piece, as opposed to stemware purchased by the place setting, is called *open stock*. However, the least expensive way to buy stemware is by the set (witness catalog sales). To make entertainment easier to plan, purchase stemware in multiples of four, and purchase extra pieces for pattern longevity.

# Handmade and Machine-made Stemware

Handmade stemware is a time-consuming, labor-intensive product made of the finest materials. The texture is thinner than machine-made glassware, the ornamentation is sharply defined, and the edges are crisp. Machine-made stemware is mass-produced in seconds from common materials, glass recognized by uniformity of design, consistent dimensions, bulkier appearance, and ornamentation with blunt, and sometimes rounded, edges.

Labor, energy, and materials determine the cost of stemware. Labor amounts to approximately 75 percent of the cost of the finished product, which means that handmade stemware will almost always be the most expensive choice. To provide uniformity of product, the furnace operates 24 hours a day, whether it is used or not, and energy represents about 20 percent of cost. Materials are about 5 percent of cost.

# How to Judge the Quality of Stemware

Quality stemware is evident by its smoothness, balance, invisible seams, and uniformity of design. To discern smoothness, run the fingers around the rim, the edge of the foot, and under the base. Stemware with good balance rests flat on the table and does not wobble. Invisible seams are just that—imperceptible to the eye. Uniformity is associated with machine-made ware. Handmade products are subject to the vagaries of human skill and exact dimensions are almost impossible to achieve; slight differences are of little concern unless they are glaringly noticeable, such as parallel lines that are not straight or a bowl that is a little larger than standard.

Allowances are made for slight variations in the glass itself and for imperfections caused by manufacture, such as seeds, cords, shear marks, and mold marks. *Seeds* are minute bubbles of air, about the size of a pinpoint, created by gas trapped in the material when it is mixed, melted, or fused; they give the glass "personality" when it is held to the light. *Cords* are slight striae caused by an uneven furnace temperature when the material is melted or undulating marks made by tools when glass is rotated. Cords are perceptible to the touch and visible in an empty glass, but not when a glass is full. *Shear marks* are slight puckers made from an overabundance of molten liquid on the pontil rod when the expanded object is cut away. *Mold marks* are ridges that occur when two pieces are joined together or when the product is removed from the mold.

## How to Judge Crystal

Clarity, sparkle, weight, and ring are the criteria used to judge crystal. *Clarity* is apparent when stemware is held against a white background. The higher the lead content, the greater the clarity of crystal. Crystal with a low lead content appears cloudy and possesses a slight tint of gray, blue, or green. Crystal with a high lead content is clear. Cyrstal is 10 to 24 percent lead. Lead crystal is 24 to 30 percent lead. Full lead crystal is 30 to 33 percent lead. Anything over that is too soft.

*Sparkle* is indicative of crystal with a high lead content. Quality lead crystal possesses permanent sparkle.

*Weight* is determined by the amount of lead in the batch. Lead is heavy, and crystal with a high lead content is heavier than crystal with a low lead content.

*Ring* is determined by the shape, weight, and size of the piece. When struck gently on the rim, delicate lead crystal stemware has a deep, sonorous ring. Heavy crystal, such as a thick bowl, does not resonate.

CHAPTER THIRTY-THREE

# THE CARE OF GLASSWARE

GLASSWARE IS MADE in three main categories: crystal, soda glass, and borosilicate glass (Pyrex). Crystal is a luxury product composed of fine materials expensive to produce and replace, and hand care is recommended to retain its clarity and brilliance and inhibit damage. Soda glass and Pyrex are produced from ordinary materials, machine-made in seconds, and when haziness or damage occur, they can be replaced at a reasonable cost.

## The Care of Crystal

- *Carry one piece of stemware in each hand.* When cleaning up after a party, carry one glass in each hand, particularly if the rim flares outward. If the rim curves inward or is almost the same width as the widest part of the bowl, it is possible to carry several pieces at a time.
- *Hold stemware by the stem.* Stemware is made in two or three pieces. Holding it by the bowl or the foot can create stress that may cause the part to detach.
- *Take your rings off before washing stemware.* Crystal is softer than soda glass and Pyrex and the surface scratches easily.
- *The sulfur content in rubber darkens precious metals.* Don't use a rubber pad to

cushion a sink or a drainboard. Instead, before washing stemware ornamented with gold, silver, or platinum, pad the area with a folded towel.

- *Place each piece in the sink separately and wash it individually.*
- *Hand-wash crystal in warm, soapy water.* Crystal contains lead, a soft metal. Abrasive detergents may scratch the finish. Use *soap* if possible, or select a mild, nonabrasive detergent and reduce the amount by half.
- *Hand-wash crystal decorated with gold or silver.* Precious metals are soft, and when subjected to hot water or the drying cycle in a dishwasher, they are easily scratched. To preclude damage, wash metal-decorated stemware in lukewarm water and allow it to cool before it is handled. Because the chemicals in detergent fade precious metals and leave a film on the surface, mild *soap* is recommended (but use as little as possible).
- *Wash the inside and outside of crystal separately.* When the interior and exterior surfaces of crystal are washed together, the action creates pressure that eventually leads to cracks.
- *Dry crystal with a lint-free towel.* Lint clogs engraved ornamentation. For best results use a tightly woven towel to dry crystal ornamented with cut decoration, a towel that will not scratch the surface of crystal.
- *Water leaves a permanent mark.* Before crystal is put away, hold each piece to the light, check for water spots, and wipe them off immediately. Water spots can leave permanent marks.
- *Acid-based foods and beverages are harmful to crystal.* To protect crystal stemware from the acid in table wine, rinse crystal soon after use. Drinks low in fruit acid and high in alcohol—aperitifs, liqueurs, and brandy—are not harmful to crystal and store in decanters almost indefinitely. If table wine is left in a decanter overnight, remove the wine as soon as possible, fill the decanter with water, add 2 teaspoons of ammonia, leave the solution in the decanter for a day or two, and pray!
- *Heat causes condensation to form inside glass, etching the surface.* When an empty decanter is left in direct sunlight, heat creates vapors that etch the surface and diminish the appearance.

# The Care of Machine-made Glass

Although machine made glassware is thicker than handmade crystal and can withstand the heat, vibrations, and rigors of a dishwasher, a few words of caution are in order.

- *Glass is sensitive to changes in temperature.* To avoid shattering, don't immerse cold glass in hot water. For example, a goblet that has held ice cubes should be allowed to come to room temperature.
- *Metal defrays heat away from glass.* Before pouring hot liquid into cold glass, defray the heat by placing a metal utensil, such as a spoon, in the glass.
- *Partially fill a glass with room-temperature water before adding ice cubes.* This will allow the glass to adjust to the temperature of the ice cubes and prevent the possibility of cracks.
- *Heat does not transfer evenly through large masses of glass.* When a sizable piece of glass is placed in warm water, such as a large bowl, the uneven transfer of heat causes internal stress that may lead to cracks. To foster the even transfer of heat, adjust the temperature of the glass article to the water by placing it in the water sideways.
- *Wipe large glass objects clean with a damp cloth wrung dry.* Massive objects are awkward to hold and wash with soap and water but are easy to wipe clean with a cleaning solution.
- *Release glasses stuck together.* Glass expands and contracts with heat. To release two glasses stuck together, fill the top glass with cool water and submerge the bottom glass in warm water. The cool water causes the upper glass to contract and the warm water expands the lower glass. After a few minutes the glasses should separate. If not, wrap the glasses in a warm towel.
- *Direct the heat from a burning candle away from stemware.* To protect stemware from the heat generated by a burning candle, do not allow the candle to burn lower than 3 inches from the top of the candleholder.
- *In a dishwasher stack glassware well apart.* The force of water causes vibration that may cause tightly packed glassware to hit one another and chip.
- *The mineral deposits in water affect the clarity of glass.* Minerals are found in

hard water or in chemicals used to treat water, notably in Florida and some parts of the Northwest. When the minerals combine with the chemicals in detergent and the heat of a dishwasher, a reaction occurs that leaves a permanent film on glass. To promote clarity and retard haziness, stop the dishwasher before the drying cycle or reduce the temperature of the drying cycle to 60°C (140°F).

- *To prevent glass from hitting the spout, use a rubber nozzle or turn the tap to the side.*
- *Flowers change water chemically.* To avoid permanent damage to glass vases, change the water daily.

## Homemade Cleaning Solutions

Although homemade cleaning solutions are not always guaranteed, they are worth a try.

- To enhance the sparkle of crystal, add a few drops of *bluing* to the water.
- For extremely cloudy glass, prepare a mixture of *fine sand and denatured alcohol,* and swish it around inside the article.
- To make large pieces of crystal glisten, dampen a cloth in four parts *water,* two parts *ammonia,* and one part *alcohol.* Wring out the cloth until almost dry, wipe the article clean, and leave it to air dry.
- To clean the grooves of cut crystal or pressed glass, dip a soft brush, like an old toothbrush, in the solution of *water, amonia,* and *alcohol.*
- Spots, haziness, and iridescence are removed or diminished when *white vinegar* is added to the rinse water. Or try soaking the article in water and white vinegar, or rub the spot with half a *lemon.* If all fails, and the piece is valuable, take it to a glasshouse for an acid bath.
- *Toothpaste* is a gentle cleaner of stained glass.
- *Alcohol* causes the evaporation of condensation. To remove condensation from inside a bottle, when the bottle is cool, pour alcohol inside.
- Wrap several *paper towels* around a pencil or straightened wire hanger and use this "stick" to dry the interior of a decanter.
- To remove a glass stopper stuck in the neck of a bottle, gently tap it with a

pencil, or loosen the stopper by running warm water or *warm soapy water* into the neck of the bottle.

- To smooth glass nicks, use a *fine sanding file* available at hardware stores. Or take the chipped piece to a glasshouse for professional grinding.

## The Storage of Glass

Proper storage is important to the longevity of glassware and requires only a few simple precautions.

- Store seldom-used glassware in a covered, zippered case fitted with adjustable plastic dividers. Or store glassware in a cabinet located away from kitchen grease.
- Pollution is inherent in the air. To keep glass grease-free, rotate use.
- Moisture-absorbing material, such as newspaper or excelsior, absorbs the sodium oxide in glass and can cause haze. Such materials are not recommended for storage of glass.
- Store crystal after it is cool and completely dry. When glass is damp or warm, moisture collects on the surface and a film forms that is impossible to remove.
- Glass can stick to glass. Do not store crystal directly on a glass shelf.
- Store stemware with the bowl facing upward. The rim is the weakest part of stemware and when the bowl is stored downward, moisture collects inside, along with shelf odors. When glass is exposed to excessive moisture and repeated changes in temperature, it is subject to deterioration.
- Store glass away from direct sunlight, heating outlets, or air conditioner vents. Because glass conducts sunlight, storage in direct sun creates stress that leads to cracks. Moreover, glass can transfer heat to another glass object, such as a glass shelf, and cause stress.
- Temperature changes cause glass to expand and contract. To avoid chips, leave enough space between the rims of stemware to allow for expansion and contraction. Make sure the bases do not touch. Provide space between glassware and the walls of the storage cabinet.

# Part V

# Table Linens

# CHAPTER THIRTY-FOUR

# TABLECLOTHS, PLACEMATS, AND TABLE RUNNERS

## Origin of the Tablecloth

The tablecloth is the first decorative accessory known to the table, an all-purpose covering known in antiquity as a *gausape,* a woolen fabric, shaggy on one side and smooth on the other, used as a napkin, towel, or sheet by Romans who dined in a reclined position on a sofa. But, when our ancestors chose to sit upright in a chair and eat before a table, a custom established in the fifth century by Merovaeus, king of the Franks and ruler of Gaul, the tablecloth evolved as a luxury item. The table originally was a board laid on two trestles, and the covering was known as a *borde cloth.* But in the sixteenth century when the nobility began to use solid tables, the covering was called a *table cloth.*

Mosaics attributed to Ravenna, Italy, circa fifth century, show the altar embellished with beautifully woven cloths. Monastic meals were taken at a cloth-covered table, possibly as a symbol of purity, a theory substantiated by the rules of the Order of St. Benedict (founded in 529), which decreed that monks who arrived late to the table must eat alone without benefit of wine or a tablecloth. Tablecloths were laid on secular tables, but only at banquets and feasts, such as one made of roses described by Venantius Fortunatus in a sixth-century poem written to Queen Radegunde.

Royalty in the Middle Ages seldom remained in one place long enough to receive vassals and liege lords but rather traveled from one territory to another as honored guests of the nobility, a subtle reminder of their presence, power, and rule. Silk tablecloths were among the refinements of royal travel, a rare fabric in the Western world, often embroidered with threads of silk, silver, and gold as a symbol of status and wealth. But flax was the most common fiber. The fabric was commonly loomed as tablecloths with blue stripes occasionally patterned with stylized designs, hemmed at both ends with a knotted fringe, a style depicted by Domenico Ghirlandajo in *The Last Supper*, in the collection of the Ognissanti Monastery, Florence.

The medieval table setting was simple, laid with salt cellars and plates made of stale bread or wood. Guests ate with their fingers and carried their own knives and spoons. Goblets were shared and placed on a sideboard. To relieve the austerity of the plain table setting, white tablecloths were folded with wide pleats, a decorative style depicted in the late Renaissance by Francisco de Zurburán in *Saint Hugh in the Refectory*. The pleated style, called *linenfold*, was adapted later to squares of wood paneling and chests carved to simulate folded linen, a style popular in the wall paneling of Tudor times and seen later in the great country houses of England and the baronial mansions of the United States. In a painting entitled *Two Epicureans*, Robert Le Vrac portrayed a white tablecloth ironed in a checkerboard pattern.

The medieval tablecloth was used on both sides, a practical custom known as *doubles*, and used to censure nobility. A less-than-chivalrous knight ate from a cloth laid on the soiled side. A seriously grave offender was not allowed to eat from the same tablecloth as his peers. A wrongdoer's space would be cut from the cloth. Hence the expression, "He and I are not of the same cloth."

To prevent unseen attack by an enemy, the trestle table was set along one side so the diners' backs were to the wall. The tablecloth hung to the floor, but only on the diners' side. This was to protect the guests' knees from drafts and keep the animals from walking over their feet. When all four sides of the tablecloth hung to the floor, the corners were knotted to keep the cloth clean, a decorative custom that continues today.

In a feudal society, everyone—the lord of the manor, honored guests, and serfs—banded together for purposes of agriculture and mutual protection from the enemy and ate together in the great hall. To designate rank, a tablecloth was laid only before the lord of the manor and honored guests.

The medieval menu consisted of roasts, stews, soups, and puddings. The meal was eaten with knife, spoon, and fingers, and the tablecloth became heavily soiled.

To foster cleanliness, the table was laid with an overcloth, an undercloth, and a cloth that draped from the side. After the first course, the overcloth was removed and the second course was served on a clean undercloth. The third cloth hung like a swag along the side and was used as a communal napkin. Dessert was served on a bare table or another cloth was provided.

Overcloths were made of white fabric, a color symbolic of purity, the original sacred meal, and the sanctity of the altar cloth. The exception was in rural areas, where top cloths were woven with colorful stripes, plaids, or checks. The undercloth was a darker color.

During the Renaissance the wealthy built grand palaces furnished with ornately carved chests and huge cupboards made for the storage of linens. By the early seventeenth century, tablecloths were a common accessory, and the chests and cupboards of a modest home might hold no fewer than forty. Inventories of holdings in royal and noble households reveal chests and cupboards filled not only with unused linens but with many ells of fabric. An *ell* is a unit of measurement. Ells woven in Holland were 27 inches in length, and those loomed in England were approximately 45 inches long and woven with "diaper designs," a term for tiny geometric patterns that repeated and overlapped, such as diamonds or lozenges. Oriental rugs were enormously popular tablecloths. Considered too valuable to lay on the floor, the rugs were protected at meals with an overcloth of white damask, which was removed afterward to reveal the rich beauty of the design.

From the sixteenth to the nineteenth centuries, royal tablecloths were made of damask, a reversible silk or linen cloth woven in Damascus. The fabric was introduced to Europe by the crusaders in the Middle Ages. Damask was woven with pictorial or "storied" motifs; themes included religious subjects, coats of arms, royal weddings, coronations, battle scenes, or various flora and fauna. In an age without electricity, the sheen of white damask offset the dark wood furniture and paneling.

But damask was costly. Louis XV sought to economize by setting the style for white tablecloths made of cotton embroidered to resemble damask. For a brief period in the early eighteenth century, fashionable tables were covered with brightly colored tablecloths made of calico, a gaily patterned cotton woven in Calicut, India.

The Industrial Revolution and the invention of the steam engine in the eighteenth century mechanized the textile industry, and toward the end of the century cotton fabric was mass-produced. The demand for hand-loomed tablecloths waned. By the nineteenth century, machine-made tablecloths were sold in the linen departments of local stores. Artificial dyes displaced vegetable dyes and tablecloths were produced in an array of colors. However, white continued as the favorite tablecloth color, and linens were often designated "white goods" by department stores.

The nineteenth century brought a mode of food presentation that affected the number of tablecloths a hostess might need, namely, *service à la russe,* or Russian service. In Russian service, serving dishes were presented to the diner from the left side, one dish at a time. In French service, serving dishes were placed on the table all at one time and required several cloths to keep the table clean, whereas Russian service required only one tablecloth. Nonetheless, the fashionable Victorian table often featured "accident cloths" laid over the ends of the tablecloth, slips of cloth removed with the tablecloth before the final course. Dessert was served on a bare table.

The development of synthetic fibers in the late 1960s promoted manufacture of easy-care cotton blends, fabrics that made tablecloths almost a disposable item. No longer were tablecloths cherished, mended, and bequeathed in family wills. Rather, by the second half of the twentieth century, heavily stained or well-worn tablecloths were considered disposable.

Today, the tablecloth is a decorative accessory that unifies the components of the table setting, a practical accoutrement that insulates the table and lowers the noise level in the room. Moreover, tablecloths provide more elbow room than placemats, and conserve space at a crowded table. The unbroken line unifies the profusion of tableware required for a multicourse formal dinner or a formal tea table heavily laded with teaware and tea equipage and is always used at both occasions. But at a formal luncheon, fewer courses are served and the cover is less crowded, so placemats are often used.

At an informal meal, fewer courses are served, less tableware is required, the table setting is simpler, and any covering is appropriate: placemats, runners, shawls, obis, rugs, rebozos, saris, throws, blankets, sheets, bedspreads, large towels, oilcloth, upholstery fabric, and natural materials, such as straw, bamboo, reed fans, or ivy. The informal table may also be left bare, a look attributed to the eighteenth century, when reflective surfaces were important; a polished mahogany table laid with glistening porcelain, glittering crystal, and gleaming silver was very pleasing to the eye in an age without electricity. Today, a bare table is used to accent the beauty of the surface material, such as wood, glass, travertine, or lacquer.

# The Right Tablecloth

The tablecloth draws ornamental inspiration from five design elements: dominance, visual weight, color, texture, and pattern.

*Dominance* refers to the prevailing design element. The right tablecloth accents the dominant color, pattern, and texture of the dinnerware and room decor.

*Visual weight* relates to the proportions of the room. In a large room, to keep the table setting from looking lost, a tablecloth woven with big, compactly arranged patterns conveys visual weight. In a small room, lightness is suggested by a tablecloth woven with an airy pattern.

*Color* is a design tool that changes the mood of the table setting without changing the tableware. The colors of formal dining are white, ivory, and ecru (although pastel tablecloths sometimes appear on formal tables). But the ground color of the dinnerware and the tablecloth are not always the same. When one is ivory and the other is pure white, use them together, but for continuity match the color of the napkins to the tablecloth. The colors of informal dining are all shades, from bright to deep to contrasting, from metallic to pastel to white. Bright colors are informal, deep colors are sophisticated, contrasting colors are dramatic, metallic fabrics are opulent, and pastels, whites, and off-whites are elegant.

The *texture* of the tablecloth should relate to the finish of the tableware and also to the dining occasion. The textures of formal dining are smooth—porcelain, crystal, silver, finishes appropriate for a tablecloth woven with a satin sheen, such as damask. Tablecloths with a heavy weight, notably double-woven damask, are harmonious with opaque porcelain and heavy baluster stemware. Sheer tablecloths, such as lace, are unified with the delicate textures of translucent porcelain and thin crystal. The textures of informal dining range from smooth to coarse. Smooth weaves are compatible with fine surfaces, such as porcelain, bone china, ironstone, semiporcelain, silver, silver plate, and stainless steel. Loosely woven heavy fabrics relate to coarse textures, such as pottery, stoneware, and pewter flatware.

The *patterns* of tablecloths range from large to small, bold to subtle, each design appropriate for a particular occasion. The patterns of formal dining are small and subtle, motifs that do not detract from the profusion of tableware; a damask tablecloth woven with a classic white-on-white jacquard weave or linen embroidered in the same color as the cloth is appropriate. For informal dining in a dining room decorated with eye-catching wallpaper and boldly patterned upholstered pieces, a solid-covered tablecloth can be used to accent the decor. But in a room decorated with painted walls, or walls papered with a subtle design, and chairs upholstered with a small-scaled pattern, a tablecloth woven with a simple design underscores the setting. The same concepts apply to outdoor table settings. In a garden profuse with blooming flowers, a solid-color cloth accents the beauty of the blossoms. But in a garden where few flowers are in bloom, a patterned tablecloth draws the eye.

## Decorative Tips for Tablecloths

- *The first purchase.* A solid-color tablecloth is suggested for the first purchase, one that matches the dinnerware or accents the dinnerware in a contrasting color.
- *Variety.* When the same tableware is used daily, vary the coverings to add interest to the settings. Use cheerful, bright-colored linens at breakfast and lunch, and create a relaxed ambience with soft-colored tablecloths at dinner.
- *Color mixing.* Add a light-hearted touch to dining with a colorful mix of tablecloths and napkins, in complimentary hues and intensities.
- *The layered look.* For decorative interest lay round or square tablecloths over circular cloths, and square cloths over oblong or oval tablecloths.
- *Open-weave tablecloths.* To emphasize the beauty of an open-weave pattern, accent the design with a colorful underliner in a shade that coordinates with the predominant hue of the dinnerware. Cool colors, such as blue or green, mix with dinnerware decorated with grayish hues. Warm colors, such as red or yellow, compliment dinnerware with yellowish undertones. Neutral colors, such as ivory, beige, or tan, are compatible with earth-tone dinnerware. Also, accent the pattern of an open-weave cloth on a bare table top, or lay the cloth on an underpad that simulates the color of the table top.

## The Length of the Tablecloth Overhang

The overhang is the distance between the top of the table and the hem of the tablecloth, a dimension that depends on the size of the table and the weight of the fabric. In general, a lengthy table requires a long overhang and a small table a short drop. However, should a long overhang dwarf the look of the table or a short drop appear skimpy, change it. The guidelines are adaptable.

The average dining table is 27 inches high, and most chair seats are 16½ inches from the floor. At a formal dinner the tablecloth overhang is luxurious and deep, approximately 10 to 15 inches, a drop that rests in the diner's lap and is tucked under the table before the napkin is lifted. When a formal dinner is served at a number of tables, usually folding tables with metal legs are rented, covered with tablecloths that extend to the floor. Because the menu at a formal luncheon is lighter than a formal dinner, the overhang of the tablecloth is shorter. But at a formal tea, most of the guests stand, and the overhang of the tablecloth is up to 18 inches deep. In a hotel or private club, when tea is served from a folding table, the tablecloth hangs to the floor to conceal the metal legs.

An informal dinner served at a smaller table is more relaxed than a formal affair, and the tablecloth overhang is several inches shorter, approximately 10 inches. But exceptions do exist, depending on the fabric, such as a lace tablecloth that makes a graceful drape with a generous drop. Because no one sits at a buffet table, the overhang may be generous, even hanging to the floor, as it does for restaurant service tables with folding metal legs.

## The Right Size Tablecloth

The size of the tablecloth is determined by the length and width of the dining table and the overhang on all four sides. A dining table extended by leaves changes shape; a round table becomes an oval, and a square table becomes a rectangle. The right size tablecloth is determined by the shape of the table that is used, and the addition or deletion of leaves calls for tablecloths of different sizes.

1. **Round tables without leaves require *round tablecloths*.**
   - Round table made for two to four people: 72-inch round tablecloth
   - Round table made for six to eight people: 86- to 90-inch round tablecloth
2. **Round tables with leaves require *oval tablecloths*.**
   - Round table extended to seat six people: 80- to 90-inch oval table-cloth
   - Round table extended to seat six to eight people: 102- to 108-inch oval tablecloth
   - Round table extended to seat ten to twelve people: 124- to 126-inch oval tablecloth
3. **Square tables without leaves require *square tablecloths*.**
   - Square table made to seat four: 52- to 54-inch square tablecloth
4. **Square tables with leaves require *oblong tablecloths*.**
   - Square table extended to seat two to four people: 70-inch oblong tablecloth
   - Square table extended to seat six people: 80- to 90-inch oblong tablecloth
   - Square table extended to seat eight to ten people: 102- to 108-inch oblong tablecloth
   - Square table extended to seat ten to twelve people: 124- to 126-inch oblong tablecloth
   - Square table extended to seat fourteen people: 144-inch oblong tablecloth
5. **Rectangular tables with or without leaves require *oblong tablecloths* in the same dimensions as mentioned for square tables.**
6. **Oval tables without leaves require *oval tablecloths*.**
   - Oval table for four people: 70-inch oval tablecloth
   - Oval table for six people: 80- to 90-inch oval tablecloth
   - Oval table for eight to ten people: 102- to 108-inch oval tablecloth
   - Oval table for ten to twelve people: 124- to 126-inch oval tablecloth
   - Oval table for twelve to fourteen people: 144-inch oval tablecloth

To calculate the yardage for a tablecloth measure the length and width of the table, the overhang, the width of the seams, and the hem allowance.

## The Silence Cloth

To insulate against noise, a protective pad is laid under the tablecloth; this liner is known as a *silence cloth*. In the nineteenth century, silence cloths were considered vulgar, except for the baize, a thick, coarse woolen fabric in a reddish-brown color, often dyed green to resemble felt. The baize insulated the table, protected the surface, and when tied to the corners prevented the tablecloth from slipping and bunching.

Today, a silence cloth is used to give the tablecloth a soft, drapey, luxurious appearance. This liner can be homemade of assorted materials, such as felt, an old wool blanket, a fluffy white fabric, or foam-backed vinyl cut to fit the table. Hard table pads made of layered insulation topped with aluminum foil and cotton flannel are available through department and specialty stores by custom order.

## Storing Tablecloths

To avoid unwanted wrinkles and an off-center crease where fabric rot may develop, wrap the tablecloth around a cardboard mailing tube that is as long as the tablecloth is wide. As an alternative, fold the tablecloth in half and use a smaller tube (however, fabric rot may develop on the crease). To touch up wrinkles with an iron, bring the ironing board to the end of the table and pull the cloth onto the table as it is ironed. Or cover the table with a heat-proof pad and iron the cloth on the table. To keep the cloth from getting dirty while it is being ironed, lay a sheet on the floor.

To prevent damage from smog and other contaminants in the air, store white, ecru, and ivory-colored tablecloths in blue acid-free tissue paper available at hand laundries. Man-made materials, such as plastic bags, trap moisture within and are not recommended for the storage of linens because they encourage the development of mildew and may change the color of the tablecloth. Seldom-used linens wrinkle when stored over a long period of time, and often it is easier to store them laundered, but unironed, rolled in a clean cotton sheet than to reiron them after storage. Moreover, never store soiled linens; the stains set and with time are harder to remove.

# Placemats

The placemat evolved in the seventeenth century when a London draper named Doyley lined an underplate with a small linen mat to keep the bowl in place. An etiquette manual written in 1906 stated placemats were acceptable because they kept the tablecloth clean. Today, placemats are used at formal luncheons and in informal dining. They are particularly suitable for families who eat on the run or dine at different hours; for young homemakers who have not yet selected "the" dining table and do not need a tablecloth; and for those whose lives are in flux.

Placemats create a broken line, give the table setting a spotty look, and are not used at a table laid with a profusion of tableware. But the spotty look does not disrupt a table setting where a simpler meal is served, and placemats are recommended for a seated meal of not more than ten people. To provide elbow room, allow a *minimum* of 4 inches between placemats.

Underpads create bulk and project slightly in a way that disturbs the symmetry of the table. Therefore fabric placemats are not insulated with underpads, unless they are made of sheer fabrics, such as organdy or handkerchief linen. However, for those who feel more secure with underpads underneath cloth placemats, they are easy to make from two layers of felt stitched together or foam-backed vinyl cut slightly smaller than the dimensions of the placemats.

The alignment of placemats with the edge of the table varies according to the way the table is finished. Placemats are laid on a bevel-edged table flush with the bevel. On a straight-edged table, placemats are laid about an inch up from the edge.

Placemats are made in assorted sizes and shapes. Large rectangular placemats approximately 12 inches wide by 18 inches long or 14 inches wide by 20 inches long hold an entire place setting and are the most popular size. Small placemats approximately 12 inches in diameter in square, oval, or round shapes hold only a dinner plate; the napkin, flatware, and stemware are laid on the table. However, small placemats extend space at a crowded table, work as hot pads, and emphasize the beauty of the table top.

# Table Runners

The table runner is a narrow length of cloth laid on top of tablecloths or on a bare table. In the fifteenth century they were used to protect the tablecloth from soil and were made of the same fabric. By the nineteenth century, table runners offered the hostess a fashionable alternative to tablecloths.

Today, table runners are used in any way the mind can conjure. They are laid down the center of the table for decoration, laid across the table to define seating, or used to carry out a theme. Luxurious metallic silks create an opulent ambience, obis give an Asian look, tapestry suggests a traditional setting, homespun weaves set a country mood, and certain patterns and colors promote a holiday theme.

To accommodate the average place setting, the table runner is approximately 14 to 17 inches wide, and the drop at the ends is about 15 inches deep. It is easier to care for than a tablecloth and a little more decorative than a placemat.

# CHAPTER THIRTY-FIVE

# NAPKINS

## A Brief History

The first napkin was a lump of dough the Spartans called *apomagdalie,* a mixture cut into small pieces and rolled and kneeded at the table, a custom that led to using sliced bread to wipe the hands. In Roman antiquity, napkins known as *sudaria* and *mappae* were made in both small and large lengths. The *sudarium,* Latin for "handkerchief," was a pocket-size fabric carried to blot the brow during meals taken in the warm Mediterranean climate. The *mappa* was a larger cloth spread over the edge of the couch as protection from food taken in a reclining position. The fabric was also used to blot the lips. Although each guest supplied his own *mappa,* on departure *mappae* were filled with delicacies leftover from the feast, a custom that continues today in restaurant "doggy bags."

In the early Middle Ages, the napkin disappeared from the table and hands and mouths were wiped on whatever was available, the back of the hand, clothing, or a piece of bread. Later, a few amenities returned and the table was laid with three cloths approximately 4 to 6 feet long by 5 feet wide. The first cloth, called a *couch* (from French, *coucher,* meaning "to lie down") was laid lengthwise before the master's place. A long towel called a *surnappe,* meaning "on the cloth," was laid over the *couch;* this indicated a place setting for an honored guest. The third cloth was a communal napkin that hung like a swag from the edge of the table. An example can be seen in *The Last Supper* by Dierik Bouts (1415–1475), which hangs in Saint Peter's Church,

Louvain, Belgium. In the late Middle Ages the communal napkin was reduced to about the size of our average bath towel.

The napkin had gone from a cloth laid on the table to a fabric draped over the left arm of a servant. The maître d' hôtel, the man in charge of feasts, as a symbol of office and rank, draped a napkin from his left shoulder, and servants of lower rank folded napkins lengthwise over their left arms, a custom that continued into the eighteenth century. Today in the United States, the napkin is placed on the left of the cover. But in Europe, the napkin is often laid to the right of the spoon.

The napkin was a part of the ritual at medieval banquets. The ewerer, the person in charge of ablutions, carried a towel that the lord and his honored guests used to wipe their hands on. The Bayeux tapestry depicts a ewerer kneeling before the high table with a finger bowl and napkin. The panter carried a *portpayne,* a napkin folded decoratively to carry the bread and knife used by the lord of the manor, a custom that distinguished his space from those of exalted guests. The folded napkin was placed on the left side of the place setting; the open end faced the lord. The spoon was wrapped in another napkin, and a third napkin was laid over the first and second napkins. To demonstrate that the water for ablutions was not poisoned, the marshal or the cup bearer kissed the towel on which the lord wiped his hands and draped the towel over the lord's left shoulder for use.

> If napkins are distributed, yours should be placed on the left shoulder or arm; goblet and knife go to the right, bread to the left.
>
> Erasmus, *De Civilitate Morum Puerilium,* 1530

By the sixteenth century, napkins were an accepted refinement of dining, a cloth made in different sizes for various events. The *diaper,* an English word for napkin, from the Greek word *diaspron,* was a white cotton or linen fabric woven with a small, repetitious, diamond-shaped pattern. The *serviette* was a large napkin used at the table. The *serviette de collation* was a smaller napkin used while standing to eat, similar to the way a cocktail napkin is used today. A *touaille* was a roller towel draped over a tube of wood or used as a communal towel that hung on the wall. It also meant a length of fabric laid on the altar or table to enclose bread, or a cloth used to protect a pillow or draped decoratively around a lady's head.

By the seventeenth century, the standard napkin was approximately 35 inches wide by 45 inches long, a capacious size that accommodated people who ate with their fingers. Essentially, napkins were approximately one-third the breadth of the tablecloth. However, when the fork was accepted by royalty in the seventeenth century, the napkin fell from use among the aristocracy and neatness in dining was emphasized. According to Ben Jonson, "Forks arrived in England from Italy 'to the saving of napkins.'" German-speaking people were reputed to be such neat diners that they seldom used a napkin.

The acceptance of the fork in the eighteenth century by all classes of society brought neatness to dining and reduced the size of the napkin to approximately 30 inches by 36 inches. Today, the napkin is made in a variety of sizes to meet every entertainment need: large for multicourse meals, medium for simple menus, small for afternoon tea and cocktails.

The French court imposed elaborate codes of etiquette on the aristocracy, among them the way to use a napkin, when to use it, and how far to unfold it in the lap. A French treatise dating from 1729 stated that "It is ungentlemanly to use a napkin for wiping the face or scraping the teeth, and a most vulgar error to wipe one's nose with it." And a rule of decorum from the same year laid out the protocol:

> The person of highest rank in the company should unfold his napkin first, all others waiting till he has done so before they unfold theirs. When all of those present are social equals, all unfold together, with no ceremony.

Fashionable men of the time wore stiffly starched ruffled collars, a style protected while dining with a napkin tied around the neck. Hence the expression "to make ends meet." When shirts with lace fronts came into vogue, napkins were tucked into the neck or buttonhole or were attached with a pin. In 1774, a French treatise declared, "the napkin covered the front of the body down to the knees, starting from below the collar and not tucked into said collar."

Around 1740, the tablecloth was made with matching napkins. According to Savary des Bruslons, "Twelve napkins, a large tablecloth and a small one, comprise what is called these days a 'table service.'"

# How to Use a Napkin

The purpose of a napkin is to blot the lips and wipe fingertips. Its shape and size are affected by the formality of the occasion, a factor that also determines the placement of the napkin, the fold, the color, texture, and pattern, and whether napkin rings are provided.

## *The Shapes and Sizes of Napkins*

Most napkins are square. Large napkins, approximately 22 to 26 inches square, are used at a multicourse meal. Medium to large napkins, approximately 18 to 24 inches square, or *lapkins*, approximately 12 inches wide by 22 inches long, are appropriate for buffet service where a one-dish menu is eaten from the lap. Medium-size napkins, approximately 18 to 20 inches square, are used at a simple dinner. Napkins approximately 14 to 16 inches square are used for luncheons. Small napkins, approximately 12 inches square, are easy to hold under a tea plate and are used at afternoon tea. For cocktails, tiny napkins approximately 9 inches square, 4 inches by 6 inches, or 6 inches by 8 inches, are used. These sizes fit under the small hors d'oeuvres plate and wrap around a cocktail glass.

## *Napkin Colors and Designs*

The ambience of the table setting is changed by the color of the napkins. At a formal table, rather than distract the eye with an array of napkins in contrasting colors, the napkins should match the color of the tablecloth in shades of white, ivory, ecru, or pastel.

Napkins chosen for formal use are not decorated with an elaborate border. Rather they are plain or feature a simple weave that does not detract the eye from the table setting.

At an informal meal, napkins in contrasting colors offer easy accent. For additional interest, alternate different patterns around the table, such as dotted napkins with plaid designs or striped napkins with a floral tablecloth. But to unify the mix of patterns, keep the scale of the designs the same.

## *Napkin Textures*

Choose napkins with an absorbent texture to properly blot the mouth. To unify the table setting, keep the texture of the linens compatible with the occasion and the finish of the tableware. The elegance of formal dining is compatible with the fine texture of matching napkins and tablecloth and the smooth finish of the porcelain, silver, and crystal. However, the repast served at afternoon tea is simpler than a formal dinner or luncheon, less tableware is required and the texture of the linens need not match; linen napkins can be paired with a lace tablecloth, for example. At an informal meal, unusual textures add interest to a plain setting, and when the table is laid with coarsely textured tableware, unify the look with loosely woven napkins.

## *The Placement of the Napkin*

At a formal affair, to conserve space at a fully appointed place setting, the napkin is centered on the service plate, a placement that brings the napkin closer to the diner. If hot soup is in place when the diner comes to the table, the napkin is placed to the left of the forks.

At an informal meal, the napkin is placed wherever and however the host chooses: in the center of the plate, to the left of the forks, above the plate, under the plate, on the bread-and-butter plate, in the wine glass, draped over the chair, wrapped around flatware on a buffet, or arranged decoratively in a container.

## *The Placement of the Napkin Fold*

The "next-to-the-fork fold" frames the place setting, and when the napkin is lifted for use the fingers do not hit the flatware. The "away-from-the-fork fold" places the four points of the napkin closer to the diner, a fold that assures a smooth movement when the napkin is placed in the lap. As the placement of the fold is a matter of personal preference, the important point is to face the fold in the same direction at each cover.

## *The Napkin Fold*

The table setting is a composite of hard surfaces. To promote a softened look, napkins are folded into shape, rather than pressed into form. Moreover, a folded napkin lies smoother on the lap than a creased napkin. But the fold of the napkin is different for formal and informal dining. At a formal affair, to accent the elaborate table setting, the napkin is folded into a simple form, such as a square, rectangle, triangle, or shield. For uniformity, the corners of the napkin meet exactly.

- *The square or rectangle folds look well on a service plate.* To make a square, fold a large square napkin in half, and fold it in half again. When an extralarge napkin is used, such as a 22- to 26-inch napkin, it may take several folds to make a medium-size square. To make a rectangle, take a large square nap-

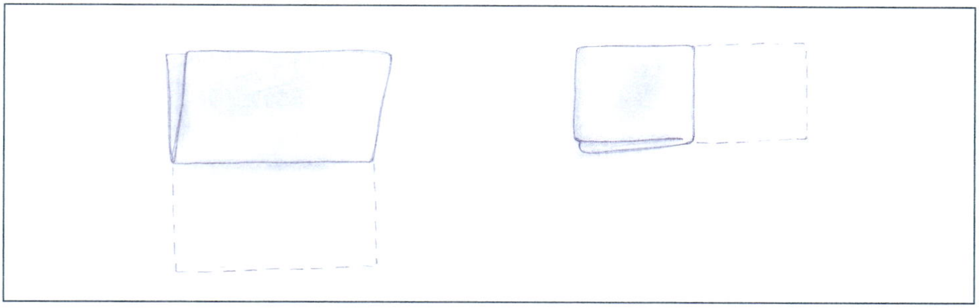

THE SQUARE STARTS WITH A SQUARE NAPKIN FOLDED IN HALF TO MAKE A RECTANGLE. THE RECTANGLE IS FOLDED IN HALF AGAIN TO MAKE A SQUARE. THE FOLD IS REPEATED AS MANY TIMES AS IS NEEDED TO MAKE THE NAPKIN THE RIGHT PROPORTION FOR THE SERVICE PLATE.

kin and fold it lengthwise in thirds, one side overlapping the other to make a long rectangle. Fold the top half over the bottom half, and roll the sides under to make a smaller rectangle.
- *The triangle fold is appropriate when the napkin is laid next to the fork.* Fold a large square napkin lengthwise in thirds to form a rectangle. Fold the rectangle in thirds to make a square. Fold the square in half diagonally to make a triangle. Lay the fold next to the fork.
- *The shield fold is laid on the service plate.* The shield fold is used when the rect-

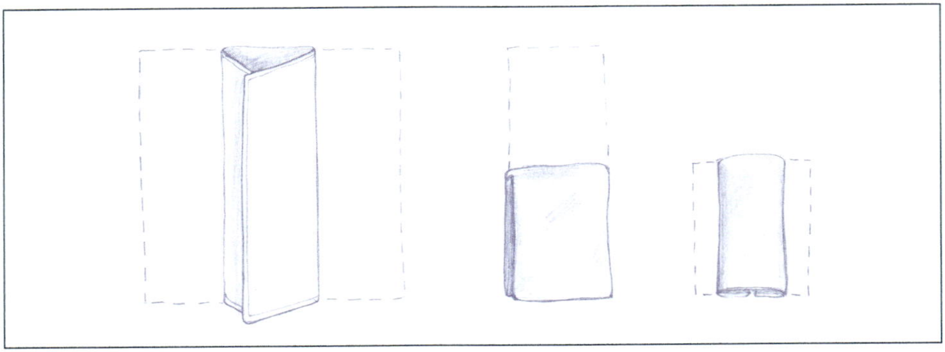

The rectangle fold begins with a square napkin folded lengthwise in thirds, one side overlapping the other. The top half is folded over the bottom half. The long sides of the napkin are rolled under.

The final fold is placed on the service plate.

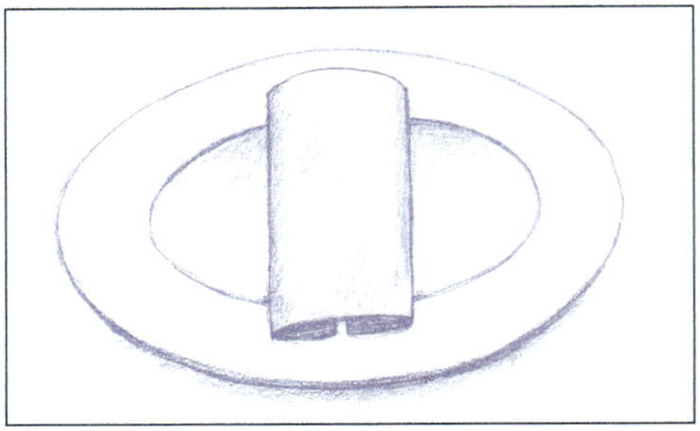

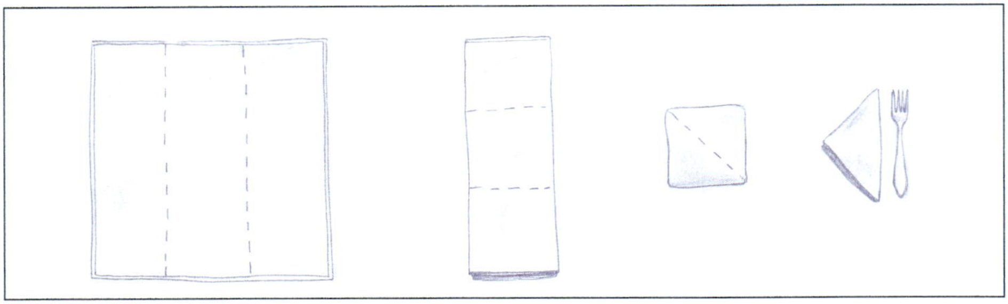

The triangle fold starts with a large square napkin folded lengthwise in thirds forming a rectangle. The rectangle is folded in thirds to make a square. The square is folded in half diagonally to make a triangle. The fold of the triangle is laid next to the fork.

angle or square fold are longer than the service plate. The large napkin is folded into a triangle. Two edges of the triangle are folded under to make a shield. The tip of the shield points toward the diner. The shield fold accents a napkin finished with a decorative edge.

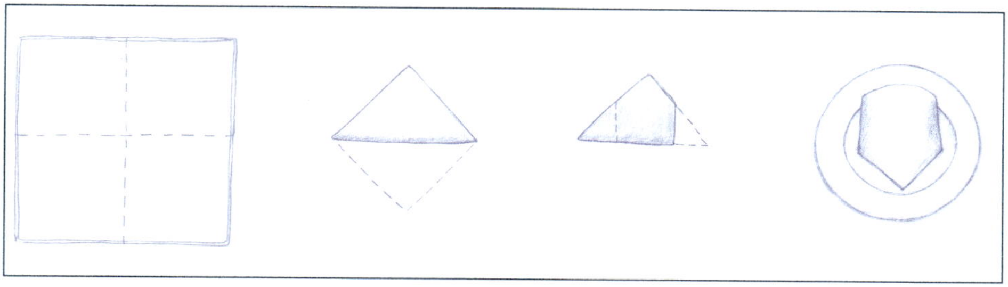

TO MAKE A SHIELD, FOLD THE NAPKIN INTO A SQUARE. FOLD THE SQUARE DIAGONALLY TO MAKE A TRIANGLE. FOLD TWO SIDES OF THE TRIANGLE UNDER AND POINT THE TIP OF THE SHIELD TOWARD THE DINER.

In the case of *monogrammed napkins,* the napkin is personalized in one of three places:

- A napkin monogrammed *in the center of one side* is folded into a rectangle. The rectangle is folded into thirds to make a square. The initial lies in the center of the square.
- A monogram *in the center of the napkin* is folded lengthwise into a rectangle. The upper and lower thirds of the napkin are folded under to form a square. The initial lies in the center of the square.
- A napkin monogrammed *in the corner* is folded into a square. The square is folded diagonally to make a triangle. The initial lies in the tip of the triangle.

At an informal meal, fewer courses are served, the table setting is simpler, and a decorative napkin fold adds interest. There are many fine books on the subject of decorative napkin folds. The folds presented here form a container, hold utensils,

TO ACCENT A MONOGRAM PLACED IN THE *CENTER OF ONE SIDE,* THE NAPKIN IS FOLDED INTO A SQUARE. THE SQUARE IS FOLDED INTO A RECTANGLE. IF THE RECTANGLE IS TOO LONG FOR THE PLATE, THE NAPKIN IS FOLDED INTO THIRDS TO MAKE A SMALLER SQUARE.

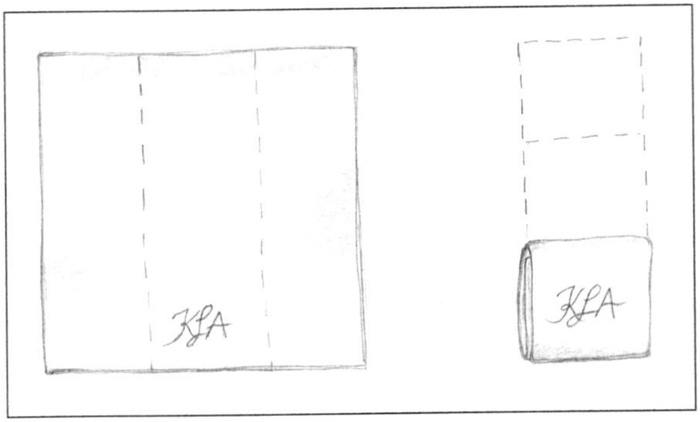


TO ACCENT A MONOGRAM IN THE *CENTER OF THE NAPKIN,* THE NAPKIN IS FOLDED LENGTHWISE TO MAKE A RECTANGLE. THE UPPER AND LOWER THIRDS OF THE RECTANGLE ARE FOLDED UNDER TO FORM A SQUARE.

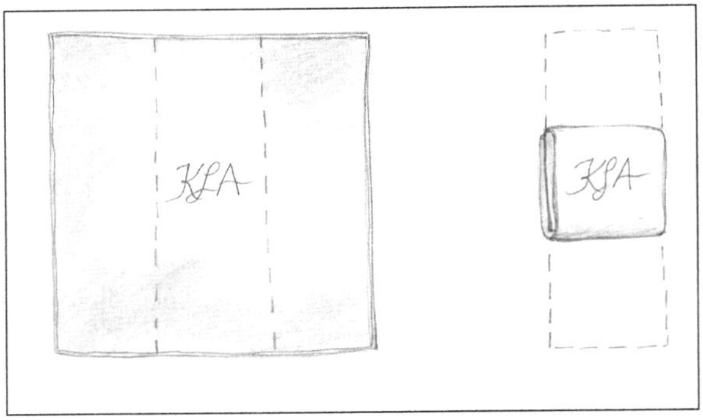


TO ACCENT A MONOGRAM IN THE *CORNER OF THE NAPKIN,* THE NAPKIN IS FOLDED INTO A SQUARE, THEN DIAGONALLY TO MAKE A TRIANGLE.

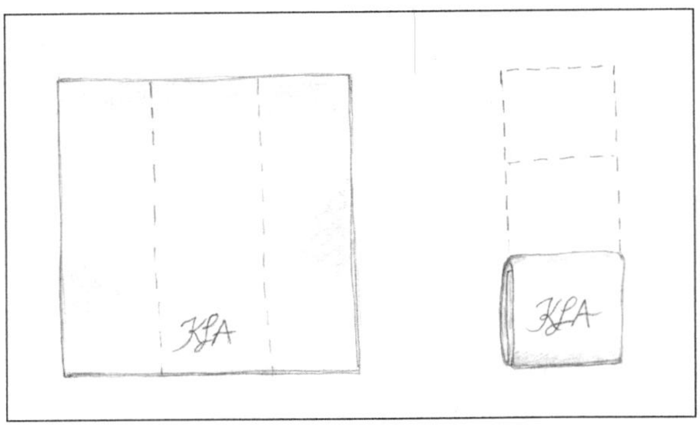

conserve space, present two napkins, and act as placemats, runners, vases, trivets, and centerpieces.

- *The water lily fold is a container that holds a roll, a wine glass, a small bowl, a party favor, or a flower.* A square napkin is ironed flat and laid on the table. The four points of the napkin are folded to the center front, a shape that forms a small square. Depending on the size of the napkin, the fold is repeated one

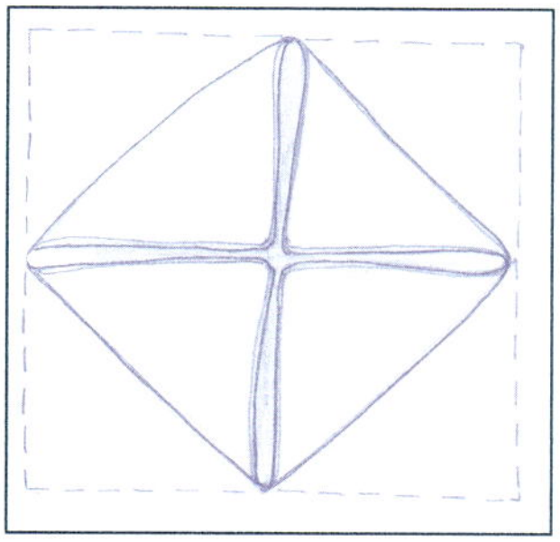

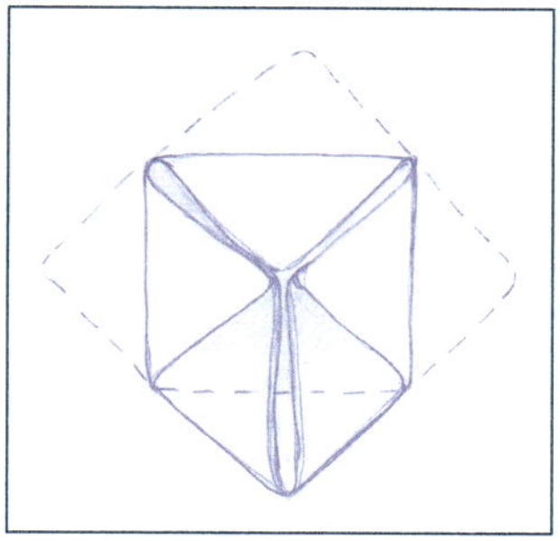

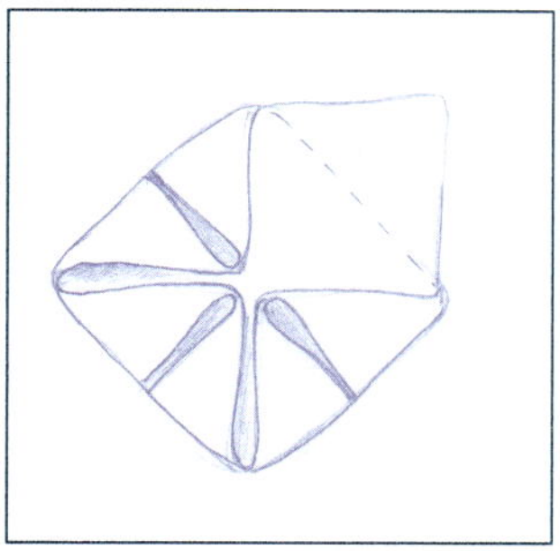

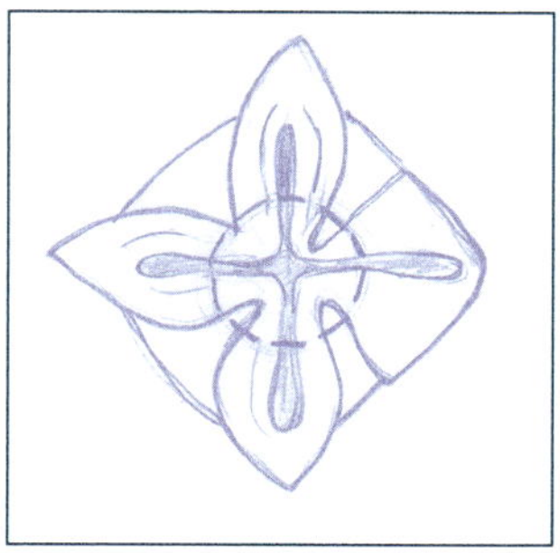

*Left to right:* It begins with a square napkin ironed flat. The four points of the napkin are folded to the center front to make a smaller square. The fold is repeated to make an even smaller square.

The napkin is turned over so the folds on the front of the napkin lie downward on the table. The corners of the upward side of the napkin are folded to the center. The folds in the center of the napkin are held in place with one hand or with a wine glass.

With the free hand, the points on the bottom side of the napkin are pulled out, forming petals similar to a water lily. The points in the top center of the napkin are folded back, exposing space for a roll, wine glass, small bowl, or party favor.

or two times. To make the final fold, the napkin is turned over so the front lies face downward on the table. The points on the top side of the napkin are folded to the center front, and held with the finger or a glass. With the free hand, the points on the bottom side are pulled up and out forming petals, a look similar to a water lily.

- *The flatware fold holds utensils on a buffet, a second napkin, or a party favor*. The four corners of the napkin are folded in to make a square. The square is

*LEFT TO RIGHT:* THE *FLATWARE FOLD* HOLDS UTENSILS FOR A BUFFET-STYLE MEAL, A SECOND NAPKIN, OR A PARTY FAVOR. FOUR CORNERS OF THE NAPKIN ARE FOLDED IN TO MAKE A SQUARE. THE SQUARE IS FOLDED IN HALF TO MAKE A RECTANGLE.

THE RECTANGLE IS FOLDED AGAIN TO MAKE A SQUARE. THE SIDES OF THE SQUARE ARE FOLDED UNDER.

THE FINAL POCKET OF THE FOLD IS FILLED WITH WHATEVER.

folded in half to make a rectangle. The rectangle is folded again to make a square. The sides of the square are folded under. The final pocket of the fold is filled with flatware, a second napkin, or a party favor.

- *The stemware fold conserves space on a crowded table*. Because the fabric may leave lint in a wine glass, the stemware fold is not suggested for an elegant meal where a special wine is served. The napkin is laid flat on the table and is folded into accordian pleats about 1 inch wide. The pleats are secured with the finger in the center, folded in half, and the bottom third is placed in a wine glass. The top pleats are fanned outward above the rim of the glass.

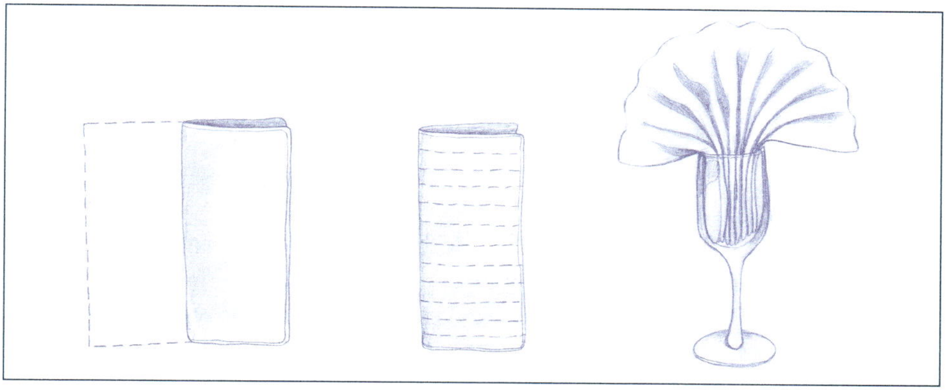

THE *STEMWARE FOLD* CONSERVES SPACE ON A CROWDED TABLE. THE NAPKIN IS LAID FLAT ON THE TABLE AND FOLDED IN HALF. THEN THE NAPKIN IS FOLDED INTO ACCORDION PLEATS ABOUT 1 INCH WIDE. THE PLEATS ARE SECURED IN THE CENTER OF THE NAPKIN WITH THE FINGER, AND THE BOTTOM HALF OF THE NAPKIN IS PLACED IN THE WINE GLASS. THE UPPER PLEATS ARE FANNED OUT ABOVE THE RIM.

- *The double napkin fold accommodates a meal eaten with fingers*. Two large napkins of the same size, preferably in contrasting colors or a solid-color napkin paired with a patterned napkin, are folded together to make a rectangle. The rectangle is folded into a square. The square is folded into a rectangle. To protect the lap from the plate, the outer napkin is unfolded and laid over the lap. The inner napkin is used in the traditional capacity.

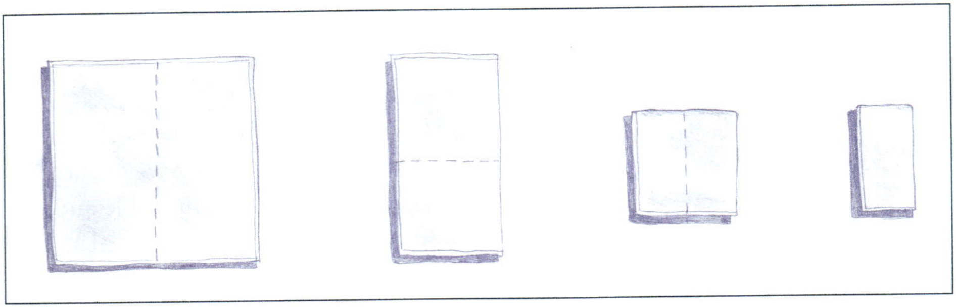

THE *DOUBLE NAPKIN FOLD* COVERS THE LAP FOR A MEAL EATEN AWAY FROM THE TABLE OR TAKEN WITH FINGERS. TWO NAPKINS OF THE SAME SIZE ARE FOLDED TOGETHER LENGTHWISE TO MAKE A RECTANGLE. THE RECTANGLE IS FOLDED INTO A SQUARE. DEPENDING ON THE SIZE OF THE NAPKIN, THE SQUARE IS FOLDED INTO A RECTANGLE.

- *Napkins as placemats.* Lay an open napkin on the table in a diamond position. The half of the diamond that faces the center of the table becomes a placemat. The lower half hangs off the table and makes a decorative overhang.
- *Napkins as runners.* An assortment of colorful napkins are folded and overlapped down the center of the table, a length that makes a runner.
- *Napkins as vases.* To turn an ordinary pot into a colorful vase, wrap a napkin around a garden pot and secure it with a ribbon, straw, or cord.
- *Napkins as trivets.* To turn an odd piece of wood into a trivet, cover it with a napkin in a patterned or plain design that harmonizes with the dinnerware.
- *Napkins as a centerpiece.* To make a colorful centerpiece, fold napkins in the shape of birds, flowers, and fruit.

Here are some final points on napkin folds.

- The 18-inch napkin is the easiest size to fold into a decorative shape.
- For shape retention, before folding a napkin, lightly starch the fabric and iron out the creases.
- Heavy fabrics hold shape well and are suggested for vertical napkin folds.
- Lightweight fabrics are recommended for horizontal napkin folds.
- Fabrics with a pattern on one side expose the reverse weave and change the appearance of the napkin fold.

## *Napkin Rings*

Before the washing machine and dryer eased and enhanced our lives, fabric napkins were laundered by hand. To conserve time and energy, at family meals napkins were enclosed in a personalized ring, often made of silver, an accessory that identified the napkin for reuse. Today, in formal dining, napkin rings are not used because they suggest the original purpose, reuse. Moreover, after World War II, paper napkins were enthusiastically endorsed, and the convenience and easy disposability made napkin rings almost obsolete. But customs change, and today at informal meals, elegant or otherwise, the napkin ring is used as a decorative accessory, an accoutrement avidly collected, from antique napkin rings, to theme napkin rings, to napkin rings made purely for fun.

For easy removal, the napkin is placed in the napkin ring with the point of the napkin facing the diner. After the napkin is removed, the napkin ring is placed at the top left of the place setting. At the end of the meal, the napkin is grasped in the center and pulled through the napkin ring, so the point of the napkin faces the center of the table.

## *Extra Napkins*

To replace overly soiled napkins, or napkins that accidentally drop to the floor, it is the wise hostess who has extra napkins at the ready. Extra napkins also double as hotpads, to insulate bread, and to catch drips when tied around the neck of wine bottles.

## *Paper Napkins*

The convenience and easy disposability of paper napkins are a boon to the host of family meals, picnics, barbecues, children's parties, large buffets, and cocktail parties. The two-ply paper napkin is more absorbent than the one-ply. At the end of a meal, rather than make a ball of a soiled napkin, fold it loosely and lay it on the table.

# PART VI

# Serving Techniques

CHAPTER THIRTY-SIX

# FORMAL DINNER SERVICE

FORMAL DINING IS a gracious, elegant, memorable event. A multicourse menu is planned to include the choicest seasonal delicacies and finest wines. The table setting is luxuriant, resplendent with translucent porcelains, sparkling crystal, gleaming silver, and pristine linens. Centerpieces profuse with peak-of-perfection flowers adorn the table in a multitude of arrangements amid fully appointed place settings defined by place cards. Menu cards are laid at each place setting or offered to guests between place settings. The ladies are beautifully gowned and coiffed and the gentlemen are in full dress. Deportment is refined, and the conversation is scintillating. After-dinner entertainment is planned.

To assure the gala ambience of the evening, the host and hostess do not assist with the meal, nor do the guests help or even offer to do the same. A chef prepares the meal and a professional staff serves—traditionally a male staff overseen by a majordomo, who also pours the wine. To make sure that the needs of the guests are met, the majordomo watches the service at a distance from behind the hostess's chair. Maids assist with formal luncheon service.

But so often enjoying good service and knowing how to direct or give it are two different things. Here are some general guidelines.

- *Never leave an empty space before a guest.* Hospitality dictates that the space before the guest must always hold a plate, and for this reason service plates are laid on the table before the guests enter the dining room. An empty cover is left before the guest very briefly only when the table is cleared for dessert.

- *Good service is quiet and unobtrusive.* When a meal comprises five or more courses, the clearance and placement of plates on the table is hardly noticed if the staff make a conscious effort to avoid noises that disrupt conversation.
- *The ratio of help to guests depends not only on the number of courses, but on the amount of special preparation required.* To serve each course at its proper temperature, provide one butler for four to six guests. When the guest list is increased by four, increase the number of butlers by one. If a course requires last-minute attention, the rate of service is slowed and extra help are engaged to assure a timely tempo. When sauce is presented, two butlers often work as a team: one to serve the course and the second to follow with sauce.
- *The server's fingers do not touch plates that hold food.* To keep fingers from the rim of the plate, the butler holds a fresh plate in the *palm* of his left hand (often a gloved hand) and slides it into place. But the server's fingers may touch the rim of the plate when it is cleared.
- *The serveware required per course depends on the number of guests.* A "service" is the serveware required to present a course, such as a platter and a sauce bowl. In general, six to eight guests require one service per course; fourteen guests, two services; and sixteen to eighteen guests, three services.
- *Service moves in a single direction.* Food service proceeds to the right, counterclockwise, starting with the guest of honor. Beverage service progresses to the left, clockwise.
- *The traffic level in the dining room is kept at a minimum.* To promote an atmosphere that is not disruptive to conversation, a butler tries not to enter and exit the dining room more than four to six times per course: to set a plate before each guest; to serve the course; to present sauce (as needed); to serve wine; to replenish water (as needed); to clear the plate.
- *Prearranged courses are served on a platter.* At a formal dinner, to make service of each course easy for the guest, individual portions are prearranged and presented on a platter.
- *The platter is held in a position that facilitates service.* To enable the guest to serve himself comfortably, the platter is held about 1 inch above the guest's

plate. To avoid spills and make access to the platter easy, the platter is held partially over the table in a level position.

- *A separate utensil is provided for each food on the platter.*
- *After service, the platter is lifted above the guest's shoulder.* Rather than lift a platter over the guest's head and risk a spill, the platter is raised above the guest's shoulder after service.
- *Sauce bowls are passed if appropriate.* When the well of a platter is not deep enough to contain fluids that flow from food, such as the juice from a roast, liquid seasoning is passed in a bowl.
- *Second helpings are not offered.* Formal dining includes multiple courses and second helpings are not offered. Once serveware is taken from the dining room, it is not returned.
- *The temperature of the plates should be appropriate for the food they contain.* To enhance and compliment the flavor of each course, food is served on a hot or cold plate. Because porcelain is naturally cold to the touch, the plates are not cooled before cold courses, such as appetizers or salad, are served.
- *Plates are served and cleared from the left side.* At a formal dinner, plates are served and cleared from one side only, the left side, a method that makes the guests feel less enclosed by someone constantly hovering about them with arms suddenly appearing left and right. The server's right hand clears a used plate, and the left hand slides a fresh plate into place. The exception is when something on the right side of the cover is removed, such as the sherry glass; rather than reach across the guest, the butler clears it from the right.
- *Plates are served and cleared one at a time.* At a formal meal, when a soiled plate is cleared, the butler immediately slides a fresh plate into place. In this way, there is never an empty space before the guest. And because both hands are engaged in the removal and service of plates, at formal affairs plates are served and cleared one at a time.

  The exception is the service and clearance of the first course and the dessert course. To expedite service of the first course, the butler carries two plates to the table at one time. After the table is crumbed, the butler carries two dessert plates to the dining room at one time.
- *Beverages are served and cleared from the right side.*
- *The goblet and wine glasses remain on the table through the entire meal so each guest*

*may enjoy whatever wine he or she chooses.* Only the sherry glass is removed at the end of the course it accompanies. If a guest informs the butler that he or she is allergic to a particular wine or simply does not care for the taste, the butler removes the wine glass with the guest's permission.

- *When the same wine is offered with consecutive courses, it is served in the same glass.*

# The Progression of Service

## *The Guest Who Is Served First*

Years ago it was traditional to serve the host and hostess first, a custom that originated in the Middle Ages to demonstrate that the food was not poisoned. Today the custom is observed only in a few instances: to demonstrate to guests from a foreign country the correct way to proceed; when a hostess is dining alone with her family; or if a hostess is dining with a group of younger women.

Customarily, the honored guest is served first, a courtesy that affords a selection of the choicest food from an untouched platter. Service begins with the lady of honor seated to the right of the host, proceeds counterclockwise, and ends with the host. But when a formal affair has no one guest of honor, service begins with the most important female guest. Depending on individual circumstances, there are several ways to serve a formal meal.

- *Ladies served first.* At a large formal dinner, or one where strict protocol is followed, service may commence with the women, starting with the lady of honor. Although this is a courteous method of service, it is slow, as each butler must circle the table numerous times and crisscross around the room.
- *Service in the order of progression.* At a small formal dinner where less help is provided, service in the order of progression commences with the lady of honor seated to the right of the host and proceeds counterclockwise around the table, ending with the host. The hostess is served in the order of progression and commences to eat as soon as she is served so that others may begin to eat while the course is at its proper temperature. The butler does not double back around the table, and the meal is not delayed.
- *Service for a single hostess and an acting host.* When a single hostess asks a gen-

tleman to act as her host, he is seated opposite her. The lady of honor is seated on his right hand and is served first. The hostess is served in the order of progression and the acting host is served last.

- *Service for a single hostess without a host.* The lady of honor is seated at the end of the table opposite the hostess, and she is served first. The order of service proceeds from the lady of honor counterclockwise. Because there is no host the hostess is served last. As the arrangement is not balanced with alternate male-female seating, this form of service is rare.
- *Service for a single host without a hostess.* A host without a hostess seats the lady of honor to his right. Service begins with her and proceeds counterclockwise around the table, ending with the host.
- *Alternating service for each course.* To avoid serving the same guest last, alternate service is provided. The first course commences with the lady of honor and proceeds counterclockwise around the table. The second course starts with the lady seated to the left of the host and progresses clockwise. Each time the host is served last.

## *Duplicate and Triplicate Service*

To ensure that each course is served at the proper temperature, when more than six guests are seated at the table, duplicate and triplicate services are presented simultaneously.

- *Duplicate service.* The lady of honor is served first, and the guest seated directly opposite her to the left of the host receives duplicate service. The remaining guests are served in the order of progression (counterclockwise on the right side of the table, clockwise on the left), regardless of gender. The host and hostess are served last. Alternatively, duplicate service begins with the lady of honor and the lady seated diagonally opposite her at the other end of the table. If the man of honor is extremely important, duplicate service begins with him.
- *Triplicate service.* When the ladies are served first, triplicate service begins with the lady of honor and two ladies seated equidistant from her. If service is in the order of progression, triplicate service begins with the lady of honor and the guests seated one-third the distance from her, regardless of gender.

### *Time Lapses between Service of Courses*

A multicourse meal takes time to prepare, serve, and clear, an interval that prompts leisurely dining and promotes good conversation. Depending on the number of courses served, and whether they require sauce or extra attention, a formal dinner may last 4 or 5 hours, or more.

### *Inspection of the Meat Platter*

Traditionally, the main course at a formal dinner is a roast of beef, fowl, or game. To expedite service, a combination of food is presented on the platter, such as prime rib with potatoes, asparagus, and parsley. Because the main course is the most important course, at a formal dinner held in a private residence, the meat platter is presented to the hostess for inspection, a courtesy that enables her to make sure nothing was omitted from the platter, that the food is arranged attractively, and that the platter is tidy. With a nod or a comment she indicates approval (or disapproval) and service begins. However, the custom is followed only for the main course. Because the courses that precede and follow the main course do not include a combination of food, the approval of the hostess is not needed. Moreover, in a club or hotel, the meat platter is not presented to the hostess for inspection; instead the job is performed by the maître d' hôtel.

### *Service of Watery Vegetables*

To absorb liquids that flow from food, vegetables that leave fluids on the bottom of a dish, such as asparagus, are served on a folded napkin.

### *When to Clear Each Course*

Years ago, so that guests didn't have to look at a table filled with soiled plates, plates were cleared as soon as each guest laid his or her eating utensils in a finished position. By the time the last guest ceased to eat, the table was cleared. However, the method tended to rush slow eaters, and the custom changed.

Now the time to clear the course depends on the number of guests seated at the table. At a small dinner party, plates are cleared after the last guest is finished. At a large dinner party, to expedite service, plates are cleared as soon as the majority of guests are finished. When dinner guests are seated at several tables, plates are cleared first from the tables at which the host and hostess are seated (as these tables are where the honored guests are seated). To speed service at a banquet, plates are cleared as soon as two or three diners at a table are finished.

### *Clearing the Table*

To keep the noise level low in the dining room, rather than stack several plates together or clear them on a tray, servers carry plates to the kitchen or pantry one at a time. However, at a large affair, to speed clearance one butler may carry a soiled plate to a sideboard, for another to take to the kitchen.

Before dessert is served the table is cleared of everything unrelated to the dessert course, starting with the largest items and working to the smallest, namely plates, stemware, flatware, and small sets of salt and pepper. Although large articles are cleared one in each hand, to expedite service small items are cleared on a small doily-lined tray. The doily prevents slippage on the tray and reduces the noise level in the room. The purpose of the doily is to keep the tableware from slipping and to absorb oils from food, such as dessert presented on a plate. Linen doilies are used in formal dining and paper doilies at informal affairs. Because heavy ware, such as a coffee service, is unlikely to slip, a large tray is not lined with a doily.

### *Crumbing the Table*

The multiple courses served at a formal dinner create crumbs. To freshen the table before dessert, the butler stands to the left of each guest and with a small thin brush or a folded napkin, brushes the crumbs onto a small plate, a tray, or a silent butler held just below the edge of the table.

### *Service of Sweets*

Special sweets, such as fine chocolates and glacéed fruit, are presented in compotes and placed on the table as part of the table decor. The compotes remain on the table throughout the meal and are offered to the guests during dessert. However, in the long lapse between courses, oftentimes the guests help themselves to a bite or two from the compote placed nearest to them.

## *Service of Demitasse, Liqueur, and Brandy*

A formal dinner lasts for hours. To allow guests to stretch, freshen up, and regroup, demitasse, liqueurs, and brandy are served in another room.

Demitasse is a stimulant and a digestive. It is traditionally taken black. Cream is not offered because it reduces the stimulating effect, and makes coffee more of a food. However, on request, sugar is added.

Demitasse is served English style or continental style. In the English method, the men and women take coffee, liqueur, and brandy in different rooms, a separation that affords a brief interlude for guests of the same gender to enjoy conversation not relevant to a mixed group, an interval of approximately 20 minutes.

The hostess leads the ladies to a separate room, such as the bedroom or the anteroom of the powder room, where a maid pours demitasse for the ladies and presents it on a small tray. As she hands a demitasse to each lady, she asks the guest if she would care for a liqueur. If so, the maid pours the liqueur and serves it on a salver.

The gentlemen remain in the dining room for coffee, brandy, and cigars, or they move to the library. Demitasse and brandy are set out on a tray on a sideboard. The butler pours demitasse for each gentleman and asks each guest in turn if he would like a brandy. If so, the butler pours brandy and serves it on a salver. Cigarettes and cigars are offered from a tray in an open humidor.

In the continental style, demitasse, liqueurs, and brandy are taken jointly by the guests, traditionally in the drawing room, a convivial custom that does not disrupt the party. At a small affair, the butler sets the coffee tray on a low table, and as a personal touch, the hostess pours, asking each guest in turn how he or she takes coffee. The guest steps forward to receive the cup, or the host hands it to the guest. At a large affair, the butler presents a coffee tray to each guest, and asks if he or she would like a cup. If the answer is yes, the butler takes a demitasse cup and saucer from the tray, places it on the table nearest the guest, and pours. The butler may also hold the tray in his left hand and pour demitasse with his right hand. The guest removes the demitasse cup and saucer from the tray. Sometimes two butlers work in pairs: The first butler carries a small tray with a demitasse pot, and the second butler follows with a larger tray of cups, saucers, and spoons. The first butler removes the demitasse cup and saucer from the larger tray, places it on the smaller tray, and pours for the guest. The guest removes the cup and saucer from the tray.

After coffee is poured, liqueur and brandy are offered. Generally two after-dinner drinks are offered, perhaps brandy and a sweet cordial, such as a cream liqueur.

### *Cigarettes and Ashtrays*

Cigarettes and ashtrays do not appear on a table except at the hostess's request. However, when cigarettes are offered, out of courtesy to those who are allergic to smoke or find the habit offensive, guests wait to light the cigarette until after dessert is finished. Years ago, it was customary to lay at each place setting an ashtray, a book of matches, and a small silver urn with several cigarettes. Today people are more health-conscious, but when cigarettes are offered at formal affairs, it is from an open box presented on a silver tray that contains a stack of small ashtrays and a cigarette lighter or a lighted taper. A lighted candle not only makes the presentation dramatic, it eliminates the chemical odor inherent in lighter fluid. The butler lights the guest's cigarette and places an ashtray to the right of the cover. When cigarettes are offered in the drawing room, they are presented after demitasse is served.

### *A Tray of Water*

Approximately a half hour after the guests are finished with after-dinner drinks, a tray of water and tumblers is set out on a side table in the drawing room, and the guests help themselves.

### *Late-Night Snack*

A formal dinner begins late in the evening, generally at 8:30 or 9:00 P.M., and lasts until well past midnight. The meal is followed by entertainment, dancing, and possibly cards. To revive the guests, at the host's option, a late-night snack is served, such as a tray of finger sandwiches and a dish of chocolates, from a nearby table.

### *Bidding Guests Good Night*

At a large affair, the host and hostess say good night to their guests in the drawing room. In the foyer the butler helps the guests into their wraps, escorts them to the door, and bids them good night. A valet brings their car and helps the guests into it.

# Service of a Formal Six-Course Dinner

Although a four-course menu is the minimum number served at a formal dinner, for illustration a six-course menu is presented step-by-step. Each course follows the same sequence of service: presentation of the course, sauce, wine, and water (replenished as needed).

## *First Course, Hot or Cold*

- *Hot soup.* To eliminate the awkwardness of ladling soup from a tureen held by a butler, the soup plate is filled in the kitchen and laid on the service plate. Soup may also be served from a cart that is rolled around the room.
- *Cold appetizer.* A cold course, such as fish, is presented to the guest on a platter. The butler places a plate before the guest who serves himself or herself from the platter.
- *Wine.* In formal dining, wine bottles are opened in the kitchen. The host's glass is filled first and the host tastes the wine for palatability. To avoid spills, the wine bottle is brought to the glass.
- *Water.* Traditionally, water is poured after the first course is served. However, at a multicourse meal that involves extensive service, water goblets are often filled before the guests come to the table. This expedites service, decreases the noise level in the room, reduces the amount of hovering about the guests, and creates a more relaxed atmosphere. Water goblets remain on the table throughout the meal. The water pitcher is brought to the goblet, and to avoid spills, the goblet is filled no more than three-quarters full. The butler carries a folded napkin in the left hand, or over the left forearm, and uses the napkin to catch drops.
- *Rolls.* Rolls are served dry in a low container lined with a linen doily or a napkin. Guests remove the roll from the container and lay it on the tablecloth. In Europe, rolls are occasionally placed in the fold of napkins or are laid on top of napkins, a method that eliminates the need to pass rolls with

the first course. However, because the roll may drop to the floor when the napkin is lifted, the method is used less today.

### *Second Course*

Immediately after the first course is cleared, the butler slides a fresh plate into place and carries the soiled plate to the kitchen. After all the plates are cleared, the second course is presented on a platter. Wine is poured. If croutons or toast are served with the second course, they are presented, usually by a second butler. Water is replenished.

### *Main Course*

After the second course is cleared and the dinner plates are in place, the meat platter is presented to the hostess for approval (only in a private residence). To steady the platter, and to insulate his hand from the heat, the butler either covers the palm of his right hand with a napkin folded in a square or a rectangle or wears white cotton gloves. In England years ago, servants wore thumb guards rather than gloves.

To eliminate traffic in the room, the meat platter is filled with a combination of foods, namely a roast, starch, vegetables, and garnish. Vegetables may also be offered separately, one or two bowls at a time. When bowls are carried two at a time, the butler presents the first bowl with the left hand, while holding the second bowl in the right hand, behind his back. After the first bowl is presented, the butler presents the second bowl in the right hand and holds the first bowl behind his back.

After the meat platter has been passed, the butler presents sauces and condiments served in sauceboats or small bowls carried on a salver. Wine is poured. Water is replenished.

### *Salad Course*

At a formal dinner, a prearranged salad is served from a platter, followed by an optional presentation of a cheese tray, toasted crackers, and butter served at room temperature. Because silver is subject to scratches, a wooden cheese board is placed on a silver tray. A separate knife is provided for each type of cheese. The guests cut a slice of cheese and place it on the side of the salad plate. The service of crackers and butter follow. The guests remove a cracker or two, place it on the salad plate, and take a slice of butter.

Because the acidic quality of salad dressing competes with wine, a new wine is not introduced with the salad course. Water is replenished.

### *Dessert Course*

To prepare the table for dessert, the butler clears items that do not relate to the dessert course, and the table is crumbed.

The butler then slides a dessert plate before the guest. A finger bowl is presented on the dessert plate or on a fruit plate. (The use of a finger bowl is discussed in Chapter 7, "Bowls: Large to Small.")

Firm dessert, such as torte, is presliced and served on a platter. Soft dessert, like parfait, is preserved in tall, narrow glasses, brought to the table on a tray, and placed before the guest. The dessert utensils are laid on the dessert plate. (The use of the dessert knife, dessert spoon, and dessert fork are discussed in Chapters 17, 18, and 19.)

Dessert wine is poured. Water is replenished.

### *Fruit Course*

At a long rectangular table, two to four bowls of fresh fruit flank the centerpiece in positions that alternate with the compotes of glacéed fruit, chocolates, and nuts and smaller floral arrangements.

The fruit plate is laid before the guest, along with a fruit fork and a fruit knife. (The use of these utensils is discussed in Chapters 19 and 17, respectively.) Guests help themselves to fruit from the fruit bowl. But if the fruit bowl is inaccessible, the butler presents it to the guest. The hostess may also request sliced seasonal fruit passed on a platter. After the fruit course, compotes of candy and nuts are passed.

CHAPTER THIRTY-SEVEN

# INFORMAL DINNER SERVICE

*A smiling face is half the meal.*

LATVIAN PROVERB

MODERN TECHNOLOGY EASES our lives with electronic conveniences that make entertaining relatively tension-free and relaxed. Today, meals are usually cooked by the hosts and served unassisted. The exception is a dinner for a large group: to expedite service the hosts may engage professional help.

An informal menu is planned to save the hostess steps; the meal has two to four courses, not more. To create a relaxed ambience, the hostess is up from the table no more than two to three times (a real challenge). To achieve a nondisruptive atmosphere when a three-course menu is served, the first course, such as soup or salad, is placed on the table before the guests are seated. The hostess rises once to clear the first course and serve the main course; a second time to offer extra helpings; and a third time to clear the plates and serve dessert. For a four-course menu, steps are saved when a first course is served away from the table, for example, cocktails with substantial hors d'oeuvres, such as caviar with toast rounds and garniture or jumbo shrimp with sauce. Dessert and coffee may be taken in another room (hopefully one that is free of preprandial paraphernalia).

To make the occasion *appear* effortless, the hosts should discuss each one's responsibilities in advance of the occasion. Ideally, one or the other is with the guests at all times (this is not always possible, but make it a goal). Generally, the host pours cocktails, passes hors d'oeuvres once, pours the dinner wine, carves the meat, assists the hostess at the buffet, offers after-dinner libations, and helps guests with their wraps. The hostess cooks, sets the table, serves the meal, clears the table, and pours after-dinner coffee. If assistance is needed during the meal, in advance of the meal the hostess may ask a friend or a relative to help. This will help to prevent all the guests from rising at one time.

The following techniques are presented only as guidelines and are open to individual interpretation.

- *The salad or first course is pre-served and on the table before the meal begins.* To save steps in clearance of the first course, salad is served as a side dish with the main course.
- *A plate is filled and then served to a guest.* To avoid a table cluttered with serving dishes, the hostess fills each dinner plate in the kitchen and serves it to the guest. Or the host and hostess prepare the dinner plates from a buffet.
- *Two dinner plates are served at one time.*
- *The host pours the wine.* The host walks around the table and fills the glasses. He places a second bottle near a gentleman seated at the opposite end of the table and asks him to refill glasses for those seated nearby. Alternatively, after the first glass is poured, the host tells the guests to help themselves to wine bottles strategically placed. Or the host fills the glasses closest to him and passes them down the table, exchanging them for unfilled glasses (not recommended for a long table), a method that also makes refills awkward.
- *Unless the menu is quite salty or spicy, at an informal meal water is not served.* But a glass of water is provided for guests who do not drink wine. To make sure everyone who wants water has a glass, a pitcher of water and a few goblets are placed on a nearby table.
- *The guests pass rolls, sauce, and condiments at the table.*
- *Second helpings are offered and encouraged.*
- *Plates are served on the left side and cleared on the right side.* Because fewer courses are served at an informal meal than at a formal affair, the left in, right out technique does not give the guests the feeling of being enclosed by a hostess whose arms are suddenly appearing right and left. However, to

avoid reaching across a guest, plates on the left side of the cover are cleared from the left side.

- *The time to clear the table depends on the number of guests.* At a small dinner, plates are cleared when the last guest is finished. At a large dinner, plates are cleared when the majority of people are finished. However, when guests are seated at several tables, the hostess clears her table and the host's table first (as these tables are where the honored guests are seated).
- *The table is cleared in an orderly fashion.* Before dessert is served, the table is cleared of items not needed for the dessert course, an order that starts with the largest pieces and works to the smallest. Serving dishes and platters are cleared first. Plates are removed second, two at a time, but to keep the noise level low in the room and to reduce the risk that a utensil may drop to the floor, plates are not stacked. Flatware and unused stemware are cleared third. Small items, such as salt and pepper sets, are cleared last, and to expedite clearance, they are placed on a small tray for easy removal.
- *The table is not crumbed before dessert.* Unless the table is quite messy, it is not crumbed when only a few courses are served. Moreover, bread-and-butter plates help to keep the table crumb-free.
- *After-dinner coffee is served in another room or at the table.* To allow the guests the opportunity to regroup, the hostess serves coffee in another room, and sets out a tray of coffee on a low table or any suitable surface, such as a desk top. However, rather than interrupt good conversation, the hostess may choose to serve coffee at the dining table. She asks each guest how he or she takes coffee, pours, and mentions the guest's name as she passes the cup.
- *After-dinner drinks are not necessary after a simple meal.* Liqueurs and brandy are served as a digestive and a stimulant following a lengthy multicourse meal. But at a simple meal digestives and stimulants are not necessary, and liqueurs and brandy are offered only as a gesture of hospitality.

Certain procedures can expedite service before the guests come to the table. For example:

- Water goblets are filled (if water is provided). To temper the glass and reduce the possibility of cracks, a few ounces of water are poured into the glass before ice cubes are added.

- The first course is placed at each place setting or served in the living room.
- Rolls are prebuttered and placed in a low container on the table. However, when dinner rolls are presented unbuttered, a butter pat is placed on each bread-and-butter plate or a butter dish is placed on the table.
- Sauce and condiments are presented in duplicate for eight or more guests, one set for each end of the table.
- Candles are lighted.
- Dinner plates are warmed.
- A coffee tray is set up ready for after-dinner service, complete with cups, saucers, spoons, creamer, sugar bowl, and sugar spoon or tong.
- When after-dinner drinks are served, liqueur and brandy are placed on a tray in advance of the meal, along with the attendant stemware.

## Service of Informal Dinners

To provide a general guideline for the service of an informal dinner, four methods are presented: host style, french style, english style, and professional style. Each method adapts easily to suit individual needs.

### *Host Style*

Guests chat while the hosts serve the meal, a method that creates a relaxed, convivial atmosphere. Although the guests are left alone temporarily at the table with an empty space in front of them, by the time the meal is served they are engaged in conversation and the absence of the hosts is unnoticed.

The host and hostess serve the meal from a buffet or the kitchen. The host carves the meat or serves the casserole. The hostess dishes up the vegetables, serves the plates, and clears the table.

### *French Style*

The meal is placed on the table all at one time and the guests pass the serving dishes. Although French service saves steps for the hostess, unless covered serveware is used, the food cools faster this way than in other service methods. Moreover, the excessive handling of serveware by the guests disrupts the conversation.

A meat platter or casserole is placed in front of the host. The plates are stacked above the meat platter, slightly to the right for easy handling. The host asks guests for the cut of meat they prefer and repeats the name of each guest as he passes the plate. Those who prefer an outside piece or a well-done cut are served before those who prefer a rare cut.

### *English Style*

A small table adjoins the dining table, and the hostess remains seated throughout the meal. Although this method enables the hostess to remain seated throughout the meal, it entails excessive handling of the plates, disrupts conversation, and is seldom used today.

A small table, such as a card table or a tea cart, is placed next to the dining table to hold a salad bowl, salad plates, dessert, and dessert plates. The meat platter or casserole is placed before the hostess, and the dinner plates and serving utensils are laid above the platter. The hostess serves the plates. The first plate is passed to the lady of honor seated to the right of the host. To reduce the number of times the guests handle the plates, the second plate is passed to the host. Service proceeds up one side of the table and down the next. The hostess is served last. At the end of each course, the guests pass their plates to the hostess, who stacks them on the adjacent table. To reduce the noise level in the room, the plates are not scraped.

### *Professional Style*

Host and hostess remain seated throughout the meal. Professional service is reserved for posh affairs cooked entirely, or partially, by the hosts. Professional help is engaged to serve and clean up. One maid serves six to eight guests. When more than eight guests are seated, the hosts and professional work together as a team to expedite service. The following variations may be adjusted as needed.

> Russian style: the most formal way to entertain informally. A maid presents each course to the guest from the left side, and returns the serveware to the kitchen.
>
> Water and wine are served in the same manner as a formal dinner.

Rolls are served by the maid and placed on a bread-and-butter plate or the rim of the plate. Butter dishes are placed at each end of the table for the guests to pass. Or a container of rolls is placed at each end of the table for the guests to pass. Or prebuttered rolls are passed.

At a table of eight people or more, the maid fills the salad plates in the kitchen before she serves them. At a small dinner of six or fewer, the maid places an empty salad plate before the guest and presents the salad bowl. Or she presents a platter filled with prearranged salads to each guest.

The roast is carved in the kitchen by the maid and presented on a platter to the guests. The platter is returned to the kitchen to keep warm. The maid carries two vegetable bowls at one time or holds a divided bowl and offers it to the guests. The main course is passed twice.

The maid serves and clears plates two at a time. The smaller plate is removed first with the right hand. The larger plate is carried with the left hand.

The table is not crumbed unless unusually messy. Dessert is presented on a platter or pre-served on individual plates. The maid serves coffee, clears the table, and cleans up.

**Host carves roast; maid exchanges the service and appetizer plates for a dinner plate; maid serves the vegetables.** This method of service is appropriate for an elegant dinner where service plates are used, a technique that does not leave an empty space before the guest, except before dessert is served.

The meat platter and dinner plates are placed before the host. The maid stands to the host's left. As the host fills a dinner plate, he hands it to the maid, who takes it to the guest and exchanges it for the service plate and appetizer plate on the cover. She takes the plates to the sideboard or the pantry, then returns to the host to receive the next dinner plate, takes it to the next guest, and continues until all the guests are served. The maid presents the vegetables. The meat platter remains on the table, and the maid offers second helpings. The maid clears the table, serves dessert, and pours coffee.

**Host carves the roast; dinner plates are used as service plates.** To fill the empty space at each cover and to expedite service, a dinner plate is laid at each setting before the guests come to the table.

The maid places the meat platter before the host and lays two dinner plates above it. She stands to the left of the host. The host fills the top plate. The maid takes the filled plate to the guest of honor, exchanges it for her dinner plate, and takes the empty plate to the host. The process of filling and exchanging plates continues counterclockwise around the table. To expedite service, the hostess is served in the order of progression. After everyone is served, one dinner plate remains before the host which is used to serve himself. The maid offers second helpings, clears the table, serves dessert, and pours coffee.

**Host carves roast; guests pass dinner plates; maid serves vegetables.** This is an expeditious technique appropriate for a small group of approximately six guests. The host carves the roast and the guests pass the plates down the table. The maid presents the vegetable bowls to them, offers second helpings, clears the table, serves dessert, and pours coffee.

**Host carves roast; hostess serves plates; maid serves vegetables.** This is a courteous method of service because the guests handle fewer plates. When meat is cooked to the same degree of doneness all the way through, such as a ham or a turkey, after the host has carved the meat the hostess serves the plates, starting with the lady of honor on the host's right. The honored male guest seated to the hostess's left is served next, followed by the remaining guests on the left side of the table. The hostess then serves the honored male guest seated to her right and proceeds with service up the right side of the table, ending with the woman on the host's left. The hostess serves herself second to last, and the host fills his plate last. The maid serves vegetables, offers second helpings, clears the table, presents dessert, and pours coffee.

**Host carves roast; the ladies are served before the gentlemen; the maid passes the vegetables.** This method of service is courteous to the ladies, but entails excessive handling of plates. The host carves the roast, and the first dinner plate is handed to the lady of honor seated on his right. The second dinner plate is handed to the lady seated on his left. The honored ladies pass the plates to the remaining ladies, a progression that ends with the hostess. After the ladies are served, a dinner plate is passed to the man of honor seated to the right of the hostess, followed by the gentleman seated to her left, and so on, ending with the host. The maid serves the vegetables in the same order as the meat, offers second helpings, clears the table, presents dessert, and pours coffee.

**Host carves roast; hostess serves vegetables; maid serves plates.** This method adds a personal touch to the meal because the host and hostess are involved in the service. However, the technique creates additional traffic in the room, and the vegetable bowls left on the table take up space.

The meat platter and plates are placed before the host, and the vegetable bowls are placed before the hostess. The maid stands to the left of the host. As the host fills a dinner plate, the maid takes it to the hostess who dishes up the vegetables. The maid serves the lady of honor. Service proceeds counterclockwise. The hostess is served second to last and the host last. The vegetable bowls remain on the table, the maid presents the course for second helpings, clears the table, serves dessert, and pours coffee.

**Hostess dresses salad at the table; maid serves the plates.** To ensure absolute freshness for the salad, the hostess dresses the greens at the table. The maid places a salad bowl, cruets, and salad plates before the hostess, who tosses the salad. The maid serves the plates.

**Hostess serves dessert at the table; maid serves the plates.** To add a personal note to a meal, the maid places serving utensils and dessert plates before the hostess who fills the plates. The maid serves the plates.

**Hostess pours coffee at the table; maid serves the cups.** At a small dinner of eight or fewer guests, rather than interrupt good conversation, the hostess may choose to pour after-dinner coffee at the table. The maid places a coffee tray in front of the hostess. The hostess asks each guest how he or she takes coffee, pours, and hands the cup to the maid, who serves the guest.

CHAPTER THIRTY-EIGHT

# DINNER SERVICE FROM A BUFFET

The first depiction of buffet-style service is from wall paintings found in ancient Egypt, artistry that reveals food was served by slaves from a central table to guests seated along the side of the room. Buffet service was introduced to Europe in the eighteenth century by Benjamin Franklin, who in his role as ambassador to France was called upon to entertain members of the French court. For lack of the right furniture to host a large group, Franklin laid a board on a trestle, placed it against the wall, covered it with cloth, and set a self-service table. The word for sideboard in French is *buffet,* hence the origin of our English meaning of the word.

Buffet entertaining, regardless of how elegant, is an informal meal. Food is prepared in advance. Help is not required, except to assist a large group. Guests serve themselves and return for second helpings.

Any flat surface is appropriate for a buffet meal: a desk, a coffee table, a piano top, a card table, a kitchen counter, or a patio table, to name a few. However, to accommodate the tableware and serveware, a minimum of 5 feet is needed. When the requisite space is unavailable, three or four smaller tables are used: one for tableware, another to hold the main course, a third to present the dessert and dessert plates, and a fourth for beverages, such as water, wine, coffee, or tea.

The placement of the buffet table is determined by the dimensions of the room. In a spacious room, the buffet table is positioned in the center. This placement accommodates service from both sides or both ends of the table, accelerates service, and reduces congestion in the room. In a small room, to allow space for the flow of traffic, a buffet table is placed against the wall.

To expedite traffic around the serving area, dining chairs are positioned against the wall. Dinner plates and the main dish are placed nearest the entrance to the dining area, a location that allows the guests to circle around the table and exit the serving area without doubling back.

The key to successful buffet entertaining is to serve a one-dish meal that requires one utensil to eat, namely a fork. However, for a large group, as a gesture of hospitality two main courses are served, such as turkey and ham.

Here are some tips for successful buffet service.

- Allow enough room beside each dish for guests to rest their dinner plate while they help themselves to food that requires two utensils to serve, for example, a tossed salad.
- Provide space to lay the serving utensils by the serveware they are meant to accompany, along with the lids of covered serving bowls.
- Arrange the flow of the tableware and the serving dishes in logical order, a sequence that proceeds from left to right.
- Stack dinner plates in groups of eight. A stack of plates higher than eight resembles a cafeteria or the service station in a restaurant.
- Arrange food in groups of related temperatures, such as hot foods together.
- Place salads near a cheese board (if one is provided).
- Set sauces and condiments next to the dishes they accompany.
- Place a basket of prebuttered rolls or sliced bread near the salt and pepper shakers.
- Because a pepper mill requires both hands to manipulate, it is not placed on a buffet table.
- At the exit end of the table, lay the flatware in a row on the table, if space permits. When flatware is placed in a stacked position, the top utensil is difficult to remove.
- Place napkins last. To conserve space, present napkins overlapped, beneath each plate, wrapped around the flatware, or on each tray.
- Station a side table to hold beverages and glassware. To avoid trying to balance a plate while lifting a heavy water pitcher, lighten the load and partially fill several pitchers or carafes with water.
- Place coffee and dessert on a side table, along with the cups, saucers, dessert plates, and flatware.

Guests serve themselves in the order in which they arrive at the buffet, and eat seated wherever they are comfortable: on chairs, floor, or stairs. When possible, supply a small folding table for each chair, and provide lap trays for guests who sit on stairs. To make room for used dinner plates, clear end tables of unneeded accessories. Protect the furniture and flooring with strategically placed coasters and ashtrays.

## Service of a Buffet Supper

Buffet service is provided unassisted or with the aid of professional help, a friend, or a relative.

### *Unassisted Buffet Service*

Guests serve themselves entirely and sit or stand to eat, a method that accommodates a large group of people with ease. The guests help themselves at the buffet. Glasses for water and wine are placed on a sideboard or a side table near the buffet. Dessert and coffee are served from the buffet table or from a separate side table. At a small party, soiled plates are placed on a side table provided for this purpose. But when space is at a premium, such as a one-room apartment, to relieve the space for enjoyment of the gathering, soiled plates are taken to the kitchen counter. At a large gathering when there is no side table for soiled plates, they are placed wherever space is found, such as on an end table.

### *Professional Assistance with Guests Seated at Preset Tables*

This method reduces the risk of spilled food and drink. When a buffet menu consists of two courses—namely, main course and dessert—the salad is considered part of the main course and the guests help themselves at the buffet. Dessert and coffee are served at the tables by a helper. If a buffet menu has three courses—namely, appetizer, main course, and dessert—the first and third courses are served at the tables by a helper. The appetizer is placed on the tables before the guests are seated. The guests help themselves to the main course at the buffet and return for second portions as they wish. Dessert and coffee are served to them.

A typical preset table includes a small centerpiece, tableware, sets of salt and pepper, place cards, and a basket of prebuttered rolls (optional). Space limitations prohibit the use of bread-and-butter plates. Ashtrays are also optional.

At a small seated affair, the host pours the wine. But at a large party, to expedite service a wine bottle is placed on each table and the guests pour for themselves.

Plates are cleared two at a time. The tables are not crumbed unless unusually messy. Dessert is pre-served on dessert plates in the kitchen and carried to the tables two at a time. Or a preapportioned dessert is served from a tray.

After-dinner coffee is served at the table, poured and passed from a tray. Cream and sugar are placed on the tables or are served from a tray. As an alternative, the guests help themselves to coffee served at a side table. At a small party the hostess may pour coffee in the living room.

### *Professional Assistance with Guests Sitting Randomly Throughout the House*

This method is more relaxed than service at preset tables. Although professional assistance is given at the buffet table, the guests sit on chairs, the floor, and stairs.

When two people are engaged to assist, one serves the main course and the second serves the salad. The guests help themselves to rolls and condiments. If the buffet is presented in duplicate on both sides of the table, each helper serves a main course, and the guests help themselves to the rest of the meal. The maids set up folding trays, replenish platters, clear plates, and serve dessert and coffee.

CHAPTER THIRTY-NINE

# SERVICE OF FORMAL AND INFORMAL LUNCHEON

THE DIFFERENCE BETWEEN luncheon and dinner is the time of day each is served and the number of courses presented. The traditional hour to serve lunch is 12:30 or 1:00 in the afternoon. Guests arrive a half hour before lunch and remain for 30 minutes to 1 hour afterward, depending on the guests' schedules and amount of leisure time.

Generally, four courses are presented at a formal luncheon, and one, two, or three courses are served at an informal luncheon. If gentlemen are present, the menu is more substantial because they generally have a greater appetite. Because a heavy meal at noon tends to make people sleepy, luncheon is lighter than dinner. Moreover, most people have less time midday to devote to lunch, and the period allotted luncheon is shorter than dinner.

In keeping with the menu, preprandial beverages are generally light, for example, white wine, champagne, bloody Marys, and nonalcoholic drinks such as cranberry juice, grapefruit juice, and mineral water. Hors d'oeuvres and canapes are not served, although optionally a few nibbles, such as mixed nuts or small assorted crackers, are placed about.

Candles are not needed for visibility in daylight hours and are not lighted at luncheon. The exception is an overcast day when a gray sky throws a dark glow indoors and lamps are turned on. To fill the void left by the absence of candles, flank the centerpiece with figurines, fruit, or small bouquets.

For a *formal luncheon,* the table is laid exactly as for a formal dinner, only less tableware is needed. Although a tablecloth is appropriate at luncheon and unifies the accoutrements of a multicourse meal, at a formal luncheon placemats in shades of white or pastel are also appropriate. A service plate is laid at each cover. Luncheon-size flatware and plates are used by those who own them, but they are not essential. Generally, the table is laid with place-size flatware and regular dinner plates. Bread is served, and bread-and-butter plates are provided. Multiple centerpieces grace the table, as do compotes of candy. Place cards are inscribed with guests' formal names. Finger bowls and menu cards are optional. Second portions are not offered because the multicourse menu precludes the need. Although one wine is sufficient, at the hostess's option two wines are poured. The table is crumbed prior to dessert. Following the meal, demitasse and liqueurs are offered in the drawing room.

An *informal luncheon* is served by the hostess. The linens range from a white tablecloth to colorful placemats. The table may also be left bare, and as ornamentation and to provide interest the napkins are folded decoratively. Service plates are not used, except as decoration or as placemats. For eight guests or more, place cards identify seating arrangements, inscribed with the guests' first names or nicknames. Bread-and-butter plates are provided. The exception is when prebuttered rolls are passed and placed on the rim of the luncheon plate. Because the menu is simple, second portions are offered. The table is not crumbed. Following dessert, hot tea or coffee are served at the table in regular-size cups.

CHAPTER FORTY

# SERVICE OF AFTERNOON TEA AND HIGH TEA

*There are few hours in life more agreeable than the hour dedicated to the ceremony known as afternoon tea.*

*Henry James*, The Portrait of a Lady, *1881*

IN THE NINETEENTH century, two meals a day were served, breakfast and dinner, the latter between 7 and 8 P.M., when workers came home. To stave off a sinking feeling that we know today as low blood sugar, in 1840, the duchess of Bedford began to take tea around four in the afternoon in her bedroom suite at Belvoir Castle. Eventually the duchess invited friends to join her, and the custom evolved into a tradition surrounded by elaborate ritual, involving the service of "empire" tea, grown in India or Ceylon, to guests attired in "tea gowns," diaphanous dresses that flowed to the ankle, a length known today as *tea length*.

A light snack was served with tea, initially toast and sweet butter often sprinkled with cinnamon. But as afternoon tea gained in popularity, the menu became more extensive and sophisticated. Soon hot buttered scones, jams, crumpets, delicate sandwiches, and elegant pastries were added to the menu. Today, the gracious custom of afternoon tea has waned in popularity and been replaced by the morning coffee break and the evening cocktail hour. But the custom gently lifts a weary psyche, and new devotees are finding afternoon tea a way to relax. Because afternoon tea is served several hours after luncheon, normally between three and four o'clock, a light repast is customary. Guests may stay for about an hour, although the invitation is generally for two hours.

## Afternoon Tea

To facilitate the flow of traffic, tea is served from a dining table. However, when one's table is too small for the tableware and serveware, tea is served from several tables: one to hold tea equipage, a second for a coffee service, and a third for sandwiches and pastries.

The differences between a formal tea and an informal tea are the number of guests invited, the seating arrangements, and the menu. A formal tea, like a formal dinner or formal luncheon, is an elegant affair that involves considerable preparation, and as such is generally given for a large group who expect to stand. Extra chairs and tables are not required. The guests help themselves to a repast of delicate finger sandwiches, pastries, assorted nuts, mints, and chocolates. The table is laid with the finest porcelain and silver. Because formal affairs are held later in the day than informal events, a formal tea is held around four o'clock, and to make the late-afternoon atmosphere cozy and intimate, the draperies are pulled and candles are lighted (as opposed to luncheon, when midday visibility precludes the need to light candles).

Afternoon tea incorporates two traditions. The most important is that the hostess pours tea for her guests. The second is that the tea table is always laid with a tablecloth. However, when a large tea is held, the number of guests to greet precludes the courtesy, and in advance the hostess asks a few friends to pour for her, stating the hour and the length of the service, generally 30 minutes. Moreover, a busy hostess may ask several friends to answer the door for a given period of time (although she remains near the door to welcome her guests, make introductions, and oversee the affair). For ease of introductions, at an extremely large affair a receiving line is formed near the door to introduce the guests to the guest of honor (if there is one). Each guest chats briefly with the honoree. On departure, cups, saucers, plates, and napkins are laid on nearby tables. If the honored guest is busy when a guest departs, good-byes are said only to the hostess.

At a formal tea, tea plates are not provided because the light repast of finger foods balances easily on a saucer. But when an extensive menu is offered, tea plates and forks are provided. To hold the teacup secure, English tea plates are made with a well that eliminates the need for a saucer and provides space for sandwiches and pastries.

The formal tea table is laid with two silver services, one for tea and the other for coffee, placed at opposite ends of the table. Because Americans drink more coffee than tea, in the United States a coffee service is placed at the entrance of the room nearest to the tea table.

The accoutrements of the formal tea service include a teapot, hot-water kettle with an alcohol burner (to keep water hot), a sugar bowl with sugar cubes, sugar tongs, a creamer with whole milk, a tea caddy with loose-leaf tea, a caddy spoon to measure tea, a tea strainer to strain tea, a waste bowl to hold the dregs of tea, and a lemon plate with sliced lemon, a lemon fork, or a lemon pick.

For easy access, the spouts of the hot-water kettle and the teapot face the pourer. The pourer uses the caddy spoon to lift tea leaves from the tea caddy and place them in the teapot. Freshly boiled water is taken from the hot-water kettle and is poured into the teapot, a brew that steeps for 3 to 5 minutes or until the infusion is quite strong. To make tea weak, a small amount of strong tea is poured into the cup and diluted with water from the hot-water kettle. On request, sugar, milk, or lemon are added.

Because the majority of people are right-handed, the teaspoons, sugar bowl, sugar tongs, creamer, and lemon plate are placed on the right side of the tea tray. Before tea is poured, the pourer places a teaspoon on the saucer, behind the cup handle in a parallel position, a placement that keeps the spoon from falling when the cup is lifted. To accommodate right-handedness and avoid the possibility of spilled milk, the creamer is placed to the right of the sugar bowl with the handle pointed toward the pourer. The left side of the tea tray holds the tea caddy, slop bowl, tea strainer (laid on a stand or over a slop bowl), plus teacups and saucers stacked in groups of two. Additional teacups are placed on the table to the left of the tray. With the left hand, the pourer lifts the teacup and uses the right hand to pour tea.

The formal coffee service features a tray, a coffeepot with an alcohol burner to keep the beverage hot, a sugar bowl with sugar cubes, sugar tongs, and a creamer filled with cream.

An informal tea is held earlier than a formal tea, usually at two or three o'clock in the afternoon, and the menu, following so soon after luncheon, is quite light, including finger sandwiches, pastries, assorted nuts, and candy. The hostess prepares and serves tea in any setting that is comfortable, such as the garden, patio, family room, living room, or dining room, and from any flat surface convenient for the occasion, such as a low table, side table, or desk, a space laid with a tablecloth and graced with a floral arrangement. Although a white tablecloth is always appropriate and is used traditionally at a formal tea, at an informal tea a colored tablecloth is festive, as are colored napkins in matching or contrasting colors. And to avoid the formal overtones of candelabra or candlesticks, at informal teas votive candles are often lighted. When the group is small, a chair is provided for each guest.

At an informal tea, a single beverage service is all that is necessary, one in keeping with the mood of the occasion, such as pottery, porcelain, silver, or stainless steel. Continuity of design is unimportant and unmatched equipage is used, an assemblage of teapot, coffeepot, hot-water pot (optional), sugar bowl, sugar cubes, sugar tongs, a small pitcher with whole milk for tea, a creamer with cream for coffee, and a tray of sliced lemon with a lemon fork or lemon pick.

## High Tea

In the early eighteenth century, copious cups of tea were considered a depressant, and to lift the spirits a splash of brandy was added to a teacup. Bottles of rum, whiskey, or liqueur were very much part of the Georgian tea table, along with small cordial glasses, a custom replaced today at high tea with a decanter of spirits.

The expression "high tea" is attributed to the nineteenth-century English Midlands, an industrial area. With the advent of the Industrial Revolution a century earlier, shopkeepers began staying open until eight or nine o'clock at night to accommodate the needs of late-shopping workers. Dinner was served after the shops closed. To stave off hunger, workers took tea at around six o'clock in the evening, a time numerically "high" in the day. The menu was usually a smattering of substantial leftovers, such as cold meat and bread, and high tea was also known as *meat tea* or *ham tea*.

Today, high tea is served later in the day than afternoon tea, around five o'clock, a time when the average person is hungry. The menu is substantial, similar to the hors d'oeuvres and canapes served at cocktails. Plates and appropriate utensils are provided to hold the ample repast. All other aspects of high tea are the same as afternoon tea.

# Part VII

# *Dining Finesse*

CHAPTER FORTY-ONE

# THE PROTOCOL OF SEATING

*It isn't so much what's on the table that matters as what's on the chairs.*

W. S. GILBERT

KING ARTHUR SOLVED the protocol of seating when he devised the round table and accorded the same rank to all seats. In the Middle Ages, the lord of the manor, honored guests, family, and servants all dined together in the great hall. To define rank, the lord and most important guest sat in the finest chairs, and ordinary chairs were reserved for the chatelaine and guests of lesser importance. Those of minor importance sat on long benches in the order of rank.

Today courtesy at a meal begins with the assignment of seats. Good conversation is the main ingredient of a successful party, and a well-planned seating arrangement encourages sparkling wit and promotes interesting conversation. The seats of honor are accorded those to the right of the host and hostess, and the second most important seats are to their left. To eliminate confusion about who sits where, use place cards when more than six guests are seated.

# Honored Guests

A seating plan begins with the honored guests, but oftentimes deciding who to honor is a dilemma. At a family gathering, but only at a family gathering, the oldest person is accorded the seat of honor. When both parents and in-laws are seated at the same table, the hostess's mother sits to the right of the host, and his mother sits to his left. The host's father sits to the right of the hostess and her father sits to her left.

A guest entertained in one's home for the first time, or a houseguest, is accorded a seat of honor, as are guests from a foreign country.

Married couples rank higher than unmarried guests. At a party of old friends, the husband of one couple is seated to the hostess's right, and the wife of another couple to the right of the host. The respective spouses sit in the middle of the table on opposite sides of the honorees. Because married couples so often tell the same stories (but relate them differently, leading to corrections and embellishments that impede conversation), they are not seated next to each other. The exception is newlyweds, defined as a couple married for less than a year, who sit next to each other. But engaged couples are seated in whatever way makes for better conversation.

A person of extreme rank, such as the president of a country or a royal personage, is seated at the head of the table and the hostess is seated to his left, an arrangement that honors the dignitary and acknowledges his prestige by seating him to the right of the hostess. The next highest ranking male and female are seated to the right of the dignitary, and so on around the table.

Both present and former government officials and their spouses are accorded the seats of honor. Both husbands and wives are granted the status of their higher-ranking spouses. Thus, if a woman is prime minister of a country, her husband is seated according to his wife's rank. The same protocol applies to local dignitaries and clergy.

## Seating the Left-handed Guest

The main concern of the left-handed guest is to avoid bumping elbows with his or her right-handed dinner partner. To allow freedom of elbow movement, when possible, seat a left-handed guest at the end of the table.

## Guidelines for Alternate Male-Female Seating

The custom of alternate male-female seating dates to the age of chivalry in the eleventh century, when couples shared a plate and a bowl. Hence the expression "to eat from the same plate." But in eighteenth-century England, ladies sat at one end of the table and gentlemen sat at the other.

> When dinner is announced, the mistress of the house requests the lady first in rank, in company, to show the way to the rest, and walk first into the room where the table is served; she then asks the second in precedence to follow . . . bringing up the rear herself. . . . The master of the house does the same with the gentlemen. . . . When they enter the dining room, each takes his place in the same order; the mistress of the table sits at the upper end, those of superior rank next to her, right and left; those next in rank following, then the gentlemen and the master at the lower end; and nothing is considered as a greater mark of ill-breeding than for a person to interrupt this order, or seat himself higher than he ought.
>
> John Trusler, *Honours of the Table,* 1788

Today, a seating plan is designed not only to honor a particular guest but to spark good conversation, and it enables the host to determine alternate male-female seating. The exception is members of the opposite sex who are not compatible with one another, and in the interests of congeniality one or the other is placed next to a person of the same gender.

As Jane Austen observed in *Mansfield Park,* "Five is the very awkwardest of all possible numbers to sit down to table." In the nineteenth century, when an even-numbered table setting was thrown off by a guest who for an unforeseen reason had to decline the invitation at the last minute, a professional guest was brought in to round out the table to an even number, a replacement known as a *quatorzième,* changing the number at table from unlucky thirteen to fourteen. Being a *quatorzième* was a highly remunerative profession.

When a guest list is divisable by 2, such as 6, 10, 14, or 18 diners (including the host and hostess), alternate male-female seating is possible. If the guest list is a multiple of 4, such as 8, 12, 16, or 20, alternate seating is impossible; to balance the arrangement, the hostess moves one seat to the left while the host remains at the head of the table; the man of honor is still on the hostess's right. Alternatively, the host and hostess sit on opposite sides of the table, with the lady of honor to the right of her host and the man of honor to the right of the hostess.

## Seating Arrangements for More Than One Table

When a meal is served at several tables, the host and hostess sit at separate tables. If the guests of honor are a married couple, the female honoree sits at the host's table, and the male honoree is seated at the hostess's table. All other husbands and wives sit at separate tables.

## Seating for Best Flow of Conversation

In the sixteenth century, a new type of gentleman evolved, one who like the medieval knight of yore was expected to right the wrongs of others, protect the honor of his lord and lady, and engage in wise and sparkling conversation at the table. In 1528, Baldassare Castiglione set forth the requirements of the courtier's conversation in his *Book of the Courtier:*

> The courtier should be one who is never at a loss for things to say that are good and well suited to those with whom he is speaking. . . . He should know how to sweeten and refresh the minds of his hearers, and move them discreetly to gaiety and laughter with amusing witticisms and pleasantries, so that, without ever producing tedium or satiety, he may continually give pleasure.

Social historians suggest the art of small talk, a contemporary expression that developed in the nineteenth century, evolved when public education was available to the masses, and light conversation about pleasant subjects prevented disruption of meals with zealous opinions. Soon the accepted mode of dinner conversation was discourse that avoided negative reference to the sense of sight, sound, touch, smell, and taste. Only agreeable topics were addressed and controversial subjects were avoided, such as illness, death, personal finances, family crisis, politics, or religion. Somerset Maugham stated it succinctly in *A Writer's Notebook:* "At a dinner party one should eat wisely but not too well, and talk well but not too wisely."

Today, good conversation avoids a sharp exchange of opposing views. To avoid bitter disagreements at a small party, do not seat together two people of the same profession, such as two doctors or two lawyers. Although they may have topics in common, it's better not to seat two employees of the same company together as they may tend to monopolize the conversation.

CHAPTER FORTY-TWO

# GIVING THANKS AND MAKING TOASTS

*When thou sit down to meat*
*Give thanks before thou eat*
*Unto him that doth give*
*The mercies thou receive*
*That such favours may be*
*Repeated unto thee.*

THE WORD *GRACE* is from the Latin *gratia,* meaning "that which is pleasing or agreeable" or simply "thanks," a prayer that began not only as a statement of gratitude but also as a way of warding off detrimental effects the food might possess. We know that Israelites offered prayers of appreciation for the day's bounty, and undoubtedly other cultures did as well. The ancient Egyptians offered food to the gods before they began eating. In the time of the English Stuarts (1602–1714), gentlemen removed their hats to say grace but replaced them to eat the meal; the king was the only man who ate bare-headed. Today, grace is a short prayer of thanks given before a meal, generally after the guests are seated and before anything on the table is touched, including the napkin. However, in some faiths a blessing is given while the guests stand behind the chairs.

Although expressing appreciation for a meal does not mean affiliation with a particular faith, to show respect for the host and the occasion, when grace is said the head is bowed, regardless of one's beliefs. The custom of bowing the head in reverence began as a way to show obedience and willingness to serve, and a person of lower rank lowered his head before a person of exalted rank. However, it is not necessary to conclude grace with a religious gesture not in keeping with one's faith, such as crossing one's self.

Grace is said by one person at the table, such as the host, hostess, a family member, a relative, or a guest. Be sure that the guest will not be embarrassed giving such a prayer. Everyone at the table joins in saying amen.

Usually grace consists of a few simple words of appreciation or a short prayer. The best-known nonsectarian blessing among English-speaking Christians is very simple:

*For what we are about to receive,*
*may the Lord make us truly thankful. Amen.*

## The Way to Give a Toast

*A toast is the only thing that can be eaten or drunk.*

The custom of raising the first glass of wine to one's health is attributed to ancient Greece, when a sip was taken to demonstrate that the drink was not poisoned. In Homer's *Iliad,* Ulysses drank to the health of Achilles. In the early Christian era, people believed that the devil entered the body through alcoholic drinks and was deterred by the sound of bells. To ward off the evil spirit, guests clinked their glasses together, making a bell-like tone that today traditionally follows a toast.

Before the Norsemen of Scandinavia took the first sip of wine, they uttered *skoal,* a word associated with success in battle when wine was drunk from the *skalle,* or skull, of a fallen enemy. The word evolved as *skaal* in Denmark and Norway and refers to a bowl-shaped cup used to make toasts. In Scotland, honored guests are toasted from a tub-shaped vessel called a *skiel.*

In the fifth century, Rowena, the beautiful daughter of Hengist, a Saxon leader in northern Germany, drank to Vortigern, a British king saying: "Louerd

King, *waes hael,*" meaning "Lord King, be of health" and through the sixteenth century in England taking a sip of wine in honor of a person was known as *drinking a health.* In time *waes hael* evolved as the Anglo-Saxon term *wassail* a word for "be well," used primarily at Christmas and New Year to toast one's health. On the twelve days of Christmas, the poor who sang Christmas carols door-to-door carried a large wooden bowl to exchange carols for wassail.

The modern word *toast* is from the Latin term *tostus* meaning "parched." In the mid-seventeenth century the word acquired its modern-day meaning, as a sentiment given to honor someone. Isaac Bickerstaffe offered this somewhat tongue-in-cheek etymology in a 1709 *Tatler*:

> It happened that on a publick day a celebrated beauty of those times was in the Cross Bath, and one of the crowd of her admirers took a glass of the water in which the fair one stood and drank her health to the company. There was in the place a gay fellow, half fuddled, who offered to jump in, and swore though he liked not the liquor, he would have the toast. He was opposed in his resolution; yet this whim gave foundation to the present honour which is done to the lady we mention in our liquor, who has ever since been called a toast.

When the Jacobites, supporters of James II after his abdication, drank a toast to Bonnie Prince Charlie—James's grandson Charles Edward Stuart, also known as the Young Pretender—they drank to "the king across the water." And when they had to drink a toast to King George II in public, they privately passed the glass over water, thus maintaining their secret pledge to Charles. An alphabet toast enunciated by Lord Duff in 1745 expressed the Jacobites' sentiments.

*A B C: A Blessed Change.*
*D E F: Damn Every Foreigner.*
*G H J: God Help James.*
*K L M: Keep Loyal Ministers.*
*N O P: No Oppressive Parliaments.*
*Q R S: Quickly Return Stuart.*
*T U V W: Truss Up Vile Whigs.*
*X Y Z: 'Xert Your Zeal.*

The custom of drinking from the slipper of a lady dates to Hungary in the eighteenth century, when a groom on his wedding night publicly drank a toast from the slipper of his bride. Afterward, the shoe was thrown to the guests as a bouquet today is thrown by the bride.

Following the American Revolution, thirteen toasts were given at official dinners and Fourth of July celebrations to honor the original colonies, a custom that commenced with a series of banquets in honor of the retirement of George Washington, toasted by Benjamin Franklin with these words:

> George Washington, commander of the American armies, who, like Joshua of old, commanded the sun and the moon to stand still, and both obeyed.

Today, a toast is given for many reasons. Here are a few examples.

- *To pay respect to the guest of honor*

  The best of happiness, honor, and fortune keep with you.
  Shakespeare, *Timon of Athens*

- *To honor a particular guest*

  *Old friends are scarce,*
  *New friends are few,*
  *Here's hoping I've found*
  *One of each in you.*

- *To pay homage to the host*

  *A toast to our host*
  *And a song from the short and tall of us,*
  *May he live to be*
  *The guest of all of us!*

- *To pay homage to the hostess*

  *Here's to our hostess*
  *Considerate and sweet;*
  *Her wit is endless,*
  *But when do we eat?*

- *To celebrate Christmas*

*Christmas is here,*
*Merry old Christmas,*
*Gift-bearing, heart-touching, joy-bringing Christmas,*
*Day of grand memories, king of the year.*

WASHINGTON IRVING

- *In reverence of pending parenthood*

*Out of a love our child will grow . . .*
*Greater than light, deeper than dark,*
*All other love is but a spark.*

A toast is short and simple (so as not to delay the meal). It is given any time after the first glass of wine is poured, but generally it lasts no longer than a few minutes at most. Even a single word suffices as a toast, such as *prosit,* German for "your health" or "cheers." When a speech is appropriate, it is reserved for the end of the meal. Customarily, the host makes the first toast to the honored guest. However, any number of toasts can be expressed at a meal.

*There's many a toast I'd like to say,*
*If I could only think it;*
*So fill your glass to anything,*
*And thank the Lord, I'll drink it!*

WALLACE IRWIN

The manner in which toasts are given varies between formal and informal dining. At a formal dinner a toast is always given. To capture the guests' attention, the host gently taps his glass with a utensil, then rises to toast the honored person. When tables are set in adjoining rooms, the host stands in the doorway, so that everyone may hear his words. He states the name of the honored guest and makes a toast. Following the toast, all but the honored guest stand, raise their glasses in the direction of the honoree, repeat his name, and take a sip of wine. But when subsequent toasts are given, the guests do not stand. The honoree remains seated and refrains from sipping wine; to do otherwise is to honor himself, as Joseph Hall pointed out in his *Virgidemiarum:* "Drink to all healths, but drink not to thine own." Nonparticipation in a toast is an offense to the honoree. But those who do not drink wine, raise a hand as if holding a glass, or raise a glass of water and take a sip.

The honoree responds with a nod of his head and a simple "Thank you." When the honoree chooses to make a toast, he responds immediately or at any time during the meal. After everyone is seated, he stands, makes his toast, and takes a sip of wine.

At an informal dinner a toast is not expected, but when one is given it adds a note of festivity to the moment. At a small party, a guest need not stand to give a toast. But at a large gathering, for audibility the person who gives the toast stands. All other aspects of the informal toast are the same as for a formal toast.

# PART VIII

# *Menu Plan*

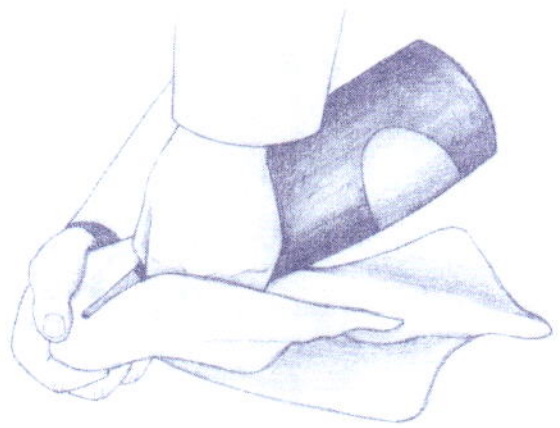

CHAPTER FORTY-THREE

# FROM FOOD TO CUISINE

*It was an odd saying of a mad Fellow, who having well dined, clapt his hand upon the board, and protested, that this eating and drinking was a very pretty invention, who ever first found it out.*

ALEXANDER POPE

TO OPEN ONE'S HOME and offer food and drink is a cornerstone of civilization, but in primitive times it was a gesture of peace. In the spirit of harmony, when a stranger was welcomed into the dwelling, food was shared. Thus, eating together evolved as a symbol of hospitality. And hospitality is associated with food.

Plutarch records that in ancient Egypt feasts often concluded with a coffin laid out with an imitation skeleton, a reminder to appreciate the bounteous gifts of life, one of them being food. Although women were not invited to social or religious banquets in Greece, both men and women gathered daily to eat food consecrated in the *prytaneum,* where a sacred fire burned. Men of Attica who sat at the sacred table were called *parasites,* from *para,* meaning "beside," and *sitos,* meaning "food."

Roman banquets often sacrificed the presentation of food to ostentation, such as a feast hosted by Emperor Heliogabalus in which peas were laced with grains of gold, lentils with precious stones, and assorted dishes with pearls and amber. In Rome, banquets were held in a special room called a *triclinium* where a three-part menu was served: appetizer, main course, and dessert, a feast laid out on a table surrounded on three sides by couches. Presentation of the food was paramount and featured dramatic surprises, such as a roasted wild boar surrounded by pastry sucklings. At the right moment the boar was stabbed in the stomach to release a bevy of thrushes captured by slaves and given to guests.

The medieval feast was a theatrical event that incorporated colorful pageantry and exotic presentation—roasted peacocks with bills and claws gilded, calves and pigs dressed with ornate garniture, swans and pheasants cooked and re-formed with hackles and tails. In the Middle Ages food was prepared as it was during the Roman occupation of western Europe; these methods were documented by Apicius, a noted epicurean, whose manuscripts were available in Latin from 1498. His recipes were studied but not adapted.

Medieval banquets were high drama, served in a lavish series of events called *courses* (from the Latin *currere,* "to run"), episodes also known as *mets* (from the French *mettre,* "to place" "to put"). Between-course activities were known as *entremets,* events that concluded with *entremets mouvants,* a French term for movable parts that included live participants. *Entremets* might also conclude with a *subtletie,* a stationary course such as a custard several feet high molded in a fanciful shape.

The typical medieval three-course menu included appetizers, such as fruit, soups, and stews, served in random order, rather than in logical sequence. The main course featured roasted food and cooked vegetables and was served in a somewhat prescribed order, such as boar's head, venison, and stuffed pig before fowl; whole large-footed birds, like swans, before smaller fowl, such as duck; sweet dishes before sour; hot foods before cold; and moist foods before dry. The dessert course was baked food and contained monumental creations called *pièces montées,* possibly forerunners of modern-day ice sculpture.

Each course in the medieval menu included seven to fifteen dishes or more, a number that depended on rank. The lord of the manor, chatelaine, and honored guests received as many as twenty dishes per course. A baron (a feudal tenant of the king) was offered half the quantity of those seated at the high table. A knight (a military servant of the king pledged to chivalrous conduct) received a quarter of the dishes served the king. All others were given an eighth of the courses (still ample by today's standards). Moreover, the quality of medieval food varied according to status. Those of highest rank received the meat of animals, and the lower class were served the entrails, especially those of deer, a dish known as *umble pie.* Hence the expression "to eat humble pie."

In the Middle Ages, the menu of the rich featured a variety of flesh foods—meat, fish, and poultry. Those who lived inland ate fish supplied by artificial ponds and moats. Birds were a favorite source of meat, particularly heron, stork, peacock, and pigeon. Squab were kept in dovecotes by noblemen granted the right to raise them. Henry IV is reported to have said: "If God grants me the usual length of life, I hope to make France so prosperous that every peasant will have a chicken in his pot on Sunday." Chickens ran at will in medieval courtyards, but not every household had poultry as easily as today, and the menu of the poor was based primarily on grains, vegetables, and dairy products.

Guillaume Tirel, nicknamed "Taillevent," rose from working as a humble kitchen boy to become master cook for King Charles VI of France (r. 1380–1422). Taillevent wrote a cookbook entitled *Le Viandier*, a tome that gives historical insight into the medieval menu. The book was not printed until 1490, however. Prior to this, recipes were handed down orally and cooking was a skill learned by repeated practice.

Cooking methods cited in *Le Viandier* involved foods that were pounded, simmered, pureed, and spiced. Pounding tenderized the tough meat of large animals, and simmering softened the tissue of small animals. Pureed food enhanced the flavor of dishes made from stale vegetables. Food that bordered on rotten was camouflaged with spices liberally applied. Seasonings were also used for decorative color: red from sandalwood, orange from saffron, blue from mulberries, and green from parsley.

In the fifteenth century, it was not uncommon to serve hundreds of people daily, and the well-staffed kitchen was divided into a dozen sections, or departments. Hospitality was a measure of power, and Richard III of England (r. 1483–1485) was known to entertain thousands, food preparation that employed hundreds of cooks and servitors. The master cook was responsible for the kitchen staff, a position that held considerable rank, and many an accomplished cook was accorded the title of squire, one who attended a knight.

In the Renaissance, the preparation of food emphasized the scientific aspects of diet and health. Renaissance menus were presented in logical sequence, "to assist the well-bred man who desires to be healthy and to eat in a decorous way, rather than he who searches after luxury and extravagance." To enhance flavor, certain dishes were served hot and others were served cold.

Bartolomeo de' Sacchi (called Platina in Latin), a Renaissance philosopher, humanist, man of letters and librarian at the Vatican, was the first to record recipes, in a book entitled *De Honesta Voluptate et Valetudine* ("Of Honest Indulgence and Good Health"), a work that set forth detailed cooking instructions. Although Platina was not a cook himself, he recorded over 250 recipes created by Martino of Como, an Italian cook who developed *rabiole,* a dish that enclosed "leftovers" in pasta served with sauce. *De Honesta Voluptate et Valetudine* was published in Rome in 1474, printed in thirty editions, and translated into German and French. In 1930, an Italian manuscript was discovered containing recipes "composed by the respected Maestro Martino, former cook to the Most Reverend Monsignor the Chamberlain and Patriarch of Aquileia." That manuscript, attributed to Platina, now resides in the Library of Congress.

The Italians blended the cooking of different regions in Italy with recipes the Crusaders had brought home from Arabia, and when 14-year-old Catherine de' Medici married Henri II in 1533, things Italian became fashionable at the French court and Italian cooks were elevated to positions of influence. In the sixteenth century, the banquet menu was divided into three parts, called *services*. The first service contained appetizers, from soup to roast. The second service was the main course, a menu based on cold roasts, vegetables, and sweets. The number of dishes provided in the second service had to equal those of the first service, and neither could total an odd number. The third service was the sweet course, consisting of petit fours and other decorated sweets, colorful ices, and assorted fruit.

Bartolomeo Scappi is considered the greatest cook of the Italian Renaissance, a chef accorded the same veneration in the field of culinary art as Michelangelo in the world of fine art. Scappi was master cook to Cardinal Campeggio, the cunning lawyer who negotiated the divorce of Henry VIII and Catherine of Aragon. In around 1574, Scappi published a cookbook entitled *Opera,* an encyclopedic volume that gave explicit instructions and exact measurements for more than 1,000 recipes. *Opera* also featured accurate drawings of cooking paraphernalia and drawings of the quintessential Renaissance kitchen filled with mechanical inventions that reflected the scientific aspect of cooking, such as an open-fire spit, turned by a propeller driven by the rising air of the heat, a device invented by Leonardo da Vinci.

Scappi was a great advocate of *stufato,* an Italian term for stew of marinated chicken baked in a sealed *stufatoro,* or stew pot, a perennial favorite of the Renaissance menu. Moreover, Scappi was the first European to experiment with Arab pastries, an interest that led to puff pastries served as a *collation,* a French word for "snack." In the sixteenth century, elegant dinners concluded with dancing, followed by *collations,* light meals of sweets, biscuits, pastries, fresh fruit, preserves, sugared nuts, and marzipan. In the sixteenth century, sweets were regarded as warming foods and laxatives and were sold at apothecaries.

In the seventeenth century leadership in culinary talent shifted from Italy to France, then the cultural center of Europe, where the preparation of food was called *cuisine,* from the French word for kitchen. French cuisine was based on the size of the kitchen, the availability of equipment, access to special ingredients, and the skill of the chef. Two types of cuisine evolved: haute cuisine and bourgeoise cuisine.

*Haute cuisine* was artful, elaborate cuisine prepared for royalty, the court, the aristocracy, and honored guests. Recipes were created by trained chefs who excelled in particular types of food, dishes that incorporated the finest seasonal delicacies, concocted in huge kitchens staffed with the latest equipment.

*Bourgeoise cuisine,* or plain cooking, was based on simple menus prepared by cooks who had little or no formal training, concocted in average-size kitchens, with ordinary equipment, from local ingredients.

The art of classical French cooking is attributed to François Pierre de La Varenne, a chef who, in a series of cookbooks, brought order and documentation to French cuisine. The first of La Varenne's books, *Le Cuisinier français,* was published in 1651 and featured recipes based on haute cuisine. This tome marks the end of the prodigious quantities of food served at medieval banquets. Courses were no longer served in random order (called disdainfully *service en confusion*), but rather *à la française,* with dishes ranked by size and placed on the table all at once in a symmetrical grand display.

La Varenne roasted the best cuts of meat but tenderized tougher cuts in a slow cooker, a method that came to be known as *bouillon,* a broth, or soup made from concentrated stock. Moreover, La Varenne was the first French cook to thicken bouillon with *roux,* a paste made of melted butter or fat mixed with flour.

French cuisine was slow to reach England, where cooks prepared food in the medieval manner and menus centered primarily on roasts, puddings, and pies. As William Forest, a chronicler of the Elizabethan period, observed: "Our English nature cannot live by roots, by water, herbs, or such beggary baggage, that may well serve for vile outlandish quarters; give Englishmen meat after their old usage, beef, mutton, veal, to cheer their courage." Meat pies were popular vehicles for practical jokes, such as the gargantuan pie of 100 turkeys baked in the diocesan kitchen of Durham Castle or the well-known meat pie set forth in the following nursery rhyme.

*Sing a song of sixpence,*
*A pocket full of rye,*
*Four and twenty black birds*
*Baked in a pie.*
*When the pie was opened,*
*The birds began to sing.*
*Oh! wasn't that a dainty dish*
*To set before a king.*

In 1660, after the restoration of Charles II from exile at the court of Louis XIV, English cooks began to experiment with foreign foods, notably, *stuffados, kickshaws,* and *olios. Stuffado* was a favorite English dish known today as *pot roast. Kickshaw* was a corruption of the French term *quelque chose,* meaning "something or other," an expression that the English took to mean "elegant French dish." Olio was an abbreviation of the Spanish *olla podrida,* Andalusian stew, or, literally, "rotten stew." In 1660, Robert May, a noted English cook, devoted four pages to *olla podrida* in a cookbook he wrote entitled *The Accomplisht Cook.* In 1699 May wrote *Acetaria,* a book devoted to salads, stating the success of the dish lay in the dressing: "oyl and vinegar beaten together, the best oyl you can get." Until May's cookbooks, English tomes focused on household management and thrifty husbandry as much as they did on tempting recipes.

In the reign of Louis XIV (r. 1643–1715), food and menu preparation were fashionable court preoccupations. Armed with La Varenne's cookbook, the French nobility developed recipes of their own, an interest that continued in the eighteenth century at the court of Louis XV, a king known to work in the kitchen under the guidance of his friend, Prince de Dombes, an accomplished cook. Although the French aristocracy cooked as a hobby, by the eighteenth century the French chef was regarded as indispensable. The writer Mercier described just such a situation in his 1780 *Tableau de Paris:*

> It will not be long now before cooks assume the title of artists in cookery. They are pampered and spoiled, their tantrums are soothed, and it is normal to sacrifice all other servants for their sake. To entice away the cook from a household is a terrible and unforgivable trick.

When Louis XV ascended the French throne in 1715, he broke with the royal tradition of dining before a large public audience and instead began to host small private suppers where wit and intellect were emphasized over pomp and circumstance. However, the change in format lay primarily in the smaller guest list—twenty people at the most—rather than in the menu. To retain the atmosphere of intimacy, notably when entertaining the queen or one of his mistresses, Louis XV installed an opening in the floor of the dining room to lower the table to the kitchen for imperceptible replenishment of dishes.

One of Louis XV's mistresses, Madame du Barry, employed a female chef, and after partaking of an exceptional meal, the king asked to meet the chef. When a woman appeared, the king, impressed by her culinary skills, awarded her the Order of the Holy Ghost, one of the highest decorations in France, an order recognized by a blue sash, or *cordon bleu*.

Novelty was important at the French court, and Menon, master cook to Louis XV, invented 100-dish menus composed of a single color. White was considered the most elegant color, and Menon devised multidish menus based on one type of meat. In 1755, Menon wrote *Les Soupers de la cour*, a three-volume work that notes a menu for thirty divided into five courses comprised of over 100 dishes. After service of the first and third courses, the table was cleared and new dishes were supplied for the second and fourth courses, the sizes of which were in proportion with the serveware that remained on the table, the latter laid in symmetrical alignment.

The eighteenth-century menu allowed time during dessert for individual guests to sing songs that praised the host's hospitality, such as the last couplet of the following song, by Marc-Antoine Desaugiers, a noted author and gastronomic poet.

*I pray that death may strike me*
*In the middle of a large meal.*
*I wish to be buried under the tablecloth*
*Between four large dishes.*
*As I desire that this short inscription*
*Should be engraved on my tombstone,*
*Here lies the first poet*
*Ever to die of indigestion.*

In the eighteenth century an eccentric American known as Count von Rumford invented the cookstove, a development that made cooking easier than before, especially for women. In England, the cookstove resulted in recipes and cookbooks by women, such as Hannah Glasse, who in 1747 wrote *The Art of Cookery Made Plain and Easy,* the most successful English cookbook of its time. In 1796, Amelia Simmons wrote *American Cookery,* the first American cookbook, a small book of 130 recipes based on local ingredients, and a departure from existing cookbooks, which featured European ingredients, often unavailable in the colonies.

In the nineteenth century, women continued to pen cookbooks. Isabella Beeton wrote *Household Management* in 1860; it was the most successful cookbook ever published in Europe. *Household Management* addressed the needs of middle-class Victorian families and was the first cookbook to give quantities, cooking times, and servings per recipe and incorporate convenience foods, such as baking powder and mushroom ketchup.

London, in the nineteenth century, had many exclusive private clubs—the Athenaeum, Brook's, the Carlton, and the Reform Club, the latter founded in 1837 by Liberal members of Parliament. The chef at the Reform Club was a Frenchman named Alexis Soyer, a creative person who designed kitchens outfitted with the latest gadgetry and equipment, such as refrigerators cooled by ice water and gas ovens that operated with accurate controls.

Soyer developed "Soyer's sauce," a liquid seasoning later purchased by Crosse and Blackwell. He was the first chef of note to direct his culinary talents toward the poor: In 1847, during the potato famine in Ireland, he set up forty soup kitchens. In 1855, he published *A Shilling Cookery for the People,* a cookbook aimed at the working class and filled with recipes for nutritive soups and dishes made from inexpensive foods. In the Crimean War, Soyer volunteered his services at Scutari Hospital in Constantinople, where he reorganized hospital and field kitchens, developed menus for the sick, transformed the food of field soldiers, and invented a campaign stove.

Haute cuisine of the nineteenth century is associated with Marie-Antoine Carême, a Frenchman known simply as Antonin Carême, possibly the greatest cook of all time. Carême simplified menus, analyzed old and new cooking methods, clarified culinary techniques, defined every aspect of food preparation, invented new sauces, and added *pièces montées* to the menu, towering desserts prepared in architectural forms, a carryover from medieval banquets. With a touch of humor, he once observed that "the fine arts are five in number, to wit: painting, sculpture, poetry, music, architecture—whose main branch is confectionery."

In turn-of-the-century America, Fannie Farmer, principal of the Boston Cooking School and author of the *Boston Cooking School Cook Book,* introduced a system of ingredients measured by *volume,* as opposed to the European way of measuring by *weight* or the French method of relying on *expérience* to dictate amount. Today, American recipes detail exact measurements and set forth instructions step-by-step, whereas French cooks rely on concepts that, once understood, adapt to many dishes.

Auguste Escoffier, "the king of chefs and the chef of kings," gained prominence at a time when top chefs no longer worked in private homes, but rather were employed by great restaurants and hotels. In 1880 Escoffier met César Ritz of the Grand Hotel in Monte Carlo, an introduction that led to an illustrious partnership.

Escoffier departed from the medieval practice of dividing the kitchen into a dozen or more departments, and instead organized the kitchen into five sections, called *parties.* Rather than balance the menu with an outlandish quantity of dishes, Escoffier balanced taste with the right combination of dishes. In 1912, Escoffier's cookbook *Le Livre des Menus* was published, a tome that presented the grand cuisine of hotels and detailed the elements of a well-planned menu, concepts that form the basis of formal menus today: food right for the occasion and appropriate for the guests, made from recipes that incorporate the finest seasonal delicacies, menus that allot time for preparation and realistically appraise the help needed to prepare and serve a multicourse meal.

In 1934, Escoffier wrote *Ma Cuisine,* a book based on bourgeois cuisine, a collection of recipes prepared in small kitchens from local ingredients. Following World War II, formal dining and haute cuisine began to disappear, and *Ma Cuisine* became the literary source of French family cooking. Today, Escoffier's concepts continue for both haute cuisine and everyday cooking.

CHAPTER FORTY-FOUR

# MENU PRIMER

*The pleasures of the table belong to all ages, to all conditions, to all countries and to every day; they can be associated with all the other pleasures and remain the longest to console us for the loss of the rest.*

ANTHELME BRILLAT-SAVARIN, PHYSIOLOGIE DU GOÛT

*He who dines well lives well.*

HORACE, EPISTLES, C. 20 B.C.

AN INVITING MENU is a balance of bland, strong, sharp, and sweet tastes, with foods of different textures, temperatures, and colors. Bland tastes, such as rice, pasta, or potatoes, contrast with strong flavors, such as meat, game, or well-seasoned vegetables, followed by the sharp taste of a vinaigrette salad, accented by a sweet dessert.

Moreover, a well-balanced menu does not duplicate taste. When cheese is served as an hors d'oeuvre, it is not incorporated in a dish served at the table. Because sweet foods dull the appetite, fruit is not served as an appetizer. The exception is grapefruit, which has a sharp taste that stimulates the palate. When a first course is served in a pastry shell, dessert with a crust is not appropriate. If creamed soup is served as a first course, creamed vegetables are not included in the main course. When sauce is served, it is presented only once.

From light to heavy, sour to sweet, each course is designed to meet a specific taste requirement. At a four-course meal, a light first course, such as hot soup or raw fish, stimulates the palate; it is followed by a combination course of cooked food, such as meat, starch, vegetables, and garnish. Afterward a light course is served, usually a crisp salad tossed with a tart dressing; it is followed by a sweet dessert. But at a simple meal, many tastes are combined in one dish, for example, a Mexican casserole made with meat, vegetables, and cheese is a spicy taste that accents the bland flavor of flour tortillas and is followed by a light dessert, such as delicate flan.

Food textures promote mastication, and the menu is designed to offer both crunchy and smooth textures. The crunchy texture of raw foods, such as carrots and celery, contrast with soft foods, such as cheese or soup. Crisp salad greens balance foods made with a smooth consistency, such as noodles in a cream sauce.

The well-balanced menu includes both hot and cold temperatures. Because hot foods stimulate the appetite, a hot dish is always included in a menu, except in extremely hot weather, when a cold menu is less obtrusive to the palate. At a four-course meal a hot first course is followed by a cold second course, then a hot main course and a cold dessert. To maintain the right temperature, hot food is served on warm plates, and cold food on cool plates. Porcelain is naturally cold to the touch, so porcelain plates are not cooled. For a hot course, they are warmed in a low oven (approximately 150 to 200°F, or 66 to 93°C). Plates can also be warmed in the drying cycle of the dishwasher.

As guests feast with their eyes as well as their palates, a well-balanced menu offers a contrast of colorful foods. Imagine an all-white-food turkey dinner, such as white meat, mashed potatoes, and creamed onions. Although the dishes may taste superb, there is nothing for the eyes to feast on. But the same dishes *are* inviting when colorful food is added, such as dark meat, cranberry sauce, string beans, and sweet potatoes.

These, then, are the subtleties of a well-balanced menu.

- The main course is the focal point of the menu, and all other foods are selected to accent the taste, temperature, texture, and colors.
- If the cocktail hour is particularly long, the palate may become dulled by hors d'oeuvres, in which case highly seasoned food is recommended for subsequent courses.

- Plan a company meal around tastes that are special, flavors obtained from the finest seasonal delicacies at their peak of perfection.
- Arrange foods attractively on the plate. The eye moves right, and for visual appeal, the dominant portion of food is placed on the right side of the plate. Make sure a particular food does not cover the plate entirely, such as a cut of prime rib. When pie is served, position the point of the wedge toward the diner.

## The Sequence of a Seven-Course Menu

*Here lie the bones of Joseph Jones,*
*Who ate while he was able;*
*But once o'er fed*
*He dropt dead,*
*And fell beneath the table.*
*When from the tomb*
*To meet his doom*
*He rises amidst sinners:*
*Since he must dwell*
*In heav'n or hell*
*Take him which gives best dinners.*

TOMBSTONE, WOLVERHAMPTON, ENGLAND, C. 1900

The following seven-course menu can be easily adapted to a four-course meal by eliminating an appetizer course, the cheese course, and the fruit course.

### *Cocktail Hour*

To keep the palate fresh for a multicourse meal, notably a formal dinner of five or more courses, do not serve appetizers with preprandial drinks. But at a simple meal of four courses or less, a ready palate is not an issue and light hors d'oeuvres or canapés can be offered with cocktails.

### *First Course*

It is said that soup is to dinner what overture is to opera, and the first course at a multicourse meal is light—perhaps a small serving of hot lentil soup, served to stimulate the appetite. At a simple meal, the first course is substantial, such as a small serving of pasta.

### *Second Course*

In the world of French cuisine, the second course is known as the *relève,* a French word for "lift," an intermediate course served to lift the palate and prepare it for the third course.

### *Third Course*

Technically, the third course is the *entrée.* Years ago when formal dinners were the norm, it was customary to serve three appetizer courses, the last one providing the *entrée,* or entrance, to the main course.

Today, people don't eat as much as they once did, and more often the third course is in fact the main course, a course often listed on restaurant menus under *entrées.* But when three appetizers are served at a multicourse meal, the third course is a light appetizer known as the *entrée.*

### *Fourth Course*

At a formal dinner, the fourth course is often the main course, a substantial course consisting of a combination of hot cooked foods, such as a roast beef surrounded by seasonal vegetables, a starch, and garnish.

*Sorbet,* essentially a fruited ice, is served to clear the palate at anytime during a meal. As the main course is the heaviest course, sorbet is usually presented before, during, or after the main course.

### *Fifth Course*

To revive the palate, the fifth course is a light course of cold or cooked food, such as endive salad, asparagus with hollandaise sauce, or a cold rôti, a French word for "roast," such as pâté de foie gras in aspic.

*Cheese it is a peevish elf,*
*It digests all things but itself.*

JOHN RAY, ENGLISH PROVERBS, 1670

Cheese is a digestive, and an assortment of cheese is presented immediately after the service of salad or fruit. To provide a contrast of taste, texture, and temperature, after the cheese board is presented, an assortment of warm crisp crackers is offered, along with butter served at room temperature.

Cheese is most flavorful at a room temperature—approximately 70 to 72°F (21 to 22°C). For greatest flavor, cheese is removed from the refrigerator approximately an hour before service. Cheese with a runny texture, like brie or camembert, is enhanced when kept three to six hours at room temperature.

Soft cheese, such as ricotta or neufchâtel, stays firm longer when placed on a chilled marble slab. Firm cheese, such as gouda or cheddar cheese, remains hard on a wooden board.

To balance the flavors of cheese, a choice of three is offered, such as the strong taste of brie, camembert, or limburger, accented by mild bel paese, muenster, edam, or gouda, and moldy blue-veined cheese, such as stilton, roquefort, gorgonzola, or blue cheese. To prevent the flavor of one cheese from invading the taste of the others, a separate knife is provided for each cheese.

To balance the textures of cheese, serve three different consistencies, such as hard cheese, like cheddar, colby, gruyère, swiss, provolone, edam, or gouda; semisoft cheese, such as port-salut, bel paese, brick, muenster, mozzarella, or blue-veined cheese; and soft cheese, like brie, camembert, ricotta, or neufchâtel.

## *Sixth Course*

The sixth course is a sweet course served to cap the appetite. In the sixteenth century, dessert was a memorable course made for display, more like a centerpiece today, a tall confection shaped in a complex ornamental shape, such as a castle or a topiary tree, surrounded by smaller edible desserts. Today dessert is a simple course, that, in keeping with past traditions, is as memorable as the final act in a play.

At a multicourse meal, a heavy menu is complimented by a light dessert with a soft texture, such as poached pears accompanied by crisp florentines and chewy macaroons. At a simple meal, a rich dessert caps the appetite with flair, for example, a smooth-textured ice-cream pie presented in a crust textured with chopped nuts.

### *Seventh Course*

Whether a meal is formal or informal, when multiple courses are served, to cleanse and refresh the palate, the meal concludes with fresh fruit. For a simple menu, the meal may conclude with a rich dessert, or with fresh fruit, such as sliced pineapple or strawberry shortcake.

## Menu Plan for a Buffet

*Kissing don't last, cookery do.*

GEORGE MEREDITH, THE ORDEAL OF RICHARD FEVEREL, 1859

A buffet meal is composed of dishes that fit on one plate. Rather than mingle sauce and salad dressing, plan a buffet menu around foods that do not run or slip off the plate (and into the guests' laps). Choose dishes that will not dry out and will maintain the right temperature for 30 to 60 minutes in a covered vegetable bowl, in a chaffing dish, or on an electric hot plate. Cover cold meat, poultry, or fish with clear aspic to maintain the chill of cold food. To keep platters attractive, serve preportioned foods, such as individually molded salads and stuffed vegetables. For a large group, serve two main courses, such as turkey and ham, and plan quantities generous enough to encourage second helpings.

# A Menu for Afternoon Tea

*What can it be, that subtle treachery that lurks in tea cakes, and is totally absent in the rude honesty of toast?*

JOHN RUSKIN

The menu for afternoon tea is planned around finger food that is neither crumbly nor sticky, foods chosen to enhance the flavor and aroma of tea, rather than overpower the appetite and take one's hunger for dinner.

Like any well-balanced menu, afternoon tea offers a contrast of taste, texture, temperature, and color. The tangy taste of lemon-curd tarts contrasts with the sweet flavor of profiteroles. The delicate flavor of thinly sliced cucumber on a soft, crustless bread provides balance and contrast with the strong flavor of watercress sandwiches on buttered rye and the piquant taste of cream cheese sandwiches seasoned with spiced chutney. Nut bread, seed cake, fruit cake, crisp cookies, and mixed nuts supply crunchy textures. Flavored butters and creamy chocolates offer smooth textures. Hot foods, such as seafood puffs or squares of lobster quiche, balance breads served at room temperature, such as gingerbread and Irish soda bread. A colorful array of jams, such as ginger-lime, orange marmalade, and cranberry, provide a festive air.

# A Menu for High Tea

High tea is served around five o'clock, a time of day when people are usually quite hungry, and the repast provided is more substantial than the light fare offered at afternoon tea. The menu is similar to hors d'oeuvres and canapes served at a cocktail hour, such as:

- Hot mushrooms on toasted English muffins
- Small cooked oysters wrapped with a half slice of bacon served on toast

- Scrambled eggs served on crustless toast, spread with anchovy paste and garnished with parsley
- Small rolls stuffed with herb-seasoned chicken or shrimp salad and bean sprouts
- Sherried liver pâté
- Smoked turkey with dijon mustard
- Large wedges of cheese
- Assorted sweets, like currant-filled Eccles cake, Dundee cake with marmalade, fruit cake topped with almonds, buttery shortbread, and spicy gingerbread

CHAPTER FORTY-FIVE

# FROM VINE TO VITICULTURE

*In water you see your own face; in wine the heart of another.*

ANONYMOUS

LEGEND TELLS US that the gods infused wine with the spirit of the lion, the ape, and the pig. Wine in moderation makes us strong, like a lion. Too much wine and we act like apes. And wine in excess makes us behave like pigs. But all agree wine is a gift from the gods.

Fermented beverages were discovered by accident millenniums ago, probably when water and kernels of grain were left to stand in clay pots. The grain fermented, and the sugar in them converted to alcohol. The first fermented beverages were made in a deliberate way when humans first began to live a settled life, farming and cultivating grain. To quote an ancient Chinese text, "The enjoyment of drinking started with tilling." With agriculture came wine.

Grapevines belong to the botanical family *Vitaceae,* a climbing woody shrub that produces berries.

The primary wine-producing vine *Vitis vinifera* is also known as the *European grape.* The exact origin of the grapevine is unknown, but the source is credited to Asia Minor, Armenia, or the region along the Caspian Sea. According to seed fossils found in the Caucasus near Mount Ararat, Turkey, *Vitis vinifera* grew wild in this region more than 9,000 years ago; archaeologists believe that it was cultivated approximately 8,000 years ago. Tomb paintings from ancient Egypt dating back 5,000 years reveal grapevines were grown on trellis-like structures that elevated the branches above the heat-parched earth. The first written record of oenology comes from predynastic tombs, on the stoppers used to seal the tall, two-handled jars called *amphorae*. But the origin of grape wine is credited to Persia. In Shiraz, a city in southern Iran about 100 miles inland from the Caspian Sea, wine was made from red syrah grapes.

The Phoenicians were great navigators and traders who transported red grapes to port cities in Crete and Greece along the northern shores of the Mediterranean. The temperate weather was right for the cultivation of grapevines in Italy, known to the Greeks as Oenotria, or the "Land of Vines." Our word *oenology,* meaning "knowledge of wine," comes from the Greek *oinos,* "wine." The word *grape* is the Old French *grape,* meaning "hook," a strong tool used to gather grapes from the vine.

"Wine is sunlight, held together by water," said Galileo. Greek wine was diluted with water, usually seawater, which clarified wine, encouraged a sweet taste, and promoted digestion. In some parts of Europe seawater is still used to cleanse and prepare wine barrels for harvest. In keeping with the motto "Nothing in excess," the Greeks diluted wine with water in a ratio of 3 to 5, resulting in a beverage with an alcohol content of about 5 to 6 percent. Undiluted wine was considered unhealthy and only drunk when prescribed. Hippocrates prescribed undiluted wine for assorted maladies, such as bee stings, snake bites, and mental illness.

To produce sweet wine, the Greeks left grapes on the vines a week beyond current-day harvest time, a practice that encouraged *Botrytis cinerea,* or "noble rot," a fungus that penetrates the grape skin, attacks the juice, and dehydrates the pulp. The juice of late-picked grapes is sweeter than grapes picked at normal harvest time, and the wine has a higher alcohol content.

The location of a vineyard is crucial to viticulture, classically located between 30° and 50° latitude in areas near water that provides humidity in drought, in regions that offer sunshine, heat, rain, and frost. Although the Greeks planted vineyards around the Mediterranean, the Romans planted vineyards in the river valleys of northern Europe. By the first century, viticulture was known in Bordeaux, by the second century in Burgundy, by the third century in the Loire Valley, by the fourth century in Champagne and in the Moselle and Rhine River valleys.

The Romans aged wine for several years or more and marked each jug, or amphora, with the names of the wine-producing region and the reign date of the consulate in the year the wine was made. They sealed the amphorae with lids of cork or fired clay held in place with cement. Vintage wines were kept over a century, sweetened with sugar as needed, and diluted with water. In 121 B.C., Lucius Opimius reigned as consul, and "Opimian wine" produced in the vineyard of Falernum was stored in private cellars, a nouveau riche form of treasure flaunted by Trimalchio in the *Satyricon,* who proudly labeled bottles: "Falernum, Opimian wine 100 years old."

Wine is part of Catholic, Protestant, and Jewish religious services. According to the Book of Genesis, when Noah's ark landed in Turkey and the animals disembarked, one of the goats began to nibble away on the wild grapes growing everywhere. After tasting the grapes himself, Noah immediately set about to plant a vineyard near Erwan, an act portrayed by Benozzo Gozzoli in a fresco seen in the Campo Santo, Pisa. In recognition of the integral part wine plays in the Christian Eucharist, signifying the blood of Christ, in the ninth century, Charlemagne deeded large parcels of land to the church for cultivation of grapevines.

By the Middle Ages, the church was the primary producer of wine, a beverage made for sacramental purposes by monks who established vineyards on the south-facing slopes of hills, among them the Côte-d'Or, France's "Golden Slope," a location that offered more hours of full sun compared to dissipation of heat over a wide area on flat ground, provided greater ventilation of the vines than did river valleys, and promoted good drainage reducing the risk of frost. Moreover, the monks were the first to notice that the chemical condition of the soil plus the texture, porosity, drainage, and depth produced wines with different characteristics. Wine made from grapes grown in the soil of Bordeaux, which was high in granite that warms quickly, produced wine lower in acidity than wine made from grapes cultivated in the chalky soil of Champagne, a cool porous type of limestone that promoted wine with a relatively high acidity.

Following the Norman conquest of England in 1066, France was the primary source of wine drunk in England, particularly red wine imported from Burgundy and Bordeaux. Burgundy, known as the *stomach of France,* is a region of hills and valleys that lies on both sides of the Saône River. Although white wine and sparkling wine are made in Burgundy, three times more red wine is produced there, primarily a fruity, full-bodied red wine called *burgundy.* After the French Revolution, the large tracts of land previously owned by the church and the nobility were redistributed to the people; Burgundy was divided into smaller parcels of land, holdings called *départements.*

Bordeaux, in southwestern France, boasts a moderate, stable climate, a region noted for production of cabernet sauvignon, a complex, full-bodied red wine. Bordeaux is composed of wine-producing estates that perform bottling operations in châteaux (French for "castles"), such as the Château Haut-Brion, Château Lafite-Rothschild, Château Latour, and Château Margaux. Although *château* is a term associated with grandeur, technically it is any small cottage located on a vineyard whose lineage boasts a long line of vintners. Prior to the establishment of chateaux, in the late seventeenth century wine production was on a crop-sharing basis.

In 1152, Eleanor of Aquitaine married Henry Plantagenet (later to be King Henry II of England), and her dowry included the region of Bordeaux. For the next 300 years, the vineyards of Bordeaux belonged to England; Guyenne, formerly called Aquitaine, is famous for its clear, blended wine, known in England as *claret.*

In Germany, the forested hills of the Moselle and Rhine River valleys provided suitable locations for terraced vineyards. The hills protected the vineyards from wind and helped the soil to retain heat through the chilly nights of northern Europe. But the cold German climate fostered a short grape-growing season, and the grapes were picked before they attained the right weight of sugar, an early harvest that makes German wines more acidic than wines produced in warmer climes, notably France and Italy.

By the Middle Ages, wine was no longer stored in clay amphorae, but in wooden casks that permitted air and bacteria to enter the pores and made aged wine turn sour. Moreover, the shape of early wine bottles was bulbous and squat, forms vertically stored, and until cork was used as a stopper at the end of the seventeenth century, wine was drunk young.

Cork was made from a slow-growing evergreen tree, *Quercus suber,* which is indigenous to Portugal and Spain. The cork tree has a thick outer bark made of a light elastic substance whose air-filled cells swell when wet. Every nine or ten years the outer bark is stripped from mature trees approximately 30 years old. Wine bottles topped with cork were binned in horizontal heaps, a position that moistened the corks, which then swelled, preventing the entrance of air, making wine with a sweeter taste, and allowing wine to age without spoiling.

In the eighteenth century wine bottles were shaped long and slim to accommodate horizontal binning. By the mid-eighteenth century, the cork-and-bottle technology had advanced the making of vintage wine, which led to the era of wine connoisseurs in the nineteenth century. However, cork allows a small amount of air, yeast, and chemicals to come in contact with wine, and today some wine makers look to synthetic cork as the answer to a perfect seal, such as those used in the medical profession.

> FALSTAFF: If I had a thousand sons, the first human principle I would teach them should be, to foreswear thin potations, and to addict themselves to sack.
>
> Shakespeare, *Henry IV,* Part II

In the sixteenth and seventeenth centuries, wine was not sipped and savored as it is today, but quaffed like a glass of water. The exception was a strong white wine called *sack,* which was fortified with alcohol distilled from brandy imported from Jerez (formerly Xeres). *Jerez* became anglicized to *sherry. Sack* is probably a corruption of the Spanish word *seco* or the French *sec,* meaning "dry."

Wine historians suggest that the Andalusians of Jerez learned distillation from the Moors of North Africa, a Muslim people of Arab and Berber descent who conquered Spain in the eighth century. The Arabs, forbidden by the Koran to drink alcoholic beverages, used distillation to make rosewater, a perfume twice-distilled from rose oil extracted from a thirty-petal damask rose grown today near Taif in western Saudi Arabia. By the sixteenth century, sherry, the first distilled and fortified wine, was produced from grapes grown in the Jerez region.

*Go and fetch a pint of port*
*But let it not be such as that*
*You set before chance-comers,*
*But such whose father-grape grew fat*
*On Lusitanian summers.*

*Lord Tennyson*

From 1689 to 1703 a political dispute raged between England and France, exacerbated by William of Orange, king of England, who levied heavy taxes on the import of French wines. To ensure a steady supply of claret, the British (who had been introduced to Portugese wine in 1662 by Catherine of Braganza, the Lusitanian princess who married Charles II) encouraged Portugese vintners to plant Bordeaux grapes in the upper valley of the Douro River. This resulted in a red wine called *port*, from the Portuguese *oporto*.

In 1703 the Methuen Treaty was passed, a commercial agreement named for John Methuen, England's envoy to Portugal, also known as the *Port Wine Treaty*. England agreed to import port at one-third less duty than French wine, and Portugal agreed to lift the ban on English textiles. Between 1707 and 1779, 95 percent of the wine imported to England was Portugese. In 1756, the Portugese government demarcated the upper valley of the Douro River, and the region became the first wine-producing area separated by boundaries.

In the hot Portugese climate, the excess sugar in the grapes accelerated the fermentation and converted the sugar to alcohol, hence port lacked sweetness. To promote a sweet taste, vintners stopped the fermentation early on, a process that also lowered the alcohol content. But port, like sherry, was fortified with alcohol distilled from brandy, a method that also raised the alcohol content.

*She's no Mistress of mine,*
*That drinks not her Wine,*
*Or frowns at my Friends drinking Motions,*
*If my Heart thou would'st gain,*
*Drink thy Bottle of Champaign,*
*'Twill serve thee for Paint and Love potions.*

*Sir George Etherege*, She would if she could, *1667*

The sparkling wine that is the "soul of France" is a bubbly wine produced in the region of Champagne. Madame de Pompadour once observed that champagne is "the only drink that leaves a woman still beautiful after drinking it." It is made by a second fermentation in the bottle, a discovery, possibly more fable than fact, that began in 1668, literally with a bang, when Dom Pierre Pérignon, a blind Benedictine cellar master at the Abbey of St. Peters, Hautvilliers, uncorked a bottle of blended wine. According to legend, in the cool autumn weather of Champagne in northeastern France, the first fermentation was halted before all the sugar converted to alcohol. But in the warm weather of spring, the dormant yeast cells reawoke and fermentation continued. In the second fermentation, the gas trapped in the casks created pressure and the bungs blew, creating a liquid explosion the monks called *devil wine.* One spring day when Dom Pérignon strolled into the cellar to check the stoppers, a few shot forth, and were followed by a crisp acidic explosion that, in Dom Pérignon's words, "tasted like stars." This eventful moment is symbolized today on the labels of champagne bottles which carry pictures of a star or a comet.

Although the legend of champagne is a bubbly tale surrounded by conjecture, it is a known fact that Dom Pérignon invented the *cuvée* method, a technique in which two or more wines made from the same or different grapes are blended, a process also known as *assemblage.* The classic blend of champagne is an assemblage of one-third chardonnay grapes, one-third pinot noir grapes, and one-third pinot meunier grapes. Moreover, Dom Pérignon was among the first to seal wine bottles with cork, a method that prevented bubbles of carbon dioxide from escaping the bottle. However, it was not until the eighteenth century that champagne was produced with a controlled amount of bubbles, a process known today as the *Méthode champénoise,* or champagne method.

Wine production was introduced to North America by Spaniards in the sixteenth century. Wine is essential to the celebration of the Eucharist, and as thanks for God's munificence, monks skilled in wine production were sent to the New World to cultivate grapes and to produce wine.

Although European wine was made from *Vitis vinifera* vines, the vines of North America were of a different type, *Vitis labrusca,* a wild grape that was indigenous to the east coast. Leif Erikson, the first European to come to America (circa 1000 A.D.), noticed that *V. labrusca* vines grew wild everywhere and named the land Vinland or Vinland the Good. Vinland has been variously located from Labrador and the Canadian maritime provinces to the northern parts of the U.S. east coast.

*V. labrusca* thrives in the cold climate of the east coast, particularly around the Finger Lakes of upstate New York. The grapes produce sweet wine with a very fruity flavor reminiscent of concord grapes. Americans termed the special *labrusca* flavor "foxy." In 1682, William Penn described "the great red grape called by ignorance, 'the fox grape' (because of the relish it hath with unskillful palates)."

The colonists who were familiar with wine made from *V. vinifera* grapes found they preferred the taste to *V. labrusca.* In 1773 Thomas Jefferson planted *V. vinifera* at Monticello, but the delicate strain did not withstand the freezing winters, hot, humid summers, pests (moths, red spiders, beetles, and mites), and mildew, and Jefferson's endeavor failed. However, *V. vinifera* thrived in California, a temperate zone similar to the Mediterranean; after the gold rush of 1849 many of the gold miners stayed on to plant *V. vinifera* grapevines; by 1863 over 12 million *V. vinifera* vines had been planted in California.

In 1860 *V. labrusca* was sent to France for grafting experiments with *V. vinifera*. But in Europe disaster struck in the form of *Phylloxera vastatrix,* a burrowing parasite transported on the leaves of *V. labrusca* vines that injected the roots of *V. vinifera* with a substance that produced root galls. As phylloxera fed on the roots they cut off the vines' circulation, and within 30 years had decimated almost every *V. vinifera* root in Europe.

Jules-Emile Planchon, professor of pharmacy at Montpellier University in France, was the first to discover that phylloxera was a native insect of the east coast of North America. Although phylloxera also attacked the labrusca vines, the roots were fully or partially immune, and the aphids produced leaf galls rather than root galls. In a historic move, vintners grafted the tops of vinifera vines to the roots of labrusca vines and the plants thrived, a practice that continues today with few exceptions and produces hybrid wine.

In 1873, phylloxera struck again, only this time on the vineyards of Sonoma County, California. To control the disease, the tops of vinifera vines were grafted to the trunks of disease-resistant labrusca vines grown in the Midwest, notably Ohio, and replanted in California. By the turn of the century, the disease was under control. It resurfaced in the late 1980s and early 1990s and more than three-quarters of the vineyards in Napa Valley, California, were replanted.

Today, the pleasures of wine increase, as do new wine-producing areas, notably in South America and Australia. Wine is a digestive sipped and savored with meals, and served at celebratory occasions, throughout the world.

CHAPTER FORTY-SIX

# THE RUDIMENTS OF WINE

*Wine is one of the most civilized things in the world and one of the natural things of the world that has been brought to the greatest perfection, and it offers a greater range for enjoyment and appreciation than, possibly, any other purely sensory thing.*

*Ernest Hemingway,* Death in the Afternoon

Wine is made from fresh or dried grapes, a fermented drink produced from elements naturally inherent in grapes, namely, sugar, acid, and yeast. When a harmonious balance of sugar and acid is attained, namely an increase in sugar and a decrease in acid, the grapes are harvested, a time that depends on the region, the climate, and the customs of the area. In the Northern Hemisphere, the growing season is from spring to fall, and harvest normally takes place in September and October, a time when the sugar reaches a particular weight, a measurement known in the United States as *Brix,* in Germany as *Oechsle,* and in France as *baumé.* In general, 1 degree Brix equals 1 percent sugar. The higher the Brix, the greater the amount of sugar for conversion to alcohol.

Alcohol (ethanol), essential to the taste and the body of wine, is created by the fermentation of the sugar in the juice, a process started by unicellular yeast cells called *saccharomyces* that live on the skins of grapes as well as in the soil and the air of the vineyards. Saccharomyces are recognized by a powder called *bloom* on the skins of grapes. The spores of the fungi break open the skins, attack the pulp and excrete a chemical substance that produces enzymes that start the fermentation process, a biochemical reaction documented in the nineteenth century by Louis Pasteur, who called wine "the most healthful and hygienic of beverages."

Fermentation converts sugar into almost equal parts alcohol and carbon dioxide, which is released in the form of bubbles. When carbon dioxide is allowed to escape, the fermented juice is called *still wine* or *table wine.* If the gas is trapped in the bottle, it creates fizz, a characteristic of sparkling wine.

Wine continues to age in the bottle. It is a living thing that stimulates the appetite and aids the digestive process, and like all living things, it has color, smell, and taste.

## The Color of Wine

All grapes produce an almost colorless juice. It is the pigment in the skins of grapes that gives wine its characteristic color, a shade determined by the length of time the skins remain on the grapes before the juice is extracted. To assess the true color of wine, hold the glass by the stem against a white background under natural light.

Although white grapes are used primarily to make white wine, occasionally red, purple, or black grapes are used to make white wine. To halt the color, the skins, seeds, and stems of grapes are removed immediately and the fruit is pressed—a method that releases only the juice for fermentation. White wine is actually a pale hue that varies with age from soft yellow to deep gold. Young white wines range in tone from pale yellow to yellow with a hint of green, the latter a color derived from the chlorophyll in the skins at the time of harvest. Mature white wines are a deeper shade—straw yellow, amber yellow, and brownish yellow, the latter a color attributed to the exposure of wine to oxygen as it matures (just as cut fruit turns brown when subjected to air). Once a bottle of white wine is opened, it gains a little color.

Champagne is made primarily from white grapes that produce wine with a pale yellow color. But occasionally black and purple grapes are used.

Rosé is made from red or black grapes that vary in tone from red to blue black. The skins and solids remain on the grapes for a few hours, a process known in France as *cuvaison courte,* "short fermentation in the vat." Rosé wine ranges in color from soft purply pink to an orange pink.

Red wine is made from red, purple, or black grapes that are crushed. The pips and skins are left on for 3 to 8 days before removal. Some wine makers, such as in Beaujolais and the Rhône, leave the stems on. The longer the skin and pips remain on the grapes, the deeper the color, and the more tannin in the taste of the wine. Red wine varies in color from bright purplish red for young wines, to deep hues for mature wines—scarlet, ruby, and mahogany red. The darker color is attributed to the tannins present in wine as it ages. Tannins are phenolic compounds naturally present in the skin, pips, stems, and wooden casks. Ripe tannins are water soluble and mellow as wine ages. When red wine is exposed to air it loses a little color.

## The Smell of Wine

The perfume of wine is known as *aroma* and *bouquet,* terms often used synonymously. Technically aroma is the odor grapes produce naturally. Bouquet is the perfume wine exudes after fermentation and aging take place; it is released by swirling wine in small movements in the glass.

To pair wine with food, vintners use an official wine aroma wheel, a descriptor that identifies the bouquet of wine with nature: *fruity* indicates a bouquet and flavor similar to fruit, such as berries, but not sweet; *earthy* wine has a faint taste of minerals, such as chalk; *grassy* wine has the aroma and taste of cut grass or herbs; a *nutty* flavor has a bouquet similar to nuts, such as almonds.

To release the bouquet, a wine glass is filled half full; this creates an empty chamber in which to gently swirl the wine. The glass is brought to the nose, and the bouquet is inhaled in a series of shorts sniffs of approximately 4 to 5 seconds. When the bouquet is inhaled for longer periods, the intensity diminishes (but returns after a short time).

## The Taste of Wine

Taste and smell are closely aligned. The nasal passage is connected to the centers of taste on the tongue and to the nerves located in the brain behind the nasal passage.

Taste is enhanced when wine is rolled around in the mouth several times, a custom the French call "chewing the wine," a short process that lasts approximately 15 seconds. Longer, and the saliva dilutes the flavor of the wine and promotes a watery taste. The chewing process enables wine to coat all parts of the mouth and releases the four components of taste: sweet, acid, salt, and bitter, flavors highlighted on certain parts of the tongue. Sweet wine is savored on the tip of the tongue. Acidity, the crisp tart flavor, is tasted on the sides of the tongue. Salty flavors are discerned at the front and sides of the tongue. Bitter flavors are noticed on the top sides of the tongue and at the center of the back of the tongue.

Alcohol adds weight in the mouth and the higher the alcohol content, the greater the texture, or weight, of wine, an element that adds taste, such as the flavor of light-bodied chenin blanc compared to the taste of full-bodied cabernet sauvignon.

## Dry Wines and Sweet Wines

Grapes contain up to one-third of their volume in sugar. Fermentation consumes sugar, either partially or wholly, and converts it to alcohol. Dry wines have a low alcohol content, 7 to 14 percent, and sweet wines have a higher alcohol content. Dry wines and sweet wines are compatible with particular foods. When the alcohol reaches a certain level, fermentation ceases, and the remaining sugar is called *residual*. Dry wines, such as burgundy or dry champagne, contain less than 0.5 percent residual sugar and compliment foods served as the main course. Although sweet wines, such as port, muscatel, tokay, and sweet champagne, do not have an overtly sweet taste, they possess more residual sugar than dry wines, approximately 1 percent, and are complimentary to dessert.

> In victory you deserve champagne, in defeat you need it.
>
> Napoleon

# Sparkling Wine and Champagne Are Dry or Sweet

The difference between sparkling wine and champagne is the method of production. Although effervescence is produced in the second fermentation of each, the second fermentation of sparkling wine occurs in large pressurized vats, a process simpler than the champagne method and less costly. Often chemicals are added to speed the process. Sparkling wine produces bubbles that are larger than those of champagne, more explosive on the palate, but the fizz is of shorter duration than that of champagne. The second fermentation of champagne occurs in the bottle in which it is sold, a long, complex, labor-intensive, and costly method. The bubbles are finer than those of sparkling wine and the effervescence lasts for a longer period of time. To start the second fermentation, sugar and yeast are added to the bottle. When the fermentation is complete, the bottle is aged. After maturation, the bottle is riddled over a period of time, then upended in a diagonal position. The dead yeast cells settle into the neck and press against the cap of the bottle. The bottle neck is frozen, and when the cap is removed the pressure of the bubbles causes the sediment to disgorge. Before the bottle is corked and wired tight, sugar is added to adjust the sweetness. Dry champagne is served before a meal as an aperitif and with a meal as a digestive. Sweet champagne is complimentary to the taste of dessert.

The dryness or sweetness of French champagne is identified on the label as *extra-brut, brut, extra-sec, sec, demi-sec,* and *doux.*

- *Extra-brut* means "very raw," a natural champagne that contains no residual sugar. The taste is the driest of all champagne.
- *Brut* means "crude," a champagne with a little less than 1.5 percent residual sugar. The taste is very dry.
- *Extra-sec* means "extra dry," a misleading expression because the taste is slightly sweeter than *brut. Extra-sec* contains 1 percent to 2 percent residual sugar. Very little sugar is added in the second fermentation.
- *Sec* means "dry," and contains 2 percent to 4 percent residual sugar. Ap-

proximately ⅔ ounce of sugar is added to the second fermentation. Because the sugar content is higher than *brut* or *extra-sec, sec* is not as dry.

- *Demi-sec* means "half dry." The amount of residual sugar is about 4 percent to 6 percent, and approximately 1 ounce of sugar is added to the second fermentation. *Demi-sec* is sweeter than *brut, extra-sec,* or *sec.*
- *Doux* means "sweet." The wine contains approximately 8 percent to 12 percent residual sugar. About 1½ ounces of sugar are added to the second fermentation. *Doux* is the sweetest of French champagnes.

## Wine Categories

Wine is divided into three categories known as *fortified wine, table wine,* and *sparkling wine,* each with special characteristics that affect service.

### Fortified Wine

Fortified wine is served as an aperitif, a dessert wine, and an after-dinner wine. Yeast cells are paralyzed in wine with an alcohol content of 20 percent, and most do not survive above 17 to 18 percent. When the alcohol content of wine is higher than 19 percent, the fermentation is halted to preserve the sweetness and the wine is fortified with alcohol made from neutral spirits or brandy.

APERITIFS From the Middle Ages to the early Renaissance, the lord of the manor, his family, and honored guests gathered before dinner and ate plums and grapes "to open the stomach." Libations were served only during and after meals. Because aperitifs do not overload the taste buds with acid, today they are served before meals to start the flow of gastric juices and stimulate the appetite.

Some wines are both aperitif and table wine, such as dry white wine and dry champagne. Because hard liquor dulls the palate for wine served with a meal, to provide a continuum of taste from preprandial libation to table wine, white wine and champagne are also served as aperitifs.

Aperitifs are flavored with herbs, barks, resins, and flowers, and are also called *aromatized wines*. Some aperitifs have a bitter taste while others are sweet.

Bitter aperitifs, such as dry Vermouth, stimulate the palate with a sharp taste and were originally taken as medicine, perhaps the origin of the expression "bitter medicine." The taste contrasts with light salty foods, such as caviar, nuts, olives, and cheese, foods the French call *amuses-gueule,* meaning "to amuse the mouth." Sweet aperitifs, such as cream sherry, are taken late in the day when sweet foods are served, such as at afternoon tea.

Vermouth is made from red or white wine infused with herbs, notably artemisia, an aromatic plant. Cinzano is a sweet red vermouth from Italy, and Noilly-Prat is a dry white vermouth from France.

Anise is made from the seeds of the star anis, a licorice-flavored member of the carrot family, with pods similar in shape to a starfish. Anise-based aperitifs include Pernod and Ricard from France and Ouzo from Greece.

Bitters are a neutral spirit infused with aromatic plants and roots. Campari is one of the best known, a reddish-brown bitters from Italy.

Aperitifs are served at various temperatures: dry sherry is served at room temperature; champagne or dry white wine is served slightly chilled, Dubonnet can be taken on the rocks, Pernod is diluted with a little cold water, and Campari is served with a twist of lemon and a dash of soda water over ice.

**Dessert Wines** Sweet flavors kill the taste buds, and to promote satiety, sweet wine is served with dessert. At one time dessert wines were reserved for royalty and called *liquid gold* or *the sweet wines of winter*. Each year on the occasion of her birthday, Franz Joseph I, king of Hungary, sent Queen Victoria cases of Tokay in an amount multiplied by her age. At age 81, Queen Victoria received 81 cases—972 bottles of Tokay.

**After-Dinner Drinks** Liqueurs, cordials, brandy, and cognac are fortified wines served after dinner, notably to stimulate and aid digestion after a multi-course meal.

Although the terms *liqueur* and *cordial* are used synonymously, technically the drinks are different. *Liqueur* is a strong drink made with alcohol, sugar syrup, and aromatic plants or herbs that also add color, such as:

- *Amaretto di Saronno:* almond-apricot-flavored; amber color
- *Bénédictine:* made from twenty-seven herbs and spices; called a *proprietary*

*liqueur* because the recipe is secret; a brownish-yellow liqueur produced by the Benedictine monks

- *Cointreau:* orange-flavored; the color of clear water
- *Crème de Cacao:* cocoa-flavored and colored
- *Drambuie:* Scotch-based liqueur the color of amber and flavored with honey and herbal oils; name derived from the Gaelic expression *an dram buidheach,* meaning "a drink that satisfies"
- *Grand Marnier:* orange-flavored; pale amber color
- *Irish Cream:* a blend of whiskey, cream, and chocolate; the color of light chocolate
- *Kahlua and Tia Maria:* coffee-flavored and -colored

*Cordial* is a liqueur infused with fruit, herbs, berries, or other flavoring. Some examples:

- *Aquavit:* spiced with Kümmel, a liqueur made of caraway seeds, anise, and cumin
- *Chambord:* black raspberry–flavored
- *Crème de Menthe:* mint-flavored

*Brandy* is an anglicized derivation of *brandewijn,* a Dutch word for "burned wine," a term attributed to the sixteenth century, when warring factions prohibited Dutch merchants from shipping wine and brandy was concentrated for restoration with water. Brandy is also known as *aqua vitae* and *eau de vie,* Latin and French terms for "water of life."

Brandy is distilled from white grapes and is aged in oak barrels rather than in bottles. Because oxygen enters the wooden barrels through the pores, the distillate lost through evaporation is called *the angels' share.*

Although brandy and cognac are terms used synonymously, cognac is the "king of brandy," and not all brandy is cognac. *Cognac* is a blend of twice-distilled brandy made in Charente and Charente-Maritime, a delimited area surrounding the medieval walled town of Cognac that lies 240 miles southwest of Paris. Within the district of Charente lie seven geographical regions where seven grades of cognac are produced, in descending order of flavor: *grand champagne, petit champagne, borderies, fins bois, bons bois, bois ordinaires,* and *bois communs.*

When the term *fine champagne* appears on a cognac label it means the blend contains at least 50 percent *grand champagne* and the balance is *petit champagne. Bois,* a French word for "wood," designates cognac with an earthy flavor, a taste less delicate than *grand champagne* or *petit champagne.*

Cognac is aged in barrels made of oak, a hardwood that imbues cognac with a unique taste, a delightful aroma, and a soft amber color. Because oak barrels have a high level of porosity, it takes 7 liters of wine to make 1 liter of cognac, and the vapor released through the pores is estimated at 25,000 bottles a day, or more than 9 million bottles a year.

## *Table Wine*

Table wine is served with meals. It contains 7 to 14 percent alcohol, a nonfortified wine served with meals to assist the assimilation of nutrients, notably protein. A totally natural nutritious product, table wine is a source of vitamins A, B, and C, calcium, chlorine, cobalt, copper, iodine, iron, magnesium, manganese, phosphorous, potassium, sodium, sulfur, and zinc. Wine is a food, a fact noted by Dr. Oliver Wendell Holmes in his address to the Massachusetts Medical Society in 1860.

The acidity of table wine produces a tart taste in the mouth that promotes saliva, and it is served with meals as a digestive. Moreover, as the taste buds become overloaded with the flavors of food, the acidic quality of table wine cleanses the palate and prepares the taste buds for the next bite.

## *Sparkling Wine*

Sparkling wine is served as an aperitif, a table wine, and a dessert wine. When table wine undergoes a second fermentation, it develops carbon dioxide gas that produces bubbles and the wine is called *sparkling.* The most famous of these is champagne. Because the stomach immediately absorbs the bubbles and deposits alcohol into the bloodstream, sparkling wine accelerates circulation to the brain and is known as a *wine of wit,* a drink appropriate for special occasions.

Sparkling wines are both dry and sweet. Dry sparkling wine is served as an aperitif before dinner and as table wine to accompany a meal or a particular course. Sweet sparkling wine is reserved for dessert.

# How to Read the Labels of Wine and Liquor Bottles

The labels of wine bottles are a prolific source of information. They include brand name, geographic location, vintage year, the type of grape (varietal or generic), alcohol content, whether it is fined or unfined and filtered or unfiltered, as well as other miscellaneous information.

*Brand name.* The brand name is the title of the company that produced or marketed the wine. Although wine growers may sell their grapes to a wine producer, the producer may sell to another company for marketing.

*Geographic location.* A specific or a nonspecific region of growth is given on the label. For example, a specific location is "Sonoma County, California," and a nonspecific region is "California."

*Vintage.* "Good wine praises itself," says the Arab proverb. Wine harvested from grapes raised in a year blessed with excellent weather is known as a *vintage wine.* When the vintage year is included on the label, it means at least 95 percent of the grapes used to produce the wine were harvested in that year. When the vintage year is not indicated on the label, it means the wine is a blend of grapes grown in several different years.

*Varietal vs. generic.* A *varietal* is a wine made from several varieties of grapes, a term that signifies 51 to 75 percent of the wine in the bottle is made from the grape designated on the label, such as chardonnay or pinot noir. By law, California varietals must contain 75 percent of the wine stated on the label. *Generic* wine is made from several types of grapes that produce a particular kind of taste when combined, such as a flavor similar to burgundy, claret, chablis, Rhine wine, etc. *Jug wine* is usually a generic wine, a term attributed to a time before Prohibition when individuals brought their own jugs to wineries for filling. Restaurant house wines are often generic.

*Alcohol content.* Each category of wine has a different alcohol content.

- *Table wines* are made with an alcohol content of 7 to 14 percent. Legally, table wines are allowed a 1.4 to 1.5 percent variation in the amount of alcohol printed on the label.
- *Champagne* is 12 percent alcohol by volume.
- *Aperitifs* range from 15 percent to 17 or 20 percent, a figure increased by fortification with brandy or neutral spirits.
- *Dessert wine* is 17 to 24 percent alcohol by volume.
- *Liqueurs* and *cordials* are 20 to 40 percent alcohol by volume.
- *Brandy* and *cognac* are 40 percent alcohol by volume.

*Fined or unfined.* To enhance the color, flavor, and aroma of wine, additional elements are added, a process known as *fined,* from the Latin *finitus,* "to finish." The finishing process is strictly regulated. Only natural products are used: egg white, gelatin, isinglass (a semiwhite gelatinous substance from the bladders of freshwater fish, notably sturgeon), bentonite (powdered clay from volcanic ash), activated carbon (reduces loss of color), ascorbic acid (retards oxidation and flavor deterioration), and sulfur dioxide (sterilizes wine and halts fermentation by killing unwanted yeast). The elements clarify or coagulate undesirable particles and induce them to collect at the bottom of the bottle. Wine made without the addition of extraneous elements is *unfined.*

*Filtered or unfiltered wine.* Wine is *filtered* to remove bacteria and unwanted yeast cells; this process acts as a clarifier and a stabilizer. However, the less processing wine undergoes, the more character it possesses, and the term *unfiltered* indicates this attribute.

*Miscellaneous terms*

- *Proprietary wine.* Wine that is made by the grower, usually a blended wine.
- *Estate-bottled.* A name for wine produced from grapes grown by the vintner and bottled on the estate.
- *Bottled at the winery:* Wine bottled at the winery where it was made.
- *Bottled by the winery.* Wine bottled by the winery, but at a different location from where it was made.

- *Produced and bottled by.* At least 75 percent of the wine in the bottle was pressed or crushed, fermented, and bottled by the winery.
- *Made and bottled by.* At least 10 percent of the wine in the bottle was fermented at the winery.
- *Cellared or prepared and bottled by.* Most of the contents of the bottle are purchased elsewhere, but some of the cellar operations, such as blending, finishing, or aging, are performed by the bottler.
- *Selected and bottled by.* The winery buys and bottles the wine but does not perform cellar operations.

## Label Designations Indicating Quality

France, Germany, and Italy are the major wine-producing regions of Europe. To protect the consumer against fraud, these countries regulate the quality of wine and identify on the label specific regions of growth where the soil and climatic conditions produce grapes with a commonality of taste.

### *French Table Wine*

The quality of French wine is divided into classifications presented in order of descending quality.

- *Appellation d'origine contrôlée (AOC or AC).* AOC is the finest French wine made according to the strict requirements of the Institut National des Appellations d'Origine (INAO). AOC on a label assures the buyer that the grapes were grown in a defined area, under certain stipulations, with maximum harvest per acre; that strict production and storage methods were followed; and that the wine was officially tasted. AOC wine emphasizes quality versus quantity; the supply is limited, and this is why fine French wines are costly. AOC is classified according to growth or vineyard, identified by the word *cru. Grand cru,* literally, "great growth," is applied to the finest wines of

Burgundy, Bordeaux, Alsace, and Champagne. *Premier cru* is "first-quality growth," the next best after *grand cru*. *Deuxième cru* is "second-quality growth."

- *Vins délimités de qualité supérieure (VDQS)*. These are wines of high quality, produced within a delimited zone, made according to rules similar to the AOC, but not as strict. VDQS wine does not possess the great individuality or character of AOC wines, and only a small number of French wines carry this status.
- *Vins du pays (VDP)*. These are regional or country wines, better-quality wines made and consumed locally, that bear the name of the controlled appellation. For example, *vins du pays de Chablis*.
- *Vin de consommation courante (VCC)*. Everyday French table wine, also known as *vin de table* or *vin ordinaire*. VCC on a label usually denotes red wine produced in anonymous vineyards throughout Europe and North Africa. The vineyards are not specified on the label.

## *French Champagne and Sparkling Wine*

There are two designations for French effervescent wines:

- *Méthode champenoise*. French sparkling wine made in the controlled region of Champagne is known as *Méthode champenoise*. By international agreement, countries that make effervescent wine by the *méthode champenoise* must market the product under a different name, but may *advertise* it as "made by the *méthode champenoise*" process, such as Spumante in Italy, Sekt in Germany, and Cava in Spain. Because the United States government did not enter into the international agreement, American champagne made by this method bears the name *Méthode Champenoise*.
- *Vins mousseux*. A French term for "foamy, frothy wine," *vins mousseux* are sparkling wines produced in France outside the Champagne region, such as in the Loire Valley, by a method known as *méthode traditionelle*.

## *German Wine*

The labels of German wines designate the grape variety and the place of origin, for example, Riesling wine produced in the Rheingau. Because of the short grape-growing season in northern Europe, grapes are harvested before they attain a full level of sugar. German wines are classified by the degree of sugar in the juice at harvest: the more natural sugar the grapes contain, the higher the quality of the wine. Because fermentation converts sugar to alcohol, the low level of sugar in German grapes makes the wines lower in alcohol than French and Italian wines; traditionally, German wines contain about 6 to 10 percent alcohol. There are three main classifications for German wine, listed here in order of descending quality.

- *Qualitätswein mit Prädikat (QmP).* "Quality wine with special attributes" or "quality wine of distinction." *Qualitätswein* is made from late-harvest grapes with a particular juice weight, a naturally sweet wine tested and analyzed by the government for the proper degree of sugar. Qualitätswein is divided in five categories identified on the label from driest to sweetest as *Kabinett, Spätlese, Auslese, Beerenauslese,* and *Trockenbeerenauslese.*
- *Qualitätswein bestimmter Anbaugebiete (QbA).* "Quality wine of designated regions," such as wine from the Rheingau. This wine may be made with the addition of sugar before fermentation, a process known as *chaptalization,* a method that raises the alcohol level of finished wine, named for Jean-Antoine Chaptal, a brilliant French chemist who served under Napoleon I as minister of the interior. Chaptalization is used only in years that produce grapes low in sugar. The method is controlled by law and never used to increase the alcohol level of well-balanced wine.
- *Tafelwein.* "Table wine," a light wine of ordinary quality, of German origin or not. Usually *Tafelwein* is a blend of wines from vineyards whose names do not appear on the label, a wine that undergoes chaptalization in years that produce grapes low in sugar. By law, 75 percent of the grapes must come from the area given on the label. *Deutscher Tafelwein* indicates wine made from German grapes where chaptalization is permitted.

## *Italian Wine*

The labels of Italian wine identify the place of origin, the name of the grape, a historic place, and more. The same name may apply to red wine, white wine, sweet wine, or dry wine. To eliminate confusion, in 1963 the Italian government divided wine into three standards of control, listed below in order of descending quality.

- *Denominazione di origine controllata e garantita (DOCG).* Wine produced in a controlled denomination where the quality of the wine is guaranteed. DOCG wine is the highest-quality Italian wine, recognized by a red government seal, a mark that indicates specific standards of quality were met and the wine was produced in the designated place of origin.
- *Denominazione di origine controllata (DOC).* Wine produced in a controlled denomination under defined methods of production. The quality of DOC is not as good as DOCG and the yield is limited.
- *Denominazione Semplice (DS).* A plain, unpretentious wine, an ordinary wine for which there is no standard.

## Storage Temperatures and Storage Areas

Cold and hot temperatures threaten the taste of wine. Cold temperatures slow the rate of fermentation, and extremely cold air increases the astringency of red wines high in tannic acid. Rather than store wine in a cold place, such as the refrigerator, store wine in a *cool, dark place,* such as a cellar, a closet, or an unused cupboard. But don't store it on the top shelf of a tall cupboard in a kitchen, because heat rises. Wines stored in warmish air mature at a faster than satisfactory rate and do not keep long.

White wine, rosé, sparkling wine, and dessert wine lose flavor and bouquet when stored in a refrigerator, but the taste is enhanced when they are *chilled* in a referigerator for several hours. When sparkling wine is stored in a refrigerator for more than 5 days, the coldness slows the action of the bubbles. Wine is affected by changes in temperature, so don't store it in a drafty area, near a heating vent, or in an area where the temperature fluctuates, such as in a kitchen. Sudden changes in temperature accelerate aging, and a constant storage temperature is essential.

Authorities differ as to the ideal storage temperature. Some oenophiles suggest a constant storage temperature of 45 to 50°F (7 to 10°C); others advocate 45 to 60°F (7 to 15°C); still others say that the best temperature is 55 to 57°F, and no more than 59°F, or the ground temperature of the earth. In general, white wine, rosé, and sparkling wine are stored at cooler temperatures than red wines. However, when wine is stored in a house where the ambient temperature is 68 to 70°F (20 to 21°C), it keeps for several months without damage.

The humidity level for wine storage is a minimum 74 percent and a maximum 95 percent. To promote humidity, place a damp sponge on a saucer. Humidity above 95 percent encourages mold.

Store wine bottles horizontally. The position keeps the corks moist. They swell and prevent air and bacteria from entering the bottles.

Wine breathes in the bottle; vibrations such as those made by a refrigerator or a dryer travel through wine and promote an unpleasant taste. Repeated vibrations, such as those made by continual outdoor traffic, foster wine lees, dead yeast cells left after fermentation that rise in the bottle and promote a sour taste. To reduce vibrations, allow space between the storage of bottles.

Wine is susceptible to odors. To promote taste, keep storage areas free of odor-producing elements, such as paint, paint remover, garlic, and onions.

Sunshine or ultraviolet light foster wine with a musty or flat flavor; incandescent light is recommended in a storage area.

## *The Right Temperature to Serve Red Wine*

Red wine has substantial weight and the bouquet vaporizes at a higher temperature than light-bodied wines. To protect red wine against vaporization and loss of bouquet, it is served at a slightly cooler temperature than the average room, or around 65°F (18°C). The expression "room temperature" is attributed to the days before central heating when most rooms were a little warmer than a cellar. Today, the average room temperature is around 68 to 72°F (20 to 22°C). Because warmth reduces the astringent taste of tannin, to lower the sharp flavor of red wine high in tannin, to wit, a young red wine, serve it at a warmer temperature than an aged red wine low in tannin. Tannin is an antioxidant that aids wine in the aging process and produces a bitter, puckery, astringent taste, a substance derived from the skins, seeds, and stems of grapes and the wooden barrels in which red wine is aged.

To *chambrer* a red wine stored in a cool place, that is, to bring it to room temperature, set it out in the area of service, such as in the dining room, and let the temperature rise slowly. When a bottle of red wine feels warm, place it in the refrigerator for a short period of time, 30 minutes to 1 hour or until it feels cool. If a bottle of red wine is too cold, warm it in a bucket of tepid water for approximately 10 minutes.

## *The Right Temperature to Serve Light-colored Wines*

White wine, rosé, sparkling wine, and dessert wine contain less tannin than red wines. The bouquets are delicate and vaporize at a cooler temperature than red wines. Therefore, light-bodied wines are served *chilled*. In general, the sweeter the table wine, the colder it is served; this reduces the cloying taste. However, if chilled too long, light-colored wines lose their bouquet and taste.

Chill white wine, rosé, and dessert wine in a refrigerator for 30 minutes to 3 hours before service. Chill champagne or sparkling wine for approximately 1 hour.

If you are using an ice bucket, chill white wine, rosé, and dessert wine in a large container filled half with water and half with ice. Add a liberal dose of salt: water speeds the melting process of ice, and salt increases the rate of chill. When wine is placed in ice alone, it takes longer to chill, because ice by itself takes longer to melt. To promote an even chill, submerge a bottle up to the neck in water. To speed the rate of chill, gently twirl the bottle so the wine comes in contact with the cool sides of the bottle. White wine, rosé, and dessert wine chill in an ice bucket in approximately 10 to 15 minutes.

To chill champagne and sparkling wine in an ice bucket, fill the container with half water and half ice, but do not add salt; the mineral causes rapid chill, which causes the flavor to deteriorate. Champagne and sparkling wine chill in an ice bucket in approximately 30 to 45 minutes.

In a freezer, chill white wine, rosé, and dessert wine for approximately 5 to 10 minutes, and champagne 10 to 20 minutes or until the bottles are cool to the touch. Set a timer as a reminder to remove them!

# Guidelines for Pairing Wine with Food

*White meat, white wine; red meat, red wine.*

FRENCH PROVERB

The best way to pair wine with food is to trust one's palate and to serve what you like, regardless of custom. Wines that match well with certain foods do so because the tastes are similar. The flavor of white wine, rosé, and sparkling wine is compatible with delicate food, and red wine with rich hearty food. But exceptions do exist. For example, both red and white wine compliment the taste of lamb, pork, poultry, and veal, but when white wine is paired with a well-seasoned dish, such as veal scallopini, the strong flavor may overpower the wine, and a soft red wine, such as merlot, may offer more compatibility. Climate also plays an important role in the right pairing of wine with food. Although red wine is a good choice for red meat, on a hot night a chilled glass of white wine may offer more compatibility. When in doubt, seek the advice of a local wine merchant.

The following is a general guideline.

*Red wine.* The dry robust flavor of red wine cuts the rich flavor of food with a high-fat content, such as red meat, duck, or game. A tart astringent taste also compliments textured foods, such as cheese and pasta.

*Rosé.* The taste of rosé is fruity, a flavor neither dry nor sweet, with the fresh smell of grapes. Although rosé is served with red meat, it also compliments foods with a light flavor, such as chicken, ham, veal, salmon, vegetables, fruit, menus served at luncheon, and cold buffets.

*White wine.* The flavor of white wine ranges from dry to sweet. Dry white wine is high in acidity and compliments appetizers and light foods, such as fish, chicken, fowl, veal, eggs, and fruit. But exceptions do exist.

- *Highly seasoned dishes.* Foods heavily flavored with onions, garlic, curry, or chili powder, such as Thai, Chinese, Indian, and Mexican dishes, often taste better with a carbonated beverage, such as beer.
- *Green salad or antipasto.* The acidic quality of vinegary salad dressing competes with the acidic quality of white wine and promotes a bitter taste. For this reason, at a multicourse meal where several wines are served, white wine is not introduced with the salad or antipasto course.
- *Foods containing citric acid.* The acidic taste of white wine is overpowered by the flavor of acidic fruits, such as lemons and oranges.
- *Overly oily fish.* The acidic level of white wine is not compatible with the taste of overly oily fish, such as sardines, anchovies, or mackerel.
- *Ice cream.* The sweet flavor of dessert wine or liqueur is more complimentary to the taste of ice cream than white wine.
- *Chocolate.* Foods high in tannin, notably chocolate, do not pair well with white wine. The exception is sherry.

*Dessert wine.* The sweet flavor of dessert wines, such as Riesling, sauterne, and muscat, pairs nicely with sweet desserts, such as cake, fruit tarts, and berries. Moreover, port compliments the flavor of chocolate. Sweet wine and sweet food may counteract one another, but the tastes are enhanced when the wine is sweeter than the dessert. Furthermore, dessert wine is compatible with foods that offer a contrast of flavor and texture, such as service with crumbly blue-veined cheese, mild, crispy crackers, and salty, crunchy nuts.

## The Order of Wine Service

*The correct order of service of wine is to begin the meal with the most temperate and progress to the headiest and most fragrant.*

ANTHELME BRILLAT-SAVARIN,
EIGHTEENTH-CENTURY FRENCH GASTRONOME

At a simple meal one wine is served, chosen to compliment the main course. When two wines are served, sparkling wine is served before still wine; dry wine before sweet wine; light wine before heavy wine; young red wine before mature red wine; and ordinary wine before fine wine.

At a multicourse dinner the menu begins with a light course or two, proceeds to the heavier main course, and ends with lighter courses. To cleanse and refresh the palate between the service of assorted wines, water is provided throughout the meal. The following order of wine is suggested for a multicourse meal:

- *Appetizers:* Aperitifs, dry sherry, dry champagne, and dry white wine
- *Soup:* White burgundy, dry champagne, chablis, or sherry (when sherry is an ingredient in soup)
- *Fish:* Dry champagne or dry white wine, such as white burgundy, chablis, chardonnay, and sauvignon blanc
- *Fowl:* Dry champagne or dry white wine, such as alsatian, pinot blanc, semillon, sylvaner, and traminer
- *Game:* Dry red wine, such as barbera, burgundy, cabernet sauvignon, gamay, pinot noir, or zinfandel
- *Red meat:* Dry red wine, such as burgundy or claret, or those listed under "Game"
- *Salad:* no wine is served
- *Cheese:* Dessert wine, such as madeira, muscatel, tawny port, sweet sherry, or tokay
- *Dessert:* Sweet champagne, such as *doux,* or dessert wine, such as madeira, malaga, marsala, port, sauterne, and sweet sherry
- *Fruit:* Dessert wine
- *Coffee:* Liqueurs, cordials, brandy, and cognac
- *Chocolate:* Port or cream sherry

# *To Decant or Not to Decant*

*Now and then it is a joy to have one's table red with wine and roses.*

OSCAR WILDE, DE PROFUNDIS, 1905

The purpose of decanting wine is to separate wine from sediment, a method that entails pouring wine out of the bottle into a decanter. *Sediment* is a bitter-tasting but harmless result of the maturation of red wine, a substance that consists partially of tannin and is recognized by crusts of wine that sit in the bottle. When the fermentation of red wine takes place, the skins, seeds, and stems from the grapes remain with the juice for 12 to 36 hours and create sediment, and red wine never fully loses its sediment. Unless red wine is very old and heavy with sediment, approximately ¼ inch thick in the bottle, decanting is unnecessary.

White wine and rosé are made from unfermented grape juice that is pressed, and fermentation occurs without the skins, seeds, and stems; these wines seldom contain sediment and they are not decanted (except for informal service from a carafe). The exceptions are white burgundy or white bordeaux, which occasionally leave a fine deposit that may require decanting. Champagne and sparkling wine lose effervescence quickly and are never decanted.

Here are some general tips for decanting red wine.

- *Settle the sediment to the bottom.* Place the bottle in an upright position for several hours to one or two days.
- *Pour wine from the bottle slowly and evenly along the inside of the decanter.* When red wine is decanted vigorously, the motion creates aeration, which brings on a loss of flavor. Bubbles that arise in the decanting process indicate wine has been poured too fast, an action that also disturbs the sediment.
- *Hold a light behind the neck of the bottle.* To ascertain the level of sediment hold a match, flashlight, or electric light behind the neck of the bottle. The moment the sediment nears the neck of the bottle, cease to decant.

- *Leave a little wine in the bottom of a bottle of red wine or in the glass.* This method avoids sediment entirely.

Red wine is decanted differently for formal service and informal meals. The refinement of dining that came into importance in the eighteenth century included elegant decanters that were kept on a sideboard. When guests wished a glass of wine, they told the footman, who took the decanter from the sideboard and poured for them. However, by the nineteenth century, wine bottles were a decorative accoutrement placed on formal dinner tables. Today in formal dining, wine is poured at the table directly from the bottle. The butler holds the bottle in his hand and faces the label toward the guest so he or she may see the vintage. The bottle is returned to the kitchen, and a decanter is not used.

At an informal meal, from patio to posh, wine is decanted or not, according to the host's preference. At an elegant meal, the host may choose to decant wine into a crystal decanter and leave it on the table, knowing that good wine is evident by bouquet and taste alone. To ensure the cool temperature of wine, chill the decanter at the same time as the wine.

## The Aeration of Red Wine

Aeration allows wine to "breathe." This is accomplished by opening a bottle of red wine in advance of service, a custom that rids wine of musty odors, such as those from an unclean barrel. However, aeration is a matter of personal preference. Some oenophiles state the narrow neck of the wine bottle does not permit sufficient aeration; rather, it speeds evaporation, lessens the bouquet, and flattens the flavor. Moreover, they state, red wine breathes as it is poured into a glass.

The amount of time red wine needs for aeration depends on the age of the wine. Young red wines, usually those under 8 years old, are strong in tannic acid and require 1 to 2 hours to aerate. Mature red wines, generally those over 8 years old, are mellow and need to breathe for approximately 30 minutes, if at all. Very old red wines require no aeration.

Wines with delicate bouquets, such as white wine, rosé, champagne, and sparkling wines are not aerated and are opened just before service.

# How to Open a Bottle

## *Still Wine*

Still table wine is opened with a spiral corkscrew. The neck is the weakest part of a wine bottle.

- Grasp the neck of the bottle to support it.
- Remove the foil. Use the blade of the corkscrew to cut the foil about ¼ inch from the top. Otherwise, as wine pours over the foil the jagged edge will impart a metallic flavor.
- To remove mold or dust that may lie underneath the capsule, wipe the outside of the lip.
- Gently insert the corkscrew in the center of the cork, but not all the way through. Otherwise small particles of cork may fall into the bottle.
- To avoid crumbling the cork, use a slow turning motion and steadily ease it from the bottle.
- In the process of removal, the cork gently presses against the sides of the bottle and may leave a deposit on the inside of the neck. Before pouring the first glass, wipe the inside and outside of the lip to remove any traces of cork.
- Save the cork to reseal the bottle.
- If the cork breaks, push it into the bottle and hold it down with a skewer or any long metal object while pouring. Or filter the wine through a fresh piece of muslin.

## *Champagne or Sparkling Wine*

The insertion of the corkscrew in cork causes the cork to compress against the neck of the bottle. If this method is used to open a bottle of sparkling wine pressure is created that makes the wine explode from the bottle. Instead, open as follows:

- Remove the metal foil.
- Twist the metal loop attached to the wire muzzle to the left.
- Remove the muzzle.
- Grasp the bottle by the neck.

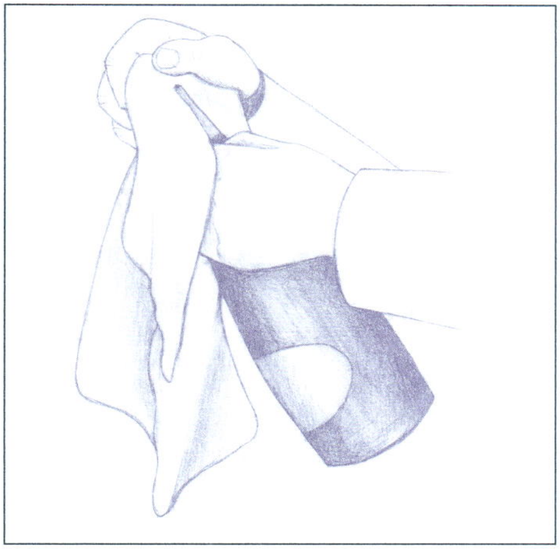

To absorb any wine that may emit from the bottle when the cork is removed, cover it with a napkin.

- To prevent the cork from shooting forth from pressure made by the bubbles, hold it in place with the thumb.
- Hold the bottle in one hand, and with the other hand turn and loosen the cork.
- To absorb any wine that may emit from the bottle when the cork is removed, cover it with a napkin.
- A tilted bottle of sparkling wine transfers pressure away from the cork and puts it against the side of the bottle. Hold the bottle at a 45-degree angle (pointed away from guests or breakable household artifacts, like antique porcelain, a window, a mirror, or a floral arrangement).

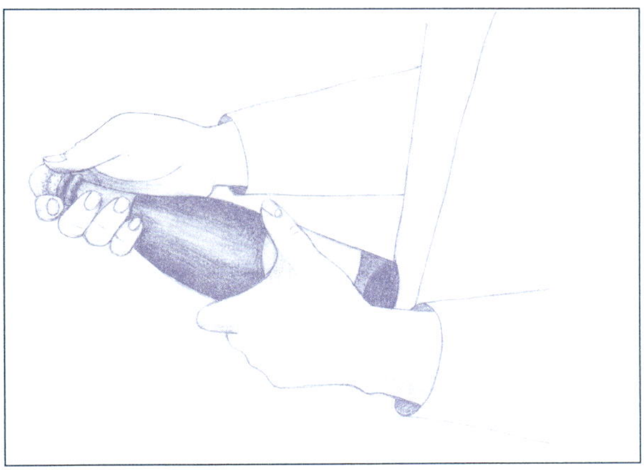

Push the cork upward with the thumb and gently ease it from the bottle.

- Push the cork upward with the thumb, and *gently* ease it from the bottle to prevent a loss of wine.
- The cork should expel with a soft sigh, rather than a loud bang.

## How to Hold and Pour a Bottle of Wine

Hold a bottle of table wine in the palm of the hand, label facing the guest, so he or she may see the vintage year. To insulate chill, wrap a napkin around the neck. To avoid spills, bring the bottle to the glass and twist the bottle over the glass to halt the drops.

Pour table wine down *the inside of a glass*. Wine with a greater alcohol content is less free flowing or more viscous than wine with a low alcohol content, a condition apparent by shapes called *tears* or *legs* that appear on the inside wall of the glass. Arches, or "cathedral windows," are a visible sign of the reduced viscosity of heavier wine made by a high level of alcohol or residual sugar.

To maintain effervescence, pour champagne soon after the bottle is opened, and in almost a trickle so as not to overly stimulate the bubbles. Pour a small amount of champagne into a glass, let the froth settle for a moment, then fill the glass approximately three-quarters full.

OXYGEN DECREASES THE FLAVOR OF WINE. TO INHIBIT AERATION, WINE IS POURED DOWN THE INSIDE WALL OF A GLASS.

To avoid spills at the table, the bottle is brought to the glass. To prevent overstimulation of bubbles, a small amount of sparkling wine is poured into the glass.

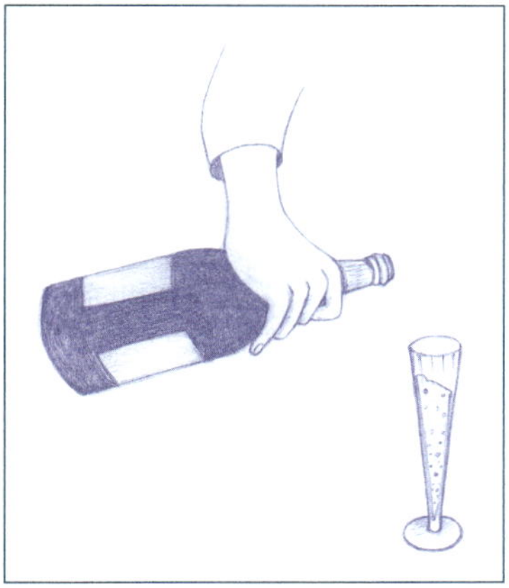

The froth is allowed to settle before the glass is filled.

## The Tradition of the Cork

Before cork was used to seal wine and halt evaporation, the necks of wine bottles were filled with oil-soaked rags, pegs of soft wood, or wax. To assure that a guest's glass was not contaminated with such materials, the first ounce of wine was poured into the host's glass. Although wine bottles today are sealed with cork, pouring the first ounce into the host's glass continues, a tradition known as *pouring the cork* or *corking the wine*. The custom prevents broken cork in the bottle from entering the guest's glass. Once all the guests are served, the host finishes filling his own glass. When cork appears in a glass, it is removed with a spoon or the tip of a knife, or a new glass is brought to the table.

Because a dry cork indicates air has entered the bottle, a condition that sours wine, the cork is pinched for moistness and laid next to the bottle so that guests may see it is wet. The exception is at a formal dinner, where the majordomo removes and pinches the cork in the kitchen and leaves it there. The wet end of the cork is smelled to determine the condition of the wine. Cork with a musty smell hints of spoiled wine. Cork with a vinegary smell suggests sour wine.

## How Much to Pour

Leave enough space in the glass to gently swirl the wine and release the bouquet. Although there is a slight difference in the amount of wine poured into a white wine glass and a red wine glass (approximately 1 ounce), the quantity is negligible. Sometimes it is easier to remember to fill a wine glass a little less than half full.

To capture the delicate bouquet of white wine and rosé, true oenophiles pour 3 ounces into the glass or fill the glass one-third full.

The bouquet of red wine is abundant and approximately 4 ounces are poured into the glass. Or, the glass is filled half full.

The effervescent quality of champagne and sparkling wine preclude swirling it in the glass, and the glass is filled three-quarters full, or around 4 ounces are poured.

Aromatic drinks have an abundant bouquet that do not require release and these glasses are filled two-thirds full or almost to the rim.

To create a chamber for the inhalation of brandy (and reduce the potent effect), only an ounce or two are poured. To enjoy the first "nose," the brandy snifter is held just below the nose in a still position, and the bouquet is inhaled. To appreciate the second "nose," the glass is held motionless, but is brought closer to the nose for inhalation. Thereafter the glass is slowly swirled to release the full bouquet.

# The Number of Servings per Bottle

*Every man hath his proper gift from God, one after this manner, and another after that. It is therefore with some misgiving that we determine how much others should eat and drink. Nevertheless, keeping in view the needs of weaker brethren, we believe that a hermina [approximately 8 ounces] of wine a day is sufficient for each. But those upon whom God bestows the gift of abstinence should know that they shall have a special reward.*

SAINT BENEDICT, RULES, 529 A.D.

In antiquity, aged wine turned sour and the Greeks served it diluted. A moderate serving was considered three glasses. With the development of corked bottles and horizontal binning in the eighteenth century, wine no longer turned sour rapidly but continued to age in the bottle. Today, a standard bottle of wine holds 750 mL, approximately six glasses, a size that enables two people to enjoy three glasses each.

The volume capacity of a bottle of table wine is designated in milliliters. A liter equals 33.8146 ounces, or a little more than 1 quart; a 750-mL bottle contains approximately 25.4 ounces.

Today vintners recognize that wine ages better in larger bottles than in smaller ones, and at festive occasions a magnum of table wine or a jeroboam of champagne is impressive. It also means there are fewer bottles to open. However, outsize bottles are heavy to hold and giant-size champagne bottles, such as the Methuselah, Salmanazar, Balthazar and Nebuchadnezzar, are made primarily for display. Here are the various sizes, based on a 750-mL bottle.

*Split:* a quarter-size bottle (2 glasses)
*Pint:* half a standard bottle (3 glasses)
*Standard*: a 750-mL bottle (6 glasses)
*Magnum:* two bottles (12 glasses)
*Jeroboam:* four champagne bottles (24 glasses)
*Rehoboam:* six champagne bottles (36 glasses)
*Methuselah:* eight champagne bottles (48 glasses)

*Salmanazar:* twelve champagne bottles (72 glasses)
*Balthazar:* sixteen champagne bottles (96 glasses)
*Nebuchadnezzar:* twenty champagne bottles (120 glasses)

When deciding the number of wine bottles to purchase for a party, buy more wine than is needed, and allow for slight overages: calculate on the basis of five glasses of wine per 750-mL bottle, rather than six. Before making your purchase, check with the liquor store to see if the unopened wine bottles are refundable. A good rule is to be generous but never pressing. Keep an extra bottle or two of white wine in the refrigerator and an unopened bottle of red wine on the sideboard.

The approximate number of servings per bottle of table wine depends on the capacity of the glass. But all glasses of the same type do not hold the same amount. American wine glasses are usually slightly larger than European glasses. To ascertain the number of wine bottles to purchase, remember that a glass is filled no more than half full, or 4 ounces. One bottle serves six people a 4-ounce drink; two bottles serves twelve people; three bottles serves eighteen people. Remember, allow for overages and have extra bottles handy.

The number of servings per bottle is determined by when the drink is taken. Aperitifs are served before meals when guests are thirsty; plan on five to six servings per bottle. When champagne is served as an aperitif, allow two glasses of champagne per person.

The amount of table wine is commensurate with the number of courses served with the meal and the length of time the guests are seated at the dinner table. At a multicourse meal, particularly a formal dinner where people sit at the table for hours and numerous wines are presented, normally one glass of white wine and two glasses of red wine are served. That is, a *minimum* of three glasses of wine is poured per person for a total of 12 ounces per guest. At a simple meal, people sit at the dinner table for approximately 30 to 45 minutes, and typically two glasses of wine are served per person, or a total of 8 ounces of wine per guest. At luncheon, one and a half glasses of wine suffice, or 4 to 6 ounces per person. When champagne is served as a table wine, three glasses a person is generous.

Because dessert wine is served at the end of the meal, one glass is sufficient. Based on a 3-ounce serving, a bottle of dessert wine holds approximately eight glasses. When champagne is served with dessert, one glass per guest is ample.

Following dessert and coffee, guests have little appetite or thirst, and a liqueur or cordial is offered in a small glass. Liqueur and cordial bottles hold approximately sixteen servings, a figure based on 1½ ounces per guest.

The average serving of brandy consists of an ounce or two. Generally one drink is served, and the average bottle of brandy holds around twelve servings based on a 2-ounce drink.

## Leftovers

Oxygen is the enemy of leftover table wine. When air penetrates table wine, the taste goes flat. To prevent loss of flavor, reduce the surface area exposed to air, and incorporate leftover wine of the same type in one bottle. Seal the bottle with one of the original corks. In France, bottles of leftover wine are filled with glass beads or marbles, a method that forces the wine to rise to the neck and eliminates oxygen.

Once a bottle of champagne is opened, some of the bubbles are lost. But when a piece of silver flatware is suspended in the neck of the bottle, such as a narrow-handled sauce ladle, leftover champagne retains enough fizz for several days of post-party pleasure. Why this works, no one knows. It simply does.

CHAPTER FORTY-SEVEN

# FROM TEA LEAVES TO TEACUPS

*You can taste and feel, but not describe, the exquisite state of repose produced by tea, that precious drink which drives away the five causes of sorrow.*

EMPEROR QIAN LONG (CH'IEN-LUNG)

THE HISTORY OF tea begins with the fables of China when Heaven and Earth were split. The world was ruled for 18,000 years by twelve emperors of Heaven. Then it was ruled for another 18,000 years by eleven emperors of Earth. For the next 45,000 years, China was controlled by nine emperors of mankind, followed by sixteen sovereigns, and finally three sovereigns: Fu Xi, Huang Ti, and Shen Nong. Tea was discoverd in the reign of Shen Nong in the twenty-eighth century B.C.

According to legend, Shen Nong was born of an earthly princess and a heavenly dragon. He was the first man to till the soil, and hence is known as the Divine Cultivator, the Divine Husbandman, and the Divine Healer. Shen Nong observed that healthy people drank boiled water, and one day as he boiled water over a fire made from a tea plant, a tea leaf accidentally fell into his cup and infused. After he drank the beverage, he felt so restored and energized that he wrote the *Shen Nong Ben Cao-jing,* the earliest materia medica in the world. In 2737 B.C. he wrote that tea

> grows in winter in the valleys by the streams and on the hills of Ichow, and does not perish in severe winter. It is gathered on the third day of the third

month and then dried. It quenches thirst. It lessens the desire for sleep. It gladdens and cheers the heart.

The first history of tea is attributed to the duke of Chou, a statesman who lived in the twelfth century B.C. But it was not until 350 A.D. that the historical information was set forth in the *Erh Ya,* a Chinese dictionary. In the fourth century, Kuo P'o identified green tea as a medicinal beverage, and by the fifth century, tea was an established medicine.

For easy transport and storage, tea leaves were dried and pressed into a "brick" form that was suspended from a rope strung through a hole pierced in the center. Tea leaves were broken from the brick and dropped into boiled water, a method of preparation that continues today. By the sixth and seventh centuries, tea bricks were a medium of exchange.

In the Tang dynasty (618–907 A.D.), tea was appreciated as much for its flavor as for its medicinal qualities, and to differentiate the beverage from drinks made of other plants, in Chinese calligraphy tea was assigned its own character. In 780, a group of tea merchants commissioned Lu Yü to write the *Cha Ching,* or *The Classic of Tea,* a three-volume work that chronicled the history of Chinese tea, the method of cultivation, and the preparation and service, a tome published still today.

Tea evolved as a social or spiritual art form in the Song dynasty (960–1280), a drink served by the cultured elite in a special tea room or teahouse, a select environment that fostered the *Ch'a Lu,* written in 1053 by Can Xiang (Tsan Hsiang), a Chinese calligrapher who mentions the preparation of green tea in powdered form. The *Ch'a Lu* was followed by the *Ta Kuan Ch'a Lun,* or *A General View of Tea,* written by Emperor Hui Tsung (r. 1101–1125), a book that described the preparation of powdered green tea with a special bamboo whisk, a utensil used to whip tea into froth.

By the Ming dynasty (1368–1644), tea leaves were infused in teapots. To enhance the color of the infusion, teacups were glazed with special colors, such as white-bodied porcelain cups to accent green tea, and brownish-black cups to compliment black tea.

In the eighth century, a group of Japanese Buddhist monks visited China and found tea so stimulating and helpful to meditation that they took home a few seeds. Initially, tea was a rare and valuable beverage only wealthy warlords and the aristocracy could afford to serve. Because tea was a scarce commodity, its use became ritualized. The first mention of a formal tea ceremony is credited to the eighth-century emperor Shomu, who held an *incha* (a religious ceremony in which tea is served to Buddha or an emperor) and invited a few monks to join him for tea prepared from a brick of tea leaves, a gift of Ganjin, a famous Chinese priest. By the early ninth century, Kukai, a monk, introduced the Japanese to the Chinese method of brewing tea from powdered green tea.

In the twelfth century, the Japanese priest Eisai Myo-an founded Zen Buddhism, which advocated truth through introspection and intuition. In 1187, Eisai went to China, and in 1191 he returned with seeds of the tea plant, which he cultivated at selected Buddhist temples. Eisai is thought to be the first Japanese to grow tea for purely religious purposes.

In the fifteenth century, Sen-no Rikyu, an Osaka merchant turned tea master, touted the Japanese tea ceremony as a mystical experience, one that fostered the four principles of Zen: harmony, purity, respect, and tranquillity. The Japanese tea ceremony, known as *Cha-no-yu,* meaning "hot water for tea," incorporated esthetics, etiquette, order, and tranquillity in a serene setting that encouraged meditation, kindled friendship between host and guests, and fostered spirituality.

But in the nineteenth century, the Japanese tea ceremony was associated with the customs of a feudal age, and masters of the tea ceremony began to lose status. The grand master of the Urasenke School of Tea saved the tradition, however. He propounded that the tea ceremony instilled obeisance, discipline, and order, qualities valuable for the success of a modern Japan. By the end of the nineteenth century, the Japanese tea ceremony was popular once again, and this led to establishment of tea schools. Today, the *Ch'a Lu* and the *Ta Kuan Ch'a Lun* form the basis of the modern tea ceremony in Japan.

The legendary discovery of tea in India is attributed to Bodhidharma, a revered Buddhist philosopher and priest, who in 520 traveled to China to teach the Zen sect of Buddhism. The emperor gave Bodhidharma sanctuary in a cave temple located in the mountains of Nanking, where according to legend he meditated for nine years facing the wall of the cave. But one day he dozed off accidentally during prayers, and when he awoke he was so distressed that to remind himself of his momentary weakness he cut off his eyelids and threw them on the ground. Magically, a tea plant took root, covered with leaves that banned the desire for sleep. Another tale relates that a frustrated Bodhidharma grabbed a handful of tea leaves, ate them, and lost the need to sleep.

Tea was introduced to Europe a little more than 300 years ago. It was imported from China along with other exotic spices and luxury products, such as silk and lacquer. In the sixteenth century, both Chinese and Indian tea were imported via land and sea routes controlled by Arab merchants. Eager to learn about Asian goods that might turn a profit, the Venetians hosted the Arabs at elaborate dinners. One evening as Giambattista Ramusio, secretary to the Venetian Council of Ten, dined with Hajji Mahommed, a Persian merchant, he learned about the curative powers of tea, and in 1559 he recorded the information in *Voyages and Travels*. This was the first European book to mention tea.

Portuguese missionaries and priests sent to China in the sixteenth century noted the taste of tea and the customs associated with the service. In 1560, Father Gasper da Cruz, the first Portuguese missionary to reach mainland China, wrote a letter that describes the taste of tea as "bitter, red, and medicinal." Father Matteo Ricci, a Jesuit priest who arrived in China in 1598, wrote about the preparation of tea and mentioned that the beverage promoted longevity and stimulated energy. Father Alvaro Samedo wrote about the social customs associated with tea, stating that the first cup honored the guest but that the third cup was a subtle suggestion to depart.

In 1607, the Dutch East India Company stimulated tea trade between Asia and Europe, commerce that included the transport of tea from Macao to Java. In 1610, the first cargo of Chinese tea was shipped by the Dutch East India Company from Java to Holland, and by midcentury transported from there to England. In England, tea was a controversial beverage, a drink touted in the seventeenth century by physicians as a cure for everything from anxiety to depression to intemperance, a beverage good for the eyes, stomach, spleen, and kidneys. However, those who disapproved of tea stated it was an addictive drug, one that promoted ill health, fostered feebleness, and undermined the British economy. Tea was outrageously expensive, costing more than $100 (£60) a pound by today's standards. The poor bought used tea leaves from the kitchens of the wealthy, and reused them until they were colorless, then ate the leaves on buttered bread sprinkled with sugar. And Jonathan Swift (in *Polite Conversations*) used his biting wit to poke fun at the miserliness of some hosts:

> Indeed, Madam, your ladyship is very sparing of your tea: I protest the last I took was no more than water bewitched.

The first public sale of tea took place in 1657 at Garway's Coffee House, London, whose owner, Thomas Garway, promoted it as a beverage that, "vanquisheth heavy dreams, easeth the Brain, and strengtheneth the Memory." He also touted it as a tonic for "Headache, Stone, Gravel, Dropsey, Scurvey, Sleepiness, Loss of Memory, Looseness or Gripping of the Guts." The Sultaness Coffee House also included tea on the menu, and advertised this in the 1658 *Mercurius Politicus:*

> That excellent and by all Physitians approved China drink, called by the Chineans Tscha, by other Nations Tay, aliea Tee, is sold at the Sultaness Head Cophee House in Sweetings Rents, by the Royal Exchange, London.

In the seventeenth century, English merchants competed with the Dutch for dominance of the tea trade, commerce assisted handsomely when Catherine of Braganza married Charles II of England in 1662, bringing in her dowry the port of Bombay and India's tea plantations. Soon the British established tea factories in Bengal and Madras, and to protect the monopoly enjoyed by the British East India Company, Parliament forbade the import of tea from the Dutch East India Company. In 1689 the British East India Company began to trade directly with China, a monopoly they held for more than 150 years.

The Golden Lyon was the first establishment to specialize in the sale of bulk tea by weight. The business was opened in 1717 by Thomas Twining and still operates today. In 1734, Twining's sold 13,114 pounds of tea, 5,137 pounds of coffee, and 2,897 pounds of chocolate.

The duty on British tea in the eighteenth and early nineteenth centuries ranged from 12½ percent to 200 percent. To support demand, between 1711 and 1810, an illegal tea industry arose. Dutch smugglers moored off the coasts of Cornwall, Dorset, Kent, and Hampshire transported tea across the channel from Holland. Tea was hidden in caves connected by underground passageways and distributed throughout England by pony cart.

The high duties prompted a second illegal industry, namely adulterated tea, one that wreaked havoc on the forests of England and the health of the population. Black tea was contaminated with "smouch," a product made from the leaves of ash trees steeped in copper water and sheep's dung. Green tea was diluted with buds from elder trees boiled in iron sulfate, sawdust, and sheep's dung.

To eliminate these illegal practices, the government repealed the tea duty in 1784 and ordered the British East India Company to import enough tea to satisfy demand without increasing the cost. However, there were those who still considered tea an addictive, intoxicating drink worthy of abstinence. Hence, the expression "teetotaller," a term attributed to Robert Turner who in 1833 urged those who drank tea not to be "tea drinkers totally."

In 1823, Major Robert Bruce, a British botanist on a trading expedition to India, noticed that wild tea plants thrived in the cooler high altitudes of Assam. This discovery led to the clearance of dense forests for tea planting in 1830 and established northeastern India and Ceylon (Sri Lanka) as major tea-producing regions.

By the eighteenth century, tea and coffee were household beverages that competed commercially for market share. Compared to coffee, which took time to roast, grind, and brew, tea was touted as faster to prepare, a beverage that required only boiled water and a few minutes to steep. To stimulate trade, the British East India Company advertised tea as a drink appropriate for both sexes to take in the outdoor setting of a tea garden that catered to families, as opposed to coffee taken indoors in the all-male coffeehouse. Soon tea gardens established in the country catered to families of all classes. In the evenings orchestras played, fireworks lit up the sky, and promenades were illuminated to encourage strolls through flower-covered arbors and romantic interludes. But the prolific use of tea in the home eventually lowered public attendance at tea gardens, and in 1850 the last one closed.

Tea leaves were a source of superstition. When boiled water was put into a teapot ahead of the leaves, it was an omen of bad luck. And teas leaves were never stirred widdershins (counterclockwise), for this forebode of a quarrel. Fortunes were told by a "tasseographer," or cup reader. As the drinker drank from the cup he or she pondered a question, leaving just enough tea in the cup to cover the leaves. Holding the teacup in the left hand, the tasseographer rotated it three times counterclockwise and poured the tea into a saucer. Next, the tasseographer rotated the cup counterclockwise three times more, ending with the cup handle pointed toward the enquirer. The reading began with the tea leaves located left of the handle. Leaves in the shape of a knife forewarned of divorce. A dot indicated money. A ball suggested the ability to overcome problems. A heart meant happiness, as did a butterfly. Two hearts implied marriage. A ladder indicated success or a promotion. And so on.

In 1618 a caravan of 300 camels carrying 600 pounds of Chinese tea embarked for Russia, an 11,000-mile journey across the Gobi Desert that took 16 months to complete. To lessen the load on the camels' backs, tea leaves were carried in cloth sacks rather than wooden chests. At night the sacks absorbed the smoke of the campfires, imbuing the leaves with a smoky taste Russians called *caravan tea.*

Russian tea was prepared from "tea essence," a dark, strong tea infused in a small teapot kept warm on the top of a *samovar,* a large metal urn with a spigot and a central tube that held charcoal for heating water. Tea essence was poured into a small glass and diluted with hot water drawn from the lower part of the samovar. As the flavor was bitter, tea was sipped through a sugar cube held between the teeth.

> There is a great deal of poetry and sentiment in a chest of tea.
>
> Ralph Waldo Emerson

The import of tea to the colonies seems to have begun with Peter Stuyvesant, the last Dutch governor of New Amsterdam (New York). In 1674, New Amsterdam became an English colony, and thereafter English customs were followed. However, the colonists were unsure how to prepare tea and often stewed the leaves for hours, producing a bitter brown drink, or ate the leaves on toast with salt.

In the eighteenth century, over 1 million pounds of tea were being exported to the colonies every year. In 1765, to help repay the cost of the French and Indian Wars (fought by the English on behalf of the colonies), King George III passed the Stamp Act, a heavy tax levied on the import of tea and other commodities, such as rum. Although Parliament rescinded the law a year later, through the Declaratory Act it reserved the right to establish taxes and laws for the colonies without their approval. The colonists deeply resented this and formed the Sons of Liberty to consider the appropriate response to the act.

A year later, in 1767, the British Parliament passed the Act of Trade and Revenue, which levied a duty on tea imported by the colonies. In defiance, the colonists refused to accept tea imported from England and smuggled in tea from Holland. Moreover, the colonists brewed "liberty tea" from herbs, roots, and leaves of local fruits, such as raspberry canes.

In 1773, Lord North, the British prime minister, passed the Tea Act, which authorized the British East India Company to export tea directly to the colonies but retained the government's right to charge 3 pence a pound. When Thomas Hutchinson, the governor of Massachusetts (a position appointed by the British government), refused to let English ships unload 18,000 pounds of tea until the colonists had paid the tax, the result was the Boston Tea Party: on the night of December 16, 1773, the Sons of Liberty, led by John Adams, Samuel Adams, and Paul Revere, dressed as Mohawk Indians, set upon 342 chests of tea with hatchets before dumping them into the sea. This was one of the events that led to the American Revolution. Coffee became the national drink of the colonies; after the revolution tea commerce resumed, but the drink was not as popular as before.

In the nineteenth century, American military officers and their wives hosted afternoon teas parties known as *kettledrums,* and served from a drum head rather than a tea table. Supposedly, the guests talked so fast and with such intensity that the din resembled the roar of a kettledrum. In 1897, the U.S. government passed a tea act that ensured uniform quality of imported tea, a measure still enforced today.

CHAPTER FORTY-EIGHT

# CHOOSING THE RIGHT TEA

*[Tea leaves] must crease like the leathern boot of Tartar horsemen, curl like the dewlap of a mightly bullock, unfold like mist rising out of a ravine, gleam like a lake touched by a zephyr, and be wet and soft like fine earth newly swept by rain.*

LU YÜ, CHA CHING, 780

NEXT TO WATER, tea is drunk more than any other beverage. It is made from the leaves of the *Camellia sinensis* plant, an evergreen tree with bright green leaves, partially serrated and slightly hairy, a botanical member of the Theaceae family. *C. sinensis* produces a tiny white flower, similar to a camellia. The size of the tea leaf varies in accordance with the variety of the plant but averages about the length of the small finger. The finest tea is made from the leaf bud and the next two leaves at the tip of the branch. Tea of medium quality is produced from the third and fourth leaves, and sometimes from the fifth leaf.

Tea plants grow in the wild to approximately 30 feet high, a height impractical for harvesting; commercially raised bushes are pruned to 3 or 4 feet. When the tea bush is 3 years old, it is "plucked," or picked. The harvest is called a *flush;* depending on the weather, tea plants flush three or more times a year. In Java and Sumatra, tea plants flush all year long and every 7 to 10 days the first four leaves at the tip of the branch are plucked.

The leading producers of tea are India, China, Indonesia, Sri Lanka, Kenya, Turkey, and Russia. The taste of the tea varies according to the soil, the climate, and the altitude. Generally, the higher the altitude, the cooler the climate, the slower the growth, the finer the taste. Tea is classified in two major groups: Assam and Chinese. Assam is raised in India, Tibet, and Burma at elevations of 3,000 to 7,000 feet. The cold climates restrict the speed of growth and produce tender leaves. In the cup, Assam infuses to a darker color than Chinese tea, and the taste is malty, deeper, and more pronounced. Chinese tea is grown on hilltops in semitropical climates; the warmer temperature and lower elevation produces delicately flavored tea that is lighter in the cup than Assam.

Tea contains enzymes, potassium, and magnesium, but the drink is enjoyed primarily for caffeine, tannin, and essential oils. Originally caffeine was called *theine,* a substance extracted in 1827 from the tea leaf. Today, the caffeine in the tea leaf and the coffee bean are recognized as one and the same, an alkaloid that stimulates the heart and nervous system, promotes blood circulation, increases energy, lifts the spirits, reduces stress, aids digestion, activates the kidneys, and promotes insomnia (for some). Although tea leaves contain more caffeine than coffee beans—approximately 2.5 to 4.5 percent caffeine in tea compared to 1 to 2 percent in coffee—a cup of brewed tea actually contains less caffeine than coffee because fewer tea leaves are used in the infusion.

Caffeine is found in most tea—black, oolong, and green—and increases with fermentation. Black tea is a fully fermented tea and contains the most caffeine. Oolong is a semifermented tea and possesses half the caffeine of black tea. Green tea is a nonfermented tea that contains one-quarter to one-third the caffeine of black tea.

The smaller the tea leaf, the stronger the extraction of caffeine. Tea bags filled with broken leaves, fannings (bits of tea), and dust (siftings) infuse faster and release twice the caffeine as whole-leaf tea. The shorter the infusion, the less caffeine per cup. In the first minute, three-quarters of the caffeine is extracted. In general, black tea infused for 3 minutes in 6 ounces of water produces 20 to 40 milligrams of caffeine, and when infused for 4 minutes produces 40 to 100 milligrams of caffeine.

Decaffeinated tea is made after the leaves are fermented and fired, a process that involves ethyl acetate, a component of ripe fruit that promotes a loss of taste. To compensate for the reduction in piquancy, decaffeinated tea is scented or flavor is added. After decaffeination is complete, the leaves retain approximately 3 percent of their original caffeine content.

Tannin gives black tea and oolong a brownish-red color and green tea a yellowish-green color. Tannin is an astringent, giving tea its puckery quality. It promotes body (the fullness of tea in the mouth), flavor (the bracing, invigorating taste), and aroma (natural or scented). Tannin is known technically as a polyphenol, an antioxidant said to reduce cell damage (that may lead to cancer) and increase the white blood cells that fight disease in the body. Because fermentation and roasting lower the polyphenol content of tea leaves, the antioxidants in green tea (an unfermented tea) are higher and more effective in reducing free radicals than those in black tea and oolong. Moreover, recent studies reveal that antioxidants, particularly those from green tea, may reduce blood cholesterol. Tannin absorbs cholesterol in the digestive tract and promotes the digestive juices. However, tea obstructs the body's absorption of iron from some foods, such as dairy products, eggs, vegetables, fruit, cereal, and nuts.

The glands of the tea leaf contain essential oils that undergo additional development in the fermentation process to promote taste, aroma, and digestion. Whole-leaf tea retains essential oils longer than broken-leaf tea, fannings, or dust.

Green tea leaves are fired, steamed, rolled, dried, and graded. After black tea and oolong are plucked, they are processed in steps known as *withering, rolling, fermentation, drying,* and *grading.* In the withering process, the tea leaves are spread on wicker trays to wilt for twenty-four hours, a period in which they partially lose moisture. To release the aroma, the leaves are crushed and bruised in a mechanical process known as rolling that destroys the membranes. Fermentation follows in a humid place and color develops. Drying eliminates residual water, and the leaves are fired or smoked, then dried, sifted, graded, selected, blended, packed, distributed, and sold.

Oolong is graded on an 18-point scale from standard quality to choice. Green tea is graded according to the age and style of the leaf when plucked, such as a bud and one leaf, a bud and two leaves, a bud and three leaves, or more. Black tea is graded in large and small sizes, as whole leaf, broken leaf, fannings, and dust. *Whole leaf* is the grade of tea that remains in the sieve after the leaves are sifted, a grade also called *leaf,* which is popular in Europe and South America but takes longer to infuse and release its flavor than broken leaf. Because of the faster infusion of slightly torn leaves, *broken-leaf tea* promotes a darker liquor and a stronger taste than whole leaf; it is used to fill tea bags and is popular in North America, Asia, and the Middle East.

Broken leaf is sorted and further graded in sizes known as *pekoe, fannings,* and *dust*. Pekoe refers to leaf size and has nothing to do with the flavor of tea or the color of the infusion. Pronounced "peck-o" rather than "peek-o," pekoe is derived from the Chinese word *pa-ko,* for "white hair," meaning the delicate white down that covers the lower part of the emerging tea leaf. Orange pekoe refers to the House of Orange and was a term Dutch traders used to denote long, thin, wiry tea leaves rolled lengthwise. Fannings are bits of tea leaves about the diameter of a pinhead that brew quickly with a dark-brown infusion, a size used primarily in tea bags made for industrial purposes. Dust denotes the siftings left over from broken-leaf tea, a grade also known as *fines*. Dust brews quickly, the flavor is strong, and the infusion is a dark-brown color. It is often used to serve a large group.

Various terms are used to describe different types of tea. *Blended tea* is a mix of different teas that create endless aromas, flavors, and colors. There may be as many as forty varieties in the mix, each type taken from a different estate and region; this method prevents the loss of one crop from affecting the final taste of the finished product. For an aromatic and healthful infusion, blended tea may contain flowers, fruit, seeds, nuts, and spices. *Specialty tea* is made from one kind of tea leaf produced in a particular region or country. Because the tea bears the name of the locale, the quality is excellent. *Instant tea* is powdered tea made from steeped and evaporated tea. *Nursery tea* is laced with generous amounts of milk and sugar and served to children. *Cream tea* is served with clotted cream, a thick, creamy yellow substance with a minimum fat content of 55 percent. Tea taken with clotted cream is associated with Devon and Cornwall in southwest England, a high-cholesterol treat served with scones and jam.

*Tea bags* are a twentieth-century innovation credited to Thomas Sullivan, a New York tea merchant, who, in 1908, sent samples of leaf tea to customers in small hand-sewn silk bags. Encouraged by the response, the merchant filled gauze bags with tea leaves and eventually enclosed tea in small bags made of paper.

## Black Tea

**Flavor** Black tea is rich, full-bodied, robust, and potent, with a sweet citric taste.

**Infusion Color** The color is dark brown with a slight reddish tint.

**Service Method** Black tea is taken plain or diluted with milk and sugar. Originally green tea was the preferred drink, taken initially as a medicinal brew without sugar. Eventually black tea gained in popularity, a strong-flavored brew that tasted better with the addition of milk and sugar. When milk is added, the tannin in the tea is fixed by the casein (protein) in the milk, and the tea loses its astringent taste. Because milk is a lighter consistency than cream, and does not curdle in hot water, milk mixes better with tea than cream.

Confusion exists over whether to add milk to the cup before or after tea is poured. In England, *warm* milk is put in the cup before tea is poured, a method that promotes a rich flavor and inhibits the discoloration of the cup by straight tea. Furthermore, warm milk tempers ceramic teacups (notably porcelain, which is naturally cold to the touch) and helps to inhibit cracks. Sugar is also added before the tea. But in the United States tea is poured before milk or sugar are added. In Asia, tea is taken neat, without milk or sugar.

In 1680, Madame de Sévigné, a noted French writer of the seventeenth century, wrote to a friend who was ailing and suggested she drink milk. She went on to state that should the temperature of cold milk mix unfavorably with the warm temperature of her friend's blood, she should add hot tea. In another letter Madame de Sévigné stated that Madame de la Sablière took tea with milk because she liked the taste. By the middle of the eighteenth century, taking tea with milk was an accepted custom in England as well as France.

### Black Breakfast Teas

- *Assam.* A strong full-bodied unblended tea from India, such as Bamonpookri, with a spicy, rich malt flavor; also ideal for service in the afternoon.
- *English breakfast tea.* A full-bodied blended tea made from small-leaf black tea grown primarily in Sri Lanka and India and, to a lesser degree, in China and Kenya.
- *Irish breakfast tea.* A robust blend of Assam and Ceylon tea, a taste and aroma more complex, more pungent, and stronger than English breakfast tea.

### Black Luncheon Teas

- *China black tea.* A mild-flavored tea that goes well with spicy foods, such as Thai.

- *Darjeeling.* An Indian word for "land of the thunderbolt," Darjeeling is the "champagne of black tea," a tea with a lovely bouquet and flavor sometimes likened to the muscat grape or honeyed fruit. However, the availability of Darjeeling is limited, and usually the tea is blended. The subtle complex taste goes well with spicy foods, such as curry and jambalaya, and also the light repast taken with afternoon tea.
- *Orange pekoe.* A high-grown black tea appropriate for lighter menus served midday, and the simple fare of afternoon tea.

#### Black Afternoon Teas

- *Coronation tea.* A blend of Indian and Ceylon tea, a mix made in 1953 to commemorate the coronation of Queen Elizabeth II. The flavor is full-bodied.
- *Earl Grey tea.* A blended tea named for the second Earl Grey, British prime minister under William IV (r. 1830–1837). In 1830, Earl Grey visited China and during the diplomatic mission one of his envoys saved the life of a mandarin. In appreciation, the Chinese official presented Earl Grey with a special blend of tea, along with the recipe. The tea is a mix of China black tea and Darjeeling flavored with oil of bergamot, an essential oil obtained from a pear-shaped citrus fruit indigenous to the Mediterranean. Earl Grey is the favorite scented tea of connoisseurs. It has a mild taste that compliments the repast served at afternoon tea and high tea.
- *Lapsang souchong.* Large-leaf black tea grown in the Lapsang district of Fujian Province. The tea leaves are fermented, grilled on hot metal plates, then placed on bamboo panels above burning pine logs, a process that promotes a smoky aroma and a flavor similar to cooked bacon. Lapsang souchong is complimentary to the light fare served at afternoon tea, the heavier repast of high tea, and the taste of salty and spicy foods.

#### Black Dinner Teas

- *Keemun.* Sometimes called the *burgundy of Chinese tea,* keemun is the finest black tea grown in China. The taste is rich, full-bodied, and strong, with smoky overtones, a flavor complimentary to Asian foods. The aroma is flowery, similar to roses or orchids. Hao Ya is the finest keemun.

- *Prince of Wales.* A blend of Chinese tea grown in Anhwei Province, made exclusively by Twinings, a taste complimentary to cheese and fruit.
- *Kenya.* High-grown tea from East Central Africa, on the Indian Ocean possesses a rich flowery aroma and brisk flavor, a taste compatible with poultry or game.

## Oolong

*Oolong* is a Chinese term for "black dragon." A blend of black and green teas, oolong was developed in the nineteenth century in Formosa (Taiwan). It possesses a less potent flavor than black tea but a taste stronger than green tea.

FLAVOR Oolong has a somewhat peachy taste.

INFUSION COLOR Its color is dark brown.

SERVICE METHOD Oolong is served black or with sugar. The exception is Jasmine tea, which is taken black or with lemon. Because oolong does not have a full-bodied flavor, milk is not added.

APPROPRIATE SERVICE TIME Oolong has a flowery scent and is not recommended as a breakfast tea. The following oolongs are appropriate for lunch, in the afternoon, or in the evening.

- *Formosa oolong.* A Taiwanese tea plant, formosa oolong is produced from April to December and usually yields five flushes. The second and third flushes are the best, processed from large-leaf and bud sets. Formosa oolong compliments the taste of spicy foods.
- *Jasmine.* A scented oolong perfumed with the petals of jasmine, a light taste appropriate in the afternoon or in the evening following dinner.
- *Russian caravan.* A blend of keemun tea from mainland China and oolong from Taiwan, Russian caravan is appropriate iced or served hot in the afternoon and evening.

# *Green Tea*

Rich in vitamin C, green tea is a natural antioxidant that aids digestion and compliments a multicourse meal, such as a Chinese dinner.

**Flavor** The tea is vegetable-like, with an astringent quality that ranges from bitter to sweet. Green tea is harmonious with Asian and sweet foods.

**Infusion Color** Green tea is pale yellowish green, never dark green.

**Service Method** Green tea is taken plain or with sugar or lemon. However, when lemon and sugar are added, sugar is added first. If lemon is added before sugar, the chemical reaction inhibits the rate at which the sugar crystals dissolve.

**Appropriate Service Time** Green tea compliments the sweeter, lighter fare served with afternoon tea. Gunpowder, gyokuro, and young hyson are among the finest green teas.

- *Gunpowder.* A name for green tea made from the smallest leaf at the tip of the stem, plucked while the white down is on the leaves. The young leaves are rolled by hand into small pellets that look like shot, that explode with flavor when infused, hence the name.
- *Gyokuro.* Green tea from Japan, and the finest available. Matcha uji, a type of gyokuro, is used in the Japanese tea ceremony. To reduce the chlorophyll in the leaves and decrease the tannin, gyokuro is raised in a garden covered for 3 weeks with black curtains or straw shades. The plant is carefully tended, and once a year in May, the tips of single buds are plucked by hand. The taste is smooth and sweet.
- *Young hyson.* Hyson or young hyson is made from trees that flourish in China. The yellow-green leaves are long and thick and promote a full-bodied taste, one more pungent than other green teas.

# *How to Prepare Tea*

*The way of tea is nothing but this; boil water, infuse tea and drink. That is all you need to know.*

SEN-NO RIKYU

A few simple steps make excellent tea.

*Draw cold fresh water from a tap.* Fresh cold water contains more oxygen than hot tap water or water previously boiled and is vital in capturing the flavor of tea. Bottled spring water is also an excellent source of fresh water, reportedly used by the Queen of England when she travels.

*Bring fresh cold water to a rolling boil.* Depending on the altitude, water boils at a temperature of approximately 212°F (100°C). By comparison, water taken "instantly hot" from a tap varies from 185 to 195°F (85 to 91°C). Be careful not to overboil the water: the longer water boils, the less oxygen it contains. Furthermore, do not allow boiled water to cool before infusion; otherwise, the water goes flat and cannot draw full flavor from the leaves.

Why not boil the water and the tea leaves together? Because tannin is insoluble in water, and when water is boiled with tea leaves, the tannic acid increases and makes the brew taste bitter.

*Preheat the teapot.* To sustain the temperature of boiled water when it is poured into the teapot, first fill the teapot with hot tap water and swish it around. Empty the water, take the teapot to the kettle, and fill it with boiling water.

*Pour boiling water over tea leaves.* The action causes the leaves to rise and open up for full infusion and promotes tea with optimum flavor and aroma.

*Just before serving, stir the leaves.* To distribute the essential oils evenly, balance the strength, and enhance the flavor and aroma of tea, just before serving stir the leaves. But before pouring tea into a cup, wait a few seconds for the leaves to settle to the bottom of the teapot.

*Pour tea through a strainer.* To keep tea leaves from entering the teacup, pour the brew through a strainer.

"Take some more tea," the March Hare said to Alice, very earnestly. "I've had nothing yet," Alice replied in an offended tone, "so I can't take more." "You mean you can't take less," said the Hatter: "It's very easy to take more than nothing."

Lewis Carroll, *Alice's Adventures in Wonderland,* 1865

How much tea should you use? A pound of tea produces approximately 200 cups of tea. To make a pot of tea from black tea or oolong, depending on strength, use one rounded or heaping teaspoon of tea per 6 ounces of water, plus one for the pot. To make a pot of green tea, use two rounded teaspoons of tea per cup, plus one for the pot. To brew tea from tea bags, use one bag per cup.

The strength of tea is determined by the time allotted for infusion. Twisted tea leaves take longer to infuse than flat leaves. Small leaves infuse quicker than coarse leaves. And tea is steeped by the clock and not by the color. In general, the best infusion time is between 3 and 5 minutes. Whole-leaf black tea steeps in 4 to 5 minutes; broken-leaf black tea steeps in 3 minutes; large-leaf oolong steeps in 7 minutes; green tea steeps in 1 to 3 minutes; and tea bags steep in 30 seconds. If after infusion the flavor of tea is too strong, dilute the strength with a little hot water. Here are some infusion tips.

- To keep a cup of tea hot during infusion, cover it with a saucer or a lid.
- To sustain the temperature of tea infused in a teapot, cover the teapot with a tea cozy.
- Discard tea leaves after infusion; otherwise, they release tannins that deliver a bitter taste. Moreover, used tea leaves produce little color.
- When tea leaves are infused in a perforated tea ball or a strainer, make sure the device is large enough to allow the leaves to swell and for the water to flow freely around them.
- Never steep a tea bag more than once. After infusion, a tea bag loses nine-

tenths of its flavor. The exception is oolong, a tea that produces a fine flavor after several infusions.

- To keep the strings and labels of tea bags from falling into the teapot, swirl and twist the strings into a single strand, and dangle the length over the outside of the pot.

## How to Make Iced Tea

Ice dilutes tea, so to compensate for diminished flavor, twice as much tea is used for iced tea as for hot tea. A good ratio is to use 1 quart of boiling water or cold tap water to 4 teaspoons of loose-leaf tea, or 8 to 10 tea bags per teapot.

To make iced tea from boiling water, pour water over the leaves, cover them, infuse the brew for 5 minutes, stir, strain, and pour the beverage into a glass filled with ice cubes or crushed ice. Glass expands and contracts when subjected to hot and cold temperatures. To defray the heat brew the tea in hot water away from the glass, and place a metal spoon inside the glass before filling it with cold tea. Because iced tea made from boiling water is usually bitter, more often the cold-water method is preferred.

Iced tea is made indoors or outdoors. To make iced tea indoors, take cold tap water and infuse the tea leaves or tea bags for 6 hours or overnight. To make iced tea outdoors, infuse tea leaves or tea bags in cold tap water for 4 or 5 hours or more. Tea made this way keeps several days in the refrigerator and never clouds.

## Tips for Storing Tea

Essential oils evaporate when exposed to light and heat and reduce the potential flavor and aroma of tea. To maximize taste, *store tea in a cool dark place* where the ambient temperature is under 85°F (29°C).

Tea leaves absorb moisture inherent in air and the flavor deteriorates. For optimum flavor, *store tea in a dry place* in a metal or ceramic container made with an airtight seal. Certain foods, like garlic and onions, herbs, and cooking odors invade the taste of tea. For best bouquet *store tea away from aromatic foods.*

Black tea and oolong store well for 18 to 24 months. Keemun stores well for a longer period, and the flavor improves with time. For maximum flavor do not store green tea longer than 6 months. Tea bags filled with fannings and dust turn stale fast. The exception is tea bags individually packaged in plastic or paper wrappers.

## Tips for Teapots

Ceramic teapots retain heat better than metal teapots, but the interiors of some ceramic teapots are porous and absorb tea oils that imbue subsequent cups of tea with flavor. For example, the famous stoneware teapots of Yixing have a characteristic taste and aroma somewhat like carnations after prolonged use. Moreover, teapots absorb the flavor of food. To enhance the taste, never use a ceramic teapot to serve anything other than tea. Although it is fun to serve clear soup from a teapot, be sure to use a teapot with a glazed interior because it is not porous. To foster the taste of specific teas, *reserve a separate pot for each type of tea*—one for black tea, one for oolong, and another for green tea.

Smooth, hard textures do not absorb the aroma of delicately scented teas, such as oolong and green tea. For optimum bouquet, *brew mildly scented tea in teapots made of glass, porcelain, or cast-iron enamel.*

To keep teapots fresh, *wash them separately* and *store unused teapots with the lids off.* But to avoid a musty smell caused by prolonged storage, place a sugar cube in the bottom of teapots that are seldom used.

CHAPTER FORTY-NINE

# FROM COFFEE BEANS TO AROMATIC BREW

THE LEGEND OF coffee begins in the sixth century with Khaldi, an Ethiopian goat herder on a plateau high above Lake Tana. Khaldi noticed that the goats danced and bleated joyously after eating the fruit of a particular evergreen tree. Curious, Khaldi ate the berries himself and found he was so stimulated, that he was able to watch over his herd all night without fatigue. One day as Khaldi was prancing with the goats, a priest named Chadely wandered by and asked the reason for the pastoral dance. Khaldi pointed to the particular evergreen tree and explained the miracle of the red fruit. Intrigued, Chadely ate the berries and found that he too was so energized that he stayed alert during his night-long prayers, and thereafter regarded the fruit as a gift from Mohammed. Whether Khaldi's story is fact or fiction, we do know that the cultivation of coffee occurred around 575 A.D. in Yemen, perhaps when the country was invaded by Ethiopia.

The myths that surround coffee continue in the thirteenth century with Sheik Hadji Omar, a Yemeni dervish, sage, and physician who introduced coffee to Mocha, the port city of Yemen. In 1258, Omar fell from favor, and for whatever reason the governor ordered him from the city. Starving and wandering aimlessly in the desert, Omar was guided by the ghost of a deceased holy master to the fruit of an evergreen tree ripe with crimson berries. Ravenous, Omar ate the berries and softened the seeds in water, then drank the bitter brew. Immediately Omar felt restored and stimulated. He spoke of the magical potion to passersby, who carried the news to the governor of Mocha. On hearing of the elixir's restorative powers, the governor welcomed Omar back to the city and ordered a monastery built for him. There Omar taught the monks how to prepare the heaven-sent brew.

Clearly coffee was a food before it was a beverage, one used by warriors of the Galla tribe, who mixed crushed coffee beans with animal fat, rolled them into bite-size balls, and ingested them to banish fatigue on long journeys. By 1000 A.D., coffee was brewed by "decoction" (from the Latin *decoctus,* "to cook"). A drink was made from unroasted coffee beans boiled with the hull. Around the twelfth century, boiled coffee was made from the fleshy outer covering of the coffee bean, a sweet beverage called *kisher* or *qishr*. A century later, coffee beans were roasted, ground into powder, and brewed to make a drink called *bounya,* from the Arabic word *bunnu* for "coffee bean."

In the Arabic world, decocted coffee was considered a medicinal beverage with religious significance. It was served in mosques to enhance the worshippers' concentration during lengthy prayers and to promote meditation. Dervishes, Sufi mystics who whirl as a means of achieving trancelike religious ecstasy, found that after a few cups of coffee they twirled faster and for longer periods of time.

In 1454, Sheik Gemaleddin Abou Muhammad Bensaid, the mufti of Aden and an expounder of religious law, approved coffee as an alternative to wine and alcohol, which was forbidden by the Koran. In 1511, the first coffeehouse opened in Mecca, a meeting place where men, comfortably seated on lush oriental rugs, could relax, socialize, listen to music, and discuss local topics over small cups of coffee. But in the same year after the coffeehouse had opened, Khair Beg, the governor of Mecca, banned coffeehouses on the premise that the stimulating and intoxicating brew violated the principles of the Koran, but when he realized that coffee provided an ample source of tax revenue, he repealed the ban. In Constantinople, coffeehouses were called *qahveh khaneh,* meaning "schools of wisdom" in Arabic. These were meeting places where men discussed art and literature.

"As with art, coffee is prepared, so one should drink it with art," says an Arab proverb. In the Middle Eastern home, the elaborate coffee ceremony rivaled the complexity of the Japanese tea ceremony. It was served with great ritual in a coffee hall called a *k'hawah,* a rug-covered area furnished with banquettes and floor cushions, a charcoal-burning fireplace, and copper pots. After exchanging greetings and imploring the blessings of Allah, with great ceremony the host roasted the coffee beans over an open fire, crushed them, prepared the brew in a small tin-lined copper pot made with a long handle, and drank the first cup to demonstrate that the beverage was not poisoned.

To control the trade, rulers would not allow coffee plants and coffee beans to leave the borders of Arabia, and until the fifteenth and sixteen centuries, coffee was barely known outside the Arabian peninsula. Although brewed coffee was sold in Arabia to foreigners, outsiders were not allowed to visit coffee plantations. Coffee is thought to have reached Asia via Muslims who returned from pilgrimages to the holy city of Mecca with a few beans in their pockets. About 1650 A.D., Baba Budan, a Muslim pilgrim, tied seven seeds around his waist and transported them to a cave-like home near Chikmagalgur in southern India. Today, most of the coffee raised in the mountainous region between Coorg and Mysore, Karnataka, a product known as *old Chick,* stems from the original beans cultivated by Baba Budan.

Coffee was brought to Europe in the sixteenth century by Venetian merchant traders. The drink was slow to receive approval in Italy. In the face of the rising power of the Ottoman Empire, Italian merchants and physicians feared the taste of coffee would incur a loss of revenue generated by wine sales and medical prescriptions. Coffee, they said, was the "bitter invention of Satan." But that perception changed when Pope Clement VII tasted the brew and declared:

> Why, this Satan's drink is so delicious that it would be a pity to let the infidels have exclusive use of it. We shall fool Satan by baptizing it, and making it a truly Christian beverage.

With papal endorsement, coffee became a social beverage, an item sold on street corners and in plazas by lemonade vendors who served it from paraphernalia carried on their backs. In 1729, Floriono Francesconi opened the celebrated Caffè Florian in the Piazza San Marco, Venice. In years to come such venerable patrons as Goethe, Dickens, and Proust would sip steaming cups of coffee in the cafe's frescoed rooms.

In an attempt to eliminate Christendom from Europe, Mohammed IV, sultan of Turkey, initiated a plan of aggression that led indirectly to the introduction of coffee to Vienna. In 1683 the city was occupied by Turkish troops. In a triumphant upset, the Viennese defeated the Turks, who left behind 500 sacks of green coffee beans. The Viennese, who knew nothing about coffee, were about to burn the beans when Franz George Kolschitzky (a hero of the Turkish-Viennese war who had once lived among the Turkish people) saved them from extinction. In an enterprising move, Kolschitzky sold the beans door-to-door, organized street vendors to hawk the brew, and in 1683 opened The Blue Bottle, the first Viennese coffeehouse. Moreover, Kolschitzky is the first European to filter coffee grounds through a strainer, to flavor coffee with cream and sweeteners, to serve coffee with *Krapfel* or *Krapfen,* a jam-filled pastry known today as a *jelly doughnut,* and also with *Kipfel,* a small roll made in a crescent shape, the symbol of Turkey.

In 1616, Dutch merchants transported coffee seeds from Mocha to Holland. By 1658, Dutch coffee was cultivated in Ceylon (Sri Lanka), and in 1697 on the island of Java. Hence, the names *java* for coffee and *mocha-java* for the famous coffee blend.

In 1706, Dutch merchants carried coffee seedlings from Batavia (Jakarta) to Amsterdam for cultivation in botanic gardens and freely distributed them to better-known conservatories throughout Europe, notably the Jardin des Plantes in Paris, the first greenhouse in Europe. In 1714, the burgomaster of Amsterdam presented a few of the coffee seedlings to Louis XIV, but the plants failed to take root, so to compensate a single, well-established 5-foot plant was sent to the king at Marly, where it thrived. In time, the Marly plant was transported back to the Jardin des Plantes. Today most of the millions of coffee trees in the Caribbean, as well as in Mexico and Central and South America, stem from that Dutch tree raised in Paris.

Gabriel Mathieu de Clieu, a 35-year-old captain in the French infantry was the first to recognize that the climate of Martinique was similar to that of Java, and probably suitable for coffee cultivation. One night in 1723, de Clieu, aided by a lady of the French court and a physician, snuck into the Jardin des Plantes and stole three seedlings for his Martinique estate. On the voyage, de Clieu enclosed the seedlings in a wooden glass-sided case, a container similar to a terrarium. But from the start, the trip was beset with adversities. Not only did de Clieu get into a scuffle with a Dutch agent at sea but the fight ended with a branch being torn from one of the plants. Moreover, the ship barely escaped capture by Tunisian pirates. And in a storm that almost destroyed the ship, the glass-sided enclosure broke and the plants were inundated with saltwater. Two of the seedlings died. To keep the third plant alive, de Clieu shared his daily ration of water with the plant.

In Martinique, de Clieu planted the seedling surrounded by thorn bushes for protection and hired armed guards to watch over it day and night. The plant took root and flourished. Three years later, 1726, the island's first crop of coffee was harvested. In appreciation, de Clieu shared 2 pounds of seeds with growers he felt would cultivate the plants with care. By the late eighteenth century over 18,000 coffee plants thrived on Martinique, all propagated from the original plant transported from Paris, a strain called *Bourbon* (named for a French colony in the Indian Ocean, now known as the island of Réunion). Today, millions of coffee trees in Guadeloupe, Haiti, Mexico, and Santo Domingo trace their origin to the single seedling planted by de Clieu.

The English taste for coffee is attributed to Conopios, a protégé of Cyril Lucaris, a religious patriarch of Constantinople, who in 1637 was strangled by a vizier of Sultan, Murad IV. In terror, Conopios fled to England where the archbishop of Laud granted him refuge at Balliol College, Oxford. Accustomed to his daily cup of coffee, Conopios arrived with a supply of coffee beans, a drink he shared with fellow students, who in time formed the Oxford Coffee Club, a forerunner of the Royal Society.

In 1652, Pasqua Rosée, the Greek servant of an English merchant, collaborated with Daniel Edwards to open the first coffeehouse in St. Michael's Alley, London, using beans imported from Smyrna (Izmir). Rosée was the first merchant to advertise coffee in England.

> The Vertue of the Coffee Drink First publiquely made and sold in England, by Pasqua Rosée . . . in St. Michael's Alley in Cornhill . . . at the Signe of his own Head.

Thereafter, the sign of a turbaned head became the widespread symbol of coffee, an emblem adopted by vendors and coffeehouses alike.

Coffee was considered a panacea for all manner of ills. Here is a list of its near-magical properties, from a 1657 *Publick Adviser*.

> Coffee closes the orifice of the Stomack, fortifies the Heat within, helpeth Digestion, quickneth the Spirits, maketh the Heart Lightsom, is good against Eye-sores, Coughs, or Colds, Rhumes, Consumptions, Head-ach, Dropsie, Gout, Scurvy, Kings Evil and many others.

In the seventeenth century, the all-male coffeehouse was so entrenched in British society that neglected housewives publicly protested, a complaint set forth in

1674 in *The Women's Petition Against Coffee.* In response to the complaint, in 1675 King Charles II issued an edict that banned coffeehouses. But 11 days later he repealed the ban.

Originally, coffeehouses were gathering places for commoners, but the establishments evolved as places where English gentlemen of rank could meet and temporarily forget social position. In the seventeenth century, coffeehouses were good sources of up-to-date information about shipping transactions and business, a place where freedom of speech was encouraged and gossip was deliciously savored.

*There is nothing done in all the world,*
*From monarch to the mouse,*
*But every day and night 'tis hurl'd,*
*Into the coffee house.*

NEWS FROM THE COFFEE HOUSE,
*A SEVENTEENTH-CENTURY NEWS SHEET*

By 1715, over 2,000 coffeehouses flourished in London, establishments called *penny universities,* where for the cost of a penny cup of coffee a person with little or no education or money might learn a great deal. For 2 pence, those who could read could buy a newspaper, a candle, and a bowl of coffee. Payment for coffee was collected in a brass-bound box inscribed with the words "to insure promptness"—hence the expression "tip," today a remuneration given in appreciation of service.

Attendance at coffeehouses was based on political persuasion, literary inclination, and commercial or professional interests. English barristers favored Tom's Coffee House in Devereaux Court. Marine underwriters and sea merchants attended Edward Lloyd's Coffee House, an establishment that spawned Lloyd's of London, the great insurance company. Garway's Coffee House was the meeting place preferred by stockbrokers of the Royal Exchange. And from a coffeehouse in 1706, Thomas Twining founded his tea company.

By the eighteenth century, coffeehouses served alcoholic drinks. However, the rowdy clientele and their inebriated conversations proved less than edifying, and the genteel, educated patron who had once conducted business from a coffeehouse sought the seclusion of private clubs as a place to transact commerce. Eventually, of course, the educated gentleman found that the most efficient place to transact business was from an office.

Coffee came to France via merchants from Marseilles who, in their travels around the Mediterranean, had developed a taste for Egyptian coffee. Initially, the sale of coffee was discouraged by French wine makers and physicians, who feared the brew would decrease their revenues from wine sales and medical prescriptions. But the protest was short-lived, and in 1671 the first French coffeehouse opened in Marseilles. Soon, coffee was a chic social beverage in Paris, a taste promoted by Suleiman Aga, the Turkish ambassador of Sultan Mohammed IV of the Sublime Porte (as Istanbul was then known), who in 1669 arrived to serve the court of Louis XIV. From an opulent palace, Suleiman Aga served coffee to those who attended his lavish, flamboyant parties. From a description by Isaac d'Israeli in *Curiosities of Literature:*

> On bended knee, the black slaves of the Ambassador, arrayed in the most gorgeous oriental costumes served the choicest Mocha coffee in tiny cups of egg-shell porcelain, hot, strong and fragrant, poured out in saucers of gold and silver, placed on embroidered silk doylies fringed with gold bullion, to the grand dames, who fluttered their fans with many grimaces, bending their piquant faces, be-rouged, be-powdered, and be-patched, over the new and steaming beverage.

Coffee was sold on street corners by Parisian vendors, trade that led to establishment of coffeehouses, and the French word *café.* In 1689, Francesco Procopio dei Coltelli, a lemonade vender from Palermo who garnered a French permit to sell spices, barley water, ices, and coffee, opened the Café de Procope, an establishment that operates still today. Located opposite the Théâtre Français, the Café de Procope has attracted luminaries in the fields of drama, art, and literature. Voltaire used to frequent the café, drinking forty cups of coffee mixed with chocolate a day. As a young officer Napoleon played chess at the café and offered his hat as collateral for his bill. By the late eighteenth century, French coffeehouses were political centers; in 1789, at the Café Foi, the orator and journalist Camille Desmoulins incited the crowd to storm the Bastille. This event marked the beginning of the French Revolution.

Germany was slow to accept coffee, and in an attempt to protect the flow of deutsche marks to foreign coffee merchants, in 1767 Frederick the Great proclaimed that all citizens should drink beer.

> It is disgusting to note the increase in the quantity of coffee used by my subjects and the amount of money that goes out of the country in consequence. Everybody is using coffee. If possible this must be prevented. My people must drink beer. His Majesty was brought up on beer, and so were his officers. Many battles have been fought and won by soldiers nourished on beer; and the King does not believe the coffee-drinking soldiers can be depended upon to endure hardships or to beat his enemies in case of the occurrence of another war.

The king declared coffee was a "devil drink" that made men sterile and women infertile. But in a gross contradiction, eventually Frederick the Great deemed coffee to be a drink appropriate for the aristocracy, but not for the poor. In the early nineteenth century, with the rise of a German middle class, coffee became a beverage for all classes, farmers, working class, and aristocracy alike. The German *Hausfrau* invited friends in for coffee, conversation, and perhaps a little gossip, a custom called a *Kaffeeklatsch,* from the German word *klatschen* meaning "to gossip."

Captain John Smith, who founded Jamestown in 1607, had knowledge of coffee from his earlier travels to Turkey. Pilgrims who traveled to the New World on the *Mayflower* brought wooden mortars and pestles, perhaps used to pulverize coffee beans. The Dutch, who wrote of coffee sweetened with sugar, honey, or cinnamon, are credited with introducing it to New Amsterdam. In 1683, William Penn, founder of Pennsylvania, noted the outrageous cost of coffee: 18 schillings, 8 pence, about $4.65 a pound.

Following the Boston Tea Party and the American Revolution, coffee became the national drink of the United States. Coffeehouses were modeled after English establishments and served as places where people met to discuss politics and events of the day. John Adams and Paul Revere met at the Green Dragon Coffee House. In the early days of the Revolution, Washington's headquarters were at the Merchants Coffee House in New York, the same establishment from which Alexander Hamilton founded the Bank of New York. The Declaration of Independence was read publicly for the first time at the Bunch of Grapes, a Boston coffeehouse.

Today coffeehouses are once again gathering places for friends, places to read a book or a periodical, discover a different taste, or simply relax over a stimulating cup of hot, aromatic brew.

CHAPTER FIFTY

# THE BASICS OF COFFEE

*The mistress of the house must always make sure that her coffee is excellent.*

ANTHELME BRILLAT-SAVARIN,
PHYSIOLOGIE DU GOÛT, 1825

TEA SOOTHES THE psyche and wine makes a fellow mellow, but coffee lifts the spirits, encourages wit, and aids in the digestion of food. The coffee plant is a member of the Rubiaceae family, a large tree with dark-green waxy leaves. The fruit bears a bean called *coava,* a name attributed perhaps to discovery of the plant in Kaffa, an Ethiopian province. *Qahwa,* Arabic for "coffee," or any nonalcoholic drink made from a plant, was known as the *wine of Islam*. The first cultivated coffee to reach Europe was called *mocha* (*al-mukha* in Arabic), after the port city in Yemen through which coffee was shipped.

The leading producers of coffee are Brazil, Colombia, Indonesia, the Ivory Coast, and Mexico. But the taste of coffee varies from country to country, a flavor affected by the soil, the elevation of the cultivation, and the climate. The ideal soil is a rocky blend of potash, nitrogen, and phosphoric acid, a mix obtained from decomposed volcanic rock, organic matter, and mold. The finest coffee is raised in elevations of 2,000 to 7,000 feet, and the higher the altitude, the more delicate the flavor and the sharper the acidity. The perfect weather is found near the equator, a semitropical climate with an average rainfall of 70 inches per year and a median daytime temperature of 70°F (21°C), one where the nights are no cooler than 50°F (10°C).

Five or six years must pass before the trees bear fruit. The ovule of the fruit is called a *berry* or a *cherry.* It is a deep crimson color when ripe and about the size and shape of a cranberry. Most berries produce a pair of flat-sided beans with an ovoid shape, but occasionally they may produce a single round bean, called a *peaberry,* a shape that roasts evenly and promotes coffee with superior taste.

The coffee bean is enveloped in a pulpy sticky mass of *mucilage* that surrounds a hard, thin, beige-colored membrane called a *parchment* and an inner skin, known as a *silverskin* or an *endocarp,* a delicate papery texture similar to an onion skin.

Although the coffee tree grows in the wild from 15 to 30 feet, to accommodate harvest the plant is pruned to about 13 feet. The tree bears ripe and unripe fruit simultaneously. When the tree is harvested too early, the beans do not develop a full mature taste, and if they are picked too late, the brew tends to have a tainted flavor. To complete the harvest, the pickers must return to the bushes up to four times a week, a labor-intensive and costly process.

Most of the world's coffee is produced from two species of plant, arabica and robusta. The finest coffee is produced from *C. arabica,* a name attributed to Linnaeus, a botanist who believed the plant came from Arabia (in fact, it was brought from East Africa to Arabia in the fifteenth century). Today, arabica is cultivated primarily in Arabia (in the Republic of Yemen), Brazil, Colombia, Ethiopia, India, Mexico and, to a lesser degree, in Asia and Kenya. The arabica bean is larger than the robusta bean and produces a light-bodied brew with greater flavor. However, it is more costly to grow and harvest because it thrives in mountainous terrain, unlike robusta, which is grown on level terrain below 2,000 feet. Moreover, arabica is more delicate than robusta and more susceptible to disease.

Robusta is a hardy strain grown primarily in West Africa. The species was discovered in 1898 in the Belgian Congo by Emil Laurent. Its genus and species name is *C. canephora,* but robusta is named for its resistance to disease. It produces full-bodied coffee with a greater caffeine content than arabica and a more bitter taste. The bean is used as a filler in blends of instant coffee and to make commercial coffee.

## Processing Method

The way coffee beans are processed affects taste and cost. Coffee is processed by wet or dry methods; in some regions, such as Sumatra, both techniques are used.

Arabica is processed by the *wet method,* a labor-intensive, costly process that is used in countries with ample moisture, for example, Costa Rica, Guatemala, Venezuela, Mexico, Kenya, and Hawaii. Fully ripe cherries are handpicked. The coffee beans are put into a tank of running water, a bath called a *sluice*. The inferior cherries, such as overripe or shriveled beans, float to the top along with the stems and leaves. The quality cherries sink to the bottom, and are sent to a pulping house where the gummy mucilage is removed by machine. The beans are fermented and dried. The parchment skin and silverskin are removed by a milling machine that blows off the skins as the beans come out of the tank. Next, they go to a separator machine that removes residual matter, such as sand, dust, and small or broken beans. The beans are then sorted until only the largest and best remain.

Robusta is processed by the *dry method.* This is the oldest and least expensive way to treat coffee; the technique is used in countries where the climate is dry and water is scarce, such as Yemen and Ethiopia. The beans are sun-dried on the tree and shaken onto cloths spread on the ground. As a result, they are exposed to the elements and the brew has an earthy flavor. The beans may also be spread in thin layers on boards and left to dry "in the husk" for 2 to 3 weeks, raked several times a day for even drying, and covered at night for protection against moisture. The beans are put in a tank where fermentation occurs without water, and the fruit is loosened from the beans. The parchment skin and silverskin are scraped off in a milling machine. The beans are then graded and shipped to roasters. The dry method promotes brew with a rich, earthy flavor, high acidity, and medium body, such as mocha from Yemen and harrar from Ethiopia.

## Color

In a natural state, coffee beans are devoid of smell and pale green, the color of hay or straw tinged with green. In the roasting process, the sugars in the coffee beans caramelize and turn brown. Short roasts produce light-brown coffee beans with high acidity and a tart taste. Long roasts result in low-acid dark-brown coffee beans with a somewhat sweeter taste.

The length of the roast influences the caffeine content. Light to medium roasts contain more caffeine than dark roasts and are served as *a stimulant during the day,* at breakfast or lunch. Such roasts are identified by non-European names, such as *cinnamon roast* and *American roast.* Dark roasts contain less caffeine and are taken as *a digestive following a heavy meal.* These roasts have European names, such as *Viennese roast* and *French roast.*

Coffee beans contain essential oils that constitute approximately 15 percent of the beans. In the roasting process, heat draws moisture from the beans and the oils rise to the surface. It is the oils that provide the aroma and most of the complex flavor in our favorite cuppa. Because light roasts undergo a short roasting period, the oils do not rise to the surface and the beans have a dry appearance. Dark roasts undergo a longer roasting period and the surface is oily. Moreover, different roasts are blended to create unique tastes, such as Viennese, a blend of two parts medium roast and one part dark roast, or European, a blend of two-thirds dark roast and one-third medium roast.

The names of roasts vary according to the region and the roaster. To eliminate confusion regarding the appropriate roast to serve at a particular hour of the day, five roasts are presented here by color.

- *Light roast.* A pale-brown color similar to cinnamon, a roast known in the United States as *cinnamon roast, New England roast, half city roast,* and *institutional roast.* Light roast has a tart taste with an astringent grainlike flavor and an almost sour acidity, a roast used often in blends. Because the caffeine content is high and the body is light, light roast is served as a stimulating beverage at breakfast.
- *Medium-brown roast.* A golden brown color similar to caramel, medium-brown roast is also known as *American roast, brown roast, medium roast, medium-high roast, regular roast,* and *city roast.* Medium-brown roast has a faint hint of sweetness , a well-balanced acidity, and a caffeine level appropriate as a stimulant at breakfast.
- *Medium-dark roast.* A shade similar to milk chocolate, medium-dark roast is also known as *full city roast* and *high roast.* The flavor is a little sweeter and

the acidity and caffeine content are a bit lower than medium-brown roast. Medium-dark roast is a good all-purpose coffee to serve at breakfast or lunch.

- *Dark-brown roast.* A color similar to semisweet chocolate, dark-brown roast is also known as *continental roast, European roast, French roast,* and *Viennese roast.* The flavor is robust with a pronounced tang, a taste between sweetness and sharpness, with bittersweet overtones. The acidity and caffeine content are lower than light roast, medium roast, and medium-dark roast. Dark-brown roast is served as a digestive after a heavy meal, such as dinner.
- *Brownish-black roast.* A color similar to bittersweet chocolate and the darkest of all roasts, brownish-black roast is also known as *dark French roast, espresso roast, heavy roast, Italian roast, New Orleans roast, Spanish roast,* and *Turkish roast.* The flavor varies from sharp to bittersweet to almost burnt, a result of a long period of carmelization. The acidity and caffeine content are the lowest of all roasts, and the flavor is the strongest. Brownish-black roast is served as a heavy-bodied brew that stimulates digestion in the late evening hours.

## The Right Coffee Grind

The coffee filter is made with fine pores or large perforations, devices that determine the choice of coffee grind. Filters lined with paper or cloth, or made of fine mesh are designed to trap colloids (insoluble coffee solids), eliminate sediment in the cup, promote coffee with clarity, and produce a light-bodied brew. Metal strainers punctured with large perforations are made to filter coarse grinds. The large holes allow insoluble solids to pass through; this leaves a little sediment in the cup, which promotes heavy-bodied brew with a pronounced taste.

Coffee grinds are extrafine, fine, medium, and coarse.

- *Extrafine-grind* "pulverized" coffee has a consistency similar to powder; it is too fine to filter and is used to boil unfiltered coffee in an open saucepan, such as a Turkish *ibrik.*

- *Fine-grind* "drip" coffee has a consistency similar to table salt; it is used in drip coffee makers, vacuum coffee makers, and espresso machines.
- *Medium-grind* "all-purpose" coffee is the consistency of sugar granules and is also used in drip coffee makers.
- *Coarse-grind* "regular" coffee is the consistency of cornmeal. It is used with a plunger pot or percolator.

## Brew Time

The brew time for each grind is different. In general, the finer the grind, the more surface area is exposed to water and the faster the essential oils are extracted. Extrafine grind brews in approximately 1 minute in an *ibrik*. Fine grind brews in about 30 to 40 seconds in an espresso machine, and around 2 to 4 minutes steeped in a pan. Medium grind brews in approximately 4 to 6 minutes in a drip coffee maker. Coarse grind, a grind that exposes less surface area to water, takes longer for extraction of essential oils and brews in about 6 to 8 minutes in a plunger pot or a percolator.

## Aroma, Acidity, Flavor, and Body

- *Aroma.* "No coffee can be good in the mouth that does not first send a sweet offering of odor to the nostrils," said Henry Ward Beecher. This "sweet offering" is the aroma that is produced when coffee grounds come in contact with water. Before the water is added, coffee grounds exude a certain bouquet. Although technically the words *aroma* and *bouquet* are not interchangeable, they are often used synonymously. Aromas vary according to the bean; some are fruity, flowery, or spicy, and some coffees have more aroma than others.
- *Acidity.* Green coffee beans have about 7 percent chlorogenic acid, an acid that produces an astringent taste. To promote a palatable flavor, the beans are roasted. Roasting breaks down the raw components in the beans and causes chemical changes to occur, a process called *pyrolysis.* The chlorogenic acid disappears, and new acids with more flavorful tastes develop.

Acidity is the rich, tart taste in the mouth, a characteristic also called *winyness*. This flavor is affected by the elevation of the cultivation. Arabica raised in mountainous terrain is more acidic than robusta, which is cultivated at lower levels. Light roasts are more acidic than dark roasts.

- *Flavor*. A combination of taste, aroma, and acidity.
- *Body*. Coffee beans are naturally high in starch and sugar. When coffee beans are roasted for a long time, the sugar in the beans carmelizes and gives the beverage "body," or weight in the mouth. Professional tasters look for body that surrounds the mouth completely, a rich flavor that lingers on the back of the tongue a few seconds after it is swallowed. Dark-roasted coffees have more body than light roasts. Because light roasts undergo a short roasting period, the sugar in the beans does not carmelize and the brew is light-bodied.

## The Finest Coffees

The name of a coffee is determined by many factors: the elevation of cultivation, the country of cultivation, the region of growth, or the port of export. The following coffees are acknowledged as exceptional.

- *Jamaican Blue Mountain*. A well-balanced brew raised above 3,000 feet. Jamaican Blue Mountain coffee possesses a lovely aroma, high acidity, rich flavor, and light body.
- *Kona*. Coffee with a lovely aroma, mild acidity, spicy yet mellow sweet taste, and light body. Kona is raised on the west side of the big island of Hawaii in the volcanic soil of the Mauna Loa volcano; it is the only coffee grown in the United States.
- *Mandheling*. A district on the west coast of Sumatra in the Malay archipelago. Mandheling is noted for beans processed by both wet and dry methods. The coffee has a rich aroma, low acidity, spicy flavor, and heavy body; it possesses an almost syrupy consistency, a hallmark of Indonesian coffee.
- *Antigua*. A district an hour or more west of Guatemala City, Guatemala. Coffee beans grown in Antigua are cultivated on volcanic slopes, terrain

that produces coffee with a distinct aroma, spicy acidity, smoky or chocolatey flavor, and heavy body with a slight bluish cast.

- *Maracaibo.* A district of Venezuela located at the northern tip of South America on the Caribbean side. Maracaibo coffee has a delicate aroma, low acidity, sweet winy flavor, and a medium body.
- *Kenya AA*. Capitalized letters are used to grade the size of coffee beans, designations that vary from country to country. In Africa, *AA* denotes coffee made from the finest and largest beans; it is followed by *A* and then *B*. Kenya AA is high-grown coffee raised at the foot of Mount Kenya on plateaus about 5,000 feet elevation. The brew has a tantalizing aroma, high acidity, a smooth winy taste, and full body.

## Caf, Decaf—What's the Difference?

*Caffeine* is a tiny, white, bitter-tasting crystal found mainly in coffee in the bean, although small quantities exist in the flowers, leaves, stems, and gummy pulp that surround the cherry. Caffeine is a xanthine, a mood-altering chemical compound that dilates the blood vessels, accelerates the heart beat, eliminates mental and muscular fatigue, stimulates digestion, fosters insomnia, acts as a diuretic, and promotes mental acuity.

> If you want to improve your understanding drink coffee.
>
> Sydney Smith, 1771–1845

Pound for pound, tea actually contains more caffeine than coffee, but less tea than coffee is used to brew a cup. The average cup of tea contains less caffeine than a cup of coffee, roughly 40 to 100 milligrams in a 6-ounce cup of black tea compared to 100 milligrams in a 6-ounce cup of coffee. Arabica contains 1.1 percent caffeine, while robusta has a caffeine content of 2.2 percent. Instant coffee contains less caffeine than regular coffee, approximately 70 milligrams in a 6-ounce cup.

*Instant coffee* is a powdered substance invented in Guatemala by an Englishman who noticed the coffee in his coffeepot left a fine condensation of powder on the end of the spout. Powdered coffee was first marketed in 1909 as a convenience food. The beans are roasted, ground, percolated in huge filtered urns, and rapidly dehydrated. Although dehydration reduces the taste and aroma of coffee, instant coffee offers instant solubility and the measurement can easily be adjusted.

*Decaffeination* removes 97 to 99.9 percent of the caffeine from coffee. Depending on the measurement, one cup of decaf contains 1 to 5 milligrams of caffeine. Decaffeination involves up to twenty-four labor-intensive steps, a procedure that is reflected in decaf's higher cost.

Coffee beans are decaffeinated by the water process or the solvent method. In the *water process,* also known as the *European* or *traditional method,* unroasted coffee beans are steamed and soaked in hot-water vats to soften them and bring the caffeine and soluble solids to the surface. The solution is drained into another tank and the caffeine is removed. The liquid containing the soluble solids is returned to the beans for absorption. The Swiss water process takes the method a step further: the coffee is percolated through a bed of activated charcoal, a technique similar to water purification. Because chemicals are not used in the water process, some afficianados believe the method is the most healthful way to decaffeinate coffee. Others feel the water process removes too many oils and soluble components and produces coffee with less taste than the solvent method.

The *solvent method* incorporates methylene chloride and ethyl acetate. Methylene chloride is a chemical solvent approved by the U.S. Food and Drug Administration. Ethyl acetate is a diluent derived from fruit, such as bananas and apples. Both solvents come in direct contact with the beans, circulate through them, bind with the caffeine, and remove it without a loss of oils. To remove any residual solvents, the beans are steamed or rinsed, then dried. Any trace solvents that remain are eliminated when the beans are roasted. Some coffee devotees fear that the solvent method promotes ingestion. However, as methylene chloride evaporates at 170°F (77°C), and coffee is roasted at 450°F (232°C), this is unlikely. Moreover, the solvent method is faster and less costly to execute than the water process.

*Flavored coffee* is made by spraying or mixing freshly roasted coffee beans with liquid flavorings, such as chocolate, cardamom, allspice, nutmeg, cinnamon, orange zest, and chicory. Coffee may also be flavored with wines and spirits, such as marsala, frangelico, sambuca, curaçao, brandy, rum, Irish whiskey, and bourbon. The result is coffee with a special taste: Irish cream, amaretto, french vanilla.

*Blended coffee* is a mix of two or more straight coffees grown in different parts of the world. Blended coffee is named for the dominant coffee in the blend, for example, Jamaica Blue Mountain blend. Often, the taste of blended coffee is more balanced than straight coffee. For example, breakfast coffee is an equal mix of mild-flavored arabica coffee from Santos blended with acidic arabica from Africa; New Orleans is a pungent mix of three parts Brazilian arabica to one part chicory; mocha-java, the oldest coffee blend, is one part arabica mocha from Yemen to two parts arabica from Java.

## How to Store Coffee

Proper storage of coffee grounds and coffee beans maximizes taste. Moisture, oxygen, and light degrade the flavor of coffee; this process starts in the roasting and continues through grinding, a period when the cells open up and absorb the moisture present in air. Because light generates heat that evaporates the essential oils, to maximize flavor, coffee is stored in a cool dark place. For the same reason, coffee purchased in a paper bag turns stale faster than coffee sold in a can.

Coffee purchased in a can is "vacuum-sealed" or "vacuum-packed" in a process that removes approximately 90 percent of the air. An unopened can of vacuum-packed coffee stays fresh for months, but once the can is opened, the grind is exposed to oxygen and turns stale in 7 to 10 days. To prolong freshness, transfer coffee packaged in a bag or a can to an opaque glass container made with an airtight seal and store it in a refrigerator or freezer.

Coffee grounds stay fresh in a refrigerator for approximately 7 to 10 days and in a freezer for about a month. However, the daily removal of grounds from the freezer permits moisture to collect inside the container. When the container is returned to the freezer, the moisture inside the jar condenses and destroys the potential flavor of the brew.

The best brew is made from freshly roasted coffee beans selected from a closed bin rather than an open burlap bag, specifically beans bought from a store that does a high-volume trade in coffee. After purchase, divide the beans into smaller quantities, such as half-pound portions, and store the beans in the refrigerator or freezer in an opaque airtight container. Whole beans stay fresh in a refrigerator for about 4 weeks, in a freezer up to 6 months, and at room temperature up to 10 days.

Because coffee beans are porous, store them away from odoriferous foods, such as cheese, onions, and fish. Roasted coffee beans do not freeze and can be ground immediately upon removal from the freezer.

## How to Make an Excellent Cup of Coffee

A superior cup of coffee is made of freshly ground coffee beans roasted within a week of transit, packaging, and shipping; cold, fresh water; and a clean coffee maker.

Cold, fresh water accounts for a great deal of the flavor of coffee. Because cold water contains more oxygen than hot water, to ensure freshness let the tap run for a few moments or use cold bottled water. When water is brought to a boil, it loses oxygen and produces coffee with a flat flavor. The best flavor is obtained from cold tap water brought to a *simmer* (approximately 200°F, or 93°C), slightly less hot than boiled water (212°F, or 100°C) and hotter than "instantly-hot" water drawn from a valve (190°F, or 88°C).

Hot tap water lies in a hot-water tank for indefinite periods of time and may acquire impurities from the pipes that bring out the tannic acid in coffee and promote a brew with a bitter taste. Because hard tap water contains alkalines that neutralize the taste of the flavor-giving acids, and artificially softened water is treated with chemicals that promote a flat flavor, use filtered water to brew a superlative cup of coffee.

To make instant coffee, lift the kettle from the burner after the water has reached a simmer. Before pouring water over the grounds, hold the kettle for a second or two to lower the temperature.

A clean coffeepot is one that is free of coffee oils that cling to the interior surface like an invisible shield and promote brew with a bitter taste. To cut the oils, disassemble a coffee maker and wash the parts in hot, soapy water. Use a nonabrasive sponge on the interior of the pot, one that will not leave scratches and grooves where oils and minerals may collect. Or soak the parts in 1 to 2 teaspoons of baking soda dissolved in hot water. Cut the buildup of lime deposits with a solution of vinegar and water.

Here are some general tips for making a choice cup of coffee.

- *Use a glass or ceramic coffee maker.* Metal does not enhance the flavor of coffee. But if you must brew in a metal pot, stainless steel is best, followed by nickel, copper, aluminum, and tin in descending order of taste.
- *Do not let coffee stand.* Oxidation robs coffee of flavor, and when the brew is left to stand it develops a bitter taste. For maximum flavor, drink coffee soon after it is made and make a fresh pot as needed. Although coffee begins to stale approximately 15 minutes after it is brewed, electric coffee makers keep coffee fresh for about an hour at temperatures of approximately 185 to 190°F (85°C to 88°C).
- *Make a full pot of coffee.* Because oxidation degrades the flavor of coffee, always brew the maximum amount a pot is made to hold. Brew eight cups of coffee in an 8-cup coffee maker, even though four cups are used, and preserve the remainder in a thermal carafe.
- *Never reheat leftover coffee.* Stale coffee has fewer soluble substances than fresh coffee, and the flavor is bitter.
- *Don't make "weak coffee."* Instead, prepare it full strength and dilute the taste with hot water, cream, or milk.

## The Ratio of Ground Coffee to Water

A first-rate cup of coffee means different things to different people. Some people like coffee with a strong taste and others prefer a mild flavor. The approved coffee measure (ACM) is 2 *level* tablespoons of ground coffee to every 5-ounce cup of water, although 6 ounces are often used. The key word here is *level* tablespoons compared to rounded or heaping. Because ground coffee retains water, coffee brewed to ACM measurements yields less than the measured amount, or approximately three-quarters of a cup of coffee. Less coffee is used to make instant coffee. Mugs hold approximately 8 to 12 ounces of water, and the measurement is adjusted upward accordingly.

The following ratio of ground coffee to water is for one 5-ounce cup of coffee, a guideline that can be adjusted to personal preference.

- *Instant coffee:* 1 teaspoon of coffee, rounded or heaping, to 5 ounces of water
- *Moderate-strength coffee:* 2 level tablespoons of coffee to 5 ounces of water
- *Strong coffee:* 2 rounded tablespoons of coffee to 5 ounces of water, plus an extra spoonful "for the pot"
- *After-dinner coffee:* 4 tablespoons of coffee to 2½ ounces of water
- *Turkish coffee:* 1 to 2 tablespoons of Turkish coffee to 1½ to 4 ounces of water

## Type of Coffee Maker

Coffee is made by decoction or infusion. *Decocted coffee* is "cooked," or boiled in an open pan; this is the oldest way to make coffee. Boiled water activates the tannic acid, promotes brew with a bitter taste, and produces a cloudy cup of coffee. Turkish coffee is made in an *ibrik* or a *cezve* (pronounced "jezwe"), a small, long-handled, conical-shaped pot made of copper or brass lined with tin. The pan is filled half-full with cold water; this allows space for a thin brown foam to develop as the coffee is cooked—a froth the Arabs call *kaimaki,* or "the face of coffee." The grounds are suspended by swishing the brew about before it is poured into the cup. The long handle and narrow upper perimeter of the pan makes this possible.

Turkish coffee is heated until it boils and removed from the burner immediately, because the brief boil robs coffee of flavor. As cold water is heavier than hot water, to halt the boil a bit of cold water is added to the pan. The pan is returned to the heat a second time, the water is brought to a boil, removed, and cold water is added again. The process is repeated, but never more than three times, because moisture and air rob coffee of oil and promote a bitter taste. After the final boil, cold water is added to settle the grounds, and the *kaimaki,* or foam, is divided equally among the guests. Approximately a tablespoon is spooned into small stemmed cups or demitasse cups. If Turkish coffee lacks foam the host loses face. Once the coffee is poured, it is not stirred. Although the grounds that pour into the cup settle to the bottom, Turkish coffee is sipped. A piece of candy, such as *rahat loukoum,* an Arabic candy made of fruit paste, is taken on the side as a sweetener.

*Infused coffee* is fairly recent, a process developed in the last 200 years. Infusion produces flavorful coffee with clarity and, depending on the coffee maker, leaves little sediment in the cup. There are five methods for making infused coffee: steeped, percolated, vacuum method, filtered, and espresso.

1. *Steeped coffee,* from the Old Norse word *steypa,* meaning "to pour out liquids," was developed from decocted coffee in the eighteenth century by the French. It is the second oldest way to brew coffee. Steeped coffee is made in a plunger pot or an open saucepan.

   A plunger pot, such as a Bodum, is used to steep coffee. The grounds are placed in the bottom, the water is added, and the brew is steeped for the desired time. Just before serving, the strainer is pressed down to the bottom of the pot; this separates the grounds from the brew and produces coffee with a rich, full-bodied taste, one that leaves little sediment in the cup.

   Coffee steeped in an open pan is prepared with cold, fresh water brought to a simmer. The water is removed from the heat and poured onto the grounds. To promote even wetness, the grounds are stirred for approximately 30 seconds. The brew is covered and allowed to steep. Just before serving, a little cold water is added to the pan to settle the grounds to the bottom. Then the brew is poured through a strainer into a cup or a mug.

   But coffee steeped in an open pan leaves sediment that clouds the brew. Additives such as egg whites, fish skins, or eggshells are put in the pan as clarifiers. The English prefer egg whites because the albumin absorbs the cloudiness as it coagulates and is easy to skim off. However, the Scandinavians prefer fish skins, although they tend to flavor the brew. And cowboys cooking eggs over an open camp fire use the crushed shell of one egg as a clarifier.
2. *Percolator* coffee, from the Latin *percolare,* "to strain through," is the third oldest way to infuse coffee. The percolator was invented in 1800 by Jean-Baptiste de Belloy, archbishop of Paris, and improved upon in 1825 by Benjamin Thompson of Woburn, Massachusetts, an eccentric American who called himself Count von Rumford.

   In the percolator, the coffee grinds are placed in the pot's metal basket and the cold water is added to the pot. The coffee maker is covered and the steam generated by the heated water creates pressure that forces the water up through the strainer and over the grounds many times. The percolator recycles the water, exposes the grounds to air, reduces the aroma, increases the tannin, and promotes brew with a bitter taste. This coffee maker is therefore not recommended by coffee connoisseurs. In the interests of flavor, electric percolators turn off automatically at the end of the brewing cycle.

3. *Vacuum coffee makers* are adapted from an invention made in 1870 by Robert Napier, a Scottish marine engineer. The coffee maker is known by such brand names as Silex and Cona. Vacuum coffee makers produce clear, sediment-free coffee with a pleasant taste and a tantalizing aroma.

   The vacuum coffee maker is made with an upper and lower globe connected by a tube that siphons water from the lower to the upper container. Although a spirit lamp rests under the lower bowl, to speed up the brewing time, the water is often heated in a kettle before it is added to the globe. As the water in the lower globe boils, it builds up steam that creates pressure and is vacuumed into the upper balloon, where it mixes with the grounds. For even infusion the grounds are stirred. After the coffee has steeped, the spirit lamp is extinguished and the coffee maker is removed from the heat. The air in the lower globe contracts and creates a vacuum that sucks the brew from the upper globe into the lower balloon, in a trickle.

4. *Filtered coffee,* also known as *drip coffee,* is the newest method of coffee infusion and the preferred method of coffee afficianados. The coffee filter was invented by Melitta Bentz, a German housewife who in 1908 filtered her husband's cup of coffee through a linen towel.

   The drip coffee maker features an upper and lower container, and the grounds are filtered through a strainer made with fine pores. Hot water of approximately 195 to 205°F (91 to 96°C) is poured over the grounds *once.* The grounds are stirred, and the brew flows into the pot below producing a mellow taste and little sediment. The filter is removed. To balance the flavor, the pot is swirled before the brew is poured.

   The drip coffee maker is made in electric and nonelectric models. Electric models, such as Melitta, Krups, and Mr. Coffee, turn off automatically. Nonelectric models take longer to brew.

5. *Espresso* is a fast-brewing machine that forces steam through a funnel into an upper container filled with dark-roasted grounds. This method produces a full-bodied brew with an almost syrupy consistency and a strong taste.

# Part IX

# Table Manners

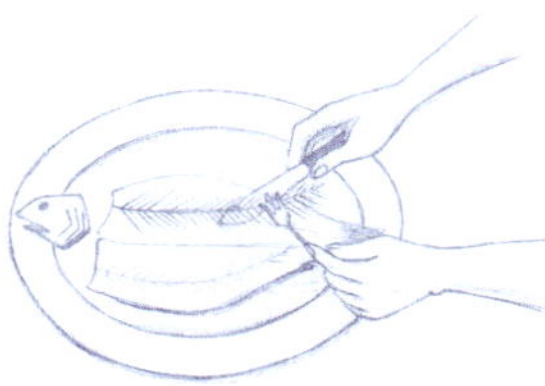

CHAPTER FIFTY-ONE

# HOW TO EAT SPECIFIC FOODS

*All things require skill but an appetite.*

GEORGE HERBERT, OUTLANDISH PROVERBS

THE WAY TO eat particular foods depends on the method of preparation and whether the meal is formal or informal. At a formal meal, utensils are used and fingers do not touch food except to eat dry rolls or crackers and hold fresh fruit. At an informal meal, both fingers and utensils are used: a hamburger in a bun is held with fingers but a meat patty on a plate is eaten with a fork. Here's how to eat certain specific foods that sometimes present difficulties.

ARTICHOKES. The artichoke is a globular, thistle-like vegetable about the size of the fist. It is indigenous to the eastern Mediterranean and harvested before it opens into a huge flower. The artichoke is served cooked and the leaves are eaten with the fingers. The base of the leaf is dipped into sauce, and the pulp or meaty part is scraped off in the mouth with the lower teeth. The discarded leaves are stacked on the side of the plate, or put on a dish laid on the table for this purpose. To separate the heart of the choke from the fuzzy part at the base of the flowerhead, leaves too thin to eat are circled with a knife and placed on a plate, and the heart is eaten with a fork, a bite at a time.

ASPARAGUS. Asparagus is indigenous to the eastern Mediterranean. It has a long narrow stalk with scalelike leaves and is eaten cooked. Depending on the size of the stalk and whether it is served with sauce, asparagus is eaten with a utensil or with fingers. At a formal meal, asparagus is served with sauce and the stalk is eaten with a fork. At an informal meal, short stalks served without sauce are eaten with fingers; long stalks are eaten with a fork.

AVOCADO. The avocado is a pear-shaped fruit indigenous to South America. It is served raw, either cut in half and sliced or mashed, or cooked in a casserole. When cut in half, the buttery flesh is scooped from the shell with a spoon. If served mashed as a dip, such as guacamole, avocado is taken with a chip. But when sliced in a salad or cooked in a recipe, avocado is eaten with a fork.

BACON. Bacon is salted, smoked, and sliced meat from the back or side of a hog. *Crisp bacon* scatters when cut and is eaten with fingers. *Limp bacon* is greasy; to prevent soiled fingers it is cut with a knife and eaten with a fork.

BEVERAGES. The protocol of beverages is often intimidating: What to do if it spills, where to place the spoon, how to cool an overly hot drink.

When a beverage spills into a saucer, replace the saucer or blot the bottom of the cup with a paper napkin and place the cup on top.

Because a soiled utensil is not placed on the table, after the spoon is used it is laid on the saucer behind the cup handle. However, mugs are made without saucers, so after a spoon is used, it is wiped clean in the mouth and placed on a nearby plate or napkin. If a saucer or napkin are unavailable, the soiled spoon is laid on the table, as long as doing so will not stain the table.

When a long-handled beverage spoon accompanies an iced-tea glass, initially the spoon is laid on the table to the right of the glass. To drink the beverage after stirring with the spoon, hold the spoon with the first two fingers against the inside rim of the glass; leave the spoon in the glass when you are done. If the iced-tea glass is placed on a coaster, however, the soiled spoon may be laid on the coaster.

At a formal meal, wait for a too-hot drink to cool. At an informal meal, transfer an ice cube from a water goblet. At a family meal, cool the beverage with an ice cube from the freezer.

BIRDS. Small birds, such as squab, quail, and pheasant, are eaten with utensils or fingers. At a formal dinner, the meat is removed from birds with a fork and a knife and fingers are not used. At an informal meal, a fork and knife are used to remove as much meat as possible; thereafter, the bones are held with the fingers and the remaining meat is taken with the teeth, *but only if the hostess does the same.* Remove bird shot from the mouth with the fingers.

BREAD PRODUCTS. Bread is broken or cut before it is eaten, depending on the texture (soft or firm), the temperature (hot or cold), and the shape (long and narrow or small and cubed).

Bread with a soft texture, such as rolls or muffins, is broken in half with fingers. A bite-size piece is pulled from the broken half, held against the side of the bread-and-butter plate, and buttered a bite at a time.

Bread with a firm texture, such as a sweet soft pastry or dry toast, is cut in half or quartered. Hot sweet rolls and toast are buttered entirely and held by the sides (rather than laid flat on the palm of the hand).

Bread sticks are made from sweet dough and do not require butter. However, when butter is applied, the length is buttered entirely or the end is buttered a bite at a time. To avoid excessive crumbs, a bread stick is broken in half gently.

Croutons are toasted cubes of buttered bread added as texture to food. Because the cubes are buttered, croutons are somewhat greasy and are spooned over food (rather than handled with fingers).

CAKE. The way to eat cake depends on the texture. Cake with a dry, crumbly texture, such as pound cake or a cupcake, is broken into small pieces and eaten a bite at a time with the fingers. Cake with a moist, gooey texture, such as cake with a custard filling, is eaten with a fork. Ice-cream cake is made in both dry and moist textures and is served with a fork and a spoon. The fork is used to hold the portion, and the spoon to cut and convey the bite to the mouth.

CANAPÉS. A canapé is a cold appetizer of cheese, meat, vegetables, or fish on a cracker, bread, toast, or pastry. Depending on the way canapés are served, they are eaten with fingers or a utensil. At a cocktail party, afternoon tea, or reception, finger food is served. But when a canapé is served as a first course at the table, for example, a light pastry filled with vegetables or fish or a wedge of pizza, it is eaten with a utensil.

CANDY IN A WRAPPER. At room temperature, candy is soft and sticky and melts easily, so to prevent soiled fingers it is presented in a paper wrapper. When a piece of candy is taken from a dish, it is removed with its wrapper. The wrapper is discarded on a nearby plate.

CASSEROLE DISHES WITH COVERS. A casserole is a covered ovenproof dish in which food is cooked and served. When a small covered casserole is presented on a dinner plate, the cover is removed, rested on the side of the plate, rim-side down, and the contents are eaten directly from the casserole. If a large covered casserole is placed above the dinner plate, the lid is removed, rested rim-side down on the underplate or dinner plate, and a portion is transferred from the casserole to the dinner plate with the accompanying serving utensil. To preserve the temperature, between servings the lid of the large casserole is replaced.

CAVIAR. Caviar is the roe, or eggs, of sturgeon, also loosely used for the roe of other fish, such as salmon or lumpfish. According to the U.S. Food and Drug Administration, when fish roe other than sturgeon is advertised as caviar, the name of the fish must preceed the word, such as "salmon caviar" or "lumpfish caviar."

> There is more simplicity in the man who eats caviar on impulse than in a man who eats Grapenuts on principle.
>
> G. K. Chesterton

Caviar is served cold in a small crystal bowl laid on a bed of cracked ice and accompanied by small rounds of toast. Caviar is scooped with a small spoon onto a toast round, along with garniture (if served), and eaten with the fingers. During Lent, Russians serve caviar with small buckwheat pancakes and sour cream, a delicacy called *blini,* which are eaten with a fork.

Because silver reacts chemically with fish roe and causes the eggs to exude a greenish fluid, a reaction that also affects the salty flavor of caviar, a small spoon made of natural material is provided, such as one made of horn, mother-of-pearl, or wood.

CELERY. Celery is served raw or cooked. Raw celery is generally served as a crudité taken with the fingers, placed on a bread-and-butter plate, and eaten with the fingers. When a bread-and-butter plate is not provided, raw celery is placed on the dinner plate. Do not sprinkle salt over celery; instead, place the seasoning on the side of the plate and dip the stalk into it.

When celery is served cooked, it is eaten with a fork.

CHEESE. Cheese is made from pressed curdled milk. In the Middle Ages, cheese was sold in a big wheel. Hence, the expression "big wheel" or "big cheese" for someone of importance. Although the rind of soft cheese, such as camembert and brie, is edible, the rind of firm cheese, such as gruyère, cheddar, jarlsberg, and romano, is generally not, and the hard covering is removed with a knife and a fork.

The way cheese is eaten depends on two things: the formality of the occasion and the texture of the cheese. At a formal dinner, a cheese tray is passed with the salad or fruit course, along with toasted crackers. Soft cheese is cut from a cheese tray, placed on a plate, spread on a cracker with a utensil, and brought to the mouth with fingers. Firm cheese is sliced, transferred to the plate, speared, and eaten with a fork. Or firm cheese is placed on a cracker and carried to the mouth with the fingers.

At an informal meal, when sliced cheese is served as an accompaniment to a particular dish, such as apple pie, it is eaten with a fork. But if cheese is served as an appetizer, such as cubes on toothpicks, it is eaten with fingers. Or a slice of cheese is cut from a wedge, placed on a cracker, and brought to the mouth with the fingers.

CHICKEN WITH BONE ATTACHED. The way to eat chicken depends on whether the meal is formal, informal, or family-style. At a formal dinner, chicken is eaten with a knife and fork. At an informal meal, the knife and fork are used to remove as much meat from the main body as possible; to eat the rest of the meat the bones are held with fingers and taken with the teeth. However, it is wise to take your lead from the hostess. At a family meal, chicken with bone attached is eaten with a fork and fingers.

CHOPS. A chop is cut from the animal's rib, loin, or shoulder. To conceal the ends of bones charred in cooking, restaurants often wrap them in a "paper skirt," a decoration held with fingers as protection from grease. The meat is cut from the bone with a knife.

Chops are eaten with a fork and a knife, but to capture a last bite or two difficult to reach with a utensil, they may be held with the fingers. Again, follow the hostess's lead. At a family meal, chops are eaten with a fork but held with fingers to reach a last bite or two difficult to spear with a fork.

CONDIMENTS. Condiments are seasonings served whole, sliced, or in thick or thin liquid consistencies. Whole condiments, such as radishes and olives, are taken with the fingers. Sliced condiments, such as pickles, are eaten with a fork. Liquid condiments with a thin consistency, such as soy sauce, are poured over food; those with a thick texture, such as salsa or chutney, are spooned over food or eaten with a fork.

COOKIES. Cookies are flat or bun-shape delicacies in varying sizes. The texture of the cookie is crumbly and best eaten with the fingers. Small cookies are eaten whole in one bite. Large cookies are broken and eaten a piece at a time. When a small plate is provided, before a cooky is eaten, it is placed on the plate. To do otherwise defeats the purpose of the plate.

CORN-ON-THE-COB. The cob is the woody ear of the corn stalk, a messy but delectable finger food served only at informal meals. The cob is held by the ends with the fingers. Large cobs are easier to eat when cut in half, and are buttered two rows at a time to control drips (but perhaps ruins the fun).

CRACKERS. A cracker is a thin crisp wafer made of unleavened dough that "cracks" when broken. Because crackers are not greasy they are eaten with the fingers.

At formal meals, toasted crackers are served with cheese and are placed on the edge of the plate or tablecloth and eaten a bite at a time. At an informal meal, large crackers are used often as a pusher to assist the fork with a particular course, such as salad. At a family meal, large crackers are broken and sprinkled over food or dropped into soup. Small crackers, such as oyster crackers, are placed on a bread-and-butter plate. If a small plate is not provided, small crackers are placed on the table.

EGGS, SOFT-BOILED, SERVED IN AN EGGCUP. Soft-boiled eggs are often served in an eggcup made with a wide rim and a bowl that is narrow at the bottom. The pointed end of the egg is placed downward in the cup. The upper part of the shell is cracked with a knife wielded in a horizontal movement, all the way around. The tip of the knife is used to lift the shell from the egg and place it on the side of the plate. Because the exposed part of the egg is relatively flat, if a dab of butter is placed on it, the butter melts and flows over the egg. A mound of salt and pepper is made on the side of the plate. With a small spoon, such as an after-dinner coffee spoon, a bite of egg is scooped from the shell and dipped into the seasonings. Alternatively, a pinch of salt and pepper may be sprinkled over each bite by hand.

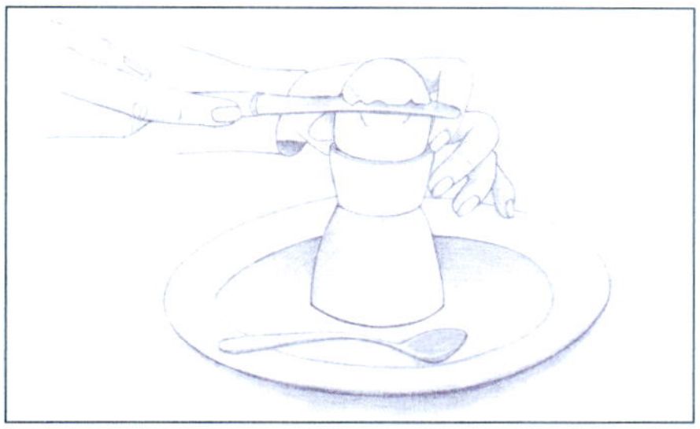

SOFT-BOILED EGG EATEN FROM AN EGGCUP IS PLACED POINTED END FACE DOWN. THE UPPER PART OF THE SHELL IS CRACKED HORIZONTALLY WITH A KNIFE, ALL THE WAY AROUND. THE KNIFE CUTS INTO THE EGG AND LIFTS THE TOP PART FROM THE SHELL.

A DAB OF BUTTER IS PLACED ON THE TOP OF THE EGG (SO IT CAN MELT OVER THE EGG).

A SMALL MOUND OF SALT AND PEPPER IS PLACED ON THE SIDE OF THE PLATE. WITH A SMALL SPOON, SUCH AS AN AFTER-DINNER COFFEE SPOON, A BITE OF EGG IS SCOOPED FROM THE SHELL AND DIPPED INTO THE SEASONINGS.

ESCARGOT. Escargot is an edible snail, a gastropod mollusk that lives on land in a spiral one-piece shell, a delicacy farmed extensively in France, Turkey, and Algeria. When escargot is served as an appetizer in garlic butter, the shell is held in a napkin-covered hand or is gripped with a scissor-like tong. A snail fork is held in the other hand and used to extract the meat with a pulling motion. To enjoy the sauce, spear a small piece of bread with the fork and dip into the buttery concoction.

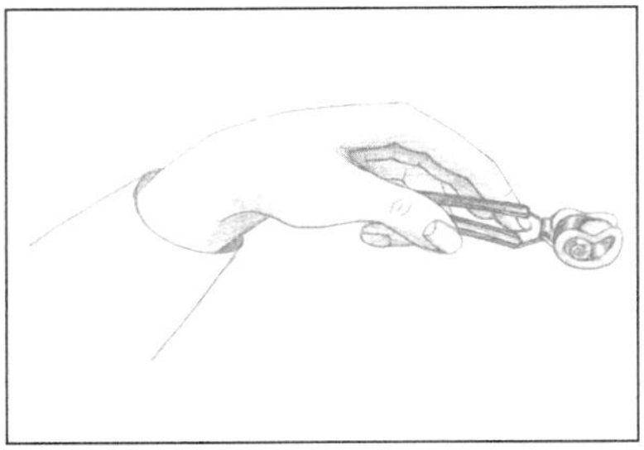

ESCARGOT SHELLS ARE HELD IN THE LEFT HAND WITH A SCISSOR TONG OR A NAPKIN-COVERED HAND.

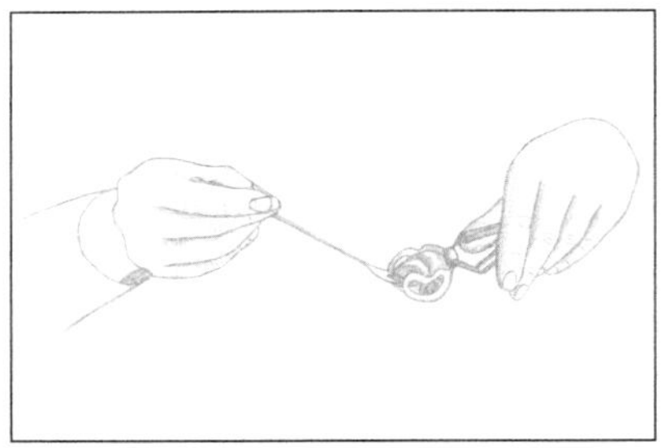

A SNAIL FORK IS HELD IN THE RIGHT HAND, AND THE MEAT IS PULLED FROM THE SHELL.

TO ENJOY THE SAUCE, SPEAR A SMALL PIECE OF BREAD WITH THE FORK AND DIP IT INTO THE BUTTERY CONCOCTION.

FISH. Although there are over 20,000 known species of fish, small freshwater fish are a challenge to eat at the table. Small freshwater fish are found in streams, rivers, and lakes, which are often stocked just so they can be harvested. Trout is one such freshwater fish and is usually served whole at the table.

- When the head of the trout is not detached in the kitchen, remove it behind the gills.
- To fillet and debone the body, hold the trout with a fork and slit from the head to the tail with a knife, then open the fish and lay it flat on the plate.
- To remove the skeleton from the body, place the tip of the knife under the backbone, lift with the fork, and place it on the side of the plate.

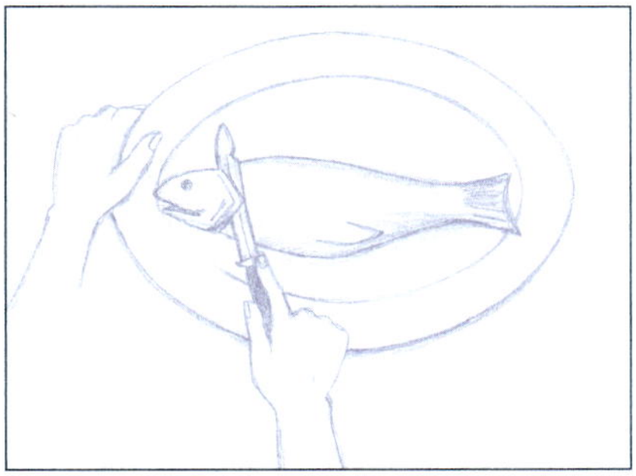

To fillet trout at the table, detach the head behind the gills.

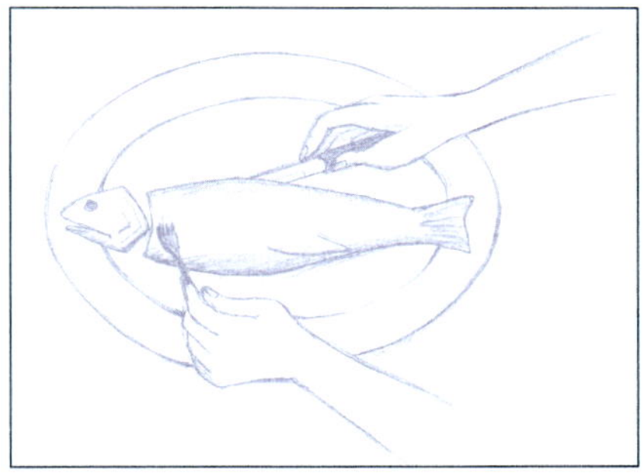

Steady the body with a fish fork, and slit the body open with the pointed tip of the fish knife.

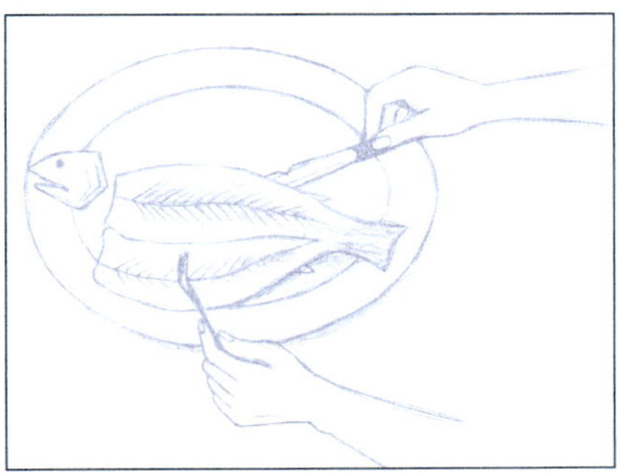

Use the fork and knife to lay the fish flat on the plate.

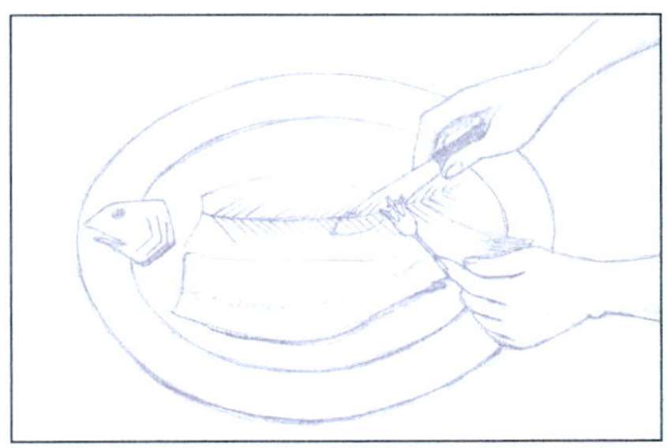

To lift the skeleton from the body, place the tip of the fish knife under the backbone, and with the fish fork lift it and place it on the side of the plate.

If you inadvertently ingest any fish bones, remove them with your fingers and place them on the side of the plate. For crab, lobster, shrimp, oysters, clams, and mussels, see *Shellfish.*

FONDUE. Fondue is a hot dish made with melted cheese and eggs, or with meat or fish. *Cheese fondue* is eaten with a long-handled fondue fork, one fork per guest. Cubed bread is speared and dipped into sauce served in a communal pot. Because the sauce is shared by everyone at the table, and the fork is redipped into the sauce many times, the tines of the fork do not pierce the cubes all the way through. Rather, the bread cube is removed from the fork with the front teeth only, and the lips and tongue do not touch the tines. *Meat fondue* and *fish fondue* are served with a fondue fork and a dinner fork, one set per guest. Bite-sized pieces of meat or fish are held on the end of the fondue fork and cooked in the stock heated in the fondue pot. Because the dinner fork is used as an eating utensil, the lips and tongue may touch the tines.

FROG LEGS. The frog is a four-legged amphibious animal with long hind legs and short forelegs; it is web-footed, has no tail, and both swims and leaps. The tender white flesh of the legs is akin to chicken in taste, and frogs are farmed. The legs are held with the fingers of one hand. The large legs are disjointed with a knife and fork.

FRUIT. Fruit is eaten at the table either peeled or unpeeled; fresh, cooked, or candied; pitted, seeded, or whole.

*Peeled fruit* is eaten cut side down on the plate, a position that allows the juice to run onto the plate and not squirt when a bite is cut. *Unpeeled fruit,* such as an apple or a grapefruit half, is eaten cut side up, so the skin can absorb the juice.

At formal affairs, fruit is served at the end of the meal. A fruit plate is laid before the diner and on it is placed a fruit knife and a fruit fork. Large and medium-size fruit, such as a pear or a peach, are quartered with the fruit knife and eaten with the fruit fork one bite at a time. Small fresh fruit, such as apricots and plums, are eaten with fingers, as are candied fruit.

At family meals, fruit is served fresh or cooked. When a slice of *fresh fruit* is served with the rind attached, such as melon, it is presented with a knife and a fork. The rind is removed by sliding the knife under the flesh and the fruit is sectioned with the knife and eaten with the fork. If a knife alone is presented, it is used to pare fruit held in the hand and eaten with fingers. *Cooked fruit* served in a bowl, such as fruit compote, is eaten with a spoon. *Canned fruit* served on a plate, such as a crab-apple, is eaten with a fork.

The *stone* is the large seed found in fleshy fruit, such as apricots, nectarines, peaches, and plums. The fruit is held with fingers and eaten close to the stone. To remove a stone from the mouth, place the thumb and first two fingers under the stone and deposit it on the plate.

The *pit* is the kernel found in small fruit, such as cherries. At an elegant meal, cherries are put into the mouth with a spoon, and the pits are cleaned in the mouth, deposited on the spoon, and placed on the plate. At an informal meal, cherries are put into the mouth with fingers. The pits are deposited into a cupped hand and placed on the plate.

AT AN ELEGANT MEAL, SMALL FRUIT IS PUT INTO THE MOUTH WITH A SPOON. THE PIT IS DEPOSITED ONTO THE SPOON AND PLACED ON A PLATE.

*Seeds* are the tiny embryos of small fruit that grow in clusters, such as grapes. Because grape seeds are too small to remove with a fork, they are deposited into a cupped hand, and put on a plate.

Here is how to eat specific fruits.

- *Apple.* A native fruit of southwest Asia, apples are eaten peeled or unpeeled. At an elegant affair, raw apple is quartered, cored, and eaten with fingers. Sliced apple eaten with cheese is taken with a fork or fingers, either together or in alternate bites. At a family meal, raw apple is eaten with fingers.
- *Apricot.* The apricot is harvested before peaches or plums. Apricots are a native fruit of China that came to Italy via Armenia, where it was known as a *plum*. Fresh apricots are eaten with the fingers, and the stone is placed on the plate.
- *Banana.* A tropical plant from Malaysia related to the lily and the orchid, bananas are served cooked or are eaten raw. At an elegant occasion, raw banana is peeled entirely before it is eaten. The peel is placed on the side of the plate, and the fruit is sliced with a knife, one bite at a time, and eaten with a fork. At a family meal, a banana is peeled totally or partially, and a small section is broken off with the fingers and eaten.
- *Berries.* The way to eat berries depends on whether the stem is removed or left on. Berries with stems removed, such as raspberries and blueberries, are usually served with cream and sugar and eaten with a spoon. Berries with stems left on, such as large strawberries, are eaten with the fingers. The fruit is held by the stem and dipped into condiments, such as powdered sugar. The stems are placed on the side of the plate.
- *Cherries.* A fruit attributed to Cerasus, Turkey, raw cherries are eaten with fingers at formal and informal meals.
- *Grapefruit.* A semitropical fruit attributed to Jamaica, grapefruit is so named because it grows in clusters like grapes. Fresh grapefruit is served cut in half or peeled. When cut in half, the segments are loosened with a knife before service and the flesh is eaten with a spoon. Because juice squirts from grapefruit when squeezed, in a social situation the juice is scooped up with a spoon. However, at a family meal, grapefruit is squeezed to capture a last spoonful of juice. Segments of peeled grapefruit are eaten with the fingers or a fork.

- *Grapes.* The origin of the grapevine is attributed primarily to the Caucasus mountains. When a large bowl of grapes is presented at the table, cut a small cluster from the main stem with the grape shears provided or break off a small stem with the fingers. Place the cluster on the plate, and eat the grapes with the fingers, one at a time. To eat the pulp of grapes only, press the fruit between the lips. The juice and the pulp enter the mouth while the seeds remain in the skin. Both are discarded on the plate.
- *Kumquat.* A native fruit of China, it is a smaller version of the orange. The kumquat is eaten whole, skin, pips, and all, in a bite or two, with the fingers.
- *Mango.* The mango is a tropical fruit from India. The skin is tough, the pulp is juicy and prone to stain, and the stone is large. Here are two ways to eat a mango, both of them somewhat messy. (1) Cut the mango around the middle (the short way around) with a sharp knife, and twist it. Remove the stone with a spoon. Hold the mango half in the palm of the hand, and eat the pulp from the shell with a serrated spoon. (2) Cut longwise down the

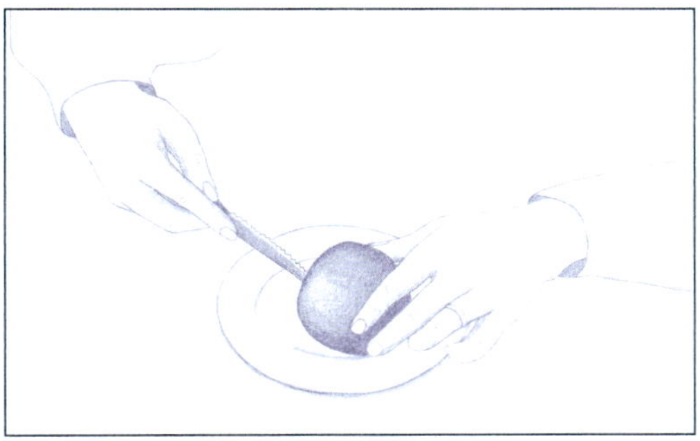

CUT THE MANGO AROUND THE CENTER THE SHORT WAY. TWIST IT OPEN AND REMOVE THE STONE WITH A SPOON.

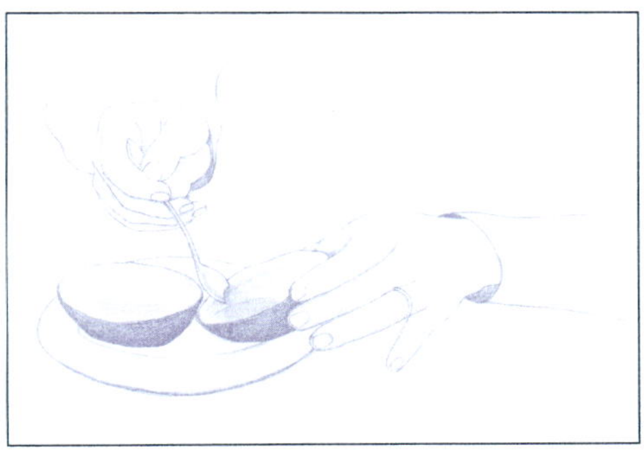

STEADY THE MANGO ON A PLATE OR HOLD IT IN THE PALM OF THE HAND AND EAT THE FLESH FROM THE CAVITY.

mango, feeling the stone as you cut around it. Open the cut with an inverted spoon, and place it over the stone. Lift the top half of the fruit from the bottom half, and remove the stone. Pull the edges of the mango skin lengthwise. The pulp will pop up ready to eat with a spoon.

- *Melon.* A tropical fruit from Asia transplanted to Italy. Melons are served in the shell, sliced, or shaped into balls. In the shell, melon is quartered with the rind attached (the seeds are removed before service), and the fruit is eaten with a spoon. Although watermelon seeds are sorted from the fruit with a fork, those that appear in the mouth are deposited in a cupped hand and placed on the plate. Sliced melon is served with the rind removed and eaten with a fork. Melon balls are eaten with a spoon.
- *Nectarine.* A native fruit of China, the nectarine is a smooth-skinned relative of the peach. At an elegant meal, the nectarine is held in one hand, and with a knife the fruit is cut to the center and twisted open. The half is quartered, cut with a knife, and eaten with a fork. At a family meal, the nectarine is held in the hand and eaten with fingers, peeled or unpeeled.
- *Orange.* A native fruit of China, oranges were introduced to Spain by the Moors. At an elegant meal, a slice of orange is peeled with a knife from top to bottom in a spiral motion. The orange is cut in half lengthwise and the segments are eaten with a fork and knife. At a family meal, the orange peel is scored, and the fruit is peeled with fingers. The segments are eaten with fingers or a fork and knife. When an orange is presented cut in half like a grapefruit, the segments are loosened before service and the fruit is eaten with a spoon.
- *Papaya.* The fruit of the papaw tree, the papaya is a pear-shaped tropical fruit attributed to Central America. It is eaten like a melon: the fruit is cut in half lengthwise, the seeds are removed from the shell, and the flesh is eaten with a spoon. Peeled papaya is eaten with a fork.
- *Peach.* The peach is a native fruit of China. At an elegant meal, the peach is held in one hand, and with a knife in the other hand, the peach is cut to the stone. Although some peaches break apart when twisted, others, such as the clingstone, do not, and the peach is cut in half and quartered. The segment is held with a fork, skin side up, and with a knife the skin is lifted and the fruit is peeled. The segments are cut into smaller pieces and eaten with a fork one bite at a time. At a family meal, a peach is usually eaten with fin-

gers. The exception is an overly ripe peach; to prevent juice from running down the hand, the fruit is cut with a knife and eaten with a fork.

- *Pear.* A native fruit of north central Asia, the pear is eaten alone or with cheese. At a formal meal, pear is peeled (optional), quartered, and cored with a knife and a fork. At an informal meal, a ripe juicy pear is eaten with a fork, but a firm pear is held with the fingers and eaten.
- *Persimmon.* Persimmons are eaten as a first course, mixed in salad, or served as dessert. As a first course, persimmon is served with the top cut off. The fruit is steadied on the plate with one hand and the pulp is scooped up with a spoon held in the other hand. Persimmon mixed in salad is peeled, cut into cubes, and eaten with a fork. Persimmon served as dessert is presented with the stem end downward. The fruit is quartered, the segment is held with the fork, and the skin is loosened with a knife and removed. The quartered sections are eaten with a fork, one bite at a time.
- *Pineapple.* A tropical fruit of Brazil, pineapple is served peeled and sliced on a plate and eaten with a knife and a fork. If cubed and served in a bowl, pineapple is eaten with a spoon.
- *Plum.* A fruit attributed to China, the plum is held in the hand and eaten close to the stone. The stone is left on the plate.
- *Pomegranate.* A native fruit of Persia and North Africa, the pomegranate is served cut in half. The fruit is steadied with one hand, and a spoon is held in the other hand to scoop out the juice and eat the seeds. Watch out for stains.

GARNISHES. Vegetables and fruit served to garnish food, such as watercress or crabapple, are eaten with a fork.

GRAVY. Gravy is the juice of meat thickened with flour and flavored with seasonings. Gravy is spooned or poured over meat and vegetables. At a meal where others use the gravy spoon, do not use it to make a well in vegetables before adding gravy. At a family meal, to savor a last delicious taste or two, break off a piece of bread with the fingers, spear it with a fork, and dip it into gravy.

HONEY. Before sugar was affordable in the nineteenth century, honey was the most common sweetener, and today it is used as a term of endearment. To capture drops of liquid honey from a container, the spoon is twisted and placed on a plate.

HORS D'OEUVRES. The phrase *hors d'oeuvres* is from the French words *hors,* meaning "outside," and *oeuvre,* for "work." These are light appetizers served as an extra course or a snack taken outside the main course. Depending on where and when hors d'oeuvres are served, they are eaten with fingers or a fork. Hors d'oeuvres served with cocktails, such as cheese and crackers, are eaten with fingers. Hors d'oeuvres served at the table as a first course, such as melon with prosciutto, are eaten with a fork.

ICE CREAM. A dessert known in ancient China as early as 3000 B.C., ice cream came to Europe in the thirteenth century via Italy. How ice cream is served determines whether it is eaten with a spoon, a fork, or both. Ice cream served in a bowl is eaten with a spoon, but on a plate, such as an ice-cream roll, it is eaten with a fork. When ice cream is served with cake, it is eaten with a fork and a spoon: the fork to hold the cake portion and the spoon to cut and lift the bite to the mouth.

KETCHUP. Ketchup is a tomato-based condiment. When served to accompany food presented on a plate, such as steak, ketchup is spooned or poured onto the plate, and placed beside the food. If food is served wrapped in a paper napkin, such as a hot dog in a bun, ketchup is poured directly on the bun. Ketchup is served at informal meals only. At a company meal, ketchup is presented in a bowl with a spoon. At a family meal, more often ketchup is served in the bottle; to protect the table, the bottle is placed on a saucer.

NUTS. Nuts are dry one-seeded fruits eaten with the fingers. At the table, a nut spoon is provided to spoon nuts from bowl to plate.

OLIVES. An edible fruit attributed to southern Europe and the Near East, olives are served as garnish, hors d'oeuvres, in cocktails, and in recipes. As a garnish or an hors d'oeuvre, olives are eaten with the fingers; small olives are eaten whole and extralarge olives are eaten in two bites. When served in a cocktail glass without a toothpick, such as a martini, the glass is tipped until the olive falls into the mouth. In a recipe, such as a casserole, olives are eaten with a fork.

PASTA. A food attributed to France, Italy, Japan, and China (introduced to Europe by Marco Polo), *pasta* is an Italian word for "dough," a type of noodle made in round, short sections, like penne; thin long strings, such as spaghetti; flat long forms, notably egg noodles; or wide shapes, such as lasagne. When pasta is served on a plate or in a shallow bowl, such as spaghetti, it is eaten with a fork, but if served in a deep bowl, such as ravioli, it is eaten with a spoon. The width and length of the noodle determine whether pasta is cut or wound around the tines of a fork. To prevent thin noodles, such as spaghetti, from falling between the tines of the fork, pasta is wound around the tines. However, to keep the bite from becoming too large, strive to pick up no more than two to three strands at one time (not always easy). For leverage, balance the tips of the tines against the side of the plate and wind the strands around them. As a base to steady the fork while the noodles are wound, sometimes a spoon is held in one hand, a technique frowned upon in Italy. When several strands of pasta dangle from the fork, suck them into the mouth (quietly), and if one noodle persists, with the fork lift the "odd man out" into the mouth. Pasta made with a broad flat noodle is stuffed with cheese or meat, such as ravioli, or layered with vegetables, meat, fish, and cheese, such as lasagne. Because wide noodles are impossible to wind around fork tines, they are cut with a fork.

PÂTÉ. Pâté is a "paste" of finely chopped or pureed meat or fish. Pâté de foie gras is made of goose liver, usually with truffles. In the eighteenth century, Sydney Smith stated, "my idea of heaven is eating pâté de foie gras to the sound of trumpets." Pâté is served before dinner as an appetizer or at a buffet as part of the main course. As an appetizer, it is spread with a knife on a small round of toast and eaten with the fingers. At a buffet, it is served cold in a terrine. A slice is cut from the terrine, placed on the plate, and eaten with a fork.

PETITS FOURS. Petits fours are small sponge cakes baked in a slow oven and decorated with fondant icing. To protect the fingers from a sticky frosting, petits fours are presented in paper wrappers. The pastry and wrapper are removed together from the tray and placed on a plate. Large petits fours of more than a few bites are eaten with a fork. Small petits fours of two bites or less are eaten with the fingers.

PIZZA. Pizza is served at informal meals as an appetizer or a main course. As an appetizer with cocktails, a small wedge of pizza is eaten with the fingers. At the table, a large wedge of pizza served as an appetizer on a plate is eaten with a fork. If in doubt, watch the host and follow suit. At a company meal, when pizza is the main course it is eaten with a fork and a knife. But at a family meal, pizza is eaten with the fingers or a utensil, whichever is more comfortable.

POTATOES. The potato is native to Bolivia and Peru. Depending on the way it is cooked and served, potato is eaten with a fork or fingers. *Baked potato* is eaten with a fork but is steadied with the fingers of one hand, while a fork is used to break open the skin in a piercing motion crosswise and lengthwise. To let the steam escape, the potato is pushed open with the fingers, and the fork is used to mix in butter and other flavorings. *Potato chips* and *shoe string potatoes* are crisp, scatter when cut, and are eaten with the fingers. *French-fried potatoes* are eaten with a fork or fingers. When french fries are served with food that requires a fork to eat, such as fish, they are eaten with a fork. If served with food eaten with fingers, such as a hamburger in a bun, they are eaten with the fingers.

SANDWICHES. The sandwich is named after John Montagu, the fourth earl of Sandwich, who rather than interrupt his wagers in an extended game of chance, ordered a meal of cold beef placed between two slices of toast.

Sandwiches are eaten with fingers or a utensil. Small tea sandwiches, and sandwiches that are not too thick, are eaten with fingers. An unwieldy sandwich, such as a club sandwich, is cut in quarters with a knife and eaten with fingers. An open-face sandwich, such as a hot roast beef sandwich with gravy, is eaten with a fork and a knife.

SAUCE. Sauce is a soft dressing served to enhance the flavor of particular foods. Because sauce is runny, only a small amount is taken at at time. Sauce is spooned from a bowl or poured from a gravy boat. Thick sauce, such as cream sauce and cheese sauce, are presented in a bowl and spooned onto vegetables. However, thicker sauces, such as cranberry sauce or horseradish, are spooned onto the plate and placed beside the appropriate food. Liquid sauce, such as béchamel, is thin and is poured from a gravy boat. But if thin sauce is served in a bowl, it is spooned onto food.

SHELLFISH. Hard shellfish, or *crustaceans,* are invertebrates, fish that have no backbones, whose bodies are protected by hard shells. These include crab, lobster, and shrimp.

Of the approximately 4,000 species of *crab,* the type commonly served at the table is one that inhabits the cold waters of the Pacific Coast. They have shells up to 9 inches wide and weigh 2 to 4 pounds. Crab is frequently served in the shell, a method that presents a challenge to the elegant diner.

- First, remove the legs and claws from the body with the fingers and break them open with a nutcracker, which is provided with the dish.
- Remove the flesh with a seafood fork or nutpick (also provided).
- Separate the body into bite-size pieces.
- Twist and break off the tail with fingers, and eat the meat with a fork.
- Discard shells in the dish provided and rinse the fingers in the finger bowl.

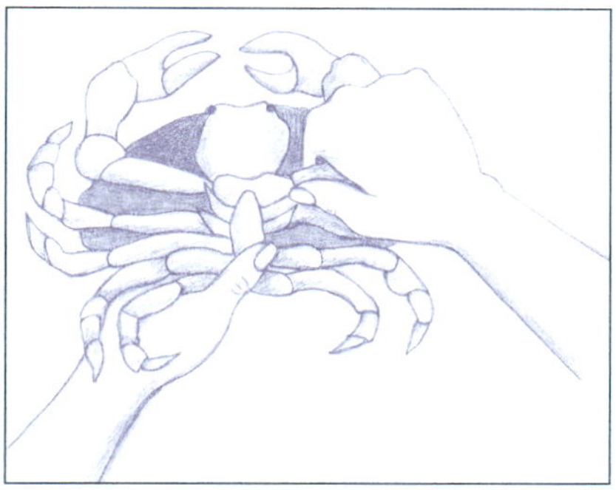

IN A RESTAURANT, CRAB IS SERVED COOKED AND CRACKED, READY TO EAT WITH A SMALL SEAFOOD FORK.
TO REMOVE THE MEAT FROM THE LEGS, CLAWS, AND TAIL, THE APPENDAGES ARE TWISTED OFF WITH FINGERS.

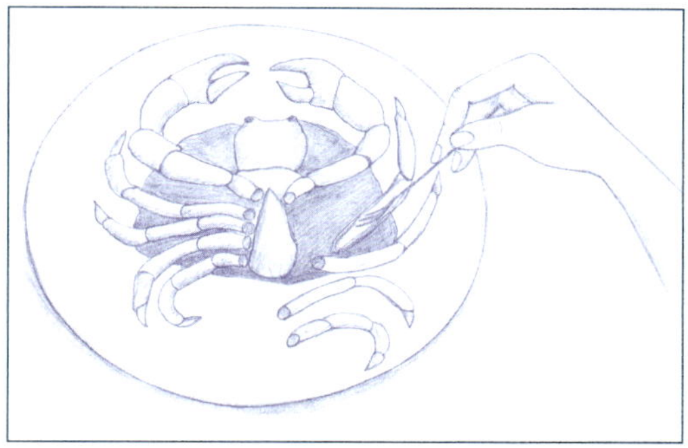

REMOVE THE FLESH FROM THE SHELL WITH A SMALL SEAFOOD FORK OR NUTPICK.

*Lobsters* have a long body and five pairs of claws for crawling among rocks. The two front claws have powerful pincers used to crush food. Lobsters are served boiled, steamed, or grilled. Lobster cooked in the shell is eaten with fingers, a small fork, a knife, and a nutcracker. A discard bowl is provided for the shells, along with a finger bowl to rinse fingertips and pat the mouth as a refresher (optional). For ease of eating, the body flesh may be loosened from the shell and then replaced in the shell before being served at the table. For flavor and eye appeal, the meat is surrounded with condiments, such as drawn butter, lemon wedges, and parsley. If the meat has not been loosened, proceed much as for crab.

- Hold the lobster over the plate with one hand. To prevent the juice from squirting from the shell, twist the large claws off slowly and open them with a nutcracker.

HOLD THE SHELL OVER THE PLATE IN ONE HAND, AND WITH THE OTHER HAND TWIST THE CLAWS, TAIL, AND LEGS OFF THE BODY.

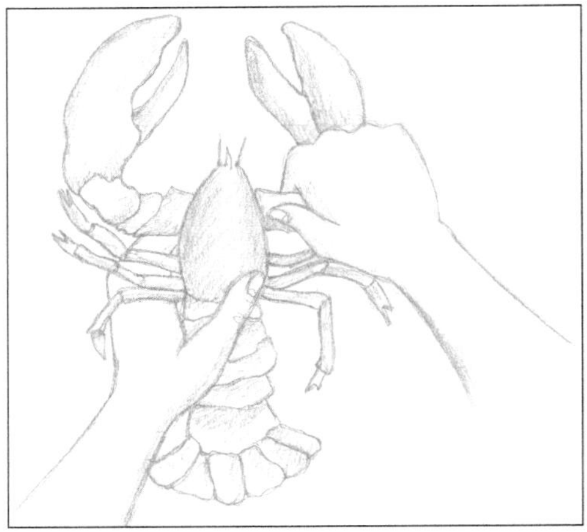

- Extract the meat and eat with the small lobster fork that has been provided.
- Twist the smaller claws off with the fingers, and suck the meat from the cavity.
- Detach the tail from the body in a twisting motion with the fingers.
- Break off the flippers at the small end of the tail with the fingers.
- Pull the meat from the tail with the small fork.
- Split the tail and use the fork to lift the meat onto the plate.
- Separate the large tail pieces into bite-size pieces with a knife and dip them into sauce with a fork.
- Crack the back shell and eat the meat with a fork.
- Eat the tomalley (the green liver of the lobster) and the roe directly from the body with a fork.
- Rinse the fingers in the finger bowl and place discarded shells in a large bowl.

*Shrimp* are small crustaceans that live in cold water, either fresh or salty. Of the nine shrimp categories, 160 species are known. A favorite at the table is the deep-water shrimp, approximately 3 to 4 inches long and cooked to a reddish-pink color. Depending on the method of service, shrimp are eaten with the fingers or a small seafood fork.

- *Shrimp served with tail attached.* The shrimp is held by the tail and eaten with fingers. The discarded tails are placed on the plate.
- *Shrimp speared on a toothpick.* The shrimp is dunked into sauce and eaten from a toothpick. Jumbo shrimp are eaten one bite at a time. However, the uneaten portion is never redipped into sauce shared by others.
- *Shrimp cocktail.* Shrimp served with sauce in a bowl or a compote is called a *cocktail,* a concoction eaten with a seafood fork. When the jumbo shrimp are too large to eat in one bite from a bowl, they are cut with a knife. However, sometimes it is awkward to manipulate a knife inside a bowl; in this instance large shrimp are speared with a fork and eaten one bite at a time. Because the cocktail sauce is not shared by others, the uneaten portion is redipped into the sauce.
- *Fried shrimp.* Fried shrimp served on a plate are eaten with a knife and fork. When served with tails attached, fried shrimp are held by the tail and eaten with the fingers. The discarded tails are placed on the side of the plate.

Thin-shelled mollusks known as *bivalves,* notably clams, oysters, and mussels, nestle among rocks and burrow into sand. Mollusks are eaten raw or cooked with fingers and a small fork. A discard bowl and a finger bowl are provided.

*Clams* are served both raw and cooked. Clams are found throughout the world, but notably in the Atlantic Ocean between Labrador and Mexico. If a clam shell is difficult to open, or is still tightly closed after being cooked, leave it alone. The clam is not good.

- *Raw clams.* Raw clams are presented on the half shell on a bed of cracked ice. The shell is steadied in one hand. A small seafood fork is held in the other hand to extract the meat.
- *Steamed clams.* Small steamed clams with no necks are taken from the shell with a fork. The clam is dipped into clam broth or melted butter served in a

separate bowl. The discarded shells are placed in a separate bowl provided for this purpose. When all the clams are eaten, the broth is spooned from the dipping bowl or drunk from the bowl.

- *Fried clams.* Fried clams are served out of the shell and sometimes dipped in batter before they are cooked. They can be eaten as finger food but are greasy to hold and are best eaten in a roll or with a fork. They may be rubbery to cut.

*Oysters* are served both cooked and raw. The oyster has a thick, rough, irregular shell. Depending on the way oysters are served, they are eaten with a fork, a spoon, or fingers.

- *Cooked oysters.* When oysters are removed from the shell and cooked, as in a sauce or soup, they are eaten with a fork or a spoon.
- *Raw oysters.* Oysters served raw on the half shell on a bed of cracked ice are usually seasoned with lemon, pepper, or a little hot sauce. The oyster is detached from the shell before service with a knife. Hold the shell in one hand and remove the oyster with a small oyster fork in the other hand. Lay the shells on the side of the plate. Alternatively, bring the shell to the mouth and quietly suck the loosened flesh from the shell.

*Mussels* are usually cooked. Mussels live in coastal waters and attach themselves in clusters to sand and rocks through a secretion of strong, silky threads known as a *beard*. Although mussels are served in a number of ways, a popular method is to steam the shells in a white wine broth *à la marinière.* The mussels are eaten with fingers, a fork, and a spoon. A discard bowl is provided for shells and a finger bowl is used to rinse fingertips.

- Hold the shell in the hand, extract the meat with a seafood fork, dip it in the broth, and eat it with one bite.
- Or bring the shell to the mouth and quitely suck the flesh from the shell, along with the juice.
- Discard the shells in the bowl provided.
- Eat the broth with a spoon or spear pieces of bread with a fork and dip them in the broth.

SHERBET. Sherbet, *sorbet* in French, is a culinary term for ice made from the syrup of fruit, a purée of fruit served to cleanse and refresh the palate between courses at a multicourse meal. At a simple meal, sherbet is served as dessert. Sherbet is served on a plate or in a cup. When served on a plate, with fruit salad or the meat course, sherbet is eaten with a fork. If presented in a cup on a plate, such as between courses or as dessert, sherbet is eaten with a spoon.

SHISH KEBAB. Shish kebab is thick cubes of meat and vegetables speared on a metal skewer and grilled. To remove the food from the skewer, the skewer is steadied between the tines of a fork with one hand, and the rod is pulled from the meat and vegetables with the other hand.

SPARERIBS. Spareribs are the thin end of pork ribs from which most of the meat is cut away. As the meat that remains on the rib is difficult to cut from the bone, the bone is held with the fingers of one hand while the meat is eaten. Because spareribs are served with sauce, they are messy to eat and are served only at informal meals (often with a bib).

TEA BAGS. To remove excess liquid from a tea bag, press the tea bag against the rim of the cup with a spoon. Use the string to place the used tea bag on the saucer.

TORTILLAS. A tortilla is a thin, flat, unleavened bread made of corn or flour, baked on an iron plate or a flat stone, and served hot. Depending on the menu, a tortilla is eaten with fingers or a utensil. When laid flat on the palm of the hand or a plate, tortillas are buttered, folded, or rolled and eaten with fingers. If filled with chopped vegetables and meat, for example, as an enchilada, tortillas are eaten with a fork and knife. However, when a crisp tortilla is filled with meat and vegetables to make a taco, it is eaten with fingers to prevent the shell from scattering when cut.

CHAPTER FIFTY-TWO

# TABLE MANNERS

*There is much in a person's mode of eating.*

OVID

TABLE MANNERS in Europe date back to the eleventh century, to the days of chivalry and knights-errant. The knights, or chevaliers, were armed horsemen, "gallant, courageous and fair"—hence our word *cavalry.* In the thirteenth century, Frederick II inaugurated courtly manners, which emphasized intellect, wit, and beauty. Our word *courtesy* is a diminutive of "courtier's customs," while *manners* comes from the Latin *manuarius,* meaning "of the hand."

*Bite not thy bread and lay it down,*
*This is not curtesy to use in town:*
*But break as much as you will eat,*
*The remnant to the poor you shall leave.*

THE BOKE OF CURTESYE, C. 1460

The fifteenth and sixteenth centuries gave birth to modern table manners. With the invention of movable type around 1440, books on social deportment based on consideration of others began to circulate. William Caxton, the first printer in England, published *The Boke of Curtesye,* around 1477, a tome that set forth the duties of knighthood and chivalrous conduct.

Renaissance women of the aristocracy played a more passive and decorative role than today, and it was gentlemen with leisure time who contemplated social deportment and wrote etiquette books. In 1528 Baldassare Castiglione, an Italian diplomat, penned *Il Libro d'Oro,* which was translated into English as *The Courtier* in 1561.

Children of the aristocracy learned table manners through menial service in noble households and from etiquette manuals. In the sixteenth century, Desiderius Erasmus, the Dutch humanist, writer, and professor of divinity at Cambridge, who believed in the education of youth, set forth the following guidelines for social deportment.

> At table or at meat, let mirth be with thee, let ribaldrie be excised; sit not down until thou have washed, but let thy nails be prepared before, and no filth stick in them, lest thou be called sloven and a great nigard. Remember the common saying, and before make water, and if need require, ease thy belly, and if thou be gird too tight, to unloose thy girdle is wisdom, which to do at table is shame. When thou wipest thy hands put forth of thy mind all grief, for at the table it become mete not to be sad, not to make others sad.

And in the sixteenth century, rules of dining were formalized.

*For rudnes it is thy pottage to sup,*
*Or speake to any, his head in the cup.*
*They knife se be sharpe to cut fayre thy meate;*
*Thy mouth not to full when thou dost eate;*
*Not smackynge thy lyppes, As commonly do hogges,*
*Nor gnawynge the bones As it were dogges;*
*Suche rudenes abhorre, Suche beastlylnes flie,*
*At the table behave thy selfe manerly . . .*
*Pyke not thy teethe at the table syttnge;*
*Nor use at they meate Over muche spytynge;*
*This rudnes of youth Is to abhorde;*
*Thy selfe manerly Behave at the borde.*

*Francis Seager,* Schoole of Vertue and Booke of Goode Nourture for Chyldren, *1557*

Court etiquette was so elaborate in the seventeenth century that it bordered on the ridiculous. Aristocrats were given tickets of admission to court ceremonies with a code of conduct printed on the reverse side. Gradually, *etiquette* came to mean a mode of behavior, not only for the French court but in social situations everywhere.

Although etiquette in Europe and England was dictated by gentlemen of leisure, in the United States men were too busy laying the foundation of a new country and providing a living for their families. It fell to the women to teach social deportment and etiquette. The exception was a young George Washington, who at age 16 wrote *Rules of Civility & Decent Behaviour in Company and Conversation,* a school exercise that included 110 rules based on a seventeenth-century book written by Francis Hawkins, *Youths Behavior, or Decency in Conversation Amongst Men,* itself based on a set of rules set forth by French Jesuits in the sixteenth century. The number one maxim that runs throughout Washington's book is consideration for others. This is the basis of modern table manners.

Nothing is as revealing about one's environment and social adjustment as table manners. A person with poor table manners usually has poor manners in other areas of life. Suffice it to say that manners must relate to one's lifestyle; otherwise they are mere affectations. Although every decade brings sweeping changes, the customs of the table prevail because they make sense and, once obtained, are never lost or taken from us. Let's start at the beginning of a meal, and work our way through to the end.

## How Long to Hold Dinner for a Late Guest

Rather than delay dinner for everyone to accommodate the arrival of a late guest, dinner is held no longer than 15 to 20 minutes.

At a formal occasion, when a guest arrives late to a dinner or luncheon, a butler or maid answers the door (so as not to interrupt the table conversation), and the hostess remains seated. The latecomer goes to the hostess immediately, offers a brief explanation, and is served the course in progress. If the latecomer arrives during dessert, as a courtesy the hostess sees that a dinner plate is made up for him or her.

At an informal meal, the host answers the door and greets the latecomer, who makes a brief explanation to the hostess. When the latecomer is a gentleman, the other men at the table remain seated. But, if the latecomer is a lady, as a courtesy, all the gentlemen rise and the man on her left helps her into her seat.

## Where to Put the Cocktail Glass When Dinner Is Announced

A cocktail glass is not brought to the dinner table because water and several wines are served with the multicourse meal. The extra glass crowds the place setting and disturbs the symmetry of the table. Moreover, the taste of grain-based spirits nullifies the flavor of wine served with the meal. Simply leave the cocktail glass in the room where cocktails are taken.

## Entering the Dining Room

At a formal dinner generally the host escorts the lady of honor into the dining room first. The remaining guests enter the dining room in whatever order they choose. The hostess enters the dining room last, accompanied by the man of honor. There are a few exceptions to this custom.

- If the guest of honor is a high-ranking male dignitary, such as the president of a country, he enters the dining room first with the hostess. The host enters the dining room second with the dignitary's wife.
- When the guest of honor is a high-ranking female dignitary, such as the prime minister of a country, she enters the dining room first with the host. The dignitary's husband follows with the hostess.

- When there are more ladies than gentlemen at a formal dinner (a rare occurrence), the hostess enters the dining room alone.

  At an informal dinner, the guests enter the dining room in whatever order is convenient. When seating arrangements are not designated by place cards, usually the hostess enters the dining room first to tell everyone where to sit.

## Where to Sit Down

Place cards identify the places people are to sit; they are used to eliminate confusion when more than six people dine together. At formal affairs, which usually involve a large group, individual places are always designated by place cards. But an informal dinner is a less structured occasion; when place cards are not provided, the hostess tells the guests where to sit or asks them to find their own places (although this is not always a good practice because mixups can occur as guests try to seat themselves in alternate male-female positions).

## When to Sit Down

At a formal meal the hostess is the last to enter the dining room, and the ladies sit down without waiting for her. At an informal meal, the ladies sit before or after the hostess is seated, whichever is convenient.

History accords the place of honor to the right side because most people are right-handed. A gentleman draws out the chair for the lady seated on his right, pushes her chair into place, and seats himself. The host seats the lady on his right. The hostess is helped by the gentleman seated on her left. To avoid congestion, it is easier if ladies approach their chairs from the right.

When all the women are seated, the men sit down.

## Where to Lay One's Purse

Because a purse on the table crowds and disturbs the symmetry of the table setting, in a private residence it is left wherever the hostess suggests, such as in a bedroom or on a chair. In a restaurant or public place, to avoid having a purse stolen, it is held on the lap or placed close at hand on a banquette. For the brave at heart, it is laid on the floor by one's chair or hung from the back of the chair (if this does not inhibit service or tempt theft).

## The Etiquette of the Napkin

At a seated meal, before unfolding the napkin, wait for the hostess to remove her napkin from the table and unfold it in her lap. The exception is at a meal served buffet-style: the napkin is unfolded when one starts to eat.

The napkin is unfolded in a smooth movement, not with a jerk, a snap, or a shake.

The size of the napkin is commensurate with the number of courses served, a dimension that affects how far it is unfolded in the lap. At a formal dinner, a large square napkin from approximately 22 to 26 inches is provided; this size covers the lap entirely, so the napkin is unfolded halfway. The weight of the fold prevents the napkin from slipping off the lap.

At a simple meal, fewer courses are served and a smaller napkin is used, approximately 18 inches square. The smaller napkin is unfolded entirely to fully cover the lap.

When messy finger food is served, such as shellfish or spareribs, before tucking the napkin under the chin or tying it around the neck, look to the host to see if he does the same.

Use the napkin to blot the lips, not to wipe the mouth.

When a napkin ring is provided, it placed at the top left of the cover, usually above the forks. At the end of the meal, the napkin is grasped in the center, pulled through the ring, and laid on the table so the point faces the center of the table.

A lady should refrain from replenishing lipstick before coming to the table in order to prevent an imprint of lipstick on the rim of a glass or a napkin.

To avoid leaving a soiled crumply napkin on the table for others to see, when you leave the table temporarily, place the napkin on the seat of the chair. If the chair seat is upholstered, to avoid staining the fabric, the napkin is laid soiled side up.

At the end of the meal the napkin is *loosely* folded. A refolded napkin suggests

FOR EASY REMOVAL, THE NAPKIN IS PLACED IN THE NAPKIN RING WITH THE POINT OF THE NAPKIN FACING THE DINER.

AFTER THE NAPKIN IS REMOVED, THE NAPKIN RING IS PLACED AT THE TOP LEFT OF THE PLACE SETTING.

AT THE END OF THE MEAL, THE NAPKIN IS GRASPED IN THE CENTER AND PULLED THROUGH THE NAPKIN RING.

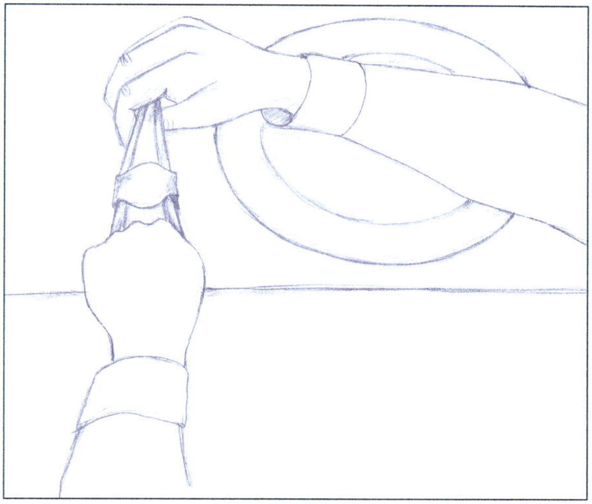

THE POINT OF THE NAPKIN FACES THE CENTER OF THE TABLE.

reuse and a crumpled napkin is unsightly. When a plate, such as a dessert plate, lies in the center of the place setting, on leaving the table lay the napkin to the left or right of the plate. But if the center of the cover is empty, the napkin is laid in the middle of the place setting. If after-dinner coffee is served at the table, the napkin remains in the lap.

## When to Commence Eating

- At a small dinner party of eight people or less, wait for the hostess to begin.
- At a large party, where a course might cool before everyone is served, commence to eat after three or four guests are served. If the party is divided into smaller tables, as is common these days, wait until everyone at the table is served. The exception is a cold course: as a courtesy to others, commence to eat after everyone is served.
- At a banquet, where throngs of people are served, in the interest of enjoying the hot courses at the right temperature, eating commences as soon as those on either side are served.
- At a meal served buffet style, eating commences when one is ready.

## The Etiquette of Eating

*Eating should be done in silence,*
*lest the windpipe act before the gullet,*
*and life be endangered.*

THE TALMUD, *C. 200 A.D.*

The essence of good table manners is unobtrusiveness, a courtesy that includes *eating quietly.* Noise impedes conversation. Scraping a plate or loudly chewing ice is unpleasant to listen to and considered impolite.

Do not bolt your food, for, as Sir Walter Raleigh observed,

*Only men in rags*
*And gluttons old in sin*
*Mistake themselves for carpet bags*
*And tumble victuals in.*

Savor the meal and eat slowly; it encourages conversation and conviviality.

Never speak with a full mouth. Not only is a full mouth offensive to see, it makes conversation difficult to hear. Before asking a question, wait until the guest is finished chewing, or almost finished. And don't smack your food in the mouth, the sound is offensive to hear.

## How Much Food to Take on a Utensil

Because people dine with their eyes as well as their palate, to avoid the sight of bulging cheeks, never pile food high on a utensil. Take only enough food to chew and swallow in one easy bite. Moreover, it makes conversation easier.

## How to Sip Beverages

To avoid leaving food on the rim of the vessel, make sure the mouth is free of food and blot the lips with a napkin before taking a sip of beverage.

## Testing Hot Foods and Liquids

*Never blow your soup if it is too hot, but wait until it cools.*

C. B. Hartley, The Gentleman's Book of Etiquette, 1873

To test the temperature of a hot beverage, take a single sip from the side of the spoon. When the sip proves too hot, give the beverage time to cool before lifting the cup to the mouth. When an extremely hot beverage is sipped, take a quick sip of water to decrease the effect of the burn.

Do not blow on hot foods or beverages—you risk offending those seated across the table. At a family meal or a casual outdoor affair, a hot beverage is often cooled with an ice cube transferred from a water goblet, if available.

## How to Remove Food from the Mouth

Food is removed from the mouth in the manner in which it is put into the mouth. Food put into the mouth with a utensil is removed with a utensil. When fingers are used to eat food, for example, plums or chicken wings, the pit or bone is removed with fingers. The exception is fish eaten with a fork: because tiny bones fall between fork tines, they are removed with fingers.

To remove spoiled food, cover the mouth with one hand, remove the morsel with the other hand, place it on the plate, and cover it with another portion of food (if possible). In a private residence, rather than embarrass the hostess by telling her that a particular dish contains foreign matter or is tainted, eat from the unspoiled portion. But if this is not possible, move the portion around on the plate so it looks as if you are eating, and leave the tainted part alone. In a restaurant, tell the server so he or she may make a replacement.

A toothpick is an offensive sight in operation. When food is caught between the teeth that is annoying or uncomfortable, wait to remove it privately.

## Sneezing, Coughing, Burping, Yawning

When sneezing or coughing at the table is unavoidable, cover your nose or mouth with a napkin and proceed as quietly as possible. Except in an emergency, don't use a napkin to blow your nose. Use a handkerchief instead, and turn your head to the side.

When a burp is coming on, cover the mouth with a napkin, quietly burp, and softly say, "Excuse me." For an attack of hiccups, excuse yourself from the table until they have passed. Rather than draw attention to the condition on return (and interrupt conversation) do not apologize in a public way. Instead, say "Sorry" quietly to the hostess and let it go at that.

In some cultures the breath is associated with man's spirit. To prevent the soul from escaping or an evil spirit from entering the body, the mouth is covered when a yawn cannot be suppressed. This custom prevails in our society today.

## How to Eat Finger Food

When finger food is taken from a tray, place it on the plate (to do otherwise defeats the purpose of the plate). Don't lick your fingers; use a napkin (that's what it's for).

When in doubt about whether to use fingers or a utensil to eat a particular food, watch those about you and proceed accordingly. If you're still in doubt, follow common sense and use a utensil, usually a fork, which is the most versatile implement.

Dunked food leaves crumbs on the rim of a cup or glass, and is frowned on at a private party or in a public place.

## The Etiquette of Utensils

Food served on a plate is eaten with a fork, and food served in a bowl is taken with a spoon. When two eating utensils or two serving utensils are presented together, such as a fork and spoon, the fork is used to steady the portion, and the spoon to cut and convey the bite to the mouth.

At one time or another everyone uses the wrong utensil, and it is not a cause of concern. Rather, remedy the situation, quietly, without apology or calling attention to the error, and forget it!

To prevent an unpleasant sight for others, refrain from half-eating or half-sipping food, such as a bite of ice cream or soup. Once a bite is placed on an eating utensil, consume the bite entirely, or not at all.

Never gesticulate with an eating utensil in the hand. You risk stabbing a dinner partner or knocking over a goblet.

In formal dining the knife is used to push food against the fork. At informal meals, a knife or a piece of bread is used as a pusher, for example, to push salad onto a fork.

In a private residence, when a place setting is laid without a necessary utensil, such as a knife, tell the hostess so she may correct it. When a serving utensil is missing, rather than use one's eating utensil, inform the hostess so she may remedy the situation for the benefit of all the guests.

In formal or informal dining, the dinner knife is used to push food against the back of the fork.

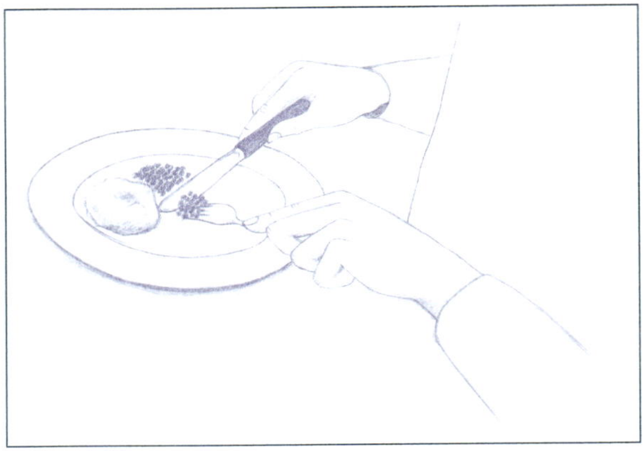

At an informal meal, a piece of bread is used as a pusher.

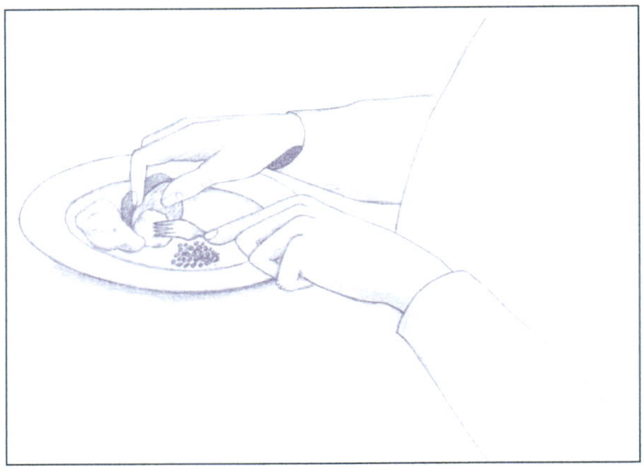

In a private residence, the table setting is a reflection of the hosts' ability; rather than embarrass the hostess by wiping a soiled utensil clean, suffer in silence. But a restaurant table setting is an impersonal expression that does not reflect on the host; if a soiled utensil is laid on the table, ask the waiter for a clean one.

At a formal affair when a utensil is dropped on the floor, leave it for the butler to retrieve—it is part of his job. He will make a replacement for you. At an informal meal, quietly retrieve a dropped utensil yourself, and if it may have caused stains or damage of any kind, offer to make a replacement or a repair.

# Miscellaneous Manners

*Do one thing at a time at the table.* If you want to sip your wine, temporarily rest your fork or knife on the plate.

*What to do if the table is improperly set.* Don't rearrange an improperly arranged place setting and offend the hostess. In a restaurant, where an improperly set table does not reflect on the skills of the host, quietly rearrange the ware for comfort.

*Where to place the hands when eating.* To avoid creating an obstruction to your dinner partner, when holding a utensil, rest your other hand in your lap. When not holding any utensils, both hands remain in the lap.

*Urges to resist.* To create a relaxed ambience, resist the urge to fidget, rearrange the silverware, twist the linens, drum on the table, and play with salt and pepper shakers. For cleanliness, keep the hands away from the face and hair.

*Posture.* Good posture at the table means sitting straight with the back rested slightly against the back of the chair. To avoid spills, lean over the plate each time you take a bite. Never tip a chair backward; the position is hard on the back chair legs and disturbs the symmetry of the table setting. Avoid wrapping your feet around the legs of the chair. Refrain from leaning back and extending your legs under the table, putting your arm on the back of a dinner partner's chair, or looping your arm around the back of the chair. To do otherwise blocks service and obstructs others from the conversation.

*Elbows and forearms off the table.* To avoid crowding one's dinner partner, during a meal the elbows remain close to the body and off the table. To prevent a barrier to conversation, the forearm and hand are not wrapped around the plate. But between courses, in the interest of hearing conversation at a crowded or noisy table, the elbows are rested on the table so one may lean forward, or the wrist and forearm are placed on the edge of the table.

In a noisy atmosphere, to better hear the conversation between courses, rest the elbows on the table and lean forward.

Or, place the wrist and forearm on the edge of the table and lean forward.

*Reaching at the table.* To keep from creating an obstruction for others, at the table reach only for ware close enough to grasp in one fluid motion. Otherwise, ask a guest to pass it to you.

*Dealing with disagreeable food.* When food that you don't like or can't eat is served, rather than make an issue and offend the hostess, take a small portion. Place the portion on the plate, dabble with it, and eat a small amount (or none at all). To compensate, take larger portions of other foods. For a severe allergy, say, "No, thank you" and after the meal, quietly explain to the hostess. At a buffet, take only the foods you like.

*Spilled food.* When a guest spills food at a formal affair, a butler takes the appropriate action. But at an informal meal, the diner quietly and quickly lifts the food with a utensil and places it on the side of his plate. However, if food is spilled on another guest, the diner apologizes and offers to pay for cleaning (but lets the other person wipe up the debris).

*Removing different foods from a platter at one time.* When a platter contains a combination of foods, such as meat, potatoes, vegetable, and garnish, take a moderate serving of each, including the garnish. However, if the removal of garnish will overly disturb the appearance of the platter, leave it. If a course is presented that contains another food underneath, such as toast or lettuce, take the entire portion.

*How large a portion to take from a platter.* When a platter of presliced food is presented, and each slice is an ample size, take one serving. But if the slices are small, and it looks as if there are enough servings for each guest to have two, take two for yourself. As a courtesy to the last guest, make sure to leave enough food on the platter so he or she has a choice from several portions.

*Which portion to take from a platter.* Rather than rummage through a platter and disturb the look of the presentation, take the portion nearest to you.

*To refuse a beverage.* Do not wave the hands about to refuse a beverage or cover up a glass or turn a cup upside down; simply say, "No thank you." To do otherwise disturbs the look of the table. When a guest refuses a glass of wine, see that he or she is given a glass of water.

*Second helpings.* At a formal affair a multicourse menu is served that precludes the need to offer second helpings. However, at an informal meal, the menu is simpler and second helpings are encouraged. If the hostess does not offer second helpings, do not ask for them. Instead, take a modest serving the first time and wait for the hostess to suggest more.

*How many pieces of food to cut at one time.* To avoid a messy plate, cut one bite at a time, and not more than two pieces.

*Assisting with service at the table.* At a formal affair domestic help is provided and guests do not assist with service, except to move the shoulders slightly to make service easier. At an informal meal, help generally is not provided and the guests assist with service by passing the dishes nearest to them. To avoid congestion, serveware is passed to the right and the guests do not delay service by helping themselves along the way (unless it is suggested that they do so).

*Thanks for service.* Each time service is provided at a multicourse meal, verbal acceptance is not necessary because it distracts from the conversation. Acceptance of the course is in itself thanks. But to refuse service, a verbal rejection of "No, thank you," is given. At a simple meal when a serving bowl is passed upon request, it is courteous for the receiver to say, "Thank you." It is not necessary for those who receive a dish in passage to say thank you.

*Greeting a butler or a maid at the table.* When a guest knows a maid or a butler, rather than draw attention to the fact and interrupt conversation, give a brief greeting, such as "Nice to see you."

*Complimenting the hostess on the food.* In the early twentieth century, even modest homes had help. Meals were prepared by a cook and it was impolite to compliment the hostess on the cuisine because it was inappropriate. Today, few people have help, hostesses delight in food preparation, and a compliment on the cuisine is appreciated. However, there are those who still hold that the conversation is more important than the food and a compliment on the menu or a particular course distracts from the discourse and is inappropriate at a party. The decision, therefore, is individual.

*Turning the table.* Years ago at a formal affair, it was customary for the hostess to begin conversation at the table with the guest seated on her right. The guests followed suit, and in this way, no one was omitted from conversation. Halfway through the meal, the hostess directed her conversation to the guest seated on her left, and the guests did the same, a custom known as *turning the table*. Today, the dinner table is no longer deliberately "turned," and a courteous guest makes sure he or she talks with the partners on both right and left sides.

*How many people does one converse with at the table?* A formal table is laid with several candelabra and multiple tall centerpieces that block cross-table visibility and make conversation with those seated on the opposite side difficult. For ease of conversation at a formal affair, guests converse with their dinner partners and chat only briefly with those seated several places away (so the person in the middle does not have to lean backward). But at an informal meal, because fewer courses are served and the table setting is simpler, cross-table visibility is not blocked and group conversation is encouraged.

*Smoking at the table.* A lighted cigarette is never taken to the table. Smoking is offensive to nonsmokers and dulls the palate. A table laid without ashtrays indicates that the hostess does not wish her guests to smoke. But if ashtrays are provided, before proceeding to smoke and as a courtesy to others, ask the hostess for permission. Because some people are allergic to smoke, wait until the table is cleared for dessert or hold off until dessert is finished. Never use a dessert plate or a saucer as an ashtray.

*Who clears the plates?* At a formal affair, plates are removed by a professional staff. But as most informal meals are served without help, the hostess clears the plates, often with the help of a guest or two. At a family meal, members clear their own plates.

*Leaving the dining room.* To signal dinner is concluded, the hostess catches the eye of the host, lays her napkin on the table, and suggests that everyone go into another room for coffee and after-dinner drinks. The hostess rises from her chair. The gentlemen help the ladies to their right and the guests leave the dining room in whatever order they wish. The host leaves last.

*When to depart a dinner party.* "With the bread eaten, up breaks the company," says Cervantes in *Don Quixote.* But such a speedy departure would not be polite. At a formal affair, guests do not depart until the honoree has left (unless they have told the hostess in advance that they must do so). Because entertainment and socializing follow a formal dinner, it is courteous to remain for at least an hour.

At an informal party, out of consideration for the hosts who have worked hard to make the occasion possible, it is polite to remain for approximately an hour. However, guests may depart within the hour and in whatever order they choose.

*Saying good-bye.* When it's time to leave, rather than detain one's host with a lengthy good-bye, make the departure brief but cordial.

CHAPTER FIFTY-THREE

# TABLE MANNERS IN A CHANGING WORLD

*The art of dining well is no slight art, the pleasure not a slight pleasure.*

*Michel de Montaigne, Essays, 1588*

TODAY THE WORLD is a smaller place. Exotic ports and distant places are only hours away. Electronic communication, mass media, global travel, and international trade expose us to cross-cultural table manners where food may be eaten with fingers rather than utensils, and seating may be on the ground rather than at the table.

Throughout the ages table manners have followed logic, a code of civility based on common sense, courtesy, and comfort, that provides a way to interact with one another in a practical manner. But so often the customs that prevail in the West are not followed in the East. Buffet service is considered impolite in many parts of the world because it is impersonal. In China, smacking one's lips is an expression of appreciation of the food and culinary skills of the chef or the host, but in the West the sound is inappropriate and considered impolite. Although an audible belch is poor manners in Western countries, in Asia it praises the munificence of the host. In the West, finger food is taken with either hand, but in the East, it is always taken with the right hand because the left hand is associated with toilet activities.

When you are unsure how to proceed in another culture, follow the logic of common sense, and remember the old dictum, "When in Rome do as the Romans do." When people from the East dine in Western homes they sit in chairs, eat from tables, and use knives and forks. Westerners who dine in an Asian or African home eat according to the customs of the host. In a sophisticated Eastern city, the Westerner sits at a table laid with flatware, but in a rural village, where the old methods prevail, he takes food with fingers from dishes laid out on the floor. Sometimes both fingers and utensils are used: for example, meat taken with fingers from a central joint cut by the host. Bread held with fingers may be used as a utensil to pick up morsels of food. In many Chinese restaurants in the West, Asians eat with utensils and Caucasians use chopsticks.

Whatever the customs, in today's changing world cross-cultural attitudes prevail, and so often menus feature a fusion of Western and Asian foods, such as Japanese-Italian dishes that require proficiency with chopsticks and forks. But, when a code of conduct ceases to apply, it is quickly forgotten and relegated to the pages of history.

The time to know and respect "thy neighbors' ways" is now, including table manners. When in doubt, follow the customs of the host country, and proceed with a certitude based on common sense, courtesy, and comfort.

# Bibliography

## Pottery and Porcelain


Battie, David, ed. *Sotheby's Concise Encyclopedia of Porcelain.* London, England: Conran Octopus, 1990.

Bedford, John. *Old Worcester China.* New York: Walker, 1966.

———. *Chelsea and Derby China.* New York: Walker, 1967.

Berges, Ruth. *From Gold to Porcelain.* South Brunswick, N.J.: Thomas Yoseloff, 1963.

Berling, K., ed. *Meissen China: An Illustrated History.* New York: Dover, 1972.

Beurdeley, Cécile, and Michel Beurdeley. *Chinese Ceramics,* trans. Katherine Watson. New York: Harper & Row.

Boger, Louise Ade. *The Dictionary of World Pottery and Porcelain.* New York: Scribner's, 1971.

———, and H. Batterson. *The Dictionary of Antiques and the Decorative Arts.* New York: Scribner's, 1957.

Bushell, Stephen W. *Chinese Art,* 2 vols. North Miami Beach, Fla.: Rare Reprints, 1977.

Charlston, Robert J., ed. *World Ceramics.* London, England: Hamlyn Publishing Group, 1971.

Clark, Kenneth. *The Potter's Manual.* Secaucus, N.J.: Chartwell Books, 1983.

Cooper, Emanuel. *A History of World Pottery.* Radnor, Pa.: Chilton, 1972.

Cox, Warren E. *The Book of Pottery and Porcelain,* 2 vols. New York: Crown, 1970.

Curtis, Edmund deForest. *Pottery: Its Craftsmanship and Its Appreciation.* New York: Harper & Brothers, 1940.

Cushion, Jan. *English Porcelain.* London, England: Charles Letts, 1982.

Divis, Jan. *European Porcelain.* New York: Simon & Schuster, 1983.

Du Boulay, Anthony. *Chinese Porcelain.* London, England: Octopus Books, 1973.

Eberlein, Harold Donaldson, and Roger Wearne Ramsdell. *The Practical Book of Chinaware.* Philadelphia: J. B. Lippincott, 1948.

Eppens, J. H. *Pottery.* New York: Universe Books, 1964.

Garrett, Wendell. *Encyclopedia of Antiques.* New York: Galahad Books, 1976.

Gilchrist, Brenda, ed. *Pottery.* Washington, D.C.: Cooper-Hewitt/Smithsonian Institution, 1981.

Godden, Geoffrey A. *British Pottery and Porcelain.* London, England: Ebenezer Baylis & Sons, 1980.
Haggar, Reginald G. *Continental Pottery and Porcelain,* 2 vols. New York: Hawthorne Books, 1960.
Hamilton, David. *The Thames and Hudson Manual of Pottery and Ceramics.* London, England: Thames and Hudson, 1974.
Hobson, R. L. *Chinese Pottery and Porcelain,* vol. 1. New York: Funk & Wagnalls, 1915.
Honey, W. B. *Dresden China.* New York: Tudor, 1934.
Howard, David, and John Ayers. *Chinese Export Porcelain.* London, England: Philip Wilson/Sotheby Parke Bernet, 1981.
Kelley, Austin P., ed. *The Anatomy of Antiques.* New York: Viking Press/Sotheby Park Bernet, 1974.
Ketchum, William C., Jr. *The Family Treasury of Antiques.* New York: A & W Publications, 1979.
Landais, Hubert. *French Porcelain.* New York: Putnam, 1961.
Mankowitz, Wolf. *Wedgwood.* London, England: Spring Books, 1966.
———, and Reginald G. Haggar. *The Concise Encyclopedia of English Pottery and Porcelain.* New York: Hawthorne Books, 1957.
Medley, Margaret. *The Chinese Potter.* New York: Scribner's 1976.
Morley-Fletcher, Hugo. *Techniques of the World's Great Masters of Pottery and Ceramics.* Secausus, N.J.: Chartwell Books, 1984.
Mudge, Jean McClure. *Chinese Export Porcelain for the American Trade.* New York: University of Delaware Press, 1962.
Nelson, Glenn C. *Ceramics.* New York: Holt, Rhinehart & Winston, 1971.
Osborne, Harold, ed. *The Oxford Companion to the Decorative Arts.* London, England: Oxford University Press, 1975.
Palmer, Arlene M. *A Winterthur Guide to Chinese Export Porcelain.* New York: Crown, 1976.
Patterson, Jerry E. *Porcelain.* Washington, D.C.: Cooper-Hewitt Museum/Smithsonian Institution, 1979.
Phillips, Phoebe. *The Encyclopedia of Antiques.* New York: Bonanza/Crown, 1972.
Ramsey, L. G. G., ed. *The Complete Encyclopedia of Antiques.* New York: Hawthorn Books, 1968.
Rhoades, Orille Bourassa. *The World of Antique Arts.* Chicago: Lightner Publishing, 1958.
Sandon, John. *English Porcelain of the 18th and 19th Centuries.* London, England: Merehurst Press, 1989.
Savage, George. *Ceramics for the Collector.* London, England: Rockcliff Publishing, 1949.
———. *Eighteenth-Century English Porcelain.* London, England: Spring Books/Westbook House, 1964.
———, and Harold Newman. *An Illustrated Dictionary of Ceramics.* London, England: Thames and Hudson, 1974.
Shackleton, Robert, and Elizabeth Shackleton. *The Book of Antiques.* New York: Tudor Publishing, 1946.
Spargo, John. *Early American Pottery and China.* Garden City, N.Y.: Garden City Publishing, 1926.
Tait, Hugh. *Porcelain.* London, England: Spring Books/Drury House, 1963.

Thomas, Gertrude Z. *Richer Than Spices.* New York: Knopf, 1965.
Williams, Peter. *Wedgwood: A Collector's Guide.* Radnor, Pa.: Wallace-Homestead/Chilton, 1992.

## Table Settings and Entertaining

Chefetz, Sheila. *Antiques for the Table.* New York: Penguin, 1993.
Cooper, Charles. *The English Table in History and Literature.* London, England: Sampson, Low, Marston, 1929.
Doran, J. *Table Traits with Something on Them.* New York: Redfield, 1855.
Earle, Alice Morse. *Homelife in Colonial Days.* New York: Jonathan David, 1975.
Freeman, John Crosby. *Victorian Entertaining.* New York: Running Press/Michael Friedman Publishing Group, 1989.
Girouard, Mark. *Life in the English Country House.* New York: Penguin, 1980.
Norman, Barbara. *Tales of the Table: A History of Western Cuisine.* Englewood Cliffs, N.J.: Prentice Hall, 1972.
Paston-Williams, Sarah. *The Art of Dining: A History of Cooking and Eating.* London, England: National Trust Enterprises, 1993.
Penner, Lucille Recht. *Eating the Plates.* New York: Macmillan, 1991.
Roberts, Patricia Easterbrook. *Table Settings, Entertaining, and Etiquette.* New York: Viking, 1967.
Visser, Margaret. *Rituals of Dinner.* New York: HarperCollins, 1991.
Wheaton, Barbara Ketcham. *Savoring the Past: The French Kitchen and Table from 1300 to 1789.* New York: Touchstone, 1983.
Willan, Anne. *Great Cooks and Their Recipes from Taillevent to Escoffier.* Boston: Little, Brown, 1992.
Wirth, Barbara. *The Elegant Table.* New York: Harry N. Abrams, 1987.

## Silver

Abbey Fine Arts, eds. *Georgian Silver.* London, England: Murray Group, 1970.
Bace, Jill. *Collecting Silver: The Facts at Your Fingertips.* London, England: Octopus Publishing Group, 1999.
Banister, Judith. *English Silver.* London, England: Hamlyn Publishing Group, 1969.
Bigelow, Francis Hill. *Historic Silver of the Colonies and Its Makers.* New York: Macmillan, 1917.
Bly, John. *Discovering Hall Marks on English Silver.* Aylesbury, Bucks, U.K.: Shire Publications, 1999.
Clayton, Michael. *Silver and Gold.* London, England: Hamlyn Publishing Group, 1985.
Fennimore, Donald L. *Silver and Pewter.* New York: Knopf, 1984.
Glanville, Philippa. *Silver History and Design.* New York: Abrams, 1997.
Gruber, Alain. *Silverware.* New York: Rizzoli, 1982.
Hackenbroch, Yvonne. *English and Other Silver in the Irwin Untermyer Collection.* New York: Metropolitan Museum, 1969.
Helliwell, Stephen. *Collecting Small Silverware.* Oxford, England: Phaidon-Christie's, 1988.
Holland, Margaret. *Silver.* London, England: Octopus Books, 1983.
Hood, Graham. *American Silver.* New York: Dutton, 1989.

Hughes, Bernard G. *Small Antique Silverware.* New York: Bramhall House/Clarkson N. Potter, 1957.

Langford, Joel. *Silver.* Secaucus, N.J.: Chartwell Books, 1991.

Mc Nab, Jessie. *Silver.* Washington, D.C.: Cooper-Hewitt Museum/Smithsonian Institution, 1981.

Osterberg, Richard F., and Betty Smith. *Silver Flatware Dictionary.* New York: Barnes, 1981.

Peterson, Harold L. *A History of Knives.* New York: Scribner's, 1966.

Pickford, Ian. *Antique Silver.* Woodbridge, Suffolk, England: Antique Collectors' Club, 1998.

Snodin, Michael. *English Silver Spoons.* London, England: Charles Letts, 1974.

Truman, Charles, ed. *Sotheby's Concise Encyclopedia of Silver.* London, England: Conran Octopus, 1993.

Turner, Eric. *English Silver from 1660.* Owing Mills, Md.: Stemmer House Publishers, 1985.

Wenham, Edward. *Old Silver for Modern Settings.* New York: Knopf, 1951.

Wills, Geoffrey. *The Guinness Book of Silver.* Middlesex, England: Guinness Superlatives, 1983.

Wyler, Seymour B. *The Book of Old Silver.* New York: Crown, 1963.

## Glass

Battie, David, and Simon Cottle, eds. *Sotheby's Concise Encyclopedia of Glass.* London, England: Conran Octopus, 1991.

Bray, Charles. *Dictionary of Glass: Materials and Techniques.* London, England: A. & C. Black, 1995.

Brooks, John A. *Glass.* Bristol, England: Camden House Books/BPCC Publishers, no date.

Buckley, Wilfred. *The Art of Glass.* New York: Oxford University Press, 1939.

Cousins, Mark. *20th-Century Glass.* Secaucus, N.J.: Chartwell Books, 1989.

Drepperd, Carl W. *The ABC's of Old Glass.* New York: Doubleday, 1949.

Gilchrist, Brenda, ed. *Glass.* Washington, D.C.: Cooper-Hewitt Museum/Smithsonian Institution, 1979.

Harshorne, Albert. *Antique Drinking Glasses.* New York: Brussel & Brussel, 1968.

Hughes, G. Bernard. *English, Scottish and Irish Table Glass: From the Sixteenth Century to 1820.* London, England: Batsford, 1956.

Isenberg, Anita, and Seymour Isenberg. *Crafting in Glass.* Radnor, Pa.: Chilton, 1981.

Lee, Ruth Webb. *Nineteenth-Century Art Glass.* New York: Barrows, 1952.

Kampfer, Fritz, and Klaus G. Beyer. *Glass: A World History.* New York: New York Graphic Society, 1966.

Middlemas, Keith. *Antique Colored Glass.* New York: Exeter Books, 1979.

Moore, N. Hudson. *Old Glass: European and American.* New York: Tudor, 1935.

Northend, Mary Harrod. *American Glass.* New York: Tudor, 1926.

Petrová, Sylva, and Jean-Luc Olivié, eds. *Bohemian Glass: 1400–1989.* New York: Abrams, 1990.

Phillips, Phoebe. *The Collector's Encyclopedia of Antiques.* New York: Crown, 1973.

———. *The Encyclopedia of Glass.* London, England: Spring Books/Octopus, 1987.

Spillman, Jane Shadel. *Glassmaking: America's First Industry.* Corning, N.Y.: Corning Museum of Glass, 1976.

———. *Glass: Tableware, Bowls, and Vases.* New York: Knopf, 1982.

Steenberg, Elisa. *Swedish Glass.* New York: Barrows, 1950.

Truman, Charles. *English Glassware to 1990.* Owings Mills, Md.: Stemmer House, 1984.

### Linens

Bendure, Zelma, and Gladys Pfeiffer. *America's Fabrics.* New York: Macmillan, 1946.
Bonneville, Françoise de. *The Book of Fine Linen.* Paris: Flammarion, 1994.
Denny, Grace G. *Fabrics.* Philadelphia: Lippincott, 1962.
Hollen, Norma, and Jane Sadler. *Textiles.* New York: Macmillan, 1955.
Lebeau, Caroline. *Fabrics: The Decorative Art of Textiles.* New York: Clarkson N. Potter, 1994.
Potter, M. David, and Bernard P. Corbman. *Fiber to Fabric.* New York: McGraw-Hill, 1959.
Stout, Evelyn E. *Introduction to Textiles.* New York: Wiley, 1970.
Walton, Perry. *The Story of Textiles.* New York: Tudor, 1936.

### Table Manners and Serving

Adams, Samuel, and Sarah Abrams. *The Complete Servant.* East Sussex, England: Southover Press, 1993.
Ager, Stanely, and Fiona St. Aubyn. *The Butler's Guide.* New York: Fireside, 1980.
Antoine-Dariaux, Geneviève. *Entertaining with Elegance.* Garden City, N.Y.: Doubleday, 1965.
Aresty, Esther B. *The Best Behavior.* New York: Simon & Schuster, 1970.
Baldrige, Letitia. *The Amy Vanderbilt Complete Book of Etiquette.* New York: Doubleday, 1978.
———. *Amy Vanderbilt's Everyday Etiquette: A Guide to Contemporary Living.* New York: Bantam, 1983.
Boehn, Max von. *Modes and Manners,* 4 vols. Philadelphia: Lippincott, 1932.
Elias, Norbert. *The History of Manners.* New York: Pantheon, 1978.
Fenwick, Millicent. *Vogue's Book of Etiquette and Good Manners.* New York: Condé Nast Publications with Simon & Schuster, 1969.
Ford, Charlotte. *Book of Modern Manners.* New York: Fireside, 1980.
Freeman, John Crosby. *Victorian Entertaining.* New York: Running Press Book/Michael Friedman Publishing, 1989.
Girouard, Mark. *Life in the English Country House.* New York: Penguin, 1980.
Iversen, William. *O the Times, O the Manners.* Toronto, Canada: McLeod, 1965.
Kasson, John F. *Rudeness and Civility: Manners in Nineteenth-Century America.* New York: Hill and Wang, 1990.
Meyer, Sylvia, Edy Schmid, and Christel Spühler. *Professional Table Service,* trans. Heinz Holtmann. New York: Van Nostrand Reinhold, 1991.
Miller, Llewellyn. *The Encyclopedia of Etiquette.* New York: Crown, 1967.
Post, Elizabeth L. *Emily Post's Etiquette.* New York: Funk and Wagnalls, 1969.
———. *The New Emily Post's Etiquette.* New York: Funk and Wagnalls, 1975.
Roosevelt, Eleanor. *Book of Common Sense Etiquette.* New York: Macmillan, 1962.
Sprackling, Helen. *The New Setting Your Table.* New York: Morrow, 1960.

### Menu Plan

Aresty, Esther B. *The Delectable Past.* New York: Simon & Schuster, 1964.
Booth, Sally Smith. *Hung, Strung, & Potted.* New York: Clarkson N. Potter, 1971.

Brasch, R. *How Did It Begin?* New York: D. McKay, 1966.
Brillat-Savarin, Jean-Anthelme. *The Philosopher in the Kitchen* (trans. *La physiologie du goût*). New York: Penguin, 1825/1984.
Chellminski, Rudolph. *The French at the Table.* New York: Morrow, 1985.
Driver, Christopher, and Michelle Berriedale-Honson. *Pepys at Table.* Berkeley: The University of California Press, 1984.
Ellwanger, George H. *The Pleasures of the Table.* New York: Doubleday, 1902.
Fortin, Jacques, ed. *The Visual Food Encyclopedia.* New York: Macmillan, 1996.
Grabhorn, Robert. *A Commonplace Book of Cookery.* San Francisco: North Point Press, 1985.
Hale, William Harlan. *The Horizon Cookbook and Illustrated History of Eating and Drinking Through the Ages.* New York: American Heritage Publishing Company, 1968.
Harrison, Molly. *The Kitchen in History.* New York: Scribner's, 1972.
Krohn, Norman Odya. *Menu Mystique.* Middle Village, N.Y.: Jonathan David, 1983.
McCully, Helen, ed. *The American Heritage Cookbook.* New York: American Heritage Publishing, 1982.
Mc Kendry, Maxime. *The Seven Centuries Cookbook.* New York: McGraw-Hill, 1973.
Mariani, John F. *The Dictionary of American Food and Drink.* New York: Ticknor and Fields, 1983.
Mead, William Edward. *The English Medieval Feast.* New York: Barnes & Noble, 1967.
Montagne, Prosper. *The New Larousse Gastronomique.* New York: Crown, 1960.
Revel, Jean-François. *Culture and Cuisine.* New York: Doubleday, 1982.
Simon, Andre L., and Robin Howe. *The Dictionary of Gastronomy.* Woodstock, N.Y.: Overlook Press, 1978.
Sokolov, Raymond. *Why We Eat What We Eat.* New York: Simon & Schuster, 1991.
Tannahill, Reay. *Food in History.* New York: Stein and Day, 1973.
Toussaint-Samat, Maguelonne. *History of Food,* trans. Anthea Bell. Malden, Mass.: Blackwell Publishers, 1992.
Wilen, Joan, and Lydia Wilen. *Food Lore & Folk Cures.* Stamford, Conn.: Longmeadow Press, 1988.
Williams, Susan. *Savory Suppers: Fashionable Feasts.* New York: Pantheon, 1985.

## Wine

Adams, Leon D. *Commonsense Book of Wine.* Boston: Houghton Mifflin, 1975.
Johnson, Hugh. *Wine.* New York: Simon & Schuster, 1966.
———. *A Complete Guide to the Wines and Spirits of the World.* New York: Simon & Schuster, 1971.
———. *Vintage: The Story of Wine.* New York: Simon & Schuster, 1989.
———. *Modern Encyclopedia of Wine.* New York: Simon & Schuster, 1991.
Joseph, Robert. *The Book of Wine.* New York: Smithmark, 1996.
Kramer, Matt. *Making Sense of Wine.* New York: Morrow, 1989.
Lichine, Alexis. *Encyclopedia of Wines and Spirits.* New York: Knopf, 1969.
Muscatine, Doris, Maynard A. Amerine, and Robert Thompson, eds. *Book of California Wine.* Berkeley: University of California Press/Sotheby Publications, 1984.
Olken, Charles E., and Earl G. Singer. *The Connoisseur's Handbook of California Wines.* New York: Knopf, 1980.
Schuster, Michael. *Beginner's Guide to Understanding Wine.* New York: Simon & Schuster, 1989.

Sichel, Allan, Leslie Seyd, H. B. Lanson, Lance K. Cock, Ian Mackenzie, and Alfred Langenbach. *A Guide to Good Wine.* London, England: Abbey Library, 1973.
Walton, Stuart. *The Book of Wine.* New York: Smithmark Publishers, 1997.
Waugh, Alec. *Wines and Spirits.* New York: Time-Life Books, 1968.
*Wines of the World.* New York: Bounty Books, no date.

## Coffee

Calvert, Catherine. *The Essential Guide to Coffee.* New York: Hearst Books, 1994.
Davids, Kenneth. *Coffee, A Guide to Buying, Brewing, and Enjoying.* Santa Rosa, Cal.: 101 Productions, 1976.
DeMers, John. *The Community Kitchen's Complete Guide to Gourmet Coffee.* New York: Simon & Schuster, 1986.
Kolpas, Norman. *A Cup of Coffee: From Plantation to Pot, a Coffee Lover's Guide to the Perfect Brew.* New York: Michael Friedman, 1993.
Kummer, Corby. *The Joy of Coffee: The Essential Guide to Buying, Brewing, and Enjoying.* Boston: Houghton Mifflin, 1997.
Perry, Sara, *The Complete Book of Coffee: A Gourmet Guide to Buying, Brewing, and Cooking.* San Francisco: Chronicle Books, 1991.
Schapira, Joel. *The Book of Coffee and Tea: A Guide to the Appreciation of Fine Coffees, Teas, and Herbal Beverages.* New York: St. Martin's Press, 1996.

## Tea

Beilenson, John. *The Book of Tea.* White Plains, N.Y.: Peter Pauper Press, 1989.
Blodfeld, John. *The Chinese Art of Tea.* London and Sydney: George Allen & Unwin, 1985.
Franklin, Aubrey. *Teatime.* New York: Frederick Fell Publishers, 1981.
Huxley, Gervas. *Talking of Tea.* London, England: Thames and Hudson, 1956.
Israel, Andrea. *Taking Tea.* New York: Weidenfeld & Nicolson, 1987.
Lu Yü, *The Classic of Tea,* trans. Francis Ross Carpenter. Boston: Little, Brown, 1974.
Manchester, Carole. *French Tea: The Pleasures of the Table.* New York: Hearst Books, 1993.
Ministry of Information. *The Book of Tea & Herbs: Appreciating the Varietals and Virtues of Fine Tea and Herbs.* Santa Rosa, Cal.: Cole Group, 1993.
Wild, Anthony. *The East India Company Book of Tea.* New York: HarperCollins, 1994.

## General History

Cooper, Charles. *The English Table in History and Literature.* London, England: Sampson, Low, Marston, 1929.
Eichler, Lillian. *The Customs of Mankind.* New York: Garden City Publishing, 1937.
*The Encyclopedia of Antiques.* New York: Crown, 1982.
Gardner, Louise. *Art Through the Ages.* New York: Harcourt, Brace & World, 1959.
Harrison, Molly. *The Kitchen in History.* New York: Scribner's, 1972.
Janson, H. W. *The History of Art.* New York: Abrams, 1962.
Kelley, Austin P. *The Anatomy of Antiques: A Collector's Guide.* New York: Viking, 1974.

Knowles, Eric. *100 Years of the Decorative Arts.* London, England: Reed Consumer Books, 1998.

Panati, Charles. *Extraordinary Origins of Everyday Things.* New York: Perennial Library, 1987.

Phillips, Phoebe. *The Collector's Encyclopedia of Antiques.* New York: Crown, 1973.

Ramsey, L. G. G. *The Complete Encyclopedia of Antiques.* New York: Simon & Schuster, 1983.

Schmit, Patricia Brady. *Nelly Custis Lewis's Housekeeping Book.* New Orleans: Historic New Orleans Collection, 1982.

Watson, Lillian Eichler. *The Customs of Mankind with Notes on Modern Etiquette and the Newest Trend in Entertainment.* Westport, Conn.: Negro Universities Press, 1924/1970.

# Photography Credits

Page 48: Tankard, c. 1715, Germany, manufactured by Meissen, stoneware, brass, gilding. Courtesy of Cooper Hewitt National Design Museum, Smithsonian Institution/Art Resource, NY. Museum purchase in memory of Mrs. John Innes Kane, 1941-43-1. Photograph by Tom Rose.

Page 49: Teapot and cover, c. 1765, Germany, manufactured by Hoechst Porcelain factory, porcelain, enameled and gilded decoration. Courtesy of Cooper Hewitt National Design Museum, Smithsonian Institution/Art Resource, NY. Gift of the Trustees of the Estate of James Hazen Hyde, 1960-1-46-a, b.

### INSERT PAGE 1

Top left: Celadon vase from Chinese Song dynasty. Courtesy of the Freer Gallery of Art, Smithsonian Institution, Washington, D.C., accession #F1937.18.

Top right: Islamic lusterware: platter with horseman. Courtesy of the Freer Gallery of Art, Smithsonian Institution, Washington, D.C., accession #F1957.21.

Bottom left: Porcelain dish with cobalt underglaze, from Chinese Yuan dynasty. Courtesy of the Freer Gallery of Art, Smithsonian Institution, Washington, D.C., accession #F1974.32.

Bottom right: *Famille rose* vase. Courtesy of The Metropolitan Museum of Art, Mr. and Mrs. Isaac D. Fletcher Collection, Bequest of Isaac D. Fletcher, 1917 (17.120.194). Photograph © 1983 The Metropolitan Museum of Art.

### INSERT PAGE 2

Silver tea kettle, salver, and tripod table. Courtesy of The Metropolitan Museum of Art. Gift of Irwin Untermeyer, 1968 (68.141.81). Photograph © 1996 The Metropolitan Museum of Art.

INSERT PAGE 3

Left: Candelabra, 1739/40, Paris, France, made by Claude Ballin, the Younger (1661–1754), silver. Courtesy of Cooper Hewitt National Design Museum, Smithsonian Institution/Art Resource, NY. Anonymous Gift, 1949-31-2-a, b. Photograph by Steve Tague.
Right: Silver tea set. Courtesy of The Metropolitan Museum of Art. Bequest of A. T. Clearwater, 1933 (33.120.543-.547). Photograph © 1977 The Metropolitan Museum of Art.

INSERT PAGE 4

Cut and engraved glass: standing cup and cover, eighteenth century, Bohemia. Courtesy of Cooper Hewitt National Design Museum, Smithsonian Institution/Art Resource, NY. Gift of the Trustees of the Estate of Jamez Hazen Hyde, 1960-1-8-1-a, b. Photograph by John White.

INSERT PAGE 5

Photograph by Billy Cunningham, from *The New Tiffany Table Settings* by John Loring and Harry B. Platt. Copyright © 1981 by Tiffany & Company, Inc. Used by permission of Doubleday, a division of Random House, Inc.

INSERT PAGE 6

Photograph © 2000 by Joshua Greene, from *Antiques for the Table* by Sheila Chefetz & Joshua Greene.

INSERT PAGE 7

Photographs © 2000 by Joshua Greene, from *Antiques for the Table* by Sheila Chefetz & Joshua Greene.

INSERT PAGE 8

Top left: Photograph by Billy Cunningham, from *The New Tiffany Table Settings* by John Loring and Harry B. Platt. Copyright © 1981 by Tiffany & Company, Inc. Used by permission of Doubleday, a division of Random House, Inc.
Center right: Courtesy of Baccarat, Inc.
Bottom left: © 2000 Joshua Greene Photography/All rights reserved.

### INSERT PAGE 9

Top: Photograph by Manfredi Bellan, from *The Tiffany Gourmet Cookbook*. Copyright © 1992 by Tiffany & Company, Inc. Used by permission of Doubleday, a division of Random House, Inc.
Bottom: Lisa Masson Photography.

### INSERT PAGES 10 AND 11

Photographs by Billy Cunningham, from *Tiffany Taste* by John Loring. Copyright © 1986 by Tiffany & Company, Inc. Used by permission of Doubleday, a division of Random House, Inc.

### INSERT PAGE 12

Top left: Photograph by Billy Cunningham, from *Tiffany Taste* by John Loring. Copyright © 1986 by Tiffany & Company, Inc. Used by permission of Doubleday, a division of Random House, Inc.
Top right: Photograph by Billy Cunningham, from *The New Tiffany Table Settings* by John Loring and Harry B. Platt. Copyright © 1981 by Tiffany & Company, Inc. Used by permission of Doubleday, a division of Random House, Inc.
Bottom left and right: Photographs by Michael Peters, from *The New Tiffany Table Settings* by John Loring and Harry B. Platt. Copyright ©1981 by Tiffany & Company, Inc. Used by permission of Doubleday, a division of Random House, Inc.

### INSERT PAGE 13

Top: Photograph © 2000 by Joshua Greene, from *City Foods* by Lee Bailey.
Bottom: Joshua Greene.

### INSERT PAGE 14

Photograph by Billy Cunningham, from *The Tiffany Gourmet Cookbook*. Copyright © 1992 by Tiffany & Company, Inc. Used by permission of Doubleday, a division of Random House, Inc.

### INSERT PAGE 15

Top: Tom Eckerle.
Bottom: Arras, StockFood Munich.

INSERT PAGE 16

Top: Arras, StockFood Munich.

Center left: Photograph by Billy Cunningham, from *Tiffany Taste* by John Loring. Copyright © 1986 by Tiffany & Company, Inc. Used by permission of Doubleday, a division of Random House, Inc.

Bottom: Patricia Barrow.

# Index